MW00785393

# HIGHWAY TO RICHES series, Volume I

# COMPOUNDING, THE WIZARD OF WEALTH BUILDING

**Jacob Sebastian,** MS, MIE, MBA.

**Published by: Dekkaan Publishing, 2021**

**HIGHWAY TO RICHES series**

## Volume I

# COMPOUNDING, the wizard of wealth building

First Global Edition, March 2021

Author: **Jacob Sebastian**

jacobsebastian@highwaytoriches.info

www.highwaytoriches.info

**Copyright © 2021 by Jacob Sebastian**

Jacob Sebastian owns the following trademarks/ copyrights:

**Yieldometer®**

**Tax Dragon®**

**Highway to Riches©**

**The Wizard of Wealth Building©**

## DISCLAIMER

While all attempts have been made to verify the information provided in this publication, neither the author nor the publisher assumes any responsibility for errors, omissions, or contrary interpretations on the subject matter herein. This book is for informational purposes only. The views expressed are those of the author alone and should not be taken as expert instructions or commands. The author or publisher is making no guarantees for earnings or any other results of any kind, nor are any liabilities assumed. The reader is entirely responsible for his or her own actions.

ISBN for Print-book in color: **978 908 3120 300; 978 908 3120 331.**

ISBN for Print-book in Black & White: **978 908 3120 324.**

ISBN for e-book: **978 908 3120 317.**

Dekkaan Publishing, Rotterdam, The Netherlands, EU.

HIGHWAY TO RICHES series, **Volume I**

# COMPOUNDING
# The wizard of wealth building

## A complete guide to the 4D-world of compounding & wealth-building

A treasure trove of mathematical secrets that can make you 30x times wealthier in 30 years and 100x times wealthier in 40 years than through conventional methods of wealth building.

Content is based on mathematical laws, timeless, and eternally valid.

Global edition, applicable in all countries & currencies.

Loaded with 70 graphs & tables to enable easy at-a-glance comprehension.

## Discover the mighty secrets of wealth-building:

- 2D-world arithmetic laws do not apply to the 4D-world of wealth building.

- 1% marginal yield rate can have more value than a 20% nominal rate.

- 20% yield rate can equal 10%+10%+10%+10% or more.

- 20% tax rate can drain 90% of your wealth through Tax Drag.

- Foreign stock markets may give you many times more returns.

- Become a millionaire with little or no capital to invest.

- Investment with borrowed money can be the airlift to super-wealth.

- Wealth-gap will always grow exponentially with time unless intervened.

- Learn which of 10 investment categories generate the highest returns.

- And many more.

**Jacob Sebastian,** MS, MIE, MBA.

GLOBAL EDITION

## DEDICATED TO

My beloved FATHER & MOTHER,

My jewels in life LEONIE, DENNIS & VALENTINE,

Mother of my children, HANNEKE,

My sisters GRACY, VALSA, PHILO & ROSA,

My brother NOBLE.

**TO THEM, I OWE EVERYTHING THAT I AM AND I HAVE TODAY.**

---

*The natural flow of Water is always from top to bottom.*

*It is the unbreakable law of Physics.*

*To get water to the top, you need to use a water pump.*

*But,*

*The natural flow of Wealth is always from bottom to top.*

*It is the unbreakable law of Mathematics.*

*To get wealth to the bottom, governments need to use a wealth pump.*

**Jacob Sebastian**

# About the Author

**Jacob Sebastian** is an engineer, born in India, and a long-time resident and citizen of the Netherlands (EU). His academic credentials include the following:

- Graduation in Mechanical Engineering (India).
- Postgraduation in Combustion Technology (IIT Madras, India).
- Postgraduation in Energy Management (Netherlands).
- MBA in International Trade and Finance (UK).

He has held senior engineering and management positions with the Government of India, an industrial conglomerate in the Middle East, and the European Division of a USA-based Fortune-500 corporation. Subsequently, he set up and operated his own businesses in software development and real estate development.

Excelling in academic, professional, and business fields, he has received several achievement awards. As chief engineer of a major petrochemical concern in the Netherlands, he has made a significant contribution to environmental protection by achieving a reduction of 300 million kg of $CO_2$ emission through innovation.

His passion for Physics and Mathematics is so strong that he embraced engineering above medical studies when he had a choice with admission granted to both. He has spent much of his life doing calculations varying from engineering projects and budget for his erstwhile employer companies to project finance for his real estate projects to coform to investment bankers' criteria and standards.

The extensive calculations and research he did for this series of books and the software "Yieldometer" are the latest testimony to his penchant for exploration. Publishing them devotionally to propagate the knowledge distilled over a long period of time is a testimony to his roots in a large family of pioneering educators and teachers.

Jacob Sebastian lives in Rotterdam, The Netherlands (EU). He can be reached at:

jacobsebastian@highwaytoriches.info

www.highwaytoriches.info

# Table of Contents

\* \* \* \*

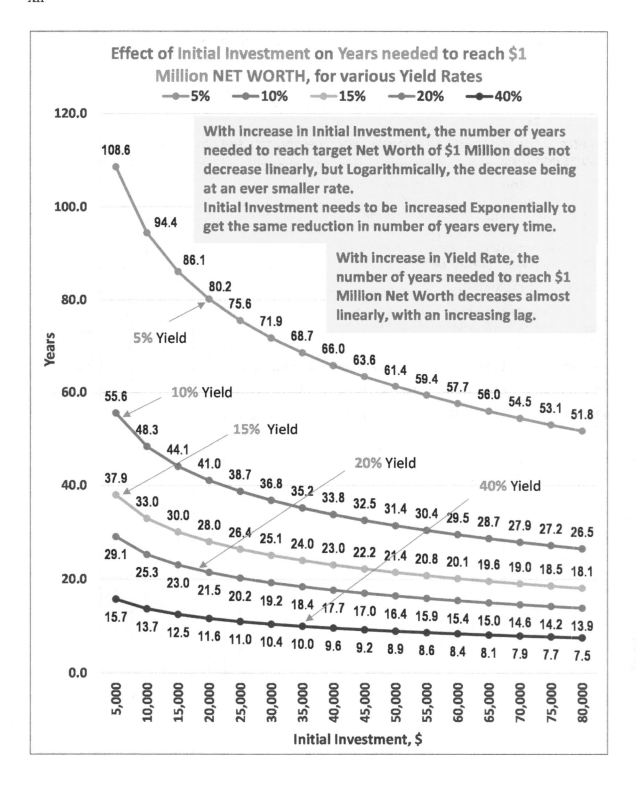

Effect of Initial Investment on Years needed to reach $1 Million NET WORTH, for various Yield Rates

# Chapter 0:

# This book in a Nutshell

**In a nutshell, this book will show you:**

1.  The secrets that all Billionaires used to get to that position.

2.  How to create a net worth that will be at least 100x times bigger in 40 years, 30x times bigger in 30 years, 10x times bigger in 20 years, and 3x times bigger in 10 years than what your net worth would be with conventional wealth building methods.

3.  How your net worth can be $30 million instead of the $1 million you aim to have in 30 years.

4.  Why a 3% differential yield rate or interest margin can be more valuable than a 20% nominal yield rate, and how to use it to build wealth faster.

5.  Why a 1% differential yield rate or interest margin can be 200x times more valuable than a 1% nominal yield rate, and how to benefit from it.

6.  Why a 20% yield rate can equal 10%+10%+10%+10% or more, and how you can use it to build your wealth faster.

7.  How a 3-fold increase in yield rate can result in a 20-fold increase in total return over time.

8.  How TAX DRAG may stealthily be draining 90% of your potential wealth with a nominal tax rate of only 20%, and how to avoid it.

9.  How to calculate the actual amounts of return, net worth, tax, tax drag, etc., in an easy way using pre-calculated tables provided in this book.

10. What it will take in initial investment, yield rate, and time to accumulate a net worth of $1 million or $1 Billion.

11. What the Influence of initial investment, yield rate, and time-period will be on your net worth in 10, 20, 30, or any number of years.

12. How investing in some stock markets abroad can increase your net worth many-fold.

13. How to convert and compare the Rate of Return in foreign stock markets with that of your domestic stock market and choose the market with the highest return to invest in.

14. How to become a millionaire even with little or no own capital to invest.

15. How borrowing to invest can put you on the Golden route to millionairedom and the only path open to Billionairedom.

16. How banks make more money for themselves with your deposit than they make for yourself, and how you can use the same technique for your own benefit.

17. Which of the ten standard investment vehicles would give you the highest and the lowest returns, and what returns you can expect from each of them.

18. Why percentages of anything can be utterly misleading, and you should never rely on them as such. If you do, you may end up losing 90% of potential returns. You should base all your decisions also on solid amounts instead of only percentages.

19. How investments with deferred tax instead of annual tax will take you to millionairedom several times faster.

20. Why government and taxpayer are both equal losers with the annual income tax system.

21. Why deferred tax system is a win-win for all, including the government, and why you should actively seek investments with deferred tax, avoiding investments with annual tax.

22. Why fixed deposit does not qualify to be in the top ten of wealth-building options but is a donkey-cart on a muddy road to millionairedom with which you will never reach your destination.

23. Why your own business in innovative fields can be the Ferrari that will take you to Millionairedom or Billionairedom in the shortest possible time.

24. How fast the other nine investment vehicles such as real estate and stock market are in taking you to millionairedom, and beyond, in the shortest time.

25. Why tax evaders live in a fool's paradise and may be losing more money than they save on taxes.

26. Why you may ultimately be earning less, instead of more, with various tax-free investment plans with stringent restrictions.

27. How you can calculate and discover that you may be better off with an investment at a 20% yield rate and 30% deferred tax than an investment with an 18% yield rate and zero tax.

28. How the infallible mathematical laws make wealth always flow from bottom to top, from poor to rich, resulting in the exponential growth of the wealth gap between rich and poor, making it an undesired natural phenomenon necessitating an artificial balancing mechanism.

29. Why the ever-increasing wealth gap between rich and poor is not the fault of the rich but due to a natural mathematical phenomenon that is beyond the ability of many politicians to understand or recognize and take balancing measures.

30. How a simple-to-use software program, titled Yieldometer, can instantly calculate all investment results, relieving you of the need to make any manual calculations and making financial decisions a lot more effortless.

31. How to create immense wealth using the financial equivalent of Albert Einstein's $E=MC^2$, in which the speed of light $C$ is substituted by the gems of Knowledge sprinkled on the pages of this book.

32. How anyone with a mediocre salary and zero net worth can become a dollar-millionaire in 15 to 20 years.

33. And numerous other insights that will help you to reach your financial goals a lot faster.

\* \* \* \*

# Chapter 1:

# Introduction to this Wealth Expedition

## Please do not skip this chapter

## 1.1     WHAT THIS SERIES OF BOOKS AND SOFTWARE ARE ABOUT

### 1.1.1     The book series "Highway to Riches"

This book you are now reading is the first of a series of books titled **"Highway to Riches."**

This first volume of the series is titled **"Compounding, the Wizard of Wealth Building"** and covers the foundation upon which all vast wealth is created.

This book is also the foundation upon which the second volume of the book series, titled **"Tax Drag, the Dragon that eats up your Wealth,"** has been developed.

This book is also the foundation for the third product in the series, a software program based on Microsoft Excel and titled **"Yieldometer."** It will automatically calculate all the results of investments, including tax and tax drag. It will measure the return or yield of an investment and its numerous derivatives, and hence the name Yield-O-Meter.

The content of both volumes of the book will surprise and fascinate you. They will entice you into taking action to create wealth for yourself, turning it into a delightful sport and hobby. Irrespective of whether you are a middle school drop-out or a Ph. D in mathematics, you will undoubtedly take many gems of knowledge and wisdom from these books, which will serve you well throughout your life. That is a promise!

Each of the books and the software program will make you a wizard in the specific fields covered by each of them.

All three products together, when released, would make you also a wizard of wealth building with formidable intellectual and calculational powers irrespective of your level of education.

You would wish that these books were taught to you earlier in your life in High School or College or at least in the MBA program if you had done one.

## 1.1.2     More on Volume II of the book series

The second Volume of the book is titled **"Tax Drag, the Dragon that eats up your Wealth."** While tax is a visible robber of your wealth, tax drag is the invisible thief that stealthily drains the pockets of all taxpayers on Earth, often draining 90% or more of your potential lifetime earnings. Yet hardly anyone knows about it. Volume II of the book series will reveal every aspect of it, and you will probably be dumbfounded.

Though that book is also already written, it is not yet published. However, tax and tax drag are introduced in this first Volume, and section 3.4 and chapter 18 of this book are also dedicated to tax drag. Further, tax and tax drag are discussed whenever they are relevant to the topics covered in this book.

Because of the importance of tax drag in any wealth-building plan and the relative mathematical complexity of its calculation, it was necessary to devote a separate dedicated volume of the book to that subject.

## 1.1.3     More on software program Yieldometer

While the books will provide you with valuable insight into the powers of compounding to create wealth and show you how to calculate investment results manually using tables and a simple calculator, this software tool will automatically calculate everything that is covered in both volumes of the book, and a lot more. This tool is the easiest, quickest, and best way to analyze and compare various investment options and choose the best one. It was also developed by the author of this book.

As a matter of fact, most of the investment results shown and discussed in both the volumes of the book-series were calculated using Yieldometer.

The software, though already developed, is not yet released. The release can be expected within three months of publication of this book. However, an introduction to Yieldometer is given in chapter 22 of this book, including some sample screenshots of the results.

## 1.2     WHAT THIS VOLUME (1) OF THE BOOK-SERIES IS ABOUT

## 1.2.1     What this book "Compounding, the wizard of wealth-building" will teach you

Compounding is one of the most fascinating mathematical phenomena that exists, but one that is also least understood by most people because much of its formidable power and many secrets are invisible to most people's eyes and brains. How fundamental and crucial it is to wealth-building will become apparent to you as you progress through the pages of this book.

When you hear the word compounding, you might be thinking only of compound interest that banks offer to you on your savings deposit and not about the complex world that exists beyond the reach of your eyes, knowledge, and imagination. It is in this hidden world that Millionaires and Billionaires operate and where vast amounts of wealth are being created using the formidable powers and hidden secrets of compounding.

Almost always, all vast personal wealth is created in this complex world of compounding. So also, that of Bill Gates, Warren Buffett, Jeff Bezos, Mark Zuckerberg, Carlos Slim (Mexico), Mukesh Ambani (India), and Tim Mia (China). They are all virtual auto-couriers on the highway to riches with superfast virtual cars of their own making, and some of them have already passed the milestone marked 100 Billion.

Compounding of wealth is the fuel that is propelling them all forward at incredible speeds. Starting with relatively small investments, it is the magic of compounding that made them so fabulously wealthy. It is said that Bill Gates started Microsoft with S1 million that he borrowed from his dad. See section 21.1 for details.

**Through this book, go with me on a short tour to explore and discover the hidden powers of compounding that made so many people so wealthy and learn how you too can use those powers to create massive wealth for yourself. At the end of the tour, you will have found the Ferrari and a safe highway that will take you to the riches of your dreams.**

During our exploration, you will come across some secrets that may shock you because you had never imagined that they existed or were even possible. When I am talking about shocking secrets, I mean mathematical secrets that are, by definition, irrefutable, infallible, and timeless, remaining valid forever.

**Mathematics never changes or lies. Therefore, the derivations, conclusions, and lessons drawn from this book, and this book itself, will remain valid and relevant for all years and ages to come, without an expiry date.**

## 1.2.2 Examples of compounding other than that of money and wealth

Compounding is the term we generally use when exponential growth occurs to money due to the compounding of interest.

Compounding or compounded growth is therefore mathematically synonymous with the exponential growth of money or wealth. In section 3.2, we will discuss what both these phenomena and their characteristics are.

But money or wealth is only one of the numerous things that compound themselves and grow exponentially all around us in our daily lives, some of which are destructive and some constructive.

### 1.2.2.1 Compounding processes that are destructive

A nuclear bomb is an excellent example of the incredible power of compounding, in which one atomic reaction by a single neutron gets compounded to a billion reactions in a second. See section 2.3 for details.

A virus infection like Covid-19 is another example of a single infected person compounding the infection to many millions of infected persons. See section 2.4 for details.

The food that gets spoiled outside the fridge in a few hours is also a real-life example of a bacteria multiplying itself through compounded growth. See section 2.5 for details.

A nominal tax rate of 20% draining off 90% of your potential wealth through tax drag is an example of compounding in reverse gear, though you may not even have heard of tax drag and are most probably a victim of it without even being aware of it. See section 3.4 and chapter 18 for details of tax drag.

### 1.2.2.2 Compounding processes that are constructive

On the positive side also, there are numerous examples of the power of compounding.

A nuclear power plant generating electricity is one. Brewing beer or other alcoholic drinks is another. Using yeast to prepare food is another.

**Building wealth is another real-life example**. Without the power of compounding, there would not have been any Billionaires in the world today, and probably no more than a handful of millionaires.

Using the hidden power of compounding to build wealth is the central theme of this Volume of the book.

### 1.2.3 Example 1.2.3

For example, did you know that if you invested $10,000 in some project at a 23% yield rate and your neighbor invested $10,000 at a 20% yield rate, after 30 years, you will have a net worth of $4.98 million, which will be 210% larger than your neighbor's $2.37 million? Over 40 years, yours will be $39.5 million, which will be 268% larger than your neighbor's $14.7 million.

Instead of investing in the project himself, if your neighbor had lent the $10,000 to you at a 20% interest rate and you invested it at a 23% yield rate, your own share of the net worth after 30 years would have been $2.61 million (= 4.98 – 2.37) which is 8% larger than your neighbor's net worth of $2.37 million. After 40 years, your net worth would have been $24.8 million (= 39.5-14.7), which is 69% larger than your neighbor's $14.7 million.

Your own initial investment, in this case, was zero because you had borrowed it all from your neighbor.

Was it then such a crazy idea, as everybody around you told you at that time, that you took this loan to invest for a mere 3% (= 23 – 20) marginal yield rate? Certainly not. On the contrary, it was a brilliant idea.

In this example, what we see is that the **differential yield rate** of 3% that lies embedded between 20% and 23% is more valuable than the 20% that lies embedded between 0% and 20%. Put it differently, this **3% yield rate of yours is bigger in value than the 20% yield rate** of your neighbor.

**Is it not correct to say that the 3% yield rate via one route is 8% or 69% bigger than the 20% yield rate via another route?**

Put it more precisely, your net worth with a **3% marginal or differential** yield rate will be **1.08x times** the size of your net worth with a **20% nominal** yield rate in 30 years and **1.69x times** in 40 years.

See chapter 7 for more information about **differential yield rates.**

Your neighbor had calculated how much you would earn for the investment service you provide. He had estimated that you would make a total of **$14,273** in 30 years and considered it an acceptable amount. How wrong he was! He had calculated with a **3% Nominal** yield rate instead of a **3% Differential** yield rate.

When some finance company or broker wants you to invest with them on a long-term basis and tells you "we will earn 25% rate of return on this project; we will keep only 5% for all our services and will give you 20% return", you can better walk out and look elsewhere for more honesty. As a knowledgeable investor, you know that your 20% return will be smaller than his 5%.

## 1.2.4    Example 1.2.4

Suppose that, in a fit of anger at your neighbor for leaving only a 3% marginal yield for you, you reject your neighbor's proposal and let the opportunity to invest with a 23% yield rate pass. Determined not to lose the 3% yield anyway, you then raise $10,000 yourself by selling some gold ornaments and deposit that amount in a Fixed Deposit at a 3% interest rate.

You are very content because you think you are earning the same as you would have made by borrowing the neighbor's money at a 3% marginal yield rate. In this case, you just landed in a fool's paradise!

In this case, your **total return** would be only **$14,273** in **30 years** and **$22,620** in **40 years.**

**$14,273** total return in **30** years with a **3% nominal yield rate** is only **0.55%** of the **$2.61 million** you would have earned with the marginal yield rate of 3% embedded between 20% and 23%, as in example 1.2.3 above. That means your earnings would have been **183x times** bigger (= 2,610,000 / 14,273) if you had accepted the offer of a 3% marginal yield rate from your neighbor.

Similarly, a **$22,620** total return in **40** years with a **3% nominal yield rate** is only **0.091%** of the **$24.80 million** you would have earned with the marginal yield rate of 3% embedded between 20% and 23%, as in example 1.2.3 above. That means your earnings would have been **1,096x times** bigger (= 24,800,000/ 22,620) if you had accepted the offer of a 3% marginal yield rate from your neighbor.

**Is it not correct to say that a 3% yield rate via one route is 183x times or 1,096x times bigger than a 3% yield rate via another route?**

Put it more precisely, your total return with a **3% marginal or differential** yield rate will be **183x times** the size of your total return with a **3% nominal** yield rate in 30 years and **1,096x times** in 40 years.

**Have you just entered the kingdom of lunatics? No, certainly not.**

**WELCOME, you have just entered the kingdom of compounding, a kingdom full of surprises and secrets like this, a kingdom where all vast wealth is created by virtue of seemingly convoluted mathematics as in the examples above.**

## 1.3      COMPOUNDING IS A PLAYGROUND IN 3D OR 4D, NOT 2D

If simple arithmetic can be considered as a game in a playground in 2D, the mathematics of compounding should be considered as a game in a playground in 3D or 4D.

A 4D playground is a lot more complex than a 2D or 3D playground. The rules that apply to a playground in 2D cannot be applied one-on-one to a playground in 3D or 4D because you will have to take also the third and fourth dimensions into account.

If you do not take the 3rd and 4th dimensions into account or do not specify them, you will get convoluted statements like 3% yield rate equals 20% yield rate.

The two dimensions of **2D** in which most people perceive, process, and calculate wealth-building are **initial investment** and **yield rate.**

The third of the **3D dimensions that adds** magic to wealth building is **time**. Time is also the parameter that makes the calculations of wealth-building too complicated for most people.

The fourth of the **4D dimensions, the one that detracts** from the magic of wealth building, is **tax and tax drag,** the notorious twins. We will treat tax and tax drag as one singular entity because tax drag is the shadow of taxation, and they are generally inseparable, with some exceptions. Tax and tax drag are also the parameters that add an extra layer of complexity to the already complex 3D calculations involving time.

Due to the lack of knowledge, most people think and calculate in simple 2D arithmetic when it is the 3D or 4D mathematics that is required. As a result, they miss the great opportunities that the 3D and 4D worlds of compounding present to build wealth. Not only that people miss great opportunities, but many people also make huge blunders and lose a lot of money, as in the examples above.

## 1.4 THE ORIGIN OF THIS SERIES OF BOOKS AND SOFTWARE PROGRAM YIELDOMETER

Much of the calculations leading to the content of this series of books were created originally for use in some of my investment projects, especially in real estate, without having any intention at that time to publish them. They were made out of necessity as there were no suitable software programs or comprehensive books available covering the topics relevant to my investment projects.

During the past 15 years, I have been making new calculations involving new aspects of investments on an ad-hoc basis, depending on the need of the time. With my engineering, project development, finance, and management background, I needed more in-depth information than what the professional accountants were able to provide, and that too wrapped in intimidating accounting jargon. Therefore, I had to make the calculations myself and develop the needed tools for it.

I enjoyed the calculation process and especially the insight into the financial future of a project that such calculations would provide. There were several occasions that I was stunned by the surprising results of such calculations, which in turn spurred me to dig deeper and to do more calculations and research.

It was only three years back that the idea dawned upon me that I should share the insight that I had accumulated this way with the rest of the world. Especially so because such insight was not readily available in the marketplace in any form, be it a book, software, or consultancy.

Therefore, when a project that I was working on had to be kept on hold three years back, I decided to devote my time and energy to bundle my works and insights in a format that can be shared with the rest of the world. Organizing it all for sharing with others in an easily digestible form proved to be a much more laborious and time-consuming task than I had imagined.

Moreover, the whole manuscript turned out to be running into about a thousand pages, necessitating drastic editing and splitting the book into two volumes.

More importantly, the complexity of calculations and formulas involved to get precise data for any investment made it necessary to develop a simple-to-use software tool for all the calculations instead of providing complex formulas in the books, which not many people would have been able to use.

As a result, the following three products have emerged and are being delivered, one at a time.

(1). The book series titled **Highway to Riches, Volume I: Compounding, the Wizard of Wealth Building** (this book).

(2). The book series titled **Highway to Riches, Volume II: Tax Drag, the Dragon that eats up your wealth**. In order to give you an idea of how much tax drag eats from your plate, one chapter from that book is included in this book. See chapter 18.

(3). **Yieldometer**, an Excel-based software program to do all the calculations described in both volumes of the book automatically and instantaneously for any investment plan. It encompasses everything that is covered in both volumes of the book series. However, in order to understand and correctly interpret the considerable number of data that the program will generate, you need to have a good understanding of the topics covered in both books. Therefore, the program will be made available only at a later stage and after the publication of both volume 1 and volume 2 of this book series. I have dubbed the program "Yieldometer" as it is the yield that ultimately counts in wealth building. In order to give you an idea of what the program can calculate, a part of the screenshot from that program is included in this book. See chapter 22.

Volume 1 of the book series is being published now. Volume 2 will be published about three months later. The software will be released soon after that.

## 1.5     HOW "COMPOUNDING, THE WIZARD OF WEALTH BUILDING" IS ORGANIZED AND HOW TO READ IT

The book is **not modular**, meaning that the chapters are not entirely independent of each other to be read isolated and fully understood. The book is built up in a logical sequence, like in a novel, starting from the first chapter, and each component of the wealth-building tool is treated in detail in each subsequent chapter.

In order to fully understand the topic covered in each chapter, some understanding of the topics covered in the previous chapters is necessary. In most chapters, there are also **cross-references** to other chapters.

Therefore, my advice is to **read the book serially**, starting from the beginning and advancing sequentially through the chapters.

However, for advanced readers with a good understanding of wealth building through compounding, random reading of individual chapters may not detract much from fully understanding the topic covered.

That said, a **quick reading** of many of the chapters is also possible by merely **eye-skating over the tables and graphs** included in the chapters. They have been added consciously and profusely in this book to facilitate quick reading through visual perception rather than textual reading.

Another way for a **quick look at this book's essence** is to go to chapter 23, titled "**In Summary.**" That chapter summarizes most of the topics covered in this book but without going into any details. For people with little time to spare, it is an easy and quick way to catch the book's essence, like going through the headings of a newspaper in the morning without reading the details. Depending on the need and availability of time, you can go to specific chapters for more in-depth information.

The **Expanded Table of Contents** given at the end of the book in Appendix-C, which also shows sub-sections at deeper levels, will serve as a substitute for an Index and may provide you with the easiest way to navigate the content of the book with precision.

In this book, most of the topics are introduced and explained **using examples** or anecdotes, as that is the easiest way to explain and understand a subject.

**Graphs, in addition to tables,** are the primary visual tool used throughout this book to project each chapter's insight most easily and understandably. The main conclusions are also included in the graph in text format to make interpreting the graph easier for the reader.

**Color** has been used abundantly in this book to enhance readability. However, the color will be lost in the Black & White print version and Black & White e-readers. Unfortunately, color printing is a lot more costly to produce, but if you can afford it, I recommend the color version in print if it is available. Reading the color version will be much easier as important points are accentuated in color.

This series of books are **timeless** and will remain valid and relevant for years and decades to come. **The content is mathematically so fundamental that it will never get outdated.**

You may find some **repetition** of specific observations in different chapters of the book. That is because the point repeated may be relevant to the topic discussed in each of those chapters. For the same reason, you may also find the same observation repeated in text format in more graphs. I endeavor to give you a complete picture of the topic covered in each chapter, avoiding distracting cross-references to other chapters as much as possible.

**American English** is used for writing this book with apologies to the Classical Englishers for all the spelling deviations you may find in the book.

## 1.6      FOR WHOM IS THIS VOLUME 1 OF THE BOOK-SERIES WRITTEN?

This book is written for any and all persons in any and all parts of the world who have a desire and ambition to become wealthy in the shortest possible time. This book will serve you equally well irrespective of whether your targeted wealth is $100 thousand or $100 Billion. This book is littered with gems of information, wisdom, and secrets that will greatly enlighten and benefit every reader irrespective of whether the reader is a Ph.D. in mathematics or a middle school graduate.

This book is written with the aim to be easily accessible and readable for anyone with education at the level of only middle school and up. Complex, difficult, and technical words have been avoided as much as possible. Complex mathematical formulas have been avoided, and only some simple formulas have been included, even though they are also not essential for reading and understanding this book. Most of the data presented in this book have also been shown in graphical form to facilitate quick and easy comprehension at a glance.

This conscious focus on simplicity and readability for the commoner might have led to some lengthy explanations and repetitions here and there. Readability and understandability for the commoner above brevity and style was a conscious choice I made while drafting this book.

This book is an international edition. The content of the book is time-proof, country-neutral, and currency-neutral. The dollar sign ($) used in the book serves only as a symbol for currency, but the book's content applies equally to all other currencies in the world. The book's content is based on mathematical fundamentals and will, therefore, remain valid forever without an expiry date.

## 1.7      TERMINOLOGY USED IN THIS BOOK

**Yield or Yield Rate**: Wherever these terms are used in this book, depending on the context, they may also be read as **Interest Rate or Rate of Return (ROR)** as appropriate.

**Interest**: As the term interest specifically implies bank deposits and loans, I have avoided using it except when specifically bank deposits and loans are discussed. Instead, I have used the broader term **Yield** wherever possible.

**Return**: The term return is used sparingly in this book as it can be confusing to the average reader. Instead, I have used the term **Yield** primarily.

**Capital Gain**: when a capital gain is involved in addition to periodic yields like dividend yield for stock market or rental yield for real estate, the capital gain is not treated separately in this book but annualized and included in the **Rate of Return (ROR)**. Instead of using the term Rate of Return, the term used in this book by default is **Yield Rate**.

**Rate of Return (ROR)**: This term has mainly been avoided, and the term **Yield Rate** or simply **Yield** is used instead. Therefore, **Yield Rate** may also be read as **Rate of Return (ROR)** as appropriate depending on the context.

**Yield Amount** or **Total Yield** or **Total Return**: These terms are used interchangeably, and they denote amounts and not percentages.

**Final Amount** or **Gross Worth** or **Net Worth**: In the context of this book, with zero tax rate, these terms represent the same amount, and therefore they have been used interchangeably depending on the context.

**ROI (Return on investment)**: This term is one of the most misinterpreted and misused words used to mislead investors and, therefore, avoided in this book. The term yield and its appropriate variations are used instead.

**CAGR (Compound Annual Growth Rate):** This term denotes the effective yield rate of investment, including capital growth as with stock or real estate. It is the rate of return (ROR) on an annual basis, in percentage, which, when compounded annually over the period considered, would yield the total results achieved in that period. However, this term is used in this book only if it is particularly relevant to a particular situation. Otherwise, the general term **yield rate** is used.

**The principal** or **initial investment**: Disregarding the contextual difference between the two terms, they have been used interchangeably in this book.

**CAF (Compound Amount Factor):** This term lies dispersed throughout this book. It is the growth factor of any investment relative to the initial investment. In other words, it is the final value of any investment as a multiplier of the initial investment. If the CAF value is 3, it means that an initial investment of $1 grew to $3.

**CYF (Compound yield Factor):** This term is also used frequently in this book. It is the total yield of any investment as a factor of the initial investment. It is merely a multiplier of the initial investment. If the CYF value is 2, it means that an initial investment of $1 grew to $3, and therefore, the total yield is $2.

**FD (Fixed Deposit)** or **CD (Certificate of Deposit)** or **TD (Term Deposit)** or **Bank Deposit**: They are different names in different countries for the same product. In this book, all these names have been used without distinction though FD is the term most frequently used.

\* \* \*

# Chapter 2:

# Fundamentals of Compounding through Examples

## Fundamentals explained through examples

To give you a real grasp of the subject, in this chapter, I am sharing a few examples of compounding. One is a legend from the ancient past, part true and part myth, but still fascinating. The second one is from my own real-life experiment that has left everyone involved in amazement.

Let us start with the legend. Do not skip it. It is incredibly insightful as well as entertaining. The first part of the anecdote is historically genuine, but the second part may be a myth.

## 2.1    THE KING, THE WIZARD, AND THE CHESS GAME

The Chessboard, as you probably know, has 64 squares on it, made up of 8 rows and 8 columns. It was originally invented in India in the 6th century AD and later copied and adapted by Persians into the present form and spread to all corners of the world. According to the myth, the ancient Indian king named Shahram was feeling bored as there was no battle to be fought at that time, and therefore, he wanted something else fascinating to entertain himself. So, he asked the wizard in his kingdom to invent something for his entertainment.

The wizard subsequently invented the wonderful chess game with 64 squares (8x8) on the Chessboard and two sets, each of king, queen, pawns, etc., each facing the other in a perceived war position. The goal of each side was to reach and capture the king on the opposite side, the perceived enemy. The game simulates war. All the rulers of the ancient past thrived on wars, and they lived and died for it. Conducting war expeditions to loot the riches of the defeated was their primary occupation as a king. The chess game, therefore, was a perfect amalgamation of the king's passion for war and the desire for entertainment. The king was exhilarated with the fantastic game the wizard had invented and decided to reward him generously for his brilliance.

The king asked the wizard to name anything he would like to receive as a reward. The wizard told the king that he was a modest man and wanted only a modest reward. All he wanted was some grains of wheat! Pointing at his Chessboard with its 64 squares, he told the king that he just wanted one single grain in the first square, double of that in the second square, double of that in the third square, and so on, until the 64th square. The 64th square would have double the number of grains that the 63rd square had. Just one single grain and doubling up every following square until the last square, that is all. The king felt offended and told him it was too silly a reward for such a splendid invention. The king spurred the wizard to change his mind and offered him jewels, palaces, dancing girls, or whatever else he might wish. No, the wizard replied with his head becomingly lowered in reverence and told the king that all he desired was those little piles of wheat grains. Marveled by the humility of the wizard, the king ordained that his wish be fulfilled.

So, the Master of the Royal Granary came with servants and a bag of wheat. They started laying them in separate piles on the Chessboard: 1, 2, 4, 8, 16, 32, 64. 128. The first row is now completed, but the Chessboard was too small to hold all the 256 grains in square 9, and so also with all the remaining 55 squares. So, he started with the second row in a separate room instead of the Chessboard. 256, 512, 1024, 2048, 4096, 8192, 16384, 32768. The Granary Master had ordered a few more bags of wheat to be brought in the meantime. Then he started with the third row: 65536, 131072, 262144, 524288. He was only at square 20, and all the grain in the Royal Granary was now finished. About half a million grains were in square 20. All the 20 squares together had about one million grains.

Ultimately, all the grain from the whole kingdom was ordered and brought to the palace. With all that grain, they reached only square 40, which had precisely 549,755,813,388 grains or about 550 Billion grains. All the 40 squares together contained about double of it, that is 1100 Billion grains. Square 41 alone would need another 1100 Billion grains! That is equal to the entire grain production in the whole kingdom next year. But even after that, there would be squares from 42 till 64 to be filled!

We do not know whether the king, taking a noble example from some ancient kings in mythologies, handed over his kingdom to the wizard, blaming himself for not paying proper attention to the math teacher when he was at school as a boy or whether the wizard was condemned to spend the rest of his life in a dungeon playing chess alone!

## 2.1.1 The exact Numbers

See Table 2.1 for the corresponding number of grains in each square on the Chessboard.

See Figure 2.1 for a graphical depiction of how the numbers grow.

The number of grains in Square 1 is 1.

It multiplies approximately 1,000x times every 10 squares (1,024x times to be exact).

> The number of grains in square 11 is approximately 1,000.
>
> The number of grains in square 21 is approximately 1 Million.
>
> The number of grains in square 61 is approximately 1 Billion Billion.
>
> The number of grains in **square 64** is approximately **9.2 Billion Billion.**

The total of all the grains in **all the squares together** is approximately **18.4 Billion Billion** (double the number in square 64 minus 1 grain, to be exact).

This quantity of 18.4 Billion Billion grains is probably more than the wheat production in the whole world in the past 100 years!

If the Chessboard were invented with 100 squares (10x10) instead of 64 squares (8x8), the wheat grains needed to meet the wizard's reward would have weighed as much as the whole Earth.

## 2.1.2    If it was compounding of all the grains, like money in a bank account

*Please take the numbers below for granted and do not rack your brains about how to calculate them until you are equipped to do it by reading till the last page of this book.*

Getting double the number of grains in the succeeding square is equivalent to getting 200% nominal interest on only the preceding square.

It is also equivalent to getting 200% nominal interest on the grains on all the squares of the Chessboard with a 50% virtual tax. Mathematically, it would be like a bank deposit with 200% nominal interest and 50% tax on interest received.

It is also equivalent to getting 100% nominal interest on the grains on all the squares of the Chessboard with zero tax. Mathematically, it would be like a bank deposit with 100% nominal interest and zero tax on interest received.

If the wizard had asked to double the total number of grains on all the preceding squares every time instead of doubling what was on the immediately preceding square only, it would have been equivalent to compounding with 200% nominal interest with no virtual tax.

In that case, just by avoiding 50% virtual tax, the wizard would have got approximately 62 Billion times more grains. What a loss due to a 50% tax! This is an example of Tax Drag at work!

Such is the incredible power of exponential growth, compounding, and tax drag.

| Number of wheat grains on a chessboard | | | | | |
|---|---|---|---|---|---|
| Square No. | Number of grains in each square | Number of grains rounded off | Square No. | Number of grains in each square | Number of grains rounded off |
| 1 | 1 | | 33 | 4,294,967,296 | |
| 2 | 2 | | 34 | 8,589,934,592 | |
| 3 | 4 | | 35 | 17,179,869,184 | |
| 4 | 8 | | 36 | 34,359,738,368 | |
| 5 | 16 | | 37 | 68,719,476,736 | |
| 6 | 32 | | 38 | 137,438,953,472 | |
| 7 | 64 | | 39 | 274,877,906,944 | |
| 8 | 128 | | 40 | 549,755,813,888 | |
| 9 | 256 | | 41 | 1,099,511,627,776 | 1,000 Billion |
| 10 | 512 | | 42 | 2,199,023,255,552 | |
| 11 | 1,024 | 1 Thousand | 43 | 4,398,046,511,104 | |
| 12 | 2,048 | | 44 | 8,796,093,022,208 | |
| 13 | 4,096 | | 45 | 17,592,186,044,416 | |
| 14 | 8,192 | | 46 | 35,184,372,088,832 | |
| 15 | 16,384 | | 47 | 70,368,744,177,664 | |
| 16 | 32,768 | | 48 | 140,737,488,355,328 | |
| 17 | 65,536 | | 49 | 281,474,976,710,656 | |
| 18 | 131,072 | | 50 | 562,949,953,421,312 | |
| 19 | 262,144 | | 51 | 1,125,899,906,842,620 | 1 Million Billion |
| 20 | 524,288 | | 52 | 2,251,799,813,685,250 | |
| 21 | 1,048,576 | 1 Million | 53 | 4,503,599,627,370,500 | |
| 22 | 2,097,152 | | 54 | 9,007,199,254,740,990 | |
| 23 | 4,194,304 | | 55 | 18,014,398,509,482,000 | |
| 24 | 8,388,608 | | 56 | 36,028,797,018,964,000 | |
| 25 | 16,777,216 | | 57 | 72,057,594,037,927,900 | |
| 26 | 33,554,432 | | 58 | 144,115,188,075,856,000 | |
| 27 | 67,108,864 | | 59 | 288,230,376,151,712,000 | |
| 28 | 134,217,728 | | 60 | 576,460,752,303,423,000 | |
| 29 | 268,435,456 | | 61 | 1,152,921,504,606,850,000 | 1 Billion Billion |
| 30 | 536,870,912 | | 62 | 2,305,843,009,213,690,000 | |
| 31 | 1,073,741,824 | 1 Billion | 63 | 4,611,686,018,427,390,000 | |
| 32 | 2,147,483,648 | | 64 | 9,223,372,036,854,780,000 | 9 Billion Billion |
| | | | Total | 18,446,744,073,709,600,000 | 18 Billion Billion |

Table 2.1: **Number of grains in each square of a Chessboard.**

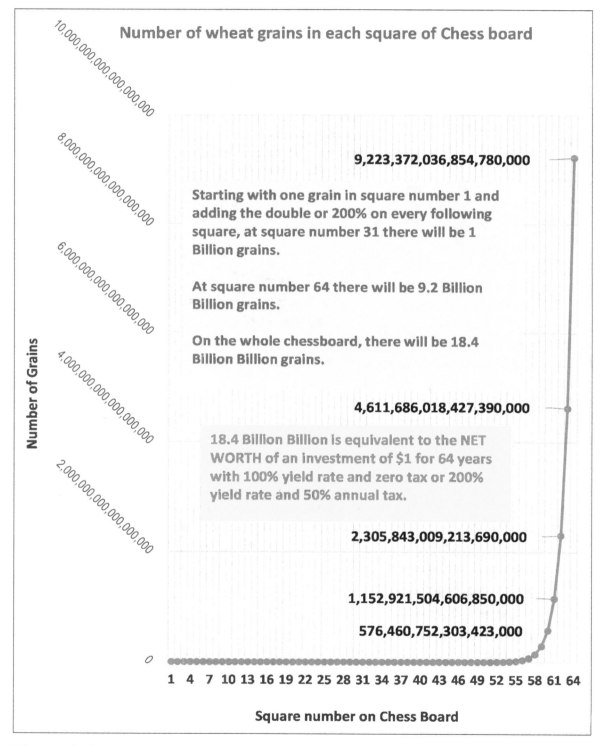

**Number of wheat grains in each square of Chess board**

9,223,372,036,854,780,000

Starting with one grain in square number 1 and adding the double or 200% on every following square, at square number 31 there will be 1 Billion grains.

At square number 64 there will be 9.2 Billion Billion grains.

On the whole chessboard, there will be 18.4 Billion Billion grains.

4,611,686,018,427,390,000

18.4 Billion Billion is equivalent to the NET WORTH of an investment of $1 for 64 years with 100% yield rate and zero tax or 200% yield rate and 50% annual tax.

2,305,843,009,213,690,000

1,152,921,504,606,850,000

576,460,752,303,423,000

Square number on Chess Board

**Figure 2.1: Number of grains in each square of a Chessboard.**

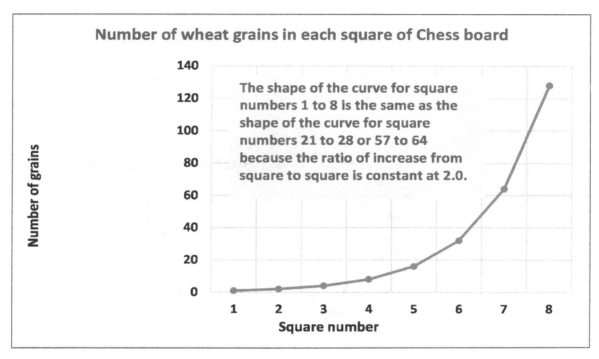

Figure 2.1a: **Number of grains in each square of a** Chessboard

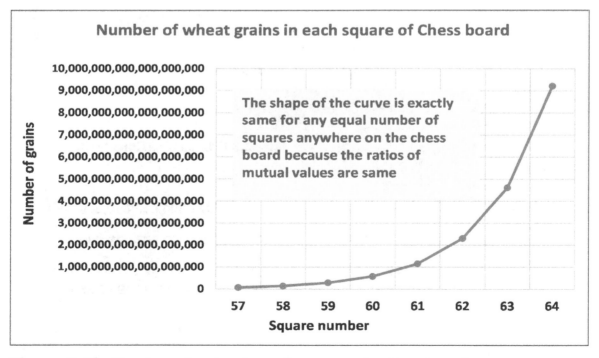

Figure 2.1b: **Number of grains in each square of a** Chessboard.

### 2.1.3     A hypothetical bank offering 100% interest rate

If there were a bank that offered a fixed deposit with a 100% nominal interest rate with zero tax and compounded annually for 63 years, and your parents had put $1 in that account upon your birth, you would have owned approximately 9.2 Billion Billion Dollars on your 63rd birthday! That is about 25,000x times (yes, 25 thousand times) the total wealth in the whole world, estimated to be USD 360 Trillion by a leading Swiss bank in 2018.

Even if you had to pay 50% tax on interest in all the years, your net worth would still have been $124 Billion, rivaling Bill Gates.

### 2.2     WIZARD'S SECOND MAGIC USING COMPOUNDING

We have seen above that the king got stuck at the 40th square and had no more grains in the whole kingdom. And he had another 24 squares to go! So, he reasoned with himself and reckoned that if the wizard would agree to a concession and accept half of the grains in each square, he would still be able to keep his promise and save his honor. The king reasoned that 40 squares are already filled, and if half from each square is taken, the remaining 24 can easily be filled.

So, the king asks the wizard if he would agree to half of one grain in the first square instead of one whole grain and then double up every square as was done before.

The wizard replied that he would be glad to give even a much higher concession and start with one-hundredth of one grain in square 1 instead of the half grain that the king had wished. Alternatively, the king could also choose to add only 150% of the number of grains to each subsequent square instead of 200% every time. The wizard told the king that It was the king's pleasure to choose.

The king reasoned that one-hundredth of one grain instead of one whole grain is a 99% concession, which is much bigger a concession than the 25% concession contained in reducing the square-to-square increase from 200% to 150%.

The king was quick to choose the 99% concession! He reasoned that he would need to give only 1% of the initially agreed number of gains instead of the 25%, which the wizard also had offered.

To make the story short, given below is a summary of both the options from which the king had to choose one.

### 2.2.1     Option 1: One-hundredth of one grain in the first square instead of one whole grain.

This is apparently a 99% concession, which the king opted to accept.

The number of grains in Square 1 is 0.01.

It multiplies approximately 1,000x times every 10 squares (1,024x times to be exact).

The number of grains in Square 11 is approximately 10.

The number of grains in Square 21 is approximately 10,000.

The number of grains in Square 61 is approximately 10 Million Billion.

The number of grains in Square 64 is approximately 92 Million Billion.

The total number of all the grains in all the squares together is approximately **184 Million Billion.**

The total number of grains in each square, and the total number of grains in all the squares together, is precisely **one-hundredth of the original number.**

With the 1,000 Billion grains which the king had and which had covered up to 40 squares previously, the king could now cover up to 46 squares but came short at square 47, let alone all the remaining 17 squares. The king's calculation went totally wrong somewhere, again.

### 2.2.2 Option 2: Only 150 % addition from square-to-square instead of 200%

This is apparently only a 25% concession, which the king opted not to accept.

The number of grains in Square 1 is 1.

The number of grains in Square 2 is 1.5 (= 150% of square 1).

The number of grains in Square 3 is 2.25.

The number of grains in Square 11 is approximately 58.

The number of grains in Square 18 is approximately 1,000.

It multiplies approximately **1,000x** times every **18 years** (985x times to be exact) instead of every 10 years in the original plan.

The number of grains in Square 35 is approximately 1 Million.

The number of grains in Square 52 is approximately 1 Billion.

The number of grains in Square 64 is approximately 124 Billion.

The total number of all the grains in all the squares together is approximately **372 Billion** (triple the number in square number 64 minus 2 grains, to be exact).

This is considerably less than the 1,000 Billion which the king already had to reach square number 40 earlier. If he had opted for this concession, he could have covered all the 64 squares with only about one-third of it and could have kept about two-thirds for his people.

**This quantity of 372 Billion grains is approximately only one fifty-millionth part of the original 18.4 Billion Billion grains, which he would have needed originally.**

Instead, he opted for a concession that would cost him one-hundredth part of the original number of 18.4 Billion Billion grains. **This mistake cost him about half a million** *times* **more grain** (= 50 million / 100) than necessary.

The king based his decision solely on percentages without calculating the actual numbers. He chose for a 99% concession instead of only 25%, a seemingly wise decision on the face of it, but one that cost him half a million times more of his asset.

## 2.2.3    The Lessons

When the king had a choice, he opted for what appeared to give him a 99% concession on the needed number of grains and rejected what seemed to give him only a 25% concession.

But instead of what looked like a gain of about 75x times (= 1% of grains versus 75% of grains required) in the required number of grains, he ended up with a loss of about 500,000x times! Overall, the king's calculation was wrong by a factor of 37.5 million (= 75 x 500,000).

In effect, what the king did is equivalent to choosing a cheque for $1 and rejecting the cheque for $500,000.

Why? The answer is ignorance. Like most of us, the king calculated everything linearly, in 2D, when calculations in 3D and 4D were necessary to get a correct picture. He had little or no knowledge of compounding or exponential growth, let alone the ability to calculate the values.

Two of the most important lessons we can draw from this blunder of the king is this:

### 2.2.3.1    Lesson 1: Never trust percentages

**Never trust and never base your financial decisions only on percentages. Percentages can be extremely deceptive black holes. Percentages are there in thousands of formats and base values. Always calculate the actual amounts and analyze and compare them before making financial decisions.**

### 2.2.3.2    Lesson 2: Learn how exponential growth and compounding work

**Learn how exponential growth, compounding, and negative compounding work and the magic they can do with numbers, percentages, amounts, and tax drag. If you are reading this, you are well on the way.**

The cornerstone of any wealth-building program is compounding. Most of the wealth possessed by most of the ultra-wealthy people on Earth results from the compounding of returns, often starting from a very modest investment base.

The purpose of this volume 1 of the 3-part series on wealth-building is to impart all-important knowledge about compounding and how it can be used effectively to accelerate your journey to millionaire status.

**We will learn how to avoid the blunders that the king made or the publicity blunder and subsequent rectification that the US officials made about a medicine that would heal "50% of all Covid-19 patients" while the correct statement would have been "50% of the 2% of all Covid-19 patients" which effectively means 1% of all patients. We will do that by learning to calculate, in the simplest way, the various wealth-building options available to us and comparing them for the highest results before making a choice.**

We will learn, for example, why 7 never equals the sum of 3+4 in the 4D mathematics of wealth building.

We will learn, for example, why a 1% yield rate can be bigger in value than a 20% yield rate, with all other variables remaining constant.

Let us now look at a couple of real-life examples of compounding.

## 2.3      NUCLEAR BOMB AND EXPONENTIAL GROWTH

This is an extreme example of exponential growth.

### 2.3.1      The chain-reaction inside the nuclear bomb

The atom of nuclear material such as enriched Uranium is hit by a neutron at a very high speed splitting the nucleus of the atom into two or more parts, and in that process of splitting, what scientifically is termed as Nuclear Fission, a tiny bit of the material is converted to an enormous amount of energy in line with Einstein's famous equation $E= mc^2$. The energy that is released is mainly in the form of heat. At the same time, due to the splitting of the heavy atom, 2 to 3 neutrons also get dislodged and fly to hit other atoms nearby, repeating this process in a nuclear chain reaction. It is the nucleus of the atom that is getting split and releases a tremendous amount of energy, and hence the name "Nuclear bomb" that is interchangeably used with the term "Atomic bomb."

Therefore, here also we have compounding taking place as with the grains on our Chessboard. One neutron releases at least another two neutrons, and those two release at least another 4. And so on. It is exponential growth, just like the grains on the Chessboard. In only 63 repetitions, we have at least 18.4 Billion Billion neutrons released and participating in the reaction and releasing a corresponding number of units of energy.

Because these neutrons travel at about 7% of the speed of light, potentially thousands of such cycles of reactions can take place within a second. Just compare it with the Chessboard. The king did not come more than 40 squares with all the grains in his kingdom. Imagine the numbers if there were thousands of squares instead of just 64, and the time available was only one microsecond! Those are the numbers and speeds involved when we are talking about a nuclear bomb! In the context of compounding, a nuclear bomb is the ultimate real-life example of extreme exponential growth.

Due to the enormous amount of heat released in a matter of microseconds, a gigantic explosion takes place, and all the remaining nuclear material is vaporized or pulverized and thrown high up into the air together with the billowing hot air and debris, which cools down quickly due to expansion and ultimately stops rising to form the mushroom-like cloud. These microparticles, which remain radioactive for very many years, eventually come down as nuclear dust spread over vast areas.

Due to the exponential nature of the chain reaction, 98% of the energy that causes the explosion may be coming from the last 5-6 reaction cycles.

### 2.3.2    The difference with nuclear power-plant

The difference between a nuclear bomb and a nuclear reactor for generating electric power is that the nuclear reaction in a power plant is kept at a steady state by limiting the number of neutrons that are allowed to participate in the chain reaction. The excessive neutrons are absorbed by suitable neutron-absorbing materials and carried away continuously. If such control mechanisms fail, including all backups, you get a Chernobyl-like or Fukushima-like catastrophe or worse. It is like a mahout controlling an elephant with the help of only a stick, and it works so long as the elephant does not go amok! If it goes amok, run!

We are not actually interested in the speed of nuclear Fission or the incredible amount of energy it generates as such, but only in how to make use of that compounding technique to create a huge amount of wealth, not energy, in the shortest possible time. Our aim is to create a wealth-multiplier using the same mathematical mechanism.

### 2.4    COVID-19 PANDEMIC AND COMPOUNDING

### 2.4.1    Spread in the first 4.5 months

This is a sinister example of the power of compounding and resultant exponential growth. Starting in Wuhan, China, by the middle of Dec 2019, it had spread to all countries in the world and infected about **3.9 million people** by the end of April 2020, all in just **4.5 months.**

From a mathematical perspective, the oil-spill-like spread can be best explained in terms of compounding, as below.

We assume that it started with just one person in Wuhan in mid-Dec 2019.

4.5 months later, by the end of April 2020, there were about 3.9 million infections worldwide.

The average period between getting infected and infecting others is about 7 days, as concluded by WHO and most scientists.

Based on the above numbers and taking the average of the 4.5 months from 16 December 2019 till 27 April 2020, it can be calculated that, on average, one infected person must have passed it on to 2.15 persons.

In just **19 steps** of compounding at a rate of only **2.15x infections per step**, the virus had spread to about **3.9 million people.**

In order to make it easier for you to grasp, the involved number of infections per step is given in Table 2.2 and Figure 2.2 below.

| Average progression of Covid-19 Infection in 4.5 months with the benefits of preventive measures | | | |
|---|---|---|---|
| **Basic Reproduction Number per infected person per period of 7 days** | | | **2.15** |
| **Period** | **Week ending on** | **Newly Infected people** | **Total infected people** |
| 0 | 16-Dec-19 | 1 | 1 |
| 1 | 23-Dec-19 | 2 | 3 |
| **2** | **30-Dec-19** | **5** | **8** |
| 3 | 06-Jan-20 | 10 | 18 |
| 4 | 13-Jan-20 | 21 | 39 |
| 5 | 20-Jan-20 | 46 | 85 |
| **6** | **27-Jan-20** | **99** | **184** |
| 7 | 03-Feb-20 | 212 | 396 |
| 8 | 10-Feb-20 | 457 | 853 |
| 9 | 17-Feb-20 | 982 | 1,834 |
| **10** | **24-Feb-20** | **2,110** | **3,945** |
| 11 | 02-Mar-20 | 4,538 | 8,482 |
| 12 | 09-Mar-20 | 9,756 | 18,238 |
| 13 | 16-Mar-20 | 20,975 | 39,213 |
| 14 | 23-Mar-20 | 45,096 | 84,309 |
| **15** | **30-Mar-20** | **96,956** | **181,266** |
| 16 | 06-Apr-20 | 208,456 | 389,722 |
| 17 | 13-Apr-20 | 448,181 | 837,903 |
| 18 | 20-Apr-20 | 963,590 | 1,801,493 |
| 19 | 27-Apr-20 | 2,071,718 | 3,873,212 |

Table 2.2: **Average progression of** Covid-19 **infections worldwide in** 4.5 months, **including the effects of all preventive measures.**

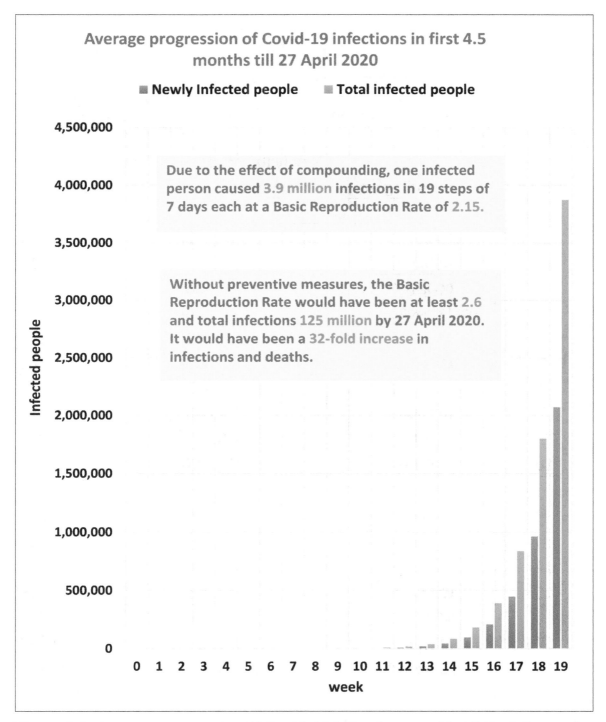

**Average progression of Covid-19 infections in first 4.5 months till 27 April 2020**

■ **Newly Infected people**      ■ **Total infected people**

**Figure 2.2: Average progression of Covid-19 infections worldwide in 4.5 months, including the effects of all preventive measures.**

All values in this Figure are taken from Table 2.2.

| Average progression of Covid-19 Infection in 4.5 months without lockdowns and social distancing | | | |
|---|---|---|---|
| Basic Reproduction Number per infected person per period of 7 days | | | 2.60 |
| Period | Week ending on | Newly Infected people | Total infected people |
| 0 | 16-Dec-19 | 1 | 1 |
| 1 | 23-Dec-19 | 3 | 4 |
| **2** | **30-Dec-19** | **7** | **10** |
| 3 | 06-Jan-20 | 18 | 28 |
| 4 | 13-Jan-20 | 46 | 74 |
| 5 | 20-Jan-20 | 119 | 192 |
| **6** | **27-Jan-20** | **309** | **501** |
| 7 | 03-Feb-20 | 803 | 1,305 |
| 8 | 10-Feb-20 | 2,088 | 3,393 |
| 9 | 17-Feb-20 | 5,430 | 8,822 |
| **10** | **24-Feb-20** | **14,117** | **22,939** |
| 11 | 02-Mar-20 | 36,703 | 59,642 |
| 12 | 09-Mar-20 | 95,429 | 155,071 |
| 13 | 16-Mar-20 | 248,115 | 403,187 |
| 14 | 23-Mar-20 | 645,100 | 1,048,286 |
| **15** | **30-Mar-20** | **1,677,259** | **2,725,546** |
| 16 | 06-Apr-20 | 4,360,874 | 7,086,420 |
| 17 | 13-Apr-20 | 11,338,273 | 18,424,693 |
| 18 | 20-Apr-20 | 29,479,510 | 47,904,203 |
| 19 | 27-Apr-20 | 76,646,727 | 124,550,930 |

Table 2.3: **Average progression of** Covid-19 **infections worldwide** without any preventive measures.

## 2.4.2        Actual situation of the first six weeks in Wuhan

The average position as shown in table 2.2 and figure 2.2 is what we got after implementing all the social distancing and lockdown measures worldwide. In the beginning, in Wuhan, there were no such containment measures. Based on the total number of infections in Wuhan in the first 1.5 months, it has been estimated that, on average, one infected person might have passed on the virus to 6 others resulting in a total of about 56,000 infections. That happened in only 6 steps of 6 transmissions each because of compounding. In a crowded megacity like Wuhan, the infection rate would be higher than in other thinner populated areas.

## 2.4.3        Actual situation worldwide by the end of April 2020, 4.5 months after the birth of Covid-19

Probably, by the end of April 2020, in some countries, the "Basic Reproduction Number," or the number of people to whom one infected person transmits the virus, had dropped below 1.0. It means that the exponential growth had been stopped, and the number of newly infected people would keep on dropping with time, even though slowly and gradually.

From a Basic Reproduction number of 6 in the beginning in Wuhan to less than 1 (one) in 19 weeks in China and some other countries is an achievement that was only possible with the drastic lockdown, social distancing, and other preventive measures implemented in those countries.

### 2.4.3.1        What if there were no lockdowns, social distancing, and other preventive measures?

See Table 2.3 for the calamitous situation if there were no preventive measures like lockdowns and social distancing worldwide.

It is estimated by WHO and other agencies that, if left uncontained by all the lockdowns and quarantine measures, the average infection rate would be approximately 2.6 at an interval rate of 7 days. If we calculate the compounding effect based on these figures, the number of infections worldwide would have been about 125 million infections instead of 3.9 million by the end of April 2020.

That means there would have been a 32-fold increase in infections and deaths by the end of April 2020.

In other words, in the first 4.5 months of the Covid-19 pandemic till the end of April 2020, we managed to contain the human toll of the virus to 3% of the potential toll if there were no preventive measures.

In theory, without the preventive measures, most of the world population would have been infected by the end of May 2020, hardly half a year from the start of the outbreak.

Luckily, scientists and statisticians with knowledge of the effects of compounding have stepped forward to persuade reluctant governments to enforce lockdown, social distancing, and many other preventive measures.

### 2.4.4    Actual situation worldwide by mid-August 2020, 8 months after the birth of Covid-19

At the time of initial writing of this sub-section 2.4.4, on 15 August 2020, the latest data from WHO shows the following:

> Total infections worldwide: 21 million.
>
> Increase in one week's time: 2 million.

From the above, it follows that the Basic Reproduction Number has dropped to 1.03 in the period May- Aug 2020. As this number is still higher than 1.0, the number of new infections will keep on increasing.

If this trend remains unchanged, the total number of infections will have reached 70 million by 31 December 2020.

You may be wondering why an additional 49 million (= 70 – 21) infections in just 4.5 months (mid-Aug to end Dec) despite all the lockdowns and other preventive measures while we had only 3.9 million in the first 4.5 months without extensive preventive measures.

The simple answer to this question is **compounding** and **resultant exponential growth**.

### 2.4.5    Actual situation worldwide by mid-Feb 2021, 6 months after the report in section 2.4.4 above

At the time of this final update, 19 Feb 2021, on the eve of publishing this book, the latest data from WHO shows the following:

> Total infections worldwide till 31 Dec 2020: 84 million.
>
> Total infections worldwide till 15 Feb 2021: 108 million.
>
> Total deaths so far, till 15 Feb 2021: 2.4 million.
>
> Average new daily infections in the third week of Feb 2021: 0.4 million per day.
>
> Average new daily infections in the last week of Dec 2020: 0.7 million per day.

#### 2.4.5.1    Conclusions

From the above data, the following conclusions can be drawn.

The average Basic Reproduction Number in the 4.5-month period, Aug-Dec 2020, was about 1.05, higher than the 1.03 in the preceding 3.5 months period.

The result of this seemingly slight increase in Basic Reproduction Number was a jump in the total number of infections from the projected **70 million to 84 million**.

The average Basic Reproduction Number in the 1.5-month period, Jan-Feb 2021, was about **0.92**, well below the 1.0 needed to "flatten the curve" or stabilize the number of new infections.

**If this pattern remains unchanged and the Basic Reproduction Number stays at 0.92, the following can be expected:**

By 31 May 2021:

- The total number of infections will have increased by "only" 22 million in 3.5 months, from the current **108 million** to **130 million.**

- New infections will have dropped from the current **0.4 million** per day to **0.12 million** per day.

By 31 Aug 2021:

- The total number of infections will have increased by "only" 7 million in 3 months, from 130 million on 31 May 2021 to **137 million** on 31 Aug 2021.

- New infections will have dropped from **120,000** per day on 31 May 2021 to **40,000** per day on 31 Aug 2021.

By 31 Dec 2021:

- The total number of infections will have increased by "only" 3 million in 4 months, from 137 million on 31 Aug 2021 to **140 million** on 31 Dec 2021.

- New infections will have dropped from **40,000** per day on 31 Aug 2021 to **10,000** per day on 31 Dec 2021.

It shows that in the world of compounding, what Covid-19 actually is, even a minute fraction of a number or percentage can have an enormous impact on the final outcome. The drop of Basic Reproduction Number from 1.05 to 0.92 can practically eradicate Covid-19 ultimately.

## 2.4.6     The lesson

The lack of this level of knowledge and insight into the effects of compounding was undoubtedly a contributing factor to the death of 50 million people worldwide due to the Spanish flu 100 years ago. To their great disadvantage, computers, which we are literally born with today, were not there at that time to facilitate the mathematical insights into compounding.

Deeper knowledge about compounding and the resultant exponential growth among scientists and statisticians has led to the timely imposition of preventive measures leading to a 97% reduction in the number of infections and deaths in the first 4.5 months of the pandemic.

This knowledge and insight into the working of compounding and resultant exponential growth can also be put into practical use today to reach your financial destination much faster.

### 2.4.6.1    Analogy with the yield rate of an investment

The Basic Reproduction Number (BRN) of Covid-19 is, in many ways, analogous to the yield rate of an investment. If the yield rate is positive, it is analogous to the BRN having a value above 1.0, and the investment will grow exponentially.

If the yield rate is negative, it is analogous to the BRN having a value below 1.0, and the investment will diminish exponentially.

If the yield rate is zero, it is analogous to the BRN having a value of exactly 1.0, and the investment will stay at the constant value just as the number of new Covid-19 infections would stabilize and remain stable at a specific number.

Just as slight variations in the BRN have tremendous consequences for the growth rate and the total number of infections, minor variations in the yield rate of investment can have a significant impact on the growth rate and resultant net worth of the investment. It will become apparent to you as you progress through the pages of this book, and you will find ways to increase the BRN of your investment substantially.

## 2.5    DECAY OF FOOD AND COMPOUNDING

Decaying of food when kept outside at room temperature is also the 'fault' of compounding. Of the many types of airborne bacteria, some of them will land on the food. When the food and other environmental conditions are ideal to a bacterium of any kind, that will settle down on the food and will make it its home. It grows and then splits itself into two daughters. And the two daughters do exactly the same: they take in food, grow, and divide themselves again into two each.

Most of the common bacteria have a doubling time of between 15 to 60 minutes in optimal conditions. One of the optimal conditions is a pleasantly warm room temperature. Let us assume that the doubling time of the bacterium on a plate of beans kept outside the fridge is 45 minutes.

A doubling time of 45 minutes means doubling of 32 times in 24 hours, 64 times in 2 days, and 96 times in 3 days. From the king's Chessboard blunder, we know the following:

After 24 hours, there will be 4 Billion bacteria on the beans.

**After 48 hours**, there will be **18 Billion Billion** bacteria on the beans! That is 4.5 Billion *times* more than the day before.

The growth is now at such an astronomical rate resulting in Billions of Billions of Billions of bacteria at the end of the third day.

But in practice, with such an enormous number of bacteria in the dish, it gets too overcrowded, the nutrients get depleted, and as a result, the multiplication process gradually stops, and at a later stage, the bacteria start dying off at an exponential rate.

This exponential growth of bacteria is the reason why the dish of beans may still look and smell relatively fresh even after 24 hours but deteriorates extremely fast after that. The decay is synchronous with the number of bacteria, both of which grow exponentially.

That is why you can prolong the preservation time of food by heating it up in between and keeping it cool again. By heating it up in between, you kill all the bacteria which were already present, resetting the cycle of exponential growth to zero.

Can we emulate this bacterial growth with our money? Doubling of money in 45 minutes is possible only in casinos, but doubling or tripling or quadrupling or even more in the span of a year, and that too structurally, is what many super-rich people have managed to achieve. So, there is hope that we can also follow them, even if at a slower speed.

## 2.6 THE BIRTHDAY TEASER

Sometimes, teasing is the most effective way to drive home a point and have fun at the same time too.

One piece of advice I often give to young people is to open a bank account in their child's name when the child is **one year**, deposit one dollar in it, and as the banks give little interest, give 100% interest themselves every year until its 31st birthday. That way, the child would have a financial base to start his own family by the time the parents retire.

Every person to whom I made this suggestion was very enthusiastic about the idea and said he would gladly do it for his child! When specifically asked whether paying a 100% interest on the balance amount would not be too big a burden, none of them saw it as a problem. On the contrary, some of them even thought that it was too meager a saving for their child.

Then, when I disclose the actual amounts involved, they get as shocked as the ancient Indian king upon discovering the number of wheat grains he would need for the Chessboard.

The mathematics involved is identical to that of the wheat grains on the Chessboard. See Table 2.1.

On the **31st birthday** of the child, the parents would have to **deposit $537 Million** in the child's bank account, which would make the total **in the account $1,074 Million.**

Like the Bacterial process in the previous example, this is also a **compounding** process with a **nominal yield rate of 100% and no tax withdrawals.**

Of course, my "advice" was not meant to be a serious one, but a teaser and a test to see if people are aware of the compounding phenomenon. I had given the "advice" only to educated young people, and each of them was startled to hear the astronomical numbers.

This anecdote again shows how mighty and misleading compound interest can be.

\* \* \* \*

# Chapter 3:

# Basic 4D-mathematics of Compounding

In this chapter, we will shortly cover some of the basics of compounding though some of the readers may be familiar with the topics covered and may find this chapter superfluous. Nevertheless, I would advise all the readers to go through this chapter, especially because of some of the new concepts introduced here.

Though it is the objective of this book that readers need not use any advanced mathematical formulas to calculate any financial result, some basic formulas are given in this chapter for the sake of those readers who might find them helpful. All the other readers can simply skip the formulas as they are not essential to understand the content of this book.

## 3.1      SIMPLE INTEREST

Let us take a quick look at Simple interest first so that we can later understand compound interest more easily.

### Example 3.1

If you put $100 in a bank account against a 10% nominal interest rate per year, you will get a total of $110 at the end of the first year.

If you withdraw the interest after a year, $10 in this example, and leave the principal of $100 in the account for another year, you will get again $10 as interest at the end of the second year.

You can repeat this process for any number of years. Let us assume you did it for five years. In 5 years, you got a total of $50 as interest, and at the end of 5 years, you got back also your initial deposit of $100.

**The total results of 5 years are as follows:**

Initial deposit: $100.00.

Total interest received: $50.00.

Tax: $0.00.

The final amount in your hands: $150.00.

The nominal interest rate that the bank had quoted was 10%. What you got as interest in 5 years was also $50, which averages to 10% interest per year.

This is an example of simple interest without compounding. If you had a huge amount of money available and no further ambitions to make it grow further, you could put that money in a deposit this way and live on the interest-only as some rich people choose to do.

### 3.1.1 Formulas for Simple interest

#### 3.1.1.1 Interest amount or yield amount

Interest amount or yield amount Y can be expressed as:

$$Y = P \times R \times N$$

In **Microsoft Excel**, the formula for interest amount or yield amount is:

=P*R*N

Where,

Y = Yield amount or interest amount.

P = Principal or initial investment.

R = Nominal interest rate or yield rate per year.

N = Number of years.

In our example with $100 deposit for 5 years at an interest rate of 10% p.a., the total amount of interest received = 100 x (10/100) x 5 = $50.

#### 3.1.1.2 Final amount or net worth

As the final amount is the resultant net worth of an investment, we will use the term net worth interchangeably with the term final amount.

Final amount or net worth = principal amount P + yield amount Y.

If there is no tax involved, net worth NW can be expressed as:

$$NW = P + Y \quad \text{or}$$

$$NW = P + (P \times R \times N) \quad \text{or}$$

$$NW = P \times [(R \times N) + 1]$$

In **Microsoft Excel**, if tax is not involved, the formula for net worth is:

=P+Y  or

=P+P*R*N  or

=P*(R*N+1)

## 3.2    COMPOUND INTEREST VERSUS EXPONENTIAL GROWTH

Most people are generally familiar with compound interest. The familiarity is limited to the knowledge that, if they deposit money in a bank for longer periods, they will get the compound interest and that compound interest has more value than simple interest.

When interest in a bank account is compounded annually, it results in an increase in your bank balance, and the rate of that increase in dollar terms goes higher and higher with time. Your bank balance will keep on increasing faster and faster, like a car accelerating on the road.

If your bank balance doubled in 5 years, it would double again in another 5 years resulting in a multiple of 4x times the initial amount. In another 5 years, it will double again, resulting in a multiple of 8x times the initial amount.

Such a steadily increasing increase of your bank balance, other assets, or anything else for that matter is what is known as **exponential growth**.

Compounding of interest would result in the exponential growth of your bank deposit or wealth.

The exponential growth of wealth has compounding of interest or yield or return as its foundation.

As we have already seen in the examples in chapter 2, compounding of interest is only one of the many forms of exponential growth that takes place around us in our everyday lives, for good and for bad.

### 3.2.1    Can the general formulas for compounding be used for all exponential growths?

Compounding of interest would result in an exponential growth of wealth. Conversely, can all exponential growth processes that occur around us then be treated as compounding?

The short answer is yes. Compounding and Exponential growth are mathematically synonymous.

The long answer is: yes, but the method of the exponential growth of, for example, Covid-19 infection can differ from the method of the exponential growth of money in a bank account. Therefore, when using the general compounding formulas for wealth-building in order to calculate the growth of Covid-19 infections, those formulas may have to be adapted accordingly.

The grains on the **chessboard** can be treated mathematically as compounding in the following way: It is equivalent to an investment of $1 for 63 years with a nominal yield rate of 200% compounded annually and a nominal tax rate of 50% paid annually. The grains that were collected in squares 1 to 63 will be the equivalent of the 50% nominal tax.

For the number of neutron collisions and energy released in a **nuclear bomb**, the relationships are the same as with the grains on the chessboard. It is equivalent to an investment of $1 with a **nominal yield rate of 200%** and a **nominal tax rate of 50%**. All the steps of collisions except the last one before the explosion constitute the virtual tax rate of 50%.

The spread of **Covid-19** pandemic in the first 4.5 months as discussed in section 2.4.1 can be treated mathematically as compounding in the following way:

Spread with a nominal spread rate of **215% compounded weekly** and a tax-equivalent **withdrawal rate of 46.5%** (= 1/ 2.15). The withdrawal of people who were infected once and had infected 2.15 people on average from further spreading the virus is the equivalent of a 46.5% tax rate.

### 3.2.2    Exponential growth of wheat grains on the chessboard

The number of grains on the chessboard was:

**1, 2, 4, 8, 16,** etc.

It can also be written as:

**1, 2, 2x2, 2x2x2, 2x2x2x2**, etc., or as

$2^0$, $2^1$, $2^2$, $2^3$, $2^4$ .... $2^{63}$.

Each number is a multiple of the previous number, and the multiplication factor, in this case, is 2.

The growth here is **exponential with a base of 2,** and the **exponent is the Square Number** on the chessboard.

If the wizard had asked for a tripling of the number of grains instead of doubling, the numbers would have been as below:

**1, 3, 9, 27, 81**, etc.

It can also be written as:

**1, 3, 3x3, 3x3x3, 3x3x3x3**, etc. or as:

$3^0$, $3^1$, $3^2$, $3^3$, $3^4$ ....$3^{63}$.

The growth here is **exponential with a multiplication factor or base value of 3.**

If the growth factor was 1.20, it would be exponential growth with a multiplication factor or base value of 1.20.

The number 16 in this example is written as $2^4$. It is spoken as "two to the power of four." The number **4** here is called the **exponent**. The number **2** is the **base.** The name exponential growth is derived from the term exponent.

The sets of numbers above, in which the exponents are whole numbers, are also said to be in geometric progression.

The terms exponential growth and geometric growth are generally used interchangeably.

## 3.3     COMPOUND INTEREST

In compound interest, if we put money in a Term Deposit in a bank, the interest received annually is not withdrawn but added to the principal. The principal generates yield in the first year, and that yield amount is added to the principal. The increased principal then goes on to generate a yield amount in the second year that will be higher than the yield amount of the first year, and that is added to the principal again. This process goes on till the maturity date of the deposit.

There is not a single dollar withdrawn and therefore stops participating in generating wealth at any point unless you have to withdraw a part of the annual yield amount to pay yearly tax.

### 3.3.1     Example of compounding

Suppose we have a term deposit of $100 in a bank account with a term of 5 years and a nominal interest rate of 10% per year compounded annually, and the interest received is tax-free.

**The total results of 5 years are as follows:**

Please do not worry about how to calculate; you will learn it in later chapters.

Total interest received in 5 years: $61.05. With simple interest, this amount would have been $50.00, as seen in example 3.1.

Withdrawn for paying tax: $0.00.

Total interest retained in the account: $61.05.

Final amount in the account after 5 years: $161.05.

### 3.3.2     Formulas for Compound interest

#### 3.3.2.1     Final amount or net worth

If there is no tax involved, net worth NW can be expressed as:

$$NW = P \times (1+R)^N$$

In Microsoft Excel, if tax is not involved, the formula for net worth NW is:

`=P*(1+R)^N`

### 3.3.2.2    Cumulative interest amount or yield amount

(Cumulative yield amount) = (Final amount or net worth) – (Principal amount).

Interest amount or yield amount Y can be expressed as:

$$Y = NW - P$$

It can also be expressed as:

$$Y = P \times (1+R)^N - P \quad \text{or as}$$

$$Y = P \times [(1 + R)^N - 1]$$

In **Microsoft Excel**, the formula for interest amount or yield amount Y is:

=P*(1+R)^N-P   or

=P*((1+R)^N-1)

Where,

Y = yield amount or interest amount.

P = principal or initial investment.

R = Nominal interest rate or yield rate per year.

N = Number of years.

### 3.3.2.3    Annual interest amount

**Method 1**

The easiest way to calculate it is to calculate the final amounts for the concerned year and the previous year. The difference between the two values is the annual interest amount you received in the concerned year.

**Method 2**

Another way to calculate it is to use the **Compound Amount Factor (CAF)** table described in chapter 4 of this book.

**Annual interest amount you will receive in** year N **will be** = $R \times P \times CAF_{(N-1)}$.

An example will illustrate how to calculate it, as shown below.

Assume $100 is invested at 10% annual interest. What would be the yearly interest amount you will be receiving in year 25?

The Annual interest amount you will receive in year 25 will be: $R \times P \times CAF_{24}$.

Let us look at the CAF table for the intersection of the 10% interest rate and year 24 (not 25). We get the CAF value of 9.85. Note that the corresponding CAF value is achieved one year earlier as we are calculating the final amount at the end of year 24 and then calculating the interest it would earn in year 25 using the above formula.

The Annual interest amount you will receive in year 25 will be: 0.10 x 100 x 9.85. =$98.50.

## Method 3

A third way to calculate it is to use a formula.

**As seen in method two above, the annual interest amount you will receive in year N will be = R x P x CAF$_{(N-1)}$.**

**Compound Amount Factor (CAF) for N years = $(1+R)^N$**

How we arrive at this formula is explained later in this book, in chapter 4.

Combining both the formulas, we get the following:

**Annual interest amount in year N will be** = P x R x $(1+R)^{(N-1)}$

In **Microsoft Excel**, the formula for Annual interest amount in year N will be:

=P*R*(1+R)^(N-1)

## Method 4

The easiest method of all is to use an appropriate software program to calculate the data.

The author of this book has developed an easy-to-use program based on MS Excel, which can compute and present all the data related to compounding, tax drag, and wealth-building. The annual interest amount is also one of the hundreds of data that the program will produce and present to you.

Nonetheless, understanding the logic and mathematics behind every such data is key to successful wealth-building. What will a monkey choose if presented with a banana and a gold bar of equal size? Some financial institutions are in the business of giving bananas to us consumers in exchange for gold bars. This series of books is intended to make us more money-smart so that we can distinguish and collect gold bars instead of bananas.

Therefore, even if you choose a software program to get the needed data for any investment computed, it is also strongly advised to go through this series of books in order to gain valuable insights required to interpret the data churned out by the software program correctly.

## 3.4    TAX & TAX DRAG

### 3.4.1    Example

Let us look at the example in the previous section 3.3.1 again in which we have a term deposit of $100 in a bank account with a term of 5 years and a nominal interest rate of 10% compounded annually. Instead of being tax-free, let us assume that there is a 30% tax obligation on the interest received yearly.

#### 3.4.1.1    The total results for 1 year are as follows

Total interest received (pre-tax): $10.00.

Total tax paid: $3.00 (this equals 30% of $10.00).

Total of interest that is retained in the account (after-tax): $7.00 (= 510.00 – 3.00).

Final amount in the account: $107.00 (= 100 + 7.00).

The total interest that would have been received if there was no tax: $10.00.

After-tax interest received as % of tax-free interest: 70.00% (= 7.00/ 10.00).

Loss of interest income due to tax: $3.00 (= 10.0 – 7.00).

TAX DRAG in 1 year = Loss of interest income due to tax as % of interest income without tax: 30.00% (= 3.00/ 10.00).

Our after-tax interest income in 1 year as % of interest income without tax: 70.00% (= 100 – 30) or (= 7.00/ 10.00).

#### 3.4.1.2    The total results for 5 years are as follows

Please do not worry about how to calculate; you will learn it in later chapters.

Total interest received (pre-tax): $57.51.

Total tax paid: $17.25 (this equals 30% of $57.51).

Total of interest that is retained in the account (after-tax): $40.26 (= 57.51 – 17.25).

Final amount in the account: $140.26 (= 100 + 40.26).

The total interest that would have been received if there was no tax: $61.05.

After-tax interest received as % of tax-free interest: 65.90% (= 40.26/ 61.05).

Loss of interest income due to tax: $20.80 (= 61.05 – 40.26).

TAX DRAG in 5 years = Loss of interest income due to tax as % of interest income without tax: 34.10% (= 20.80/ 61.05).

Our after-tax interest income in 5 years as % of interest income without tax: 65.90 (= 100 – 34.10) or (= 40.26/ 61.05).

Instead of 5 years, if we had continued our investment for 30 years, till retirement, for example, the results would have been as below.

### 3.4.1.3      The total results for 30 years are as follows

Please do not worry about how to calculate; you will learn it in later chapters.

Total interest received (pre-tax): $944.

Total tax paid: $283 (this equals 30% of $944).

Total of interest that is retained in the account (after-tax): $661 (= 944 – 283).

Final amount in the account: $761 (= 100 + 661).

The total interest that would have been received if there was no tax: $1645.

After-tax interest received as % of tax-free interest: 40.20% (= 661/ 1645).

Loss of interest income due to tax: $984 (= 1645 – 661).

**TAX DRAG in 30 years = Loss of interest income due to tax as % of interest income without tax: 59.80% (= 984/ 1645).**

**Our after-tax interest income in 30 years as % of interest income without tax: 40.20% (= 100 – 59.80) or (= 661/ 1645).**

### 3.4.1.4      The total results for 50 years are as follows

If we continue this account for 50 years, as some people who are married to term deposits do, the results would be as follows:

**TAX DRAG in 50 years = Loss of interest income due to tax as % of interest income without tax: 75.60% (= 8793/ 11639).**

**Our after-tax interest income in 50 years as % of interest income without tax: 24.40% (= 100 – 75.60) or (= 2846/ 11639).**

### 3.4.2      Summary of results

In summary, what we have observed from the above examples is the following:

Tax drag starts with the nominal tax rate in the first year but increases with time.

In this example, tax drag increased from 30% in year 1 to 75.6% in 50 years.

The net return from the investment decreased from 70% in year 1 to 24.4% in 50 years.

That means, due to tax and tax drag, in this example, your net income from this investment is only 24.4% of what you would have had if there were no tax.

If you nevertheless had a net worth of **$1 million** in 50 years after annual tax, it would have been **$4 million** if there were no tax and **$2.8 million** if the 30% nominal tax were **deferred tax or capital gains tax** instead of annual tax or income tax.

### 3.4.3    Explanation of tax drag

As viewed from the perspective of wealth-building, tax is a withdrawal from your accumulated wealth if you are paying tax annually. Tax is precisely the **opposite** of receiving annual payments of interest because it is being **withdrawn** instead of being **added** to your wealth.

When interest gets compounded annually, your wealth grows exponentially. This is **positive** compounding.

On the opposite side, in the same way, your potential wealth decreases exponentially when tax withdrawals get compounded annually. This is **negative** compounding.

When interest is received, it adds to your wealth. Therefore, it carries a **(+)** sign.

When tax is withdrawn, it subtracts from your wealth. Therefore, it carries a **(-)** sign. Therefore, you can also consider tax withdrawals as **negative interest**.

If **positive interest gets compounded**, it is logical that **negative interest also gets compounded**.

Tax Drag is the name given to the compounding of negative interest or loss of interest due to tax.

Compounding of yield or interest received can make you very wealthy, as we can see throughout this book.

Similarly, tax drag, working in the same way but traveling in the opposite direction to that of compounding of interest, can drag you down to a turtle-paced slow speed on the highway to riches and millionairedom. Mathematical relationships produce the same magnitudes irrespective of whether a number carries a positive or negative sign. Tax, or any other periodic withdrawal for that matter, bears a negative sign and will eat up a lot of your potential wealth.

**Tax Drag is like an escalator running towards you in the opposite direction.**

Tax drag with an **annual tax or income tax** is like you trying to reach an upper floor, the millionaires' floor, by climbing an escalator that is coming down and which increases its speed every time you climb one step!

Tax drag with **deferred tax or capital gains tax** is also like you trying to reach an upper floor, the millionaires' floor, by climbing an escalator that is coming down, but one with a constant speed.

See chapter 18 for more information about tax drag.

For a complete treatise on tax drag, please see volume II of this series titled "**Tax Drag, the Dragon that eats up your wealth,**" which will be published soon.

## 3.5     NOMINAL INTEREST VERSUS NET INTEREST AND TAX RATES

### 3.5.1     Formula for net interest or yield rate

Net interest or yield rate = Nominal interest or yield rate x (1 – Tax rate).

For example, if nominal interest rate is 10% and tax rate 30%, net interest rate will be 7% [= 0.10 x (1-0.30)].

If nominal interest rate is 16% and tax rate 25%, net interest rate will be 12% [= 0.16 x (1-0.25].

If nominal interest rate is 25% and tax rate 20%, net interest rate will be 20% [= 0.25 x (1-0.20].

Net interest rate, instead of Nominal interest rate, can be used directly for all calculations involving net (after-tax) yield and net worth.

### 3.5.2     Formula for net tax rate

Net tax rate = Nominal interest or yield rate x Nominal Tax rate.

For example, if nominal interest rate is 10% and nominal tax rate 30%, net tax rate will be 3% (= 0.10 x 0.30 ) of the capital under tax.

If nominal interest rate is 16% and nominal tax rate 25%, net tax rate will be 4% (= 0.16 x 0.25) of the capital under tax.

If nominal interest rate is 25% and nominal tax rate 20%, net tax rate will be 5% (= 0.25 x 0.20) of the capital under tax.

### 3.5.3     The formulas for the net (after-tax) final amount or net worth

To calculate the net (after-tax) final amount or net worth of an investment, you can use the following formulas. The formulas are the same as in section 3.3.2.1, with the only difference being the use of net interest rate here instead of the nominal interest rate.

**Final amount or net worth** $NW = P \times (1+R)^N$

In **Microsoft Excel,** the formula for net worth **NW** is:

    =P*(1+R)^N

Where,

> P = principal or initial investment.
>
> R = net interest or yield rate per year.
>
> N = Number of years.

### 3.5.4    The formulas for net (after-tax) accumulated interest or total net yield

To calculate the net (after-tax) accumulated interest or yield amount of an investment, you can use the following formulas. The formulas are the same as in section 3.3.2.2, with the only difference being the use of net interest rate here instead of the nominal interest rate.

> **Net Interest or net yield amount** $NY = P \times (1+R)^N - P$
>
> **It can also be expressed as** $NY = P \times [(1 + R)^N - 1]$

In **Microsoft Excel**, the formula for net interest amount or net yield amount $NY$ is:

> =P*(1+R)^N-P  or
>
> =P*((1+R)^N-1)

Here also, R is the Net interest rate and not the Nominal interest rate.

### 3.5.5    Formula for the actual amount of tax paid or was payable

The actual amount of tax paid or was payable in any particular year is always the amount you get when the nominal tax rate is applied to the actual pre-tax yield amount realized in that year.

Similarly, the actual amount of tax paid or was payable in any particular period, 5 or 10 years, for example, is always the amount you get when the nominal tax rate is applied to the actual pre-tax yield amount realized in that period.

Using formulas in section 3.5.4 above, we can calculate the net (after-tax) amount of interest or yield realized from any investment. From that data, we can derive or back-calculate the total amount of tax paid or was payable using the following formula:

**The actual tax amount paid or was payable as annual tax or income tax in any year or period is:**

> = (Net Yield Amount received) x (Nominal Tax rate) / (1- Nominal Tax rate).

Or,

> = (Net Yield Amount received) x (Net Tax rate) / (Net Yield rate).

**Example**

Let us take the values from the example in section 3.4.1.2.

We had invested **$100** in a term deposit for **5 years** at a **10%** nominal interest rate and **30%** annual tax on earned interest.

Using the formula in section 3.5.1 above, we get **the net interest or yield rate** as **7%** [= 0.10 x (1-0.3)].

Using the formula in section 3.5.4 above and using the net interest rate of 7%, we get the accumulated **net interest amount** as **$40.26.**

Using the first formula above, we get the following:

Actual tax amount paid or payable = 40.26 x (30%/70%) = **$17.25.**

Using the second formula above, the tax amount = 40.26 x (3%/7%) = **$17.25.**

That means, in the course of 5 years, we paid a total amount of $17.25 as tax.

## 3.6    NOMINAL INTEREST RATES VS EFFECTIVE INTEREST RATES

Banks in various countries have varying standards and intervals for compounding. However, it is the annual interest rate that is generally quoted by the banks, and it is usually referred to as the Nominal interest rate. It does not take the effect of compounding into account.

**Effective interest rate is the one that also takes compounding into account.** For quarterly compounding, the Effective rate will be a bit higher than the rate for half-yearly compounding; for monthly compounding, the Effective rate will be still a bit higher than the rate for quarterly compounding, and so on.

## 3.6.1    Half-yearly, Quarterly, Monthly or Daily Compounding

For using the compounding formulas given in section 3.3, interest rate R becomes half of the annual nominal rate for half-yearly compounding, one-fourth for quarterly compounding, one-twelfth for monthly compounding, and one-365th for daily compounding.

If 6.0% is the nominal interest rate, for half-yearly compounding, it becomes 3.0%, for monthly compounding 0.50%, and so on.

The value of the number of periods N increases correspondingly. For a 2-year deposit compounded quarterly, the number of periods N becomes 8. If the compounding is done monthly, the number of periods becomes 24 for 2 years. Some typical values:

For a **10.0% nominal** interest rate, if compounded **half-yearly**, the Effective interest rate becomes **10.25 %** p.a.

If compounded **quarterly**, the Effective interest rate becomes **10.38%** p.a.

If compounded monthly, the Effective interest rate becomes 10.47% p.a.

If compounded daily, the Effective interest rate becomes 10.52% p.a.

## 3.7    SIMPLE ANNUAL YIELD

With a term deposit of $100 for 15 years at a nominal interest rate of 10% compounded annually, the cumulative interest received in 15 years will be approximately $318. That gives an annual average of approximately $21.20 (= 318/15). On a $100 deposit, $21.20 average interest means a yearly average interest rate of 21.2% over 15 years.

This 21.2% is labeled as **Simple Annual Yield** by several major banks all over the world, especially in developing countries where laws to protect consumers are relatively weak and law enforcement is often corruption-ridden.

In our example, the nominal interest rate is 10%. The corresponding simple annual yield is 21.2%, but that is the case only if the deposit is maintained for the entire 15 years.

In contrast to a 10% annual interest, 21.2% average annual yield sounds great and may even be technically correct, but it is pretty misleading to the common people, especially in countries with relatively low literacy!

**Beware**

All over the world, unscrupulous brokers, financial and commercial institutions, Real Estate marketers, and even some banks mislead potential investors by accentuating simple annual yield instead of the nominal interest rate.

## 3.8    SOME NOTES ON INTEREST RATES

**Note-1:** Banks will compound negative interest, that is, the interest that you owe to the bank as a borrower or debtor, generally monthly if not daily. When the bank owes you interest as a depositor, generally, they compound the interest not monthly, but only on a quarterly or half-yearly basis or even yearly basis. This discrimination is to the advantage of the banks and to the disadvantage of customers.

**Note-2:** Credit Card debt is generally compounded even daily. The daily compounding adds up considerably also because of the extremely high interest rates on Credit Card debt. For a nominal interest rate of 20% p.a., upon daily compounding, the Effective interest rate becomes 22.1% p.a.

**Note-3:** With Credit Card debt, you will surely be on the super-highway to riches, but the only problem is that you are in reverse gear! It is the bank that is in forward-gear, as you will see in chapter 9.

\* \* \* \*

# Chapter 4:

# Use of Tables to calculate 4D Investment Results

## Use of Tables to calculate Final Amount and Total Return of investment.

As we have just seen in chapter 3, the formulas for calculating the final amounts and yields involving compounding are a bit complex and will need, in addition to the mathematical knowledge, a calculator or PC to calculate them and practical skills to use the calculator or PC.

A much simpler way that can be used by anybody without advanced education in mathematics is the use of tables in which the needed values are already computed for a series of interest rates and periods of investment. The formulas given in chapter 3 have been used to develop these tables.

With the help of these tables, all that you need to do to get the desired results of an investment is to do simple multiplication, division, addition, or subtraction, or a combination of those. Complex calculations using formulas can be avoided that way.

There are two sets of tables developed which are very similar, like twins, but still with slightly different values with respect to each other.

They are:

1. **Compound Amount Factor table (CAF table)**
2. **Compound Yield Factor table (CYF table)**

The full Compound Amount Factor table (CAF table) is attached as Appendix-A to this book.

The Compound Yield Factor table (CYF table) is attached as Appendix-B to this book.

For easy reference, a sample page of the CAF table is taken up in this section itself as Table 4.1, and a sample page of the CYF table is taken up as Table 4.2.

It is the CAF table that we will be using most of the time for various calculations.

The reason is that the CAF table is derived directly using the primary compounding equation, and the values are in exponential progression, making computations easier. CYF table is derived from the CAF table, and the values are not in exponential progression.

Using either of these tables is the easiest way to calculate the results of any investment for those who do not have an app or program installed on their mobile device or PC to compute the results or those who do not want to get involved in the mathematics or are aversive to using any formula.

## 4.1 COMPOUND AMOUNT FACTOR (CAF) TABLE

The CAF table gives how much the final amount or net worth will be if you invest $1 (or any other currency) for N number of years at a nominal yield or interest rate of R% on a compound basis. The results are given as a Factor (multiplier) and not as a percentage.

See Table 4.1 for a sample page. Appendix-A carries the whole table.

It gives CAF values for interest rates ranging from **1% to 100%** and investment periods ranging from **1 to 60.** The periods could be years, but in principle, they could be of any length of time like a quarter, month, or week or even days.

The CAF table gives, for any combination of interest rate and period of investment, a factor (multiplier) by which the principal amount would have grown in that period at that interest rate. It is merely a value with which you multiply the principal amount to get the final amount.

If the table gives a value of 5.0, you simply multiply your initial deposit with 5.0 to get the final amount.

**Final amount = principal amount x CAF value**

### Example 4.1

If you invested $1,000 today in a scheme that offered 15% interest compounded annually for 30 years, how much will be the final amount after 30 years?

To get the result, look at the value at the intersection of the row for 30 years and column for 15%. The table gives a value of 66.2. Therefore, your $1,000 would become $66,200 (1,000 x 66.2) at the end of 30 years.

## 4.2 COMPOUND YIELD FACTOR (CYF) TABLE

A Compound yield Factor (CYF) table can equally be called Compound Interest Factor (CIF) table, but for the sake of consistency, we will use the term CYF throughout this book.

The CYF table gives how much the accumulated yield amount will be if you invest $1 (or any other currency) for N number of years at a nominal yield or interest rate of R% on a compound basis. The results are given as a Factor (multiplier) and not as a percentage.

See Table 4.2 for a sample page. Appendix-B carries the whole table.

The layout and the range of the CYF table are exactly the same as the CAF table. However, for an easy visual distinction between the two tables, the colors are made distinctly different.

The CYF table gives, for any combination of interest rate and period of investment, a factor (multiplier) by which the principal amount would have to be multiplied to get the total cumulative yield for that period at that interest rate. It is merely a value with which you multiply the principal amount to get the total yield.

If the table gives a value of 4.0, you simply multiply your initial deposit with 4.0 to get the total yield.

**Total yield = principal amount x CYF value**

## Example 4.2

How much will be the total yield if you put $1 in an account for 30 years at an interest rate of 20% compounded annually?

To get the result, look at the value at the intersection of the row for 30 years and column for 20%. The value is 236.4. This is the CYF value. Your $1 investment would yield, or return, $236.40 in total.

| Year (N) | Yield Rate ( R ) | | | | | | | | | |
|---|---|---|---|---|---|---|---|---|---|---|
| | 5.50% | 6.00% | 6.50% | 7.00% | 7.50% | 8.00% | 8.50% | 9.00% | 9.50% | 10.00% |
| 0 | 1.000 | 1.000 | 1.000 | 1.000 | 1.000 | 1.000 | 1.000 | 1.000 | 1.000 | 1.000 |
| 1 | 1.055 | 1.060 | 1.065 | 1.070 | 1.075 | 1.080 | 1.085 | 1.090 | 1.095 | 1.100 |
| 2 | 1.113 | 1.124 | 1.134 | 1.145 | 1.156 | 1.166 | 1.177 | 1.188 | 1.199 | 1.210 |
| 3 | 1.174 | 1.191 | 1.208 | 1.225 | 1.242 | 1.260 | 1.277 | 1.295 | 1.313 | 1.331 |
| 4 | 1.239 | 1.262 | 1.286 | 1.311 | 1.335 | 1.360 | 1.386 | 1.412 | 1.438 | 1.464 |
| 5 | 1.307 | 1.338 | 1.370 | 1.403 | 1.436 | 1.469 | 1.504 | 1.539 | 1.574 | 1.611 |
| 6 | 1.379 | 1.419 | 1.459 | 1.501 | 1.543 | 1.587 | 1.631 | 1.677 | 1.724 | 1.772 |
| 7 | 1.455 | 1.504 | 1.554 | 1.606 | 1.659 | 1.714 | 1.770 | 1.828 | 1.888 | 1.949 |
| 8 | 1.535 | 1.594 | 1.655 | 1.718 | 1.783 | 1.851 | 1.921 | 1.993 | 2.067 | 2.144 |
| 9 | 1.619 | 1.689 | 1.763 | 1.838 | 1.917 | 1.999 | 2.084 | 2.172 | 2.263 | 2.358 |
| 10 | 1.708 | 1.791 | 1.877 | 1.967 | 2.061 | 2.159 | 2.261 | 2.367 | 2.478 | 2.594 |
| 11 | 1.802 | 1.898 | 1.999 | 2.105 | 2.216 | 2.332 | 2.453 | 2.580 | 2.714 | 2.853 |
| 12 | 1.901 | 2.012 | 2.129 | 2.252 | 2.382 | 2.518 | 2.662 | 2.813 | 2.971 | 3.138 |
| 13 | 2.006 | 2.133 | 2.267 | 2.410 | 2.560 | 2.720 | 2.888 | 3.066 | 3.254 | 3.452 |
| 14 | 2.116 | 2.261 | 2.415 | 2.579 | 2.752 | 2.937 | 3.133 | 3.342 | 3.563 | 3.797 |
| 15 | 2.232 | 2.397 | 2.572 | 2.759 | 2.959 | 3.172 | 3.400 | 3.642 | 3.901 | 4.177 |
| 16 | 2.355 | 2.540 | 2.739 | 2.952 | 3.181 | 3.426 | 3.689 | 3.970 | 4.272 | 4.595 |
| 17 | 2.485 | 2.693 | 2.917 | 3.159 | 3.419 | 3.700 | 4.002 | 4.328 | 4.678 | 5.054 |
| 18 | 2.621 | 2.854 | 3.107 | 3.380 | 3.676 | 3.996 | 4.342 | 4.717 | 5.122 | 5.560 |
| 19 | 2.766 | 3.026 | 3.309 | 3.617 | 3.951 | 4.316 | 4.712 | 5.142 | 5.609 | 6.116 |
| 20 | 2.918 | 3.207 | 3.524 | 3.870 | 4.248 | 4.661 | 5.112 | 5.604 | 6.142 | 6.727 |
| 21 | 3.078 | 3.400 | 3.753 | 4.141 | 4.566 | 5.034 | 5.547 | 6.109 | 6.725 | 7.400 |
| 22 | 3.248 | 3.604 | 3.997 | 4.430 | 4.909 | 5.437 | 6.018 | 6.659 | 7.364 | 8.140 |
| 23 | 3.426 | 3.820 | 4.256 | 4.741 | 5.277 | 5.871 | 6.530 | 7.258 | 8.064 | 8.954 |
| 24 | 3.615 | 4.049 | 4.533 | 5.072 | 5.673 | 6.341 | 7.085 | 7.911 | 8.830 | 9.850 |
| 25 | 3.813 | 4.292 | 4.828 | 5.427 | 6.098 | 6.848 | 7.687 | 8.623 | 9.668 | 10.83 |
| 26 | 4.023 | 4.549 | 5.141 | 5.807 | 6.556 | 7.396 | 8.340 | 9.399 | 10.59 | 11.92 |
| 27 | 4.244 | 4.822 | 5.476 | 6.214 | 7.047 | 7.988 | 9.049 | 10.25 | 11.59 | 13.11 |
| 28 | 4.478 | 5.112 | 5.832 | 6.649 | 7.576 | 8.627 | 9.818 | 11.17 | 12.69 | 14.42 |
| 29 | 4.724 | 5.418 | 6.211 | 7.114 | 8.144 | 9.317 | 10.65 | 12.17 | 13.90 | 15.86 |
| 30 | 4.984 | 5.743 | 6.614 | 7.612 | 8.755 | 10.06 | 11.56 | 13.27 | 15.22 | 17.45 |
| 31 | 5.258 | 6.088 | 7.044 | 8.145 | 9.412 | 10.87 | 12.54 | 14.46 | 16.67 | 19.19 |
| 32 | 5.547 | 6.453 | 7.502 | 8.715 | 10.12 | 11.74 | 13.61 | 15.76 | 18.25 | 21.11 |
| 33 | 5.852 | 6.841 | 7.990 | 9.325 | 10.88 | 12.68 | 14.76 | 17.18 | 19.98 | 23.23 |
| 34 | 6.174 | 7.251 | 8.509 | 9.978 | 11.69 | 13.69 | 16.02 | 18.73 | 21.88 | 25.55 |
| 35 | 6.514 | 7.686 | 9.062 | 10.68 | 12.57 | 14.79 | 17.38 | 20.41 | 23.96 | 28.10 |
| 36 | 6.872 | 8.147 | 9.651 | 11.42 | 13.51 | 15.97 | 18.86 | 22.25 | 26.24 | 30.91 |
| 37 | 7.250 | 8.636 | 10.28 | 12.22 | 14.52 | 17.25 | 20.46 | 24.25 | 28.73 | 34.00 |
| 38 | 7.649 | 9.154 | 10.95 | 13.08 | 15.61 | 18.63 | 22.20 | 26.44 | 31.46 | 37.40 |
| 39 | 8.069 | 9.704 | 11.66 | 13.99 | 16.79 | 20.12 | 24.09 | 28.82 | 34.45 | 41.14 |
| 40 | 8.513 | 10.29 | 12.42 | 14.97 | 18.04 | 21.72 | 26.13 | 31.41 | 37.72 | 45.26 |
| 41 | 8.982 | 10.90 | 13.22 | 16.02 | 19.40 | 23.46 | 28.35 | 34.24 | 41.30 | 49.79 |
| 42 | 9.476 | 11.56 | 14.08 | 17.14 | 20.85 | 25.34 | 30.76 | 37.32 | 45.23 | 54.76 |
| 43 | 9.997 | 12.25 | 15.00 | 18.34 | 22.42 | 27.37 | 33.38 | 40.68 | 49.52 | 60.24 |
| 44 | 10.55 | 12.99 | 15.97 | 19.63 | 24.10 | 29.56 | 36.22 | 44.34 | 54.23 | 66.26 |
| 45 | 11.13 | 13.76 | 17.01 | 21.00 | 25.90 | 31.92 | 39.30 | 48.33 | 59.38 | 72.89 |
| 46 | 11.74 | 14.59 | 18.12 | 22.47 | 27.85 | 34.47 | 42.64 | 52.68 | 65.02 | 80.18 |
| 47 | 12.38 | 15.47 | 19.29 | 24.05 | 29.94 | 37.23 | 46.26 | 57.42 | 71.20 | 88.20 |
| 48 | 13.07 | 16.39 | 20.55 | 25.73 | 32.18 | 40.21 | 50.19 | 62.59 | 77.96 | 97.02 |
| 49 | 13.78 | 17.38 | 21.88 | 27.53 | 34.60 | 43.43 | 54.46 | 68.22 | 85.37 | 106.7 |
| 50 | 14.54 | 18.42 | 23.31 | 29.46 | 37.19 | 46.90 | 59.09 | 74.36 | 93.48 | 117.4 |
| 51 | 15.34 | 19.53 | 24.82 | 31.52 | 39.98 | 50.65 | 64.11 | 81.05 | 102.4 | 129.1 |
| 52 | 16.19 | 20.70 | 26.44 | 33.73 | 42.98 | 54.71 | 69.56 | 88.34 | 112.1 | 142.0 |
| 53 | 17.08 | 21.94 | 28.15 | 36.09 | 46.20 | 59.08 | 75.47 | 96.30 | 122.7 | 156.2 |
| 54 | 18.01 | 23.26 | 29.98 | 38.61 | 49.67 | 63.81 | 81.89 | 105.0 | 134.4 | 171.9 |
| 55 | 19.01 | 24.65 | 31.93 | 41.32 | 53.39 | 68.91 | 88.85 | 114.4 | 147.2 | 189.1 |
| 56 | 20.05 | 26.13 | 34.01 | 44.21 | 57.39 | 74.43 | 96.40 | 124.7 | 161.1 | 208.0 |
| 57 | 21.15 | 27.70 | 36.22 | 47.30 | 61.70 | 80.38 | 104.6 | 135.9 | 176.4 | 228.8 |
| 58 | 22.32 | 29.36 | 38.57 | 50.61 | 66.33 | 86.81 | 113.5 | 148.2 | 193.2 | 251.6 |
| 59 | 23.54 | 31.12 | 41.08 | 54.16 | 71.30 | 93.76 | 123.1 | 161.5 | 211.6 | 276.8 |
| 60 | 24.84 | 32.99 | 43.75 | 57.95 | 76.65 | 101.3 | 133.6 | 176.0 | 231.7 | 304.5 |
| | 5.5% | 6.0% | 6.5% | 7.0% | 7.5% | 8.0% | 8.5% | 9.0% | 9.5% | 10.0% |

Compound Amount Factor (CAF) table, page 2

Table 4.1: **Sample page of Compound Amount Factor (CAF) table. The whole table is given in Appendix-A.**

| Year (N) | Compound Yield Factor (CYF) table, page-2 Yield Rate ( R ) | | | | | | | | | |
|---|---|---|---|---|---|---|---|---|---|---|
| | 5.50% | 6.00% | 6.50% | 7.00% | 7.50% | 8.00% | 8.50% | 9.00% | 9.50% | 10.00% |
| 0 | 0.000 | 0.000 | 0.000 | 0.000 | 0.000 | 0.000 | 0.000 | 0.000 | 0.000 | 0.000 |
| 1 | 0.055 | 0.060 | 0.065 | 0.070 | 0.075 | 0.080 | 0.085 | 0.090 | 0.095 | 0.100 |
| 2 | 0.113 | 0.124 | 0.134 | 0.145 | 0.156 | 0.166 | 0.177 | 0.188 | 0.199 | 0.210 |
| 3 | 0.174 | 0.191 | 0.208 | 0.225 | 0.242 | 0.260 | 0.277 | 0.295 | 0.313 | 0.331 |
| 4 | 0.239 | 0.262 | 0.286 | 0.311 | 0.335 | 0.360 | 0.386 | 0.412 | 0.438 | 0.464 |
| 5 | 0.307 | 0.338 | 0.370 | 0.403 | 0.436 | 0.469 | 0.504 | 0.539 | 0.574 | 0.611 |
| 6 | 0.379 | 0.419 | 0.459 | 0.501 | 0.543 | 0.587 | 0.631 | 0.677 | 0.724 | 0.772 |
| 7 | 0.455 | 0.504 | 0.554 | 0.606 | 0.659 | 0.714 | 0.770 | 0.828 | 0.888 | 0.949 |
| 8 | 0.535 | 0.594 | 0.655 | 0.718 | 0.783 | 0.851 | 0.921 | 0.993 | 1.067 | 1.144 |
| 9 | 0.619 | 0.689 | 0.763 | 0.838 | 0.917 | 0.999 | 1.084 | 1.172 | 1.263 | 1.358 |
| 10 | 0.708 | 0.791 | 0.877 | 0.967 | 1.061 | 1.159 | 1.261 | 1.367 | 1.478 | 1.594 |
| 11 | 0.802 | 0.898 | 0.999 | 1.105 | 1.216 | 1.332 | 1.453 | 1.580 | 1.714 | 1.853 |
| 12 | 0.901 | 1.012 | 1.129 | 1.252 | 1.382 | 1.518 | 1.662 | 1.813 | 1.971 | 2.138 |
| 13 | 1.006 | 1.133 | 1.267 | 1.410 | 1.560 | 1.720 | 1.888 | 2.066 | 2.254 | 2.452 |
| 14 | 1.116 | 1.261 | 1.415 | 1.579 | 1.752 | 1.937 | 2.133 | 2.342 | 2.563 | 2.797 |
| 15 | 1.232 | 1.397 | 1.572 | 1.759 | 1.959 | 2.172 | 2.400 | 2.642 | 2.901 | 3.177 |
| 16 | 1.355 | 1.540 | 1.739 | 1.952 | 2.181 | 2.426 | 2.689 | 2.970 | 3.272 | 3.595 |
| 17 | 1.485 | 1.693 | 1.917 | 2.159 | 2.419 | 2.700 | 3.002 | 3.328 | 3.678 | 4.054 |
| 18 | 1.621 | 1.854 | 2.107 | 2.380 | 2.676 | 2.996 | 3.342 | 3.717 | 4.122 | 4.560 |
| 19 | 1.766 | 2.026 | 2.309 | 2.617 | 2.951 | 3.316 | 3.712 | 4.142 | 4.609 | 5.116 |
| 20 | 1.918 | 2.207 | 2.524 | 2.870 | 3.248 | 3.661 | 4.112 | 4.604 | 5.142 | 5.727 |
| 21 | 2.078 | 2.400 | 2.753 | 3.141 | 3.566 | 4.034 | 4.547 | 5.109 | 5.725 | 6.400 |
| 22 | 2.248 | 2.604 | 2.997 | 3.430 | 3.909 | 4.437 | 5.018 | 5.659 | 6.364 | 7.140 |
| 23 | 2.426 | 2.820 | 3.256 | 3.741 | 4.277 | 4.871 | 5.530 | 6.258 | 7.064 | 7.954 |
| 24 | 2.615 | 3.049 | 3.533 | 4.072 | 4.673 | 5.341 | 6.085 | 6.911 | 7.830 | 8.850 |
| 25 | 2.813 | 3.292 | 3.828 | 4.427 | 5.098 | 5.848 | 6.687 | 7.623 | 8.668 | 9.835 |
| 26 | 3.023 | 3.549 | 4.141 | 4.807 | 5.556 | 6.396 | 7.340 | 8.399 | 9.587 | 10.92 |
| 27 | 3.244 | 3.822 | 4.476 | 5.214 | 6.047 | 6.988 | 8.049 | 9.245 | 10.59 | 12.11 |
| 28 | 3.478 | 4.112 | 4.832 | 5.649 | 6.576 | 7.627 | 8.818 | 10.17 | 11.69 | 13.42 |
| 29 | 3.724 | 4.418 | 5.211 | 6.114 | 7.144 | 8.317 | 9.653 | 11.17 | 12.90 | 14.86 |
| 30 | 3.984 | 4.743 | 5.614 | 6.612 | 7.755 | 9.063 | 10.56 | 12.27 | 14.22 | 16.45 |
| 31 | 4.258 | 5.088 | 6.044 | 7.145 | 8.412 | 9.868 | 11.54 | 13.46 | 15.67 | 18.19 |
| 32 | 4.547 | 5.453 | 6.502 | 7.715 | 9.117 | 10.74 | 12.61 | 14.76 | 17.25 | 20.11 |
| 33 | 4.852 | 5.841 | 6.990 | 8.325 | 9.876 | 11.68 | 13.76 | 16.18 | 18.98 | 22.23 |
| 34 | 5.174 | 6.251 | 7.509 | 8.978 | 10.69 | 12.69 | 15.02 | 17.73 | 20.88 | 24.55 |
| 35 | 5.514 | 6.686 | 8.062 | 9.677 | 11.57 | 13.79 | 16.38 | 19.41 | 22.96 | 27.10 |
| 36 | 5.872 | 7.147 | 8.651 | 10.42 | 12.51 | 14.97 | 17.86 | 21.25 | 25.24 | 29.91 |
| 37 | 6.250 | 7.636 | 9.279 | 11.22 | 13.52 | 16.25 | 19.46 | 23.25 | 27.73 | 33.00 |
| 38 | 6.649 | 8.154 | 9.947 | 12.08 | 14.61 | 17.63 | 21.20 | 25.44 | 30.46 | 36.40 |
| 39 | 7.069 | 8.704 | 10.66 | 12.99 | 15.79 | 19.12 | 23.09 | 27.82 | 33.45 | 40.14 |
| 40 | 7.513 | 9.286 | 11.42 | 13.97 | 17.04 | 20.72 | 25.13 | 30.41 | 36.72 | 44.26 |
| 41 | 7.982 | 9.903 | 12.22 | 15.02 | 18.40 | 22.46 | 27.35 | 33.24 | 40.30 | 48.79 |
| 42 | 8.476 | 10.56 | 13.08 | 16.14 | 19.85 | 24.34 | 29.76 | 36.32 | 44.23 | 53.76 |
| 43 | 8.997 | 11.25 | 14.00 | 17.34 | 21.42 | 26.37 | 32.38 | 39.68 | 48.52 | 59.24 |
| 44 | 9.546 | 11.99 | 14.97 | 18.63 | 23.10 | 28.56 | 35.22 | 43.34 | 53.23 | 65.26 |
| 45 | 10.13 | 12.76 | 16.01 | 20.00 | 24.90 | 30.92 | 38.30 | 47.33 | 58.38 | 71.89 |
| 46 | 10.74 | 13.59 | 17.12 | 21.47 | 26.85 | 33.47 | 41.64 | 51.68 | 64.02 | 79.18 |
| 47 | 11.38 | 14.47 | 18.29 | 23.05 | 28.94 | 36.23 | 45.26 | 56.42 | 70.20 | 87.20 |
| 48 | 12.07 | 15.39 | 19.55 | 24.73 | 31.18 | 39.21 | 49.19 | 61.59 | 76.96 | 96.02 |
| 49 | 12.78 | 16.38 | 20.88 | 26.53 | 33.60 | 42.43 | 53.46 | 67.22 | 84.37 | 105.7 |
| 50 | 13.54 | 17.42 | 22.31 | 28.46 | 36.19 | 45.90 | 58.09 | 73.36 | 92.48 | 116.4 |
| 51 | 14.34 | 18.53 | 23.82 | 30.52 | 38.98 | 49.65 | 63.11 | 80.05 | 101.4 | 128.1 |
| 52 | 15.19 | 19.70 | 25.44 | 32.73 | 41.98 | 53.71 | 68.56 | 87.34 | 111.1 | 141.0 |
| 53 | 16.08 | 20.94 | 27.15 | 35.09 | 45.20 | 58.08 | 74.47 | 95.30 | 121.7 | 155.2 |
| 54 | 17.01 | 22.26 | 28.98 | 37.61 | 48.67 | 62.81 | 80.89 | 104.0 | 133.4 | 170.9 |
| 55 | 18.01 | 23.65 | 30.93 | 40.32 | 52.39 | 67.91 | 87.85 | 113.4 | 146.2 | 188.1 |
| 56 | 19.05 | 25.13 | 33.01 | 43.21 | 56.39 | 73.43 | 95.40 | 123.7 | 160.1 | 207.0 |
| 57 | 20.15 | 26.70 | 35.22 | 46.30 | 60.70 | 79.38 | 103.6 | 134.9 | 175.4 | 227.8 |
| 58 | 21.32 | 28.36 | 37.57 | 49.61 | 65.33 | 85.81 | 112.5 | 147.2 | 192.2 | 250.6 |
| 59 | 22.54 | 30.12 | 40.08 | 53.16 | 70.30 | 92.76 | 122.1 | 160.5 | 210.6 | 275.8 |
| 60 | 23.84 | 31.99 | 42.75 | 56.95 | 75.65 | 100.3 | 132.6 | 175.0 | 230.7 | 303.5 |
| | 5.5% | 6.0% | 6.5% | 7.0% | 7.5% | 8.0% | 8.5% | 9.0% | 9.5% | 10.0% |

**Table 4.2: Sample page of Compound Yield Factor (CYF) table. The whole table is given in Appendix-B.**

## 4.3     THE DIFFERENCE BETWEEN CAF TABLE AND CYF TABLE

In the above example, $236.40 is only the total yield or return and does not include your initial deposit of $1. Your bank balance will, however, include the initial investment of $1 and show the amount as $237.40. This is your net worth assuming that you owe no tax on this earning.

The CYF table shows the value of total yield, i.e., 236.40. If you look up in the CAF table instead, you will find a corresponding value of 237.40. The difference in value between the CYF and CAF table is just 1 (one) because both the tables are based on an initial investment of $1 across the entire spectrum.

The difference of just 1 (one) between the CYF value and the corresponding CAF value is negligibly small when the values are high, like 236.40 and 237.40, respectively, but huge when the values are small, like 0.20 and 1.20, respectively.

The differences between the CAF value and CYF value can be summarized as follows.

1. **CAF value is the Cumulative Growth Factor of the initial investment**. The net worth of an investment can be calculated directly by multiplying the initial investment with the CAF value in the CAF table.

2. **CYF value is the Cumulative Yield Factor of the initial investment**. The total yield of an investment can be calculated directly by multiplying the initial investment with the CYF value in the CYF table.

3. The difference between the CAF value in the CAF table and the corresponding CYF value in the CYF table is always 1.00 (one).

4. For any combination of yield rate and time-period, **CYF = CAF – 1.00.** Put it differently, **CAF = CYF + 1.00.** The CAF value is thus higher than the corresponding CYF value.

5. This difference of exactly 1.00 between the two values arises because the net worth of any investment also includes the initial investment, but net yield does not include the initial investment.

**Net worth is, therefore, consistently higher than net yield by 1x time the initial investment.**

### Example 4.3

If you invest $10,000 today and it grows to $1 million sometime in the future, your net worth will be $1,000,000, and the corresponding CAF value will be 100.

But your total yield will be only $9, 90,000 and the corresponding CYF value will be 99.

But if it is the $1 Million net yield that you wanted, thus $1 Million additional net worth in addition to your existing net worth, you will need to have a CYF value of 100, and the corresponding CAF value will be 101.

If you would be using only one table for all the calculations and that is the CAF table, calculate as below for any combination of yield rate and time-period:

**Net worth = CAF value x initial investment.**

**Net yield = (CAF value – 1.00) x initial investment.**

If you would be using only one table for all the calculations and that is the CYF table, calculate as below for any combination of yield rate and time-period:

**Net worth = (CYF value + 1.00) x initial investment.**

**Net yield = CYF value x initial investment.**

## 4.4     CAF VALUE IS YOUR FINANCIAL GPS ON THE HIGHWAY TO RICHES

You will come across the words "CAF" and "CYF value" and actual CYF values all throughout this book. It is because CAF value is probably the most important of all derived analytical data of an investment giving you your exact position in the 4D world of wealth building. It is your virtual GPS on the highway to riches.

CAF value is even a better indicator of your financial location than the CYF value due to its relative simplicity and straightforwardness of calculation compared to the CYF value.

Drawing an analogy with an altimeter when you are flying an airplane, and you want to fly at a steady 10 km altitude, the CAF will give you the altitude with reference to the sea-level directly, but the CYF meter will provide you with two values: your altitude with reference to the ground below you and the altitude of the ground with reference to the sea level. In the latter case, you will have to add up the two values to see how high you are above sea level.

\* \* \* \*

# Chapter 5:

# Exponential Effect of Time on Investment Results

## Effect of Time on Final Amount, Total Return, and Compound Amount Factor.

We will use examples again to illustrate and explain the effect of time on various aspects of compounding, some of which are certain to surprise you.

**Example 5.1**

Let us assume that we had put $100 in a Fixed Deposit with 10% interest compounding annually for 15 years first and extended it later to a total of 45 years. The interest was deposited by the bank to your account every year, and you received interest-on-interest also every year. That way, the bank balance grew every year, and it also grew faster and faster every year because of the ever-increasing interest-on-interest you received.

The details of the interest received in your account annually, cumulative interest received, and balance amount in the account each year have been calculated and are given in Table 5.1 below. Figure 5.1 shows the results graphically.

As you can see in Table 5.1 and Figure 5.1, the **annual interest** received increased gradually from $10 in the first year to $38 in year 15 and $41.8 in year 16. That is an increase by a factor of 4.18 in 15 years.

We can see that the bank balance after 15 years is $418. Depending on the context, in this book, we call it interchangeably the **final amount, final asset, net worth, or gross worth.**

From an initial deposit of $100, which we call interchangeably as **principal or initial investment**, the final amount has grown to $418 in 15 years. We can say that the principal has multiplied 4.18 times in 15 years due to a compound interest of 10%. This 4.18 is the **Compound Amount Factor** or **CAF**, which we have covered in chapter 4 of this book.

| | $100 in Fixed Deposit at interest rate of 10% p.a. | | | | |
|---|---|---|---|---|---|
| Year | Annual Intertest Amount, $ | Cumulative Interest Amount, $ | Final Amount in Account, $ | Compound Amount Factor | Simple Annual Yield, % p.a. |
| 0 | | | 100 | 1.00 | |
| 1 | 10 | 10 | 110 | 1.10 | 10.0% |
| 2 | 11 | 21 | 121 | 1.21 | 10.5% |
| 3 | 12 | 33 | 133 | 1.33 | 11.0% |
| 4 | 13 | 46 | 146 | 1.46 | 11.6% |
| 5 | 15 | 61 | 161 | 1.61 | 12.2% |
| 6 | 16 | 77 | 177 | 1.77 | 12.9% |
| 7 | 18 | 95 | 195 | 1.95 | 13.6% |
| 8 | 19 | 114 | 214 | 2.14 | 14.3% |
| 9 | 21 | 136 | 236 | 2.36 | 15.1% |
| 10 | 24 | 159 | 259 | 2.59 | 15.9% |
| 11 | 26 | 185 | 285 | 2.85 | 16.8% |
| 12 | 29 | 214 | 314 | 3.14 | 17.8% |
| 13 | 31 | 245 | 345 | 3.45 | 18.9% |
| 14 | 35 | 280 | 380 | 3.80 | 20.0% |
| 15 | 38 | 318 | 418 | 4.18 | 21.2% |
| 16 | 42 | 359 | 459 | 4.59 | 22.5% |
| 17 | 46 | 405 | 505 | 5.05 | 23.8% |
| 18 | 51 | 456 | 556 | 5.56 | 25.3% |
| 19 | 56 | 512 | 612 | 6.12 | 26.9% |
| 20 | 61 | 573 | 673 | 6.73 | 28.6% |
| 21 | 67 | 640 | 740 | 7.40 | 30.5% |
| 22 | 74 | 714 | 814 | 8.14 | 32.5% |
| 23 | 81 | 795 | 895 | 8.95 | 34.6% |
| 24 | 90 | 885 | 985 | 9.85 | 36.9% |
| 25 | 98 | 983 | 1,083 | 10.83 | 39.3% |
| 26 | 108 | 1,092 | 1,192 | 11.92 | 42.0% |
| 27 | 119 | 1,211 | 1,311 | 13.11 | 44.9% |
| 28 | 131 | 1,342 | 1,442 | 14.42 | 47.9% |
| 29 | 144 | 1,486 | 1,586 | 15.86 | 51.3% |
| 30 | 159 | 1,645 | 1,745 | 17.45 | 54.8% |
| 31 | 174 | 1,819 | 1,919 | 19.19 | 58.7% |
| 32 | 192 | 2,011 | 2,111 | 21.11 | 62.9% |
| 33 | 211 | 2,223 | 2,323 | 23.23 | 67.3% |
| 34 | 232 | 2,455 | 2,555 | 25.55 | 72.2% |
| 35 | 255 | 2,710 | 2,810 | 28.10 | 77.4% |
| 36 | 281 | 2,991 | 3,091 | 30.91 | 83.1% |
| 37 | 309 | 3,300 | 3,400 | 34.00 | 89.2% |
| 38 | 340 | 3,640 | 3,740 | 37.40 | 95.8% |
| 39 | 374 | 4,014 | 4,114 | 41.14 | 102.9% |
| 40 | 411 | 4,426 | 4,526 | 45.26 | 110.6% |
| 41 | 453 | 4,879 | 4,979 | 49.79 | 119.0% |
| 42 | 498 | 5,376 | 5,476 | 54.76 | 128.0% |
| 43 | 548 | 5,924 | 6,024 | 60.24 | 137.8% |
| 44 | 602 | 6,526 | 6,626 | 66.26 | 148.3% |
| 45 | 663 | 7,189 | 7,289 | 72.89 | 159.8% |

Table 5.1: $100 in Fixed Deposit at an interest rate of 10% p.a.

**This Table is the same as Table 6.1 in chapter 6.**

The values are rounded off to the nearest whole number.

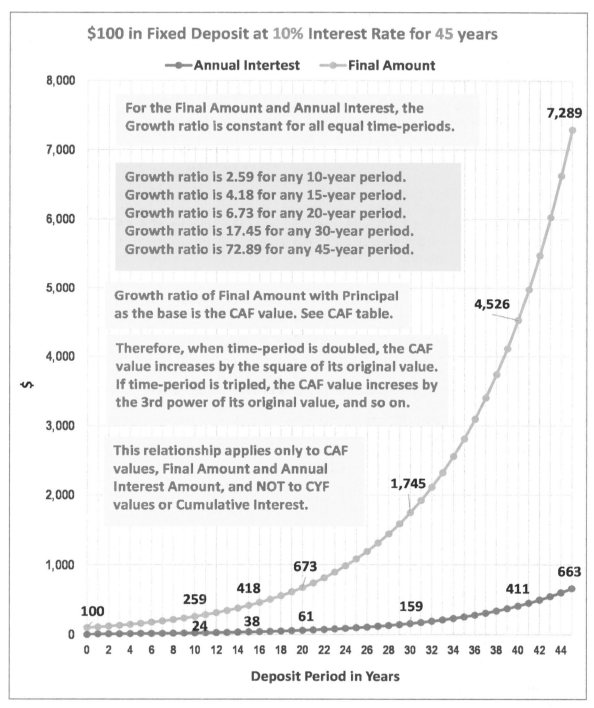

**$100 in Fixed Deposit at 10% Interest Rate for 45 years**

Annual Intertest — Final Amount

For the Final Amount and Annual Interest, the Growth ratio is constant for all equal time-periods.

Growth ratio is 2.59 for any 10-year period.
Growth ratio is 4.18 for any 15-year period.
Growth ratio is 6.73 for any 20-year period.
Growth ratio is 17.45 for any 30-year period.
Growth ratio is 72.89 for any 45-year period.

Growth ratio of Final Amount with Principal as the base is the CAF value. See CAF table.

Therefore, when time-period is doubled, the CAF value increases by the square of its original value. If time-period is tripled, the CAF value increses by the 3rd power of its original value, and so on.

This relationship applies only to CAF values, Final Amount and Annual Interest Amount, and NOT to CYF values or Cumulative Interest.

7,289

4,526

1,745

673

663

418

411

259

159

100

61

38

24

**Deposit Period in Years**

**Figure 5.1: Final amount and Annual interest for $100 in FD at 10% interest rate for 45 years.**

**This Figure is the same as Fig 6.1 in chapter 6.**

If you look in the CAF table, you can see that 4.18 is exactly the value that appears at the intersection of the column for 10% and the row for 15 years. In other words, the value of the principal multiplies 4.18 times in 15 years.

Between **15 and 30 years**, you can see in Table 5.1 that the final amount grew from $418 to $1,745. That is again growth by a **factor of 4.18** (= 1745/418).

Between **30 and 45 years**, you can see in Table 5.1 that the final amount grew from $1,745 to $7,289. That is again growth by a **factor of 4.18** (= 7289/1745).

That means, in the first period of **15 years**, the asset grew by a **factor of 4.18**. When the 15-year period was doubled to **30 years**, the total growth in the entire 30-year period was by a factor of **17.45,** which is precisely the **square of 4.18** (= 4.18 x 4.18). When the 15-year period was tripled to **45 years**, the total growth in the entire 45-year period was by a factor of **72.89,** which is precisely **4.18 to the power of 3** (= 4.18 x 4.18 x 4.18).

If you look in the CAF table, you can see that **17.45** is precisely the value that appears at the intersection of the column for 10% and row for 30 years. Similarly, you can see that **72.89** is exactly the value that appears at the intersection of the column for 10% and row for 45 years.

## 5.1    CAF VALUE (COMPOUND AMOUNT FACTOR)

Between year 15 and year 30, the Compound Amount Factor has increased from **4.18** to **17.45**. This is an increase by a factor of **4.18 or 418%** too. This is the same growth factor as during the first 15 years. Therefore, the growth factor for the entire 30-year period is the square of the growth factor in either of the 15-year periods, and it becomes **17.45** (= 4.18 x 4.18). In other words, when the time-period doubles, the CAF value for the entire period not simply doubles but becomes the square of the original CAF value.

In a similar way, the growth factor for the entire 45-year period is the third power of the growth factor in any of the 15-year periods, and it becomes **72.89** (= 4.18 x 4.18 x 4.18). In other words, when the time-period triples, the CAF value for the entire period not simply triples but becomes the third power of the original CAF value.

### 5.1.1    Square of a CAF value that is higher than 2.0 can be much bigger than its double

Note that the square of a CAF value does not necessarily mean that the square value is more than double or 2 times higher. It can also be less than double. For the **square of any value**, the **magical number** at which it flips is **2.00.**

For any CAF value that is less than 2, the square of it will always be less than its double. For example, referring to Table 5.1, for any investment with a 10% annual return, the growth factor or CAF value for **5 years** is **1.61**. If we double the investment period to **10 years**, the growth factor does not double to **3.22** (= 1.61 x 2) but is lower at **2.59,** which is the square of 1.61 (= 1.61 x 1.61).

But on the other side of the magical number of 2, just the opposite happens. For any CAF value that is higher than 2, the square of it will always become more than its double. For example, referring to Table 5.1, for any investment with a **10%** annual return, the growth factor or CAF value for **20 years** is **6.73**. If we double the investment period to **40 years**, the growth factor not only doubles but makes a giant leap from 6.73 to **45.26**. It is a leap that is **6.73 times** its size instead of merely 2 times.

But if we have an investment with a **20%** annual return, for example, investment in the stock market or real estate, the leap in growth factor or CAF value would be from **38.34 in 20 years** to **1,470 in 40 years**. It is a leap that is **38.34 times** its size instead of merely 2 times.

But if we have an investment with a **30%** annual return, for example, again investment in the stock market or real estate, the leap in growth factor or CAF value would be from **190 in 20 years** to **36,119 in 40 years**. It is a leap that is **190 times** its size instead of merely 2 times.

But if we have an investment with a **40%** annual return, for example, with investment in our own business or participation in a growing venture, the leap in growth factor or CAF value would be from **837 in 20 years** to **700,038 in 40 years**. It is a leap that is **837 times** its size instead of merely 2 times.

**Herein lies the hidden power of compounding to build enormous wealth.**

## 5.2      FINAL AMOUNT

Between year 15 and year 30, the final amount has increased from **$418** to **$1,745.** This is an increase by a factor of **4.18 or 418%.** This is the same growth factor as during the first 15 years. Therefore, the growth factor for the entire 30-year period is the square of the growth factor in either of the 15-year periods, which becomes **17.45** (= 4.18 x 4.18). In other words, when the time-period doubles, the growth factor for the final amount for the entire period not simply doubles but becomes the square of the original growth factor.

In a similar way, between year 30 and year 45, the final amount has increased from **$1745** to **$72,890**. This is an increase by a factor of **4.18 or 418%**. Again, this is the same growth factor as during the first and second 15-year periods. Therefore, the growth factor for the entire 45-year period is the third power of the growth factor in any of the 15-year periods, and it becomes **72.89** (= 4.18 x 4.18 x 4.18). In other words, when the time-period triples, the CAF value for the entire period not simply triples but becomes the third power of the original CAF value.

**Again, herein lies the power of compounding to build enormous wealth.**

Note that the CAF value or the Compound Amount Factor is the growth factor of the final amount. Therefore, all the numerical relationships that exist between the growth of CAF value and time-periods as described in the previous section 5.1 apply equally to the growth of the final amount.

Let us take a closer look at the behavior of final amount, CAF value, annual interest amount, CYF value, and cumulative interest amount when time-period or time-interval changes.

### 5.3    EFFECT OF INCREASE OF TIME-PERIOD ON CAF VALUE AND FINAL AMOUNT

With a doubling of time, the final amount would multiply by the square of the original Compound Amount Factor (= original CAF x original CAF)

With a tripling of time, the final Asset would multiply by the 3rd power of the original Compound Amount Factor (= original CAF x original CAF x original CAF).

Regarding the time-period of any investment with compounded yield or interest, we can make the following general statements.

1.  **When the time period is increased by a factor X, the Compound Amount Factor CAF grows exponentially to the power of X (= $CAF^X$ or CAF^X), resulting in a corresponding exponential growth of the final amount.**

2.  **When the time period is doubled, the Compound Amount Factor CAF grows exponentially by the square of its original value (= $CAF^2$ or CAF^2), resulting in a corresponding exponential growth of the final amount.**

3.  **When the time period is tripled, the Compound Amount Factor CAF grows exponentially by the 3rd power of its original value (= $CAF^3$ or CAF^3), resulting in a corresponding exponential growth of the final amount.**

4.  **When the time period is quadrupled, the Compound Amount Factor CAF grows exponentially by the 4th power of its original value (= $CAF^4$ or CAF^4), resulting in a corresponding exponential growth of the final amount.**

5.  **When the time period is increased by a factor of 2.5, the Compound Amount Factor CAF grows exponentially to the power of 2.5 (= $CAF^{2.5}$ or CAF^2.5), resulting in a corresponding exponential growth of the final amount.**

### 5.4    EFFECT OF DECREASE OF TIME-PERIOD ON CAF VALUE AND FINAL AMOUNT

What applies to an increase of time-period and related growth of the CAF value and final amount applies equally to any decrease of time-period and the corresponding reduction of the final amount.

1. **When the time period is** reduced to half, **the Compound Amount Factor CAF shrinks exponentially by the Square Root of its original value (= CAF$^{0.5}$ or CAF^0.5), resulting in a corresponding exponential decrease of the final amount.**

2. **When the time period is** reduced to one-third, **the Compound Amount Factor CAF shrinks exponentially by the 3rd Root of its original value [= CAF$^{1/3}$ or CAF^(1/3)], resulting in a corresponding exponential decrease of the final amount.**

## 5.5 RELATIONSHIP BETWEEN TIME-INTERVALS AND GROWTH RATIOS OF CAF VALUE, FINAL AMOUNT, AND ANNUAL INTEREST AMOUNT

Looking at the above mathematical relationship between time-period and growth of any investment in a different way, and probably a more straightforward method for some of the readers, we can observe the following.

The growth ratio of CAF value and final amount in the first 15 years in our example was 4.18. The $100 grew to become $418 in 15 years, and the CAF value increased from 1.00 to 4.18.

The growth ratio in the subsequent 15 years, that is, from 15 to 30 years, was also exactly the same: 4.18. The $418 at the end of the first 15-year period grew to become $1,745 in another 15 years, and that ratio is precisely 4.18.

If it is left to grow another 15 years, that is, from 30 to 45 years, it would again increase by a factor of 4.18, and the $1,745 would become $7,289.

In a similar way, the growth ratio in the first 5 years in our example was 1.61. The $100 grew to become $161 in 5 years.

The growth ratio in the subsequent 5 years, that is, from 5 to 10 years, was also exactly the same: 1.61. The $161 at the end of the first 5-year period grew to become $259 in another 5 years, and that ratio is precisely 1.61.

If it is left to grow another 5 years, that is, from 10 to 15 years, it will increase again by a factor of 1.61, and the $259 would become $418.

**Therefore, as a general rule, we can make the following statement:**

In any investment with compounding of interest, the **growth ratios** of the **asset, CAF values, and annual interest amounts** will be constant for all equal time-intervals provided the interest rate remains unchanged.

For example, if an asset grew by a factor of 3 in the first 7 years, it would grow by a factor of 3 between any other 7-year intervals anywhere.

A 15-year time interval from 85 to 100 years will have the same growth ratios as the 15-year interval from 5 to 20 years. The corresponding **ratios of CAF values, final amounts, and annual interest amounts** will be all equal, 4.18 in this example.

Note that we are stating that the ratio of growth of CAF values will be equal for equal time-intervals, but that does not apply to the value of growth of CAF values.

For example, the CAF value for 30 years is 17.45, and that for 15 years is 4.18. The ratio of growth between the two is 4.18 (= 17.45/4.18), but the value of growth is $13.27 (= 17.45 - 4.18).

Similarly, the CAF value for 30 years is 17.45, and that for 45 years is 72.89. The ratio of growth between the two is 4.18 (= 72.89/17.45), but the value of growth is $55.44 (= 72.89 - 17.45).

In both the 15-year intervals above, the ratio of growth is equal at 4.18, while the value of growth is as wide apart as $13.27 and $55.44.

## 5.6    RELATIONSHIP BETWEEN TIME-PERIODS AND ANNUAL YIELD AMOUNTS

All the relationships that exist between time-periods and final amount, as described in the previous sections, apply equally also to annual interest amounts.

In our example 5.1 with $100 deposited with 10% nominal interest compounded annually, we can observe the following:

Annual interest in year 1 is $10.

Annual interest in year 16 is $41.80. This is 4.18x times the interest of year 1 received 15 years ago.

Similarly, the following can also be observed:

- Growth ratio of Annual interest amount for 15 years from year 10 to 25:  4.18 (= 98/24).
- Growth ratio of final amount for 15 years from year 5 to 20:  4.18 (= 673/161).
- Growth ratio of CAF value for 15 years from year 13 to 28:  4.18 (= 14.42/3.45).

Note that it is irrelevant where the 15-year time-interval lies in the time scale. A 15-year time interval from 85 to 100 years will have the same ratios as the 15-year interval from 1 to 16 years. The corresponding ratios of CAF values, final amounts, and Annual interest amounts will all be equal, in this case, 4.18.

Individual **annual interest**, thus, has the same relationship and ratios with time as **CAF value** and **final amount**. It also undergoes the same exponential growth as the CAF value and final amount.

**These relationships apply only to the individual interest amount of the particular year and** not to any cumulative value of interest.

With this knowledge and with the help of the CAF table, you can easily calculate the annual interest amount you will be receiving in any particular year in the life cycle of your investment.

Please see section 3.3.2.3 also for details about calculating annual interest amounts.

## 5.7 RELATIONSHIP BETWEEN TIME-PERIODS, CUMULATIVE YIELD AMOUNTS, AND CYF VALUES

Cumulative yield amounts or CYF values do not synchronize precisely with any change of time-period or time-interval. Only the final amount, the CAF value, and the annual interest amount synchronize precisely with a change of time-period or time-interval and grow exponentially with time.

However, when the CAF and corresponding CYF values are exceedingly high, the CYF values and cumulative yield amounts also approach the above exponential relationship very closely, but at extremely low values, they differ very widely.

## 5.8 OTHER OBSERVATIONS

The exponential relationships between time-period and CAF value as described in previous sections apply universally to all compounding situations and to the whole spectrum of yield rates or interest rates and time-periods irrespective of the height of their values.

You can find this exponential relationship of CAF value with time-period if you track, in the CAF table, the CAF values down in a column for any particular interest rate. For example, compare the values between 5 years and 10 years and between 30 years and 60 years. CAF value for 10 years will be the square of CAF value for 5 years. Likewise, the CAF value for 60 years will be the square of the CAF value for 30 years. CAF value for 60 years will also be the 3rd power of CAF value for 20 years or the 4th power of CAF value for 15 years, or the 10th power of CAF value for 6 years.

**The relationships with time-periods and time-intervals described in the foregoing sections apply only to the CAF values and not to the CYF values. In other words, they apply to the final amount and the individual annual yield amount, but not to the cumulative yield amount.**

However, when the CAF and corresponding CYF values are extremely high, the CYF values also approach the above relationship very closely, but at extremely low values, they differ very widely. As you can see in Figure 5.2, the curves for the final amount and cumulative yield amount converge ever closer as the values go up.

We will see later in this book that the time period is the most dominant of all the wealth-building components, even more dominant than yield rate, initial investment, or tax exemption. Time-period is the king in the kingdom of compounding.

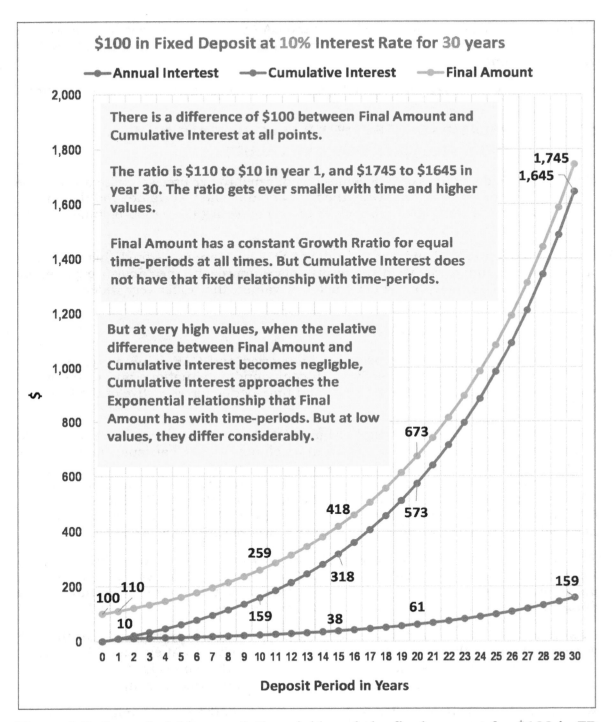

Figure 5.2: **Annual yield, cumulative yield, and the final amount for $100 in FD at a 10% interest rate for 30 years.**

## 5.9        EXAMPLES OF INVESTMENT AND EXPONENTIAL GROWTH

### Example 5.9.1

Suppose you have an investment that **doubles in 5 years**. It is possible with a **14.9%** annual yield.

In **5 years**, it would be 2x times bigger (= $2^1$ or 2^1).

In **10 years**, thus, in 2x times the original time, it would be 4x times bigger (=2x2 or $2^2$ or 2^2). We can also say that it grew 2x times in the first 5-year period, and again 2x times in the second 5-year period.

In **15 years**, thus, in 3x times the original time, it would be 8x times bigger (=2x2x2 or $2^3$ or 2^3). We can also say that it grew 2x times in the first 5-year period, again 2x times in the second 5-year period, and again 2x times in the third 5-year period.

In **20 years**, thus, in 4x times the original time, it would be 16x times bigger (=2x2x2x2 or $2^4$ or 2^4). We can also say that it grew 2x times in the first 5-year period, again 2x times in the second 5-year period, again 2x times in the third 5-year period, and again 2x times in the fourth 5-year period.

And so on.

### Example 5.9.2

Suppose you have an investment that **triples in 5 years**. It is possible with a **24.6%** annual yield.

In **5 years**, it would be 3x times bigger (= $3^1$ or 3^1).

In **10 years**, thus, in 2x times the original time, it would be 9x times bigger (=3x3 or $3^2$ or 3^2). We can also say that it grew 3x times in the first 5-year period, and again 3x times in the second 5-year period.

In **15 years**, thus, in 3x times the original time, it would be 27x times bigger (=3x3x3 or $3^3$ or 3^3). We can also say that it grew 3x times in the first 5-year period, again 3x times in the second 5-year period, and again 3x times in the third 5-year period.

In **20 years**, thus, in 4x times the original time, it would be 81x times bigger (=3x3x3x3 or $3^4$ or 3^4). We can also say that it grew 3x times in the first 5-year period, again 3x times in the second 5-year period, again 3x times in the third 5-year period, and again 3x times in the fourth 5-year period.

And so on.

**Example 5.9.3**

Suppose you have an investment that multiplies by a factor of **1.77x times in 6 years**. It is possible with a **10.0%** annual yield.

In **6 years**, it would be 1.77x times bigger (= $1.77^1$ or 1.77^1).

In **12 years**, thus, in 2x times the original time, it would be 3.14x times bigger (=1.77x1.77 or $1.77^2$ or 1.77^2). We can also say that it grew 1.77x times in the first 6-year period, and again 1.77x times in the second 6-year period.

In **15 years**, thus, in 2.5x times the original time, it would be 4.18x times bigger (=$1.77^{2.5}$ or 1.77^2.5). We can also say that it grew 1.77x times in the first 6-year period, again 1.77x times in the second 6-year period, and again 1.331x times in the last 3-year period. The CAF value for 10% and 3 years is 1.331, as can be seen in the CAF table.

In **30 years**, thus, in 5x times the original time, it would be 17.45x times bigger (=$1.77^5$ or 1.77^5). We can also say that it grew 1.77x times each in 5 six-year periods.

And so on.

Note that this example with its 10.0% annual yield is the one that we also considered in example 5.1 earlier in this chapter, for which the values are shown in Table 5.1 and Figures 5.1 & 5.2.

## 5.10    INFLUENCE OF TIME-PERIOD ON GROWTH OF WEALTH IN A NUTSHELL

**For equal time-periods, the** growth ratios **of net worth, CAF values, and annual yields are equal.** That means, if in a time period of 8 years, the net worth grew 10-fold from $1 Million to $10 Million, it will also take 8 years for net worth to grow 10-fold from 100 Million to 1,000 Million or from 1 Billion to 10 Billion.

That also means that for every doubling of time-period, the CAF value increases by its square; for a tripling of time-period, the CAF value increases by its 3rd power; for N-fold increase in time-period, the CAF value increases by its Nth power, and so on.

Conversely, that also means that **for every equal growth ratio of net worth, the time-period needed will be equal.** That means, if it takes 12 years for net worth to grow 10-fold from $1 Million to $10 Million, it will take 12 years for it to grow 10-fold from 100 Million to 1,000 Million.

The above relationship applies strictly only to the CAF value, net worth, and the annual yield amount but **not** to the CYF value, or cumulative yield amount, or total return.

\* \* \* \*

# Chapter 6:

# Effect of Time & Yield Rate on Investment Results

## Effect of Time & Yield Rate on Final Amount, Compound Amount Factor, and Simple Annual Yield.

**6.1      EXAMPLE 6.1**

Let us take the same example as in chapter 5 with $100 kept in Fixed Deposit, but for 45 years and with a compound interest rate of 20%, 30%, and 40% p.a. in addition to 10%.

Tables 6.1, 6.2, 6.3 & 6.4 show the results for all the 45 years with 10%, 20%, 30% & 40% yield rates, respectively.

Figures 6.1, 6.2, 6.3 & 6.4 show the results for final amounts and annual interest amounts in graphical form for 10%, 20%, 30% & 40% yield rates, respectively.

In the Figures themselves, please read the annotations for observations and conclusions drawn from the graphs.

| | \$100 in Fixed Deposit at interest rate of 10% p.a. | | | | |
|---|---|---|---|---|---|
| Year | Annual Intertest Amount, \$ | Cumulative Interest Amount, \$ | Final Amount in Account, \$ | Compound Amount Factor | Simple Annual Yield, % p.a. |
| 0 | | | 100 | 1.00 | |
| 1 | 10 | 10 | 110 | 1.10 | 10.0% |
| 2 | 11 | 21 | 121 | 1.21 | 10.5% |
| 3 | 12 | 33 | 133 | 1.33 | 11.0% |
| 4 | 13 | 46 | 146 | 1.46 | 11.6% |
| 5 | 15 | 61 | 161 | 1.61 | 12.2% |
| 6 | 16 | 77 | 177 | 1.77 | 12.9% |
| 7 | 18 | 95 | 195 | 1.95 | 13.6% |
| 8 | 19 | 114 | 214 | 2.14 | 14.3% |
| 9 | 21 | 136 | 236 | 2.36 | 15.1% |
| 10 | 24 | 159 | 259 | 2.59 | 15.9% |
| 11 | 26 | 185 | 285 | 2.85 | 16.8% |
| 12 | 29 | 214 | 314 | 3.14 | 17.8% |
| 13 | 31 | 245 | 345 | 3.45 | 18.9% |
| 14 | 35 | 280 | 380 | 3.80 | 20.0% |
| 15 | 38 | 318 | 418 | 4.18 | 21.2% |
| 16 | 42 | 359 | 459 | 4.59 | 22.5% |
| 17 | 46 | 405 | 505 | 5.05 | 23.8% |
| 18 | 51 | 456 | 556 | 5.56 | 25.3% |
| 19 | 56 | 512 | 612 | 6.12 | 26.9% |
| 20 | 61 | 573 | 673 | 6.73 | 28.6% |
| 21 | 67 | 640 | 740 | 7.40 | 30.5% |
| 22 | 74 | 714 | 814 | 8.14 | 32.5% |
| 23 | 81 | 795 | 895 | 8.95 | 34.6% |
| 24 | 90 | 885 | 985 | 9.85 | 36.9% |
| 25 | 98 | 983 | 1,083 | 10.83 | 39.3% |
| 26 | 108 | 1,092 | 1,192 | 11.92 | 42.0% |
| 27 | 119 | 1,211 | 1,311 | 13.11 | 44.9% |
| 28 | 131 | 1,342 | 1,442 | 14.42 | 47.9% |
| 29 | 144 | 1,486 | 1,586 | 15.86 | 51.3% |
| 30 | 159 | 1,645 | 1,745 | 17.45 | 54.8% |
| 31 | 174 | 1,819 | 1,919 | 19.19 | 58.7% |
| 32 | 192 | 2,011 | 2,111 | 21.11 | 62.9% |
| 33 | 211 | 2,223 | 2,323 | 23.23 | 67.3% |
| 34 | 232 | 2,455 | 2,555 | 25.55 | 72.2% |
| 35 | 255 | 2,710 | 2,810 | 28.10 | 77.4% |
| 36 | 281 | 2,991 | 3,091 | 30.91 | 83.1% |
| 37 | 309 | 3,300 | 3,400 | 34.00 | 89.2% |
| 38 | 340 | 3,640 | 3,740 | 37.40 | 95.8% |
| 39 | 374 | 4,014 | 4,114 | 41.14 | 102.9% |
| 40 | 411 | 4,426 | 4,526 | 45.26 | 110.6% |
| 41 | 453 | 4,879 | 4,979 | 49.79 | 119.0% |
| 42 | 498 | 5,376 | 5,476 | 54.76 | 128.0% |
| 43 | 548 | 5,924 | 6,024 | 60.24 | 137.8% |
| 44 | 602 | 6,526 | 6,626 | 66.26 | 148.3% |
| 45 | 663 | 7,189 | 7,289 | 72.89 | 159.8% |

Table 6.1: \$100 in Fixed Deposit at an interest rate of 10% p.a.

**This Table is the same as Table 5.1 in chapter 5.**

The values are rounded off to the nearest whole number.

| | **$100 in Fixed Deposit at interest rate of 20% p.a.** | | | | |
|---|---|---|---|---|---|
| **Year** | **Annual Intertest Amount, $** | **Cumulative Interest Amount, $** | **Final Amount in Account, $** | **Compound Amount Factor** | **Simple Annual Yield, % p.a.** |
| 0 | | | 100 | 1.00 | |
| 1 | 20 | 20 | 120 | 1.20 | 20.0% |
| 2 | 24 | 44 | 144 | 1.44 | 22.0% |
| 3 | 29 | 73 | 173 | 1.73 | 24.3% |
| 4 | 35 | 107 | 207 | 2.07 | 26.8% |
| 5 | 41 | 149 | 249 | 2.49 | 29.8% |
| 6 | 50 | 199 | 299 | 2.99 | 33.1% |
| 7 | 60 | 258 | 358 | 3.58 | 36.9% |
| 8 | 72 | 330 | 430 | 4.30 | 41.2% |
| 9 | 86 | 416 | 516 | 5.16 | 46.2% |
| 10 | 103 | 519 | 619 | 6.19 | 51.9% |
| 11 | 124 | 643 | 743 | 7.43 | 58.5% |
| 12 | 149 | 792 | 892 | 8.92 | 66.0% |
| 13 | 178 | 970 | 1,070 | 10.70 | 74.6% |
| 14 | 214 | 1,184 | 1,284 | 12.84 | 84.6% |
| 15 | 257 | 1,441 | 1,541 | 15.41 | 96.0% |
| 16 | 308 | 1,749 | 1,849 | 18.49 | 109.3% |
| 17 | 370 | 2,119 | 2,219 | 22.19 | 124.6% |
| 18 | 444 | 2,562 | 2,662 | 26.62 | 142.4% |
| 19 | 532 | 3,095 | 3,195 | 31.95 | 162.9% |
| 20 | 639 | 3,734 | 3,834 | 38.34 | 186.7% |
| 21 | 767 | 4,501 | 4,601 | 46.01 | 214.3% |
| 22 | 920 | 5,421 | 5,521 | 55.21 | 246.4% |
| 23 | 1,104 | 6,525 | 6,625 | 66.25 | 283.7% |
| 24 | 1,325 | 7,850 | 7,950 | 79.50 | 327.1% |
| 25 | 1,590 | 9,440 | 9,540 | 95.40 | 377.6% |
| 26 | 1,908 | 11,348 | 11,448 | 114.48 | 436.4% |
| 27 | 2,290 | 13,637 | 13,737 | 137.37 | 505.1% |
| 28 | 2,747 | 16,384 | 16,484 | 164.84 | 585.2% |
| 29 | 3,297 | 19,681 | 19,781 | 197.81 | 678.7% |
| 30 | 3,956 | 23,638 | 23,738 | 237.38 | 787.9% |
| 31 | 4,748 | 28,385 | 28,485 | 284.85 | 915.7% |
| 32 | 5,697 | 34,082 | 34,182 | 341.82 | 1065.1% |
| 33 | 6,836 | 40,919 | 41,019 | 410.19 | 1240.0% |
| 34 | 8,204 | 49,122 | 49,222 | 492.22 | 1444.8% |
| 35 | 9,844 | 58,967 | 59,067 | 590.67 | 1684.8% |
| 36 | 11,813 | 70,780 | 70,880 | 708.80 | 1966.1% |
| 37 | 14,176 | 84,956 | 85,056 | 850.56 | 2296.1% |
| 38 | 17,011 | 101,967 | 102,067 | 1,020.67 | 2683.4% |
| 39 | 20,413 | 122,381 | 122,481 | 1,224.81 | 3138.0% |
| 40 | 24,496 | 146,877 | 146,977 | 1,469.77 | 3671.9% |
| 41 | 29,395 | 176,273 | 176,373 | 1,763.73 | 4299.3% |
| 42 | 35,275 | 211,547 | 211,647 | 2,116.47 | 5036.8% |
| 43 | 42,329 | 253,877 | 253,977 | 2,539.77 | 5904.1% |
| 44 | 50,795 | 304,672 | 304,772 | 3,047.72 | 6924.4% |
| 45 | 60,954 | 365,626 | 365,726 | 3,657.26 | 8125.0% |

**Table 6.2: $100 in Fixed Deposit at an interest rate of 20% p.a.**

The values are rounded off to the nearest whole number.

| | | $100 in Fixed Deposit at interest rate of 30% p.a. | | | |
|---|---|---|---|---|---|
| Year | Annual Intertest Amount, $ | Cumulative Interest Amount, $ | Final Amount in Account, $ | Compound Amount Factor | Simple Annual Yield, % p.a. |
| 0 | | | 100 | 1.00 | |
| 1 | 30 | 30 | 130 | 1.30 | 30.0% |
| 2 | 39 | 69 | 169 | 1.69 | 34.5% |
| 3 | 51 | 120 | 220 | 2.20 | 39.9% |
| 4 | 66 | 186 | 286 | 2.86 | 46.4% |
| 5 | 86 | 271 | 371 | 3.71 | 54.3% |
| 6 | 111 | 383 | 483 | 4.83 | 63.8% |
| 7 | 145 | 527 | 627 | 6.27 | 75.4% |
| 8 | 188 | 716 | 816 | 8.16 | 89.5% |
| 9 | 245 | 960 | 1,060 | 10.60 | 106.7% |
| 10 | 318 | 1,279 | 1,379 | 13.79 | 127.9% |
| 11 | 414 | 1,692 | 1,792 | 17.92 | 153.8% |
| 12 | 538 | 2,230 | 2,330 | 23.30 | 185.8% |
| 13 | 699 | 2,929 | 3,029 | 30.29 | 225.3% |
| 14 | 909 | 3,837 | 3,937 | 39.37 | 274.1% |
| 15 | 1,181 | 5,019 | 5,119 | 51.19 | 334.6% |
| 16 | 1,536 | 6,554 | 6,654 | 66.54 | 409.6% |
| 17 | 1,996 | 8,550 | 8,650 | 86.50 | 503.0% |
| 18 | 2,595 | 11,146 | 11,246 | 112.46 | 619.2% |
| 19 | 3,374 | 14,519 | 14,619 | 146.19 | 764.2% |
| 20 | 4,386 | 18,905 | 19,005 | 190.05 | 945.2% |
| 21 | 5,701 | 24,606 | 24,706 | 247.06 | 1171.7% |
| 22 | 7,412 | 32,018 | 32,118 | 321.18 | 1455.4% |
| 23 | 9,636 | 41,654 | 41,754 | 417.54 | 1811.0% |
| 24 | 12,526 | 54,180 | 54,280 | 542.80 | 2257.5% |
| 25 | 16,284 | 70,464 | 70,564 | 705.64 | 2818.6% |
| 26 | 21,169 | 91,633 | 91,733 | 917.33 | 3524.4% |
| 27 | 27,520 | 119,153 | 119,253 | 1,192.53 | 4413.1% |
| 28 | 35,776 | 154,929 | 155,029 | 1,550.29 | 5533.2% |
| 29 | 46,509 | 201,438 | 201,538 | 2,015.38 | 6946.1% |
| 30 | 60,461 | 261,900 | 262,000 | 2,620.00 | 8730.0% |
| 31 | 78,600 | 340,499 | 340,599 | 3,405.99 | 10983.9% |
| 32 | 102,180 | 442,679 | 442,779 | 4,427.79 | 13833.7% |
| 33 | 132,834 | 575,513 | 575,613 | 5,756.13 | 17439.8% |
| 34 | 172,684 | 748,197 | 748,297 | 7,482.97 | 22005.8% |
| 35 | 224,489 | 972,686 | 972,786 | 9,727.86 | 27791.0% |
| 36 | 291,836 | 1,264,522 | 1,264,622 | 12,646.22 | 35125.6% |
| 37 | 379,387 | 1,643,908 | 1,644,008 | 16,440.08 | 44430.0% |
| 38 | 493,203 | 2,137,111 | 2,137,211 | 21,372.11 | 56239.8% |
| 39 | 641,163 | 2,778,274 | 2,778,374 | 27,783.74 | 71237.8% |
| 40 | 833,512 | 3,611,786 | 3,611,886 | 36,118.86 | 90294.7% |
| 41 | 1,083,566 | 4,695,352 | 4,695,452 | 46,954.52 | 114520.8% |
| 42 | 1,408,636 | 6,103,988 | 6,104,088 | 61,040.88 | 145333.1% |
| 43 | 1,831,226 | 7,935,215 | 7,935,315 | 79,353.15 | 184539.9% |
| 44 | 2,380,594 | 10,315,809 | 10,315,909 | 103,159.09 | 234450.2% |
| 45 | 3,094,773 | 13,410,582 | 13,410,682 | 134,106.82 | 298012.9% |

Table 6.3: $100 in Fixed Deposit at an interest rate of 30% p.a.

The values are rounded off to the nearest whole number.

| Year | Annual Interest Amount, $ | Cumulative Interest Amount, $ | Final Amount in Account, $ | Compound Amount Factor | Simple Annual Yield, % p.a. |
|---|---|---|---|---|---|
| | $100 in Fixed Deposit at interest rate of 40% p.a. | | | | |
| 0 | | | 100 | 1.00 | |
| 1 | 40 | 40 | 140 | 1.40 | 40% |
| 2 | 56 | 96 | 196 | 1.96 | 48% |
| 3 | 78 | 174 | 274 | 2.74 | 58% |
| 4 | 110 | 284 | 384 | 3.84 | 71% |
| 5 | 154 | 438 | 538 | 5.38 | 88% |
| 6 | 215 | 653 | 753 | 7.53 | 109% |
| 7 | 301 | 954 | 1,054 | 10.54 | 136% |
| 8 | 422 | 1,376 | 1,476 | 14.76 | 172% |
| 9 | 590 | 1,966 | 2,066 | 20.66 | 218% |
| 10 | 826 | 2,793 | 2,893 | 28.93 | 279% |
| 11 | 1,157 | 3,950 | 4,050 | 40.50 | 359% |
| 12 | 1,620 | 5,569 | 5,669 | 56.69 | 464% |
| 13 | 2,268 | 7,837 | 7,937 | 79.37 | 603% |
| 14 | 3,175 | 11,012 | 11,112 | 111.12 | 787% |
| 15 | 4,445 | 15,457 | 15,557 | 155.57 | 1030% |
| 16 | 6,223 | 21,680 | 21,780 | 217.80 | 1355% |
| 17 | 8,712 | 30,391 | 30,491 | 304.91 | 1788% |
| 18 | 12,197 | 42,588 | 42,688 | 426.88 | 2366% |
| 19 | 17,075 | 59,663 | 59,763 | 597.63 | 3140% |
| 20 | 23,905 | 83,568 | 83,668 | 836.68 | 4178% |
| 21 | 33,467 | 117,036 | 117,136 | 1,171.36 | 5573% |
| 22 | 46,854 | 163,890 | 163,990 | 1,639.90 | 7450% |
| 23 | 65,596 | 229,486 | 229,586 | 2,295.86 | 9978% |
| 24 | 91,834 | 321,320 | 321,420 | 3,214.20 | 13388% |
| 25 | 128,568 | 449,888 | 449,988 | 4,499.88 | 17996% |
| 26 | 179,995 | 629,883 | 629,983 | 6,299.83 | 24226% |
| 27 | 251,993 | 881,876 | 881,976 | 8,819.76 | 32662% |
| 28 | 352,791 | 1,234,667 | 1,234,767 | 12,347.67 | 44095% |
| 29 | 493,907 | 1,728,574 | 1,728,674 | 17,286.74 | 59606% |
| 30 | 691,469 | 2,420,043 | 2,420,143 | 24,201.43 | 80668% |
| 31 | 968,057 | 3,388,101 | 3,388,201 | 33,882.01 | 109294% |
| 32 | 1,355,280 | 4,743,381 | 4,743,481 | 47,434.81 | 148231% |
| 33 | 1,897,392 | 6,640,773 | 6,640,873 | 66,408.73 | 201236% |
| 34 | 2,656,349 | 9,297,122 | 9,297,222 | 92,972.22 | 273445% |
| 35 | 3,718,889 | 13,016,011 | 13,016,111 | 130,161.11 | 371886% |
| 36 | 5,206,444 | 18,222,456 | 18,222,556 | 182,225.56 | 506179% |
| 37 | 7,289,022 | 25,511,478 | 25,511,578 | 255,115.78 | 689499% |
| 38 | 10,204,631 | 35,716,109 | 35,716,209 | 357,162.09 | 939898% |
| 39 | 14,286,484 | 50,002,593 | 50,002,693 | 500,026.93 | 1282118% |
| 40 | 20,001,077 | 70,003,670 | 70,003,770 | 700,037.70 | 1750092% |
| 41 | 28,001,508 | 98,005,178 | 98,005,278 | 980,052.78 | 2390370% |
| 42 | 39,202,111 | 137,207,289 | 137,207,389 | 1,372,073.89 | 3266840% |
| 43 | 54,882,955 | 192,090,244 | 192,090,344 | 1,920,903.44 | 4467215% |
| 44 | 76,836,138 | 268,926,382 | 268,926,482 | 2,689,264.82 | 6111963% |
| 45 | 107,570,593 | 376,496,974 | 376,497,074 | 3,764,970.74 | 8366599% |

Table 6.4: $100 in Fixed Deposit at an interest rate of 40% p.a.

The values are rounded off to the nearest whole number.

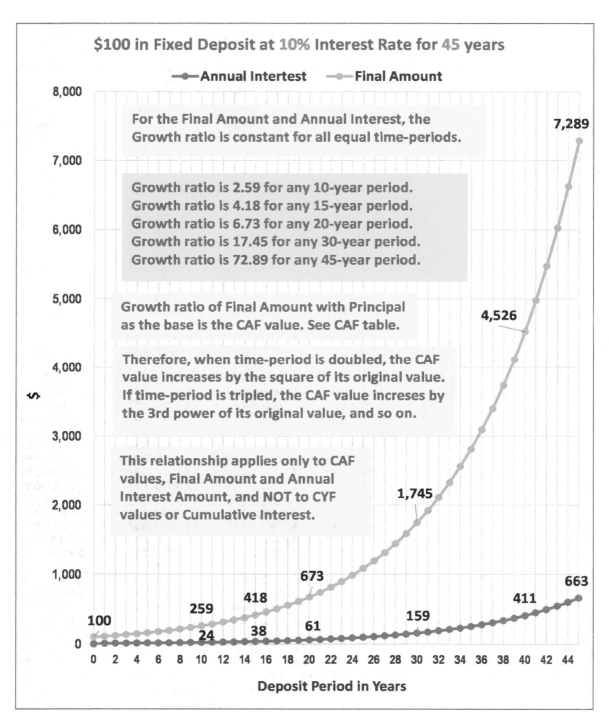

Figure 6.1: **Final amount and Annual interest for** $100 **in Fixed Deposit at** 10% **interest rate for** 45 years.

**This Figure is the same as Fig 5.1 in chapter 5.**

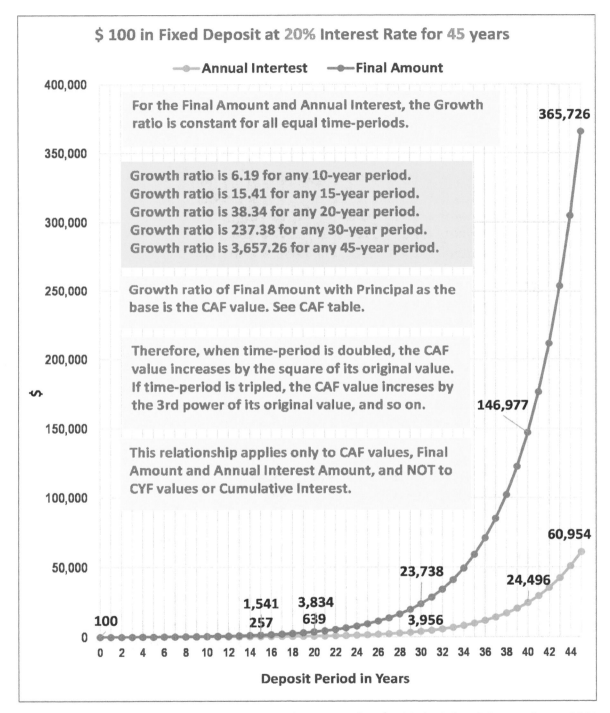

**Figure 6.2: Final amount and Annual interest for** $100 **in Fixed Deposit at** 20% **interest rate for** 45 years.

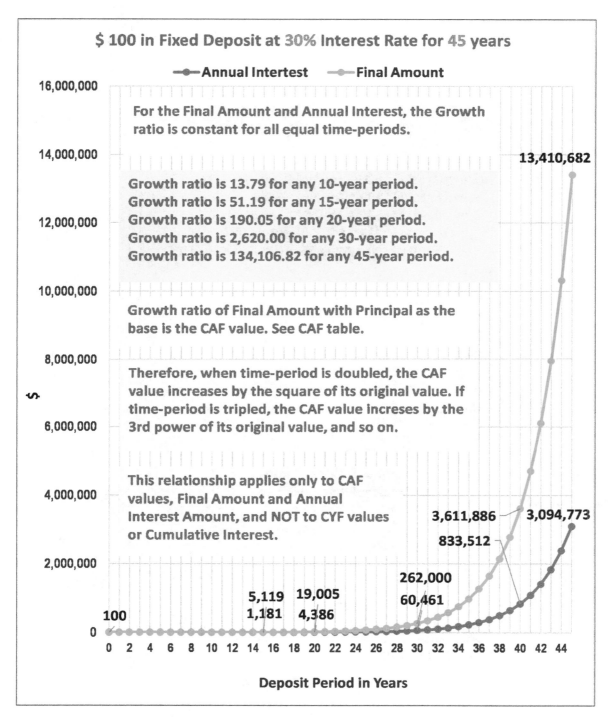

**Figure 6.3: Final amount and Annual interest for $100 in Fixed Deposit at 30% interest rate for 45 years.**

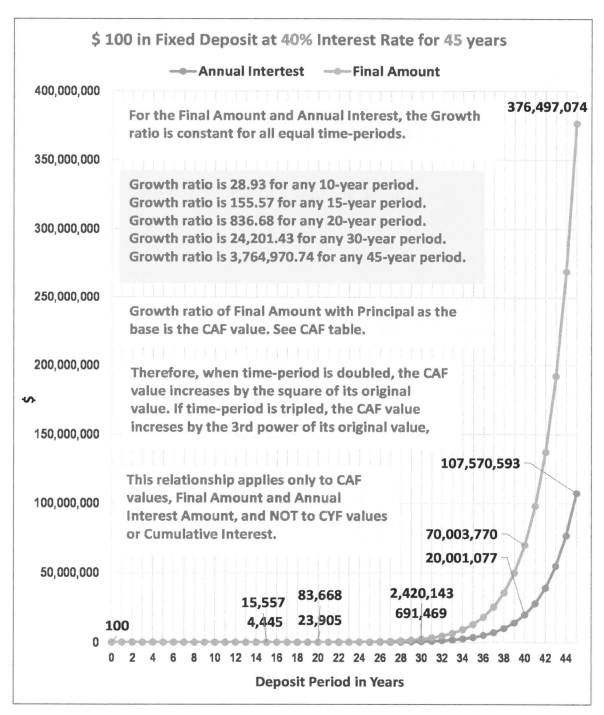

Figure 6.4: **Final amount and Annual interest for** $100 **in Fixed Deposit at** 40% **interest rate for** 45 years.

## 6.2      EFFECT OF CHANGE OF YIELD RATE AND TIME-PERIOD ON FINAL AMOUNT

Let us put the values in a table again and plot the graphs in a different way to highlight the effect of change of yield rate on the results.

In table 6.5 below, the CAF values are given for years 1 to 60 and yield rates of 10%, 20%, 30% & 40%. As we have seen in chapter 4, the CAF value gives the final amount of an investment of $1.00.

### 6.2.1      Final amounts for $1 invested with 1% to 30% yield rates for 15, 30 & 45 years

Figure 6.5 shows the pattern in which the final amount increases when the yield rate is increased from 1% to 30% for an investment period of 15 years.

Figure 6.6 shows the pattern in which the final amount increases when the yield rate is increased from 1% to 30% for an investment period of 30 years.

Figure 6.7 shows the pattern in which the final amount increases when the yield rate is increased from 1% to 30% for an investment period of 45 years.

In this section, we have not included the 40% yield rate as the values are relatively too large to fit them together with 10%, 20% & 30% yield rates into a single graph.

However, in section 6.2.2, we have also included the 40% yield rate together with 10%, 20% & 30% yield rates by using a different format for the graphs.

In the Figures themselves, please read the annotations for observations and conclusions drawn from the graphs.

| | Compound Amount Factor (CAF) or Asset Growth Factor | | | |
|---|---|---|---|---|
| **Year** | **Yield Rate** | | | |
| | 10% | 20% | 30% | 40% |
| 0 | 1.00 | 1.00 | 1.00 | 1.00 |
| 1 | 1.10 | 1.20 | 1.30 | 1.40 |
| 2 | 1.21 | 1.44 | 1.69 | 1.96 |
| 3 | 1.33 | 1.73 | 2.20 | 2.74 |
| 4 | 1.46 | 2.07 | 2.86 | 3.84 |
| 5 | 1.61 | 2.49 | 3.71 | 5.38 |
| 6 | 1.77 | 2.99 | 4.83 | 7.53 |
| 7 | 1.95 | 3.58 | 6.27 | 10.54 |
| 8 | 2.14 | 4.30 | 8.16 | 14.76 |
| 9 | 2.36 | 5.16 | 10.60 | 20.66 |
| 10 | 2.59 | 6.19 | 13.79 | 28.93 |
| 11 | 2.85 | 7.43 | 17.92 | 40.50 |
| 12 | 3.14 | 8.92 | 23.30 | 56.69 |
| 13 | 3.45 | 10.70 | 30.29 | 79.37 |
| 14 | 3.80 | 12.84 | 39.37 | 111.12 |
| 15 | 4.18 | 15.41 | 51.19 | 155.57 |
| 16 | 4.59 | 18.49 | 66.54 | 217.80 |
| 17 | 5.05 | 22.19 | 86.50 | 304.91 |
| 18 | 5.56 | 26.62 | 112.46 | 426.88 |
| 19 | 6.12 | 31.95 | 146.19 | 597.63 |
| 20 | 6.73 | 38.34 | 190.05 | 836.68 |
| 21 | 7.40 | 46.01 | 247.06 | 1,171.36 |
| 22 | 8.14 | 55.21 | 321.18 | 1,639.90 |
| 23 | 8.95 | 66.25 | 417.54 | 2,295.86 |
| 24 | 9.85 | 79.50 | 542.80 | 3,214.20 |
| 25 | 10.83 | 95.40 | 705.64 | 4,499.88 |
| 26 | 11.92 | 114.48 | 917.33 | 6,299.83 |
| 27 | 13.11 | 137.37 | 1,192.53 | 8,819.76 |
| 28 | 14.42 | 164.84 | 1,550.29 | 12,347.67 |
| 29 | 15.86 | 197.81 | 2,015.38 | 17,286.74 |
| 30 | 17.45 | 237.38 | 2,620.00 | 24,201.43 |
| 31 | 19.19 | 284.85 | 3,405.99 | 33,882.01 |
| 32 | 21.11 | 341.82 | 4,427.79 | 47,434.81 |
| 33 | 23.23 | 410.19 | 5,756.13 | 66,408.73 |
| 34 | 25.55 | 492.22 | 7,482.97 | 92,972.22 |
| 35 | 28.10 | 590.67 | 9,727.86 | 130,161.11 |
| 36 | 30.91 | 708.80 | 12,646.22 | 182,225.56 |
| 37 | 34.00 | 850.56 | 16,440.08 | 255,115.78 |
| 38 | 37.40 | 1,020.67 | 21,372.11 | 357,162.09 |
| 39 | 41.14 | 1,224.81 | 27,783.74 | 500,026.93 |
| 40 | 45.26 | 1,469.77 | 36,118.86 | 700,037.70 |
| 41 | 49.79 | 1,763.73 | 46,954.52 | 980,052.78 |
| 42 | 54.76 | 2,116.47 | 61,040.88 | 1,372,073.89 |
| 43 | 60.24 | 2,539.77 | 79,353.15 | 1,920,903.44 |
| 44 | 66.26 | 3,047.72 | 103,159.09 | 2,689,264.82 |
| 45 | 72.89 | 3,657.26 | 134,106.82 | 3,764,970.74 |
| 46 | 80.18 | 4,388.71 | 174,338.86 | 5,270,959.04 |
| 47 | 88.20 | 5,266.46 | 226,640.52 | 7,379,342.65 |
| 48 | 97.02 | 6,319.75 | 294,632.68 | 10,331,079.71 |
| 49 | 106.72 | 7,583.70 | 383,022.48 | 14,463,511.60 |
| 50 | 117.39 | 9,100.44 | 497,929.22 | 20,248,916.24 |
| 51 | 129.13 | 10,920.53 | 647,307.99 | 28,348,482.74 |
| 52 | 142.04 | 13,104.63 | 841,500.39 | 39,687,875.83 |
| 53 | 156.25 | 15,725.56 | 1,093,950.50 | 55,563,026.16 |
| 54 | 171.87 | 18,870.67 | 1,422,135.65 | 77,788,236.63 |
| 55 | 189.06 | 22,644.80 | 1,848,776.35 | 108,903,531.28 |
| 56 | 207.97 | 27,173.76 | 2,403,409.25 | 152,464,943.79 |
| 57 | 228.76 | 32,608.52 | 3,124,432.03 | 213,450,921.30 |
| 58 | 251.64 | 39,130.22 | 4,061,761.64 | 298,831,289.83 |
| 59 | 276.80 | 46,956.26 | 5,280,290.13 | 418,363,805.76 |
| 60 | 304.48 | 56,347.51 | 6,864,377.17 | 585,709,328.06 |

Table 6.5: **Compound Amount Factor (CAF) for yield rates of** 10%, 20%, 30% & 40%.

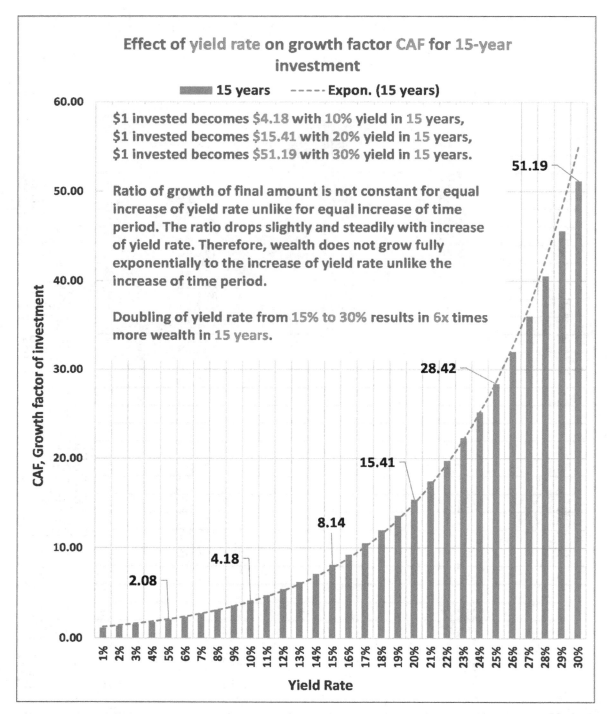

## Effect of yield rate on growth factor CAF for 15-year investment

**15 years**    - - - - **Expon. (15 years)**

$1 invested becomes $4.18 with 10% yield in 15 years,
$1 invested becomes $15.41 with 20% yield in 15 years,
$1 invested becomes $51.19 with 30% yield in 15 years.

Ratio of growth of final amount is not constant for equal increase of yield rate unlike for equal increase of time period. The ratio drops slightly and steadily with increase of yield rate. Therefore, wealth does not grow fully exponentially to the increase of yield rate unlike the increase of time period.

Doubling of yield rate from 15% to 30% results in 6x times more wealth in 15 years.

*CAF, Growth factor of investment* (y-axis)

*Yield Rate* (x-axis)

**Figure 6.5: Final amount of $1 investment in 15 years for yield rates from 1% to 30% p.a.**

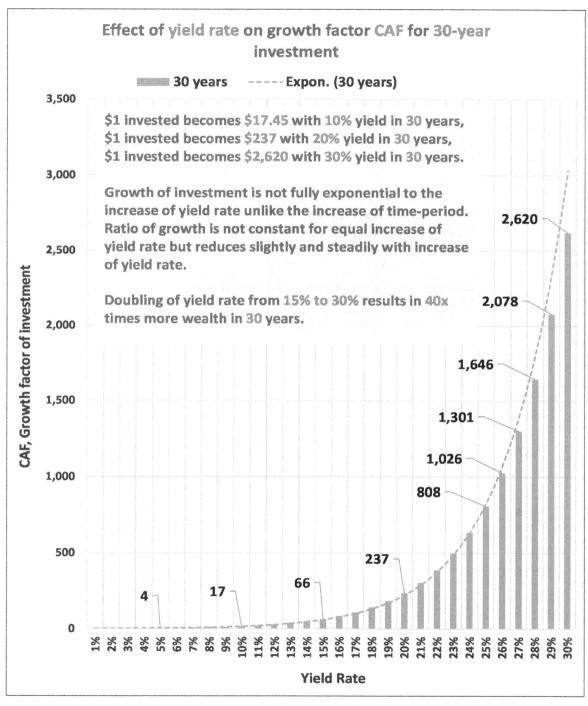

**Effect of yield rate on growth factor CAF for 30-year investment**

$1 invested becomes $17.45 with 10% yield in 30 years,
$1 invested becomes $237 with 20% yield in 30 years,
$1 invested becomes $2,620 with 30% yield in 30 years.

Growth of investment is not fully exponential to the increase of yield rate unlike the increase of time-period. Ratio of growth is not constant for equal increase of yield rate but reduces slightly and steadily with increase of yield rate.

Doubling of yield rate from 15% to 30% results in 40x times more wealth in 30 years.

Figure 6.6: **Final amount for $1 investment in 30 years for yield rates from 1% to 30% p.a.**

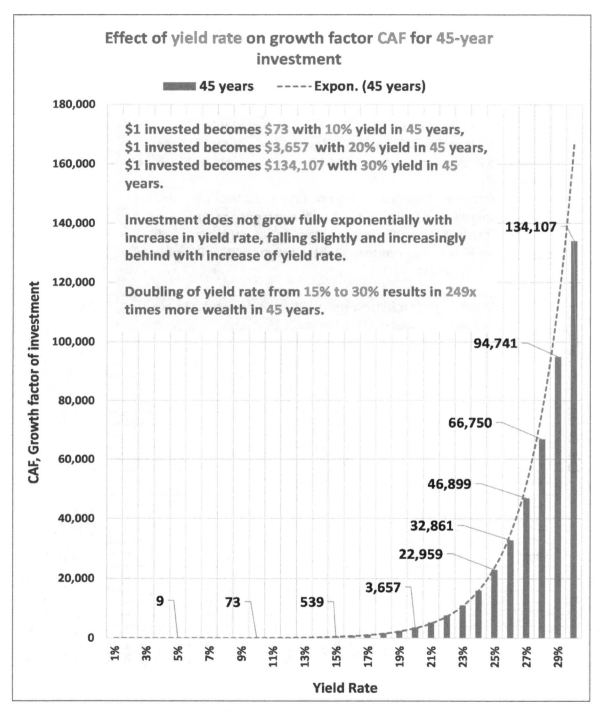

Figure 6.7: **Final amount for** $1 **investment in** 45 years **for yield rates from** 1% **to** 30% **p.a.**

## 6.2.2     Final amounts for $1 invested with 10%, 20%, 30% & 40% yield rates for 1 to 45 years

In section 6.2.1, we had not included the 40% yield rate as the values were relatively too large to fit them together with 10%, 20% & 30% yield rates into a single graph.

In this section, we have also included the 40% yield rate together with 10%, 20% & 30% yield rates by using a different format for the graphs.

Figure 6.8 shows, for yield rates of 10%, 20%, 30% & 40%, how the value of an investment of $1 increases exponentially as the investment period increases from 1 to 45 years.

Figure 6.9 shows the first 15 years of Figure 6.8 magnified.

In the Figures themselves, please read the annotations for observations and conclusions drawn from the graphs.

Please note how the 40% yield rate utterly dwarfs even the 30% yield rate and literally obliterates 10% and 20% yield rates from the graphs at higher investment periods.

If you understand these graphs, you can understand how Jeff Bezos became the richest man on earth by investing probably only a few thousand dollars of his own money to start Amazon. Amazon stock had appreciated by an average of 44% per year in the past 5 years.

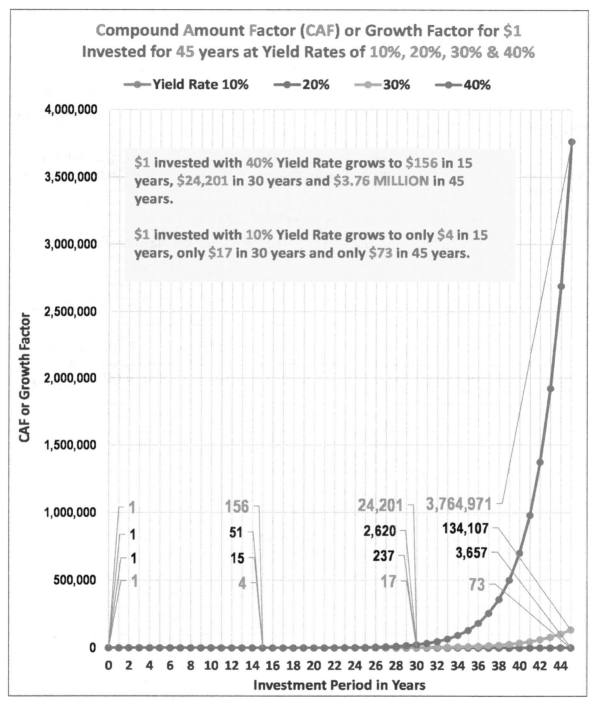

Figure 6.8: **Exponential growth of final amount with yield rates** 10%, 20%, 30% & 40% **for investment period up to** 45 years.

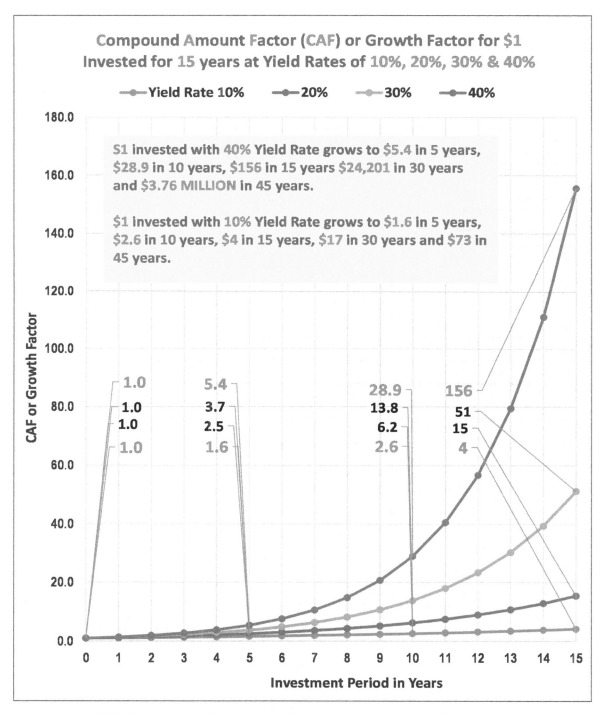

## Compound Amount Factor (CAF) or Growth Factor for $1 Invested for 15 years at Yield Rates of 10%, 20%, 30% & 40%

— Yield Rate 10%  — 20%  — 30%  — 40%

$1 invested with 40% Yield Rate grows to $5.4 in 5 years, $28.9 in 10 years, $156 in 15 years $24,201 in 30 years and $3.76 MILLION in 45 years.

$1 invested with 10% Yield Rate grows to $1.6 in 5 years, $2.6 in 10 years, $4 in 15 years, $17 in 30 years and $73 in 45 years.

| | 1.0 | 5.4 | 28.9 | 156 |
| | 1.0 | 3.7 | 13.8 | 51 |
| | 1.0 | 2.5 | 6.2 | 15 |
| | 1.0 | 1.6 | 2.6 | 4 |

CAF or Growth Factor

Investment Period in Years

Figure 6.9: **This is a magnified image of the** first 15 years of Figure 6.8. **It shows the Exponential growth of the final amount with yield rates of** 10%, 20%, 30% & 40% **for an investment period up to** 15 years.

## 6.3    SUMMARY

| Compound Amount Factor (CAF) or Growth Ratio of $1 Investment | | | | |
|---|---|---|---|---|
| | Interest or Yield Rate | | | |
| Year | 10% | 20% | 30% | 40% |
| 0 | 1 | 1 | 1 | 1 |
| 15 | 4 | 15 | 51 | 156 |
| 30 | 17 | 237 | 2,620 | 24,201 |
| 45 | 73 | 3,657 | 134,107 | 3,764,971 |
| 60 | 304 | 56,348 | 6,864,377 | 585,709,328 |

**Table 6.6: Summary of results of $1 invested at 10%, 20%, 30% & 40% yield p.a.**
All values are rounded off to the nearest whole number.

Table 6.6 is an extract of results from Tables 6.1 to 6.5 for the duration of investment of 15, 30, 45 & 60 years, with all the values rounded off to the nearest whole number.

The purpose of this table is to provide you with a better overview of the effects of yield rate and duration of investment on the growth of your wealth.

Please take note that the values in this table, though rounded off, are exactly the same as in the Compound Amount Factor (CAF) table given in Appendix-A of this book.

### Explanation of Table 6.6

$1 invested at a **10%** yield rate grows to become $4 in 15 years, $17 in 30 years, $73 in 45 years, and $304 in 60 years.

$1 invested at a **20%** yield rate grows to become $15 in 15 years, $237 in 30 years, $3,657 in 45 years, and $56,348 in 60 years.

$1 invested at a **30%** yield rate grows to become $51 in 15 years, $2.620 in 30 years, $134,107 in 45 years, and $6,864,377 in 60 years.

$1 invested at **40%** yield rate grows to become $156 in 15 years, $24,201 in 30 years, $3,764,971 in 45 years and $585,709,328 in 60 years.

## 6.3.1      Effect of change of yield rate on the final amount

Let us look at the numbers in a different way. Let us see how much more wealth you would have if you invested with a 20% yield rate instead of 10%, 30% instead of 10%, and 40% instead of 10%. Put it differently, if you would have $1 million net worth with a 10% yield rate, how many millions would you have with 20%, 30%, and 40% yield rates.

Table 6.6 above gives a summary of the final amounts in absolute values. For easy comparison, let us make the final value of the 10% yield rate as the base and see how yield rates of 20%, 30%, and 40% compare with respect to the 10% yield rate. We can do this by dividing all the 15-year values by 4 as in table 6.7 below, dividing all the 30-year values by 17 as in table 6.8 below, dividing all the 45-year values by 73 as in table 6.9 below, and dividing all the 60-year values by 304 as in table 6.10 below.

Tables 6.7, 6.8, 6.9 & 6.10 below give, for investment periods of 15 years, 30 years, 45 years, and 60 years respectively, the factor by which the final amount increases when yield rate is increased from 10% to 20%, 30%, and 40%.

### 6.3.1.1      15-year investment

| Final Amount in 15 years with 10%, 20%, 30% & 40% yield rates as ratio of Final Amount with 10% yield rate | | | | |
|---|---|---|---|---|
| | **Interest or Yield Rate** | | | |
| | 10% | 20% | 30% | 40% |
| **Initial Investment in Year 0 (zero)** | 1.00 | 1.00 | 1.00 | 1.00 |
| **Final Amount (FA) in 15** years | 4 | 15 | 51 | 156 |
| **Ratio of FA to FA with 10% Yield** | 1.0 | 3.7x | 12.3x | 37.2x |

**Table 6.7: Final amounts with** 10%, 20%, 30% & 40% **yield rates as a** ratio **of the final amount with** 10% **yield rate for an investment period of** 15 years.

Please look at the figures in Table 6.7 above, in which $1 is invested for 15 years at yield rates of 10%, 20%, 30%, & 40%.

In 15 years, $1 grows to only $4 with a 10% yield rate, but to $15 with 20%, to $51 with 30 %, and to $156 with a 40% yield rate.

By increasing the yield rate to **2x times**, namely, from 10% to 20% p.a., the $1 will grow from $4 to $15, which is an increase of **3.7x times** as can be seen in the table.

Similarly, by increasing the yield rate to **3x times**, namely, from 10% p.a. to 30% p.a., the $1 will grow from $4 to $51, which is an increase of **12.3x times.**

By increasing the yield rate to **4x times**, namely, from 10% p.a. to 40% p.a., the $1 will grow from $4 to $156, which is an increase of **37.2x times**.

### 6.3.1.2    30-year investment

| Final Amount in 30 years with 10%, 20%, 30% & 40% yield rates as ratio of Final Amount with 10% yield rate | | | | |
|---|---|---|---|---|
| | Interest or Yield Rate | | | |
| | 10% | 20% | 30% | 40% |
| Initial Investment in Year 0 (zero) | 1.00 | 1.00 | 1.00 | 1.00 |
| Final Amount (FA) in 30 years | 17 | 237 | 2,620 | 24,201 |
| Ratio of FA to FA with 10% Yield | 1.0 | 13.6x | 150x | 1,387x |

Table 6.8: **Final amounts with** 10%, 20%, 30% & 40% **yield rates as a** ratio **of the final amount with** 10% **yield rate for an investment period of** 30 years.

Please look at the figures in Table 6.8 above in which $1 is invested for 30 years at yield rates of 10%, 20%, 30% & 40%.

In 30 years, $1 grows to only $17 with 10% yield rate, but to $237 with 20%, to $2,620 with 30 %, and to $24,201 with 40% yield rate.

By increasing the yield rate to **2x times**, namely, from 10% to 20% p.a., the $1 will grow from $17 to $237, which is an increase of **13.6x times** as can be seen in the table.

Similarly, by increasing the yield rate to **3x times**, namely, from 10% p.a. to 30% p.a., the $1 will grow from $17 to $2,620, which is an increase of **150x times.**

By increasing the yield rate to **4x times**, namely, from 10% p.a. to 40% p.a., the $1 will grow from $17 to $24,201, which is an increase of **1,387x times.**

## 6.3.1.3     45-year investment

| Final Amount in 45 years with 10%, 20%, 30% & 40% yield rates as ratio of Final Amount with 10% yield rate | | | | |
|---|---|---|---|---|
| | Interest or Yield Rate | | | |
| | 10% | 20% | 30% | 40% |
| Initial Investment in Year 0 (zero) | 1.00 | 1.00 | 1.00 | 1.00 |
| Final Amount (FA) in 45 years | 73 | 3,657 | 134,107 | 3,764,971 |
| Ratio of FA to FA with 10% Yield | 1.0 | 50x | 1,840x | 51,652x |

Table 6.9: **Final amounts with** 10%, 20%, 30% & 40% **yield rates as a** ratio **of the final amount with** 10% **yield rate for an investment period of** 45 years.

Please look at the figures in Table 6.9 above in which $1 is invested for 45 years at yield rates of 10%, 20%, 30% & 40%.

In 45 years, $1 grows to only $73 with 10% yield rate, but to $3,.657 with 20%, to $134,107 with 30 %, and to $3,764,971 with 40% yield rate.

By increasing the yield rate to 2x times, namely, from 10% to 20% p.a., the $1 will grow from $73 to $3,657, which is an increase of 50x times as can be seen in the table.

Similarly, by increasing the yield rate to 3x times, namely, from 10% p.a. to 30% p.a., the $1 will grow from $73 to $134,107, which is an increase of 1,840x times.

By increasing the yield rate to 4x times, namely, from 10% p.a. to 40% p.a., the $1 will grow from $73 to $3,764,971, which is an increase of 51,652x times.

## 6.3.1.4    60-year investment

| Final Amount in 60 years with 10%, 20%, 30% & 40% yield rates as ratio of Final Amount with 10% yield rate | | | | |
|---|---|---|---|---|
| | Interest or Yield Rate | | | |
| | 10% | 20% | 30% | 40% |
| Initial Investment in Year 0 (zero) | 1.00 | 1.00 | 1.00 | 1.00 |
| Final Amount (FA) in 60 years | 304 | 56,348 | 6,864,377 | 585,709,328 |
| Ratio of FA to FA with 10% Yield | 1.0 | 185x | 22,544x | 1,923,627x |

**Table 6.10: Final amounts with** 10%, 20%, 30% **&** 40% **yield rates as a** ratio **of the final amount with** 10% **yield rate for an investment period of** 60 years.

Please look at the figures in Table 6.10 above in which $1 is invested for 60 years at yield rates of 10%, 20%, 30% & 40%.

In 60 years, $1 grows to only $304 with 10% yield rate, but to $56,.348 with 20%, to $6,864,377 with 30 %, and to $585,709,328 (approximately $586 Million) with 40% yield rate.

By increasing the yield rate to 2x times, namely, from 10% to 20% p.a., the $1 will grow from $304 to $56,348, which is an increase of 185x times as can be seen in the Table.

Similarly, by increasing the yield rate to 3x times, namely, from 10% p.a. to 30% p.a., the $1 will grow from $304 to $6,864,377, which is an increase of 22,544x times.

By increasing the yield rate to 4x times higher, namely, from 10% p.a. to 40% p.a., the $1 will grow from $304 to $585,709,328, which is an increase of 1,923,627x times (approximately 1.9 million times).

## 6.4      LIFETIME WEALTH BUILDING LIKE WARREN BUFFETT OR JEFF BEZOS

Let us consider a wealth-building period of 60 years! Just imagine, for the time being, that you are Warren Buffet. Like him, you can also work on wealth-building for 60 years if you want. From 25 to 85 years must be possible with a bit of blessing from above. A wealth-building period of 45 years must be feasible for most people.

Looking at Table 6.10 above, with the 10% yield rate per year, I am not excited about the growth of $1 to only $304 in 60 years, which would be my entire active lifetime. If I invest $1,000 today, 60 years, and all the inflation later, my final asset would be only $304,000. But 10% per annum is the maximum yield I can hope to get from any Term Deposit in any bank, even in the best of times.

If I can invest the money in a profitable business and earn 4x times that much yield rate annually, that is, **40% p.a.**, my $1 will grow to **$585.7 Million in 60 years** instead of a meager **$304** with only a 10% yield rate.

If I invest $1,000 today at 40% yield per annum, after 60 years, I will have about **$586 BILLION**!!! That is more than the net worth of Bill Gates and Warren Buffett and Jeff Bezos combined as of December 2020.

Fantasy? No. Amazon stock grew on an average by 44% per year in the past 5 years (September 2015 to August 2020). The growth rate in the past one year alone (September 2019 to August 2020) was even 100%.

## 6.5      THE SECRET OF WEALTH-BUILDING THROUGH HIGHER YIELD RATES AND LONGER TIME-PERIODS

The increase of the final amount or yield amount in any investment with compounding is not linear to the increase of yield rate but **almost exponential.**

As a result, the total yield amount from an investment with a 20% yield rate will not be equal to 2x times the total yield amount from a similar investment with a 10% yield rate.

The value of 20% yield rate is NOT EQUAL TO the sum of the values of yield rates of 10% + 10%, but it can be wildly higher.

How much higher depends on the height of the yield rates involved and the time period of investment.

**The higher the yield rates involved, the higher the difference in values.**

**The longer the time period of investment, the higher the difference in values.**

Catching the essence of our observations, and for easy memorization, we can write some shocking formulas as below as examples.

### 6.5.1    In compounding, 9% + 3% = 9.84%

For the final amount or total yield of any investment for 30 years:

9% + 3% IS NOT EQUAL TO 12% as in simple arithmetic addition.

**For the final amount of any investment for 30 years:**

9% + 3% = 9.84%.

**Let us see how we arrived at this formula.**

CAF values, or Growth Factors, from the CAF table, are as below:

CAF value for 30 years at 3% yield rate = 2.43.

CAF value for 30 years at 9% yield rate = 13.27.

CAF value for 30 years at 12% yield rate = 29.96.

CAF value for 30 years at 4.2% yield rate = 3.42.

Sum of CAF values for (3% + 9%) = (2.43 + 13.27) = 15.70.

Calculating the yield rate that generates a CAF value of 15.70 in 30 years, we get 9.84% as the result. Hence the formula 9% + 3% = 9.84%.

### 6.5.2    In compounding, 12% = 9% + 9% + 4.2%

**For the final amount of any investment for 30 years:**

9% +9% + 4.2% IS NOT EQUAL TO 22.2% as in simple arithmetic addition.

9% + 9% + 4.2% = 12.0% in the mathematics of compounding.

If you are a money manager, the not-so-literate client can suspect you of having pocketed 10.2% (= 22.2 − 12) for yourself!

Put differently, it is:

12% = 9% + 9% + 4.2%.

In this case, the not-so-literate client shall admire you as a magician who can make money multiply from 12% to 22.2%.

**Let us see how we arrived at these formulas.**

Sum of CAF values for (9% + 9% + 4.2%) = (13.27 + 13.27 + 3.42) = 29.96.

29.96 is exactly the CAF value for a 12% yield rate. Hence these formulas.

### 6.5.3      General Insight

Simple Arithmetic laws do not always apply when calculating compounding values. As we have seen in section 1.3, simple arithmetic laws apply to a world in 2D but not to the 3D and 4D worlds of compounding and tax drag.

Due to the near-exponential increase of the final amount with every **nominal** increase of yield rate, the **effective** values of two equal sequential increases in yield rate will never be equal except for the first year. Their **effective** values will be near-exponentially higher or lower depending on their numerical positions, just as it is with the value of an increase in time-period.

For example, a 1% **differential yield rate** embedded between 21% and 22% **nominal yield rates** will have a higher effective value than the 1% differential yield rate embedded between 20% and 21% nominal yield rates, and a hugely higher effective value than the 1% differential yield rate embedded between 2% and 3%.

When you add up nominal yield rates to bundle them to a bigger value, the effective sum will always be less than the arithmetic sum (example: **9% + 3% = 9.84%, which is less than 12**). It is as if you lose some yield when you add them up, but you are losing nothing. The values remain unchanged before and after adding up. Only the label gets smaller, in this example, from **12% arithmetic sum to 9.84% effective sum in 30 years.** See section 6.5.1 above for details.

Therefore, for a **30-year investment period**, we can state the following:

**9% nominal yield rate + 3% nominal yield rate = 9.84% nominal yield rate.**

When you split a yield rate into smaller parts, just the opposite happens. When you add up the split components, the arithmetic sum will always be more than the effective sum (example: **9.84% = 9% + 3%, which is more than 9.84**). It is as if you gain some extra yield when you split a nominal yield rate, but you will be gaining nothing. The values remain unchanged before and after the splitting. Only the arithmetic sum of the labels gets bigger, in this example, from **9.84% effective to 12% arithmetic.**

**Do not under-estimate the power of just a seemingly tiny 1% extra yield rate. It can be mightier than a 20% nominal yield rate, as we will see in chapter 7.**

This is an insight that most people do not have, and as a result, potential financial gains are lost to them.

### 6.6      WHICH ONE IS MORE DOMINANT: TIME-PERIOD OR YIELD RATE? IT IS TIME-PERIOD

We had already seen in chapter 5 that, with a doubling of the time period, the final amount would multiply by the square of the asset growth factor or CAF value. By a tripling of time-period, the final asset would multiply by the third power of the CAF value, i.e., $(CAF)^3$.

Putting it differently, the growth ratio of wealth between two equal time periods will be the same across the whole range of time-periods as long as the interest rate does not change.

Likewise, we have seen earlier in this chapter that, for a given time period, a doubling of the interest rate also has an almost-exponentially increasing effect on the final amount or Compound Amount Factor. But by how much? As much impact as a doubling of the time-period?

The answer is: **Yield rate does not have as much impact on the final amount as the time-period.**

A change in the time period of investment has more impact on the final amount than a proportionate or equal percentage change in yield rate or interest rate.

A closer analysis will show that the impact of increasing the interest rate is less dominant than a proportionate increase of time-period. Time-period is ***always*** more dominant than the interest rate at all time-periods and all interest rates except for the first year or first compounding period when they are both equal.

In the kingdom of compound interest, the time period is always king. Interest rate is, of course, the second most powerful. It is like the king and queen on a chessboard.

Though the supremacy of time-period over interest rate is universal in the kingdom of compounding, the dominance is not evenly distributed. At very lower interest rates, the impact of time-period is only marginally higher than that of interest rate, but at higher interest rates, the difference grows bigger and bigger. At exceedingly high interest rates, the impact of any change of time-period on yield amount is so dominant that it dwarfs the impact of a proportionate change of interest rate.

This higher impact of time-period with respect to the impact of interest rate can be seen by comparing the CAF values in the CAF table in Appendix-A. Take any combination of interest rate and time-period and record the CAF value. Then record the values at double the time-period and double the interest rate and compare the two values! You will notice that the CAF value for double the time-period is always higher than the CAF value for double the yield rate.

## 6.7      WHAT IS MORE IMPORTANT TO WEALTH BUILDING: TIME-PERIOD OR YIELD RATE? IT IS YIELD RATE

We had seen earlier that, in a virtual competition between time-period and yield rate to produce more wealth, time-period is the more powerful of the two. The only exception is the first year when both these partners are equal in power. After that, compounding comes into play and makes the time-period steadily more powerful. Time-period gets ever more dominant as time passes.

But beware!

Our target is to become a Dollar millionaire in the shortest possible time. Therefore, there is no question of choosing between time-period and yield rate.

Firstly, we should always go for the highest yield rate that is possible within a given time period.

After that, as a second step only, we should see if we can also extend the time period to twice or thrice or whatever maximum is possible, at the same time keeping the yield rate also as maximum as possible.

If you had an investment that grew 5 times in 5 years, and you succeed to get the same yield rate for another 15 years, your initial investment would grow to a total of 625x times (= 5 to the power of 4) in 20 years as we had seen with exponential growth in chapter 5.

Therefore, the answer to the above question is to go for the highest yield rate first and then go for the longest possible time period.

## 6.8        THE WEALTH-BUILDERS' FORMULA

1.  In order to get ultra-wealthy, you should invest the **maximum possible amount** for the **highest possible yield rate**.

2.  The only sure way to achieve the highest yield rate is by **setting up your own business** and not by swapping your time and intellectual resources for a salary, or your financial resources for interest, from someone else's business.

3.  Investment should be maximized with any cheaper money available, and that is **borrowed money** in the first instance and **share capital** in the last instance.

4.  Additionally, this investment should be coupled with a **long investment period** with **little or no annual tax.**

5.  If tax is not avoidable and the tax rates are high, you should consider **investments with deferred tax** even if the pre-tax Rate of Return is lower.

6.  It is the **amount of after-tax return** and not the **percentage** that ultimately counts in wealth-building.

7.  Likewise, it is also **not the percentage or amount of tax** that you pay, but only the amount of after-tax return that you get to hold for yourself that ultimately counts in wealth-building.

Essentially, the above is the secret and sacred formula used by all multi-Billionaires to amass enormous wealth. They differ from each other only in the instruments they use to generate the high yield rate. The instrument used by Jeff Bezos was Amazon; for Bill Gates, it was Microsoft; for Warren Buffett, it was the stock market, and for Trump, it was real estate.

Please note that tax is not considered in the examples discussed and analyzed in this chapter. However, tax is an all-important and elaborate topic in any wealth-building strategy. It is therefore treated separately and elaborately in volume II of this series of books on wealth building.

## 6.9     WHAT DOES IT TAKE TO HAVE $1 MILLION NET WORTH IN 30 YEARS?

Please see chapter 11 for a detailed discussion of this topic.

If you have approximately **$4,250** today to invest at a **20%** yield rate, you can be a millionaire in **30 years,** assuming that no tax is due!

If you double your investment to **$8,500,** you will become a millionaire in **26.2 years** or will have a **$2 million** net worth in 30 years.

If **20% annual tax** is due, you will need a gross return rate of **25%** p.a. (= 20/ 0.80) to reach **$1 million** net worth in 30 years.

But if **no tax** is due and the rate of return remains **25%** p.a., your net worth in 30 years will be **$3.4 million**.

In chapter 21 of this book, you will discover where and how you can get a 20% or more Rate of Return!

\* \* \* \*

# Chapter 7:

# Why 1% Differential Yield Rate can be more valuable than 20% Nominal Yield Rate

## The value of a 1% Difference in yield rate varies widely depending on its numerical position.

The content of this chapter may be surprising to you. But the subject was already discussed briefly in section 6.5.3.

## 7.1      DIFFERENTIAL YIELD RATE

The 1% difference in yield rate that lies between 3% & 4% yield rates is called a differential yield rate of 1%. So is also the 1% difference that lies between 20 & 21% or the 2% that lies between 11% & 13%.

The differential yield rate is also referred to as the marginal yield rate.

The effect of a 1% differential yield rate on the total yield or final amount of any investment varies widely depending on the numerical position of the 1% differential yield rate.

With the period of investment constant, an increase of 1% in interest rate gives a widely varying increase in total yield depending on at what level of interest rate the increase was made.

An increase of 1% from 20% to 21% yield rate in a 30-year investment has a much higher value than an increase from 3% to 4% yield rate with the same investment-period.

## 7.2      EXAMPLE 7.2

An increase in the interest rate from 16% to 17% gives a much bigger increase in the final amount than a 1% increase from 6% to 7%. In order to illustrate this point, this 1% increase has been computed for a deposit of $100 in a Fixed Deposit, and the results are given in Table 7.1 and depicted graphically in Figures 7.1 & 7.2.

On a $100 investment, the increase in the interest rate from 6% to 7% resulted in an increase in the final amount as follows.

In **10 years**, the final amount increased from $179 to $197. That is an increase of **$18 or 18%** of the principal amount.

In **20 years**, the final amount increased from $321 to $387. That is an increase of **$66 or 66%** of the principal amount.

In **30 years**, the final amount increased from $574 to $761. That is an increase of **$187 or 187%** of the principal amount.

But the increase in the interest rate from **16% to 17%** on the **$100 investment** resulted in an increase in the final amount as follows.

In **10 years**, the final amount increased from $441 to $481. That is an increase of **$40 or 40%** of the principal amount.

In **20 years**, the final amount increased from $1,946 to $2,311. That is an increase of **$364 or 364%** of the principal amount.

In **30 years**, the final amount increased from $8,585 to $11,106. That is an increase of **$2,521 or 2,521%** of the principal amount.

As you can see, the difference in additional return between the two situations is enormous.

In a wealth-building period of **30 years**, the 1% difference in nominal yield rate between **16 % & 17%** has **13.5x times** (= 2,521/ 187) more value than the 1% difference in nominal yield rate between **6% and 7%**. On any investment, this difference in value is **23.3x times** (= 25.21 – 1.87) the principal amount.

| | Effect of 1% increase in interest rate on Final Amount for $100 in Fixed Deposit | | | | | |
|---|---|---|---|---|---|---|
| Year | Final Amount at 6% interest | Final Amount at 7% interest | Difference in Final Amount between 6% & 7% | Final Amount at 16% interest | Final Amount at 17% interest | Difference in Final Amount between 16% & 17% |
| 0 | 100 | 100 | 0 | 100 | 100 | 0 |
| 1 | 106 | 107 | 1 | 116 | 117 | 1 |
| 2 | 112 | 114 | 2 | 135 | 137 | 2 |
| 3 | 119 | 123 | 3 | 156 | 160 | 4 |
| 4 | 126 | 131 | 5 | 181 | 187 | 6 |
| 5 | 134 | 140 | 6 | 210 | 219 | 9 |
| 6 | 142 | 150 | 8 | 244 | 257 | 13 |
| 7 | 150 | 161 | 10 | 283 | 300 | 18 |
| 8 | 159 | 172 | 12 | 328 | 351 | 23 |
| 9 | 169 | 184 | 15 | 380 | 411 | 31 |
| 10 | 179 | 197 | 18 | 441 | 481 | 40 |
| 11 | 190 | 210 | 21 | 512 | 562 | 51 |
| 12 | 201 | 225 | 24 | 594 | 658 | 64 |
| 13 | 213 | 241 | 28 | 689 | 770 | 81 |
| 14 | 226 | 258 | 32 | 799 | 901 | 102 |
| 15 | 240 | 276 | 36 | 927 | 1,054 | 127 |
| 16 | 254 | 295 | 41 | 1,075 | 1,233 | 158 |
| 17 | 269 | 316 | 47 | 1,247 | 1,443 | 196 |
| 18 | 285 | 338 | 53 | 1,446 | 1,688 | 242 |
| 19 | 303 | 362 | 59 | 1,678 | 1,975 | 297 |
| 20 | 321 | 387 | 66 | 1,946 | 2,311 | 364 |
| 21 | 340 | 414 | 74 | 2,257 | 2,703 | 446 |
| 22 | 360 | 443 | 83 | 2,619 | 3,163 | 544 |
| 23 | 382 | 474 | 92 | 3,038 | 3,701 | 663 |
| 24 | 405 | 507 | 102 | 3,524 | 4,330 | 806 |
| 25 | 429 | 543 | 114 | 4,087 | 5,066 | 978 |
| 26 | 455 | 581 | 126 | 4,741 | 5,927 | 1,186 |
| 27 | 482 | 621 | 139 | 5,500 | 6,935 | 1,435 |
| 28 | 511 | 665 | 154 | 6,380 | 8,113 | 1,733 |
| 29 | 542 | 711 | 170 | 7,401 | 9,493 | 2,092 |
| 30 | 574 | 761 | 187 | 8,585 | 11,106 | 2,521 |

**Table 7.1: Effect of** 1% **increase in the interest rate from** 6% to 7% **and** 16% to 17% **on the final amount for** $100 **in Fixed Deposit for** 30 years.

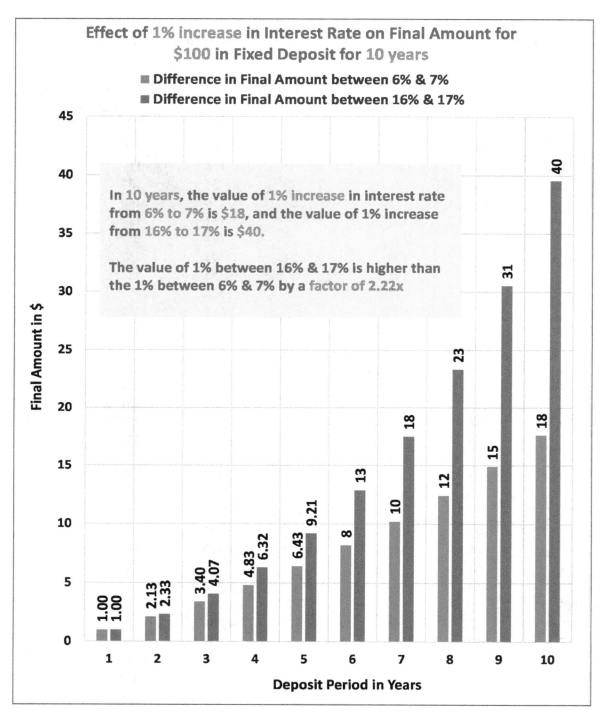

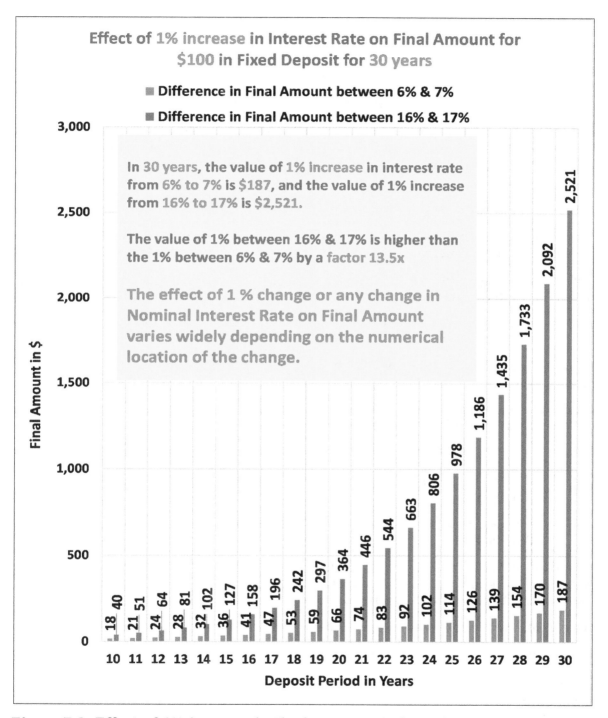

Figure 7.2: **Effect of** 1% **increase in the interest rate from** 6% **to** 7% **and** 16% **to** 17% **on the final amount for** $100 **in Fixed Deposit for** 30 years.

### 7.3    EXAMPLE 7.3

Similarly, in a wealth-building period of 45 years, the 1% difference in nominal yield rate between 29 % & 30% has 1,603x times (= 39,366/ 25) more value than the 1% difference in nominal yield rate between 9% & 10%. On any investment, this difference in value is 39,341x times (= 39,366 – 25) the principal amount. These values are derived from the CAF table in Appendix-A.

### 7.4    OUR OBSERVATIONS CAN BE SUMMARIZED AS FOLLOWS

The longer the deposit period, the bigger the difference becomes for the same nominal change in interest rate.

Put it differently, the longer the deposit period, the higher the value of a given differential interest rate.

The higher the interest rate, the bigger the difference becomes for the same nominal change in interest rate.

Put it differently, the higher the interest rate, the higher the value of a given differential interest rate.

Catching the essence of our observations, and for easy remembrance, we can also write some shocking formulas as below.

- ✓ 1% differential yield rate is NOT EQUAL TO 1% differential yield rate.

- ✓ 1% differential yield rate = 13.5 x 1% differential yield rate (as in Example 7.2 above).

- ✓ 1% differential yield rate = 1,603 x 1% differential yield rate (as in Example 7.3 above).

You can see this pattern if you look at the Compound Amount Factor table in Appendix-A. As the interest rate increases, the CAF value increases, not linearly, but increasingly faster in near-exponential progression.

We can also make the following general statement:

In the kingdom of Compounding, no one is equal. Everyone is ranked.

If you are talking about 1%, its rank and value depend on where it is positioned. If it is between 16% and 17%, it is a lot stronger than the 1% locked between 6% and 7%. If it is 1% locked between 29% and 30%, it is of a much higher rank and value than the 1% jammed between 9% and 10%.

## 7.5    CAF TABLE IS A MATRIX BOARD WITH EVERY POINT ON IT RANKED AND VALUED

If you can imagine the Table of Compound Amount Factor as a matrix board, or even as a chessboard, with interest rates on the horizontal axis or the bottom and topsides, and interest rates increasing from left to the right, and deposit periods on the vertical axis or the left and right sides and deposit periods increasing from top to bottom, then you have a matrix board with every point in it ranked.

A point at the top left corner is of the lowest rank and value, and the point at the bottom right corner is the one with the highest rank and value.

## 7.6    VALUE OF DIFFERENTIAL YIELD RATE IS LIKE THE VALUE OF THE DIGIT ZERO

We can also make the following general statement.

The value of any **change** in the nominal yield rate of any investment is like the value of the digit ZERO: it depends on its position.

The matrix of compounding is somewhat comparable to the value of digit zero. When a Zero is standing next to another zero, it has zero value. When standing next to a "1", it has a value of ten. When the same zero stands next to a "1,000", it has added a value of 9,000 to it, making it 10,000. The value of the Zero depends on where it stands.

Likewise, the value of any change in nominal interest rate depends on where it stands on the matrix board of compound interest.

In a similar way, the value of any change in the length of the investment period depends on where it stands on the matrix board of compound interest.

An increase in investment period of 1 year from 30 to 31 years has a much higher value than a one-year increase from 3 to 4 years.

## 7.7    PRACTICAL APPLICATIONS OF THIS INSIGHT IN REAL-LIFE AND WEALTH-BUILDING

### 7.7.1    Investment decisions

When you are considering choosing from a number of long-term investment options, fight for every fraction of yield rate, even if it is only one-tenth of a percent if it is a long-term investment with high yield rates involved. It can make a huge difference in your net worth.

But if the investment is for short-term or the yield rates involved are not remarkably high, you can give concessions on the yield rate, for example, 1% or 2% less, in exchange for other favors, like more shareholding in the project or more governing control. The financial value of 1% or 2% less yield rate will not be much in this case, but what you can get in exchange for the swap may be financially a lot more valuable!

## 7.7.2        Taking a loan with your Term Deposit as security is a recipe for loss

This subject is important for wealth-building and therefore treated in more detail in chapter 8 below.

## 7.7.3        Taking a loan to invest can be attractive

This subject is vital for wealth-building and therefore treated in more detail in chapter 10.

* * * *

## Chapter 8:

## Why you should never take any Loan with Term Deposit as Security

### It will be a recipe for a net loss of wealth.

When a bank advises you to keep your money in a Term Deposit and take a mortgage loan instead for 30 years at only a 3% higher interest rate so that you can avail of tax benefits, beware!

I was given such a piece of advice long ago by a certified financial advisor when we wanted to buy our first house. It took quite some calculations at that time to discover that the advice was a terrible one that would result in a substantial loss to us. Financial intermediaries get a handsome commission for a mortgage loan, and that is what was probably driving her advice.

As such practices are still widespread, I am explaining the mathematics involved in some detail below.

### 8.1    ANALYSIS OF THE BANK'S OFFER

For example, you may be getting a 9% interest rate on your Term Deposit, and you may be offered 12% interest on a mortgage loan. Let us assume that your mortgage loan amount equals your Term Deposit.

Use the CYF Table in this case, as we are comparing interest amounts here and not the net worth. From the CYF Table, we get the following.

CYF value for 12% interest rate and 30 years is 28.96. This means you will pay 28.96x times the mortgage amount as interest in 30 years.

CYF value for 9% interest rate: 12.27. This means you will get 12.27x times the Term Deposit amount as interest in 30 years.

CYF value of the 3% differential interest rate = 16.7 (28.96 – 12.27). This means you will have to pay 16.7x times the mortgage amount as extra interest to the bank in 30 years.

The nominal interest rate that corresponds to a CYF value of 16.7 in 30 years is 10.0%.

Therefore, for a 30-year period, the 3% differential interest between 9% and 12% is equal to 10% nominal interest in value.

**Therefore, using what we had learned in section 6.5, we can write the relationship for nominal interest rates in this case as below:**

12% = 9% + 10%.

The following equation can be made to put this out-of-the-world equation in its proper context:

For a 30-year period, 12% Nominal interest rate = 9% Nominal interest rate + 10% Nominal interest rate.

CYF value for 3% interest rate and 30 years is 1.43. This means, what the bank implied to you is that you would pay only 1.43x times the mortgage amount as an extra interest in 30 years.

But the interest amount that you would actually be paying, as a ratio of what the bank implied to you, will be 11.7x times (= 16.7/ 1.43) or 1,170% more.

## 8.1.1    In summary

The value of the 3% differential interest rate that lies between 9% & 12% over a 30-year period is 11.7x times the value of the 3% nominal interest rate that lies between 0% and 3%.

The value of the 3% differential interest rate that the bank offers to you is actually equal to a 10% nominal interest rate.

Therefore, if you agree to the bank's advice and keep your own money in the Term Deposit and take a separate mortgage loan from the bank for a 3% differential interest rate, you will end up losing 10% per year on the whole amount.

The 10% nominal interest you would be paying unnecessarily to the bank has a CYF value of 16.7, which means you will pay 16.7x times the mortgage amount as unnecessary interest in 30 years.

Instead, if you withdraw your own money from the Term Deposit to pay for the house, you can avoid losing 10% per year on interest payments for 30 years. No tax saving of any kind can make up for that loss, as you can see below.

## 8.1.2    Bank's advice to you, when bared naked, is this in essence

"You give us your money as a deposit. We will then lend back the same money to you. Therefore, you will not get any interest paid to you on your deposit. For this service, you need to pay us 10% nominal interest per year. You will benefit from this transaction because you can get a tax deduction for what you pay to us."

If you are not alert and knowledgeable, you will be losing a lot of money, namely 10% per year, all of which ultimately flows to the bank.

### 8.1.3    30% tax benefit on mortgage

It is possible that you may be getting a tax deduction due to the loan, but all of it will be going to the bank through the back door which they have opened for you. If you are availing of tax deduction in this scenario, you will be acting as a siphon for the bank to siphon off public money.

Let us assume that you get a tax deduction of 30% on the 3% differential or 10% nominal interest you are paying for the mortgage. The CYF value against 10% for 30 years is approximately 16.7. That means, over a 30-year period, **you will be paying $16.70 as interest for every dollar you had received as a mortgage loan**.

The government picks up 30% of it through tax deduction, and you pay 70% from your own pocket.

CYF value of the government's 30% share in interest payment: 5.0 (= 16.7 x 0.3). This is equivalent to a nominal interest rate of 6.2%.

CYF value of your own 70% share in interest payment: 11.7 (= 16.7 x 0.7). This is equivalent to a nominal interest rate of 8.8%.

Taking the lesson from section 6.5 again, we can write the relationship for these nominal interest rates as below:

10.0% = 8.8% + 6.2%.

Therefore, your after-tax net loss in this transaction is the equivalent of 8.8% nominal interest per year.

In addition, you get a tax benefit to the equivalent of 6.2% nominal interest per year. But you are passing it on entirely to the bank so that the bank keeps getting its full 10% nominal interest. If you do not get the tax deduction, you would be paying the complete 10% to the bank from your own pocket.

In effect, in this example, the bank is siphoning off 8.8% nominal interest from your own pocket and is using you to siphon off another 6.2% nominal interest from the government.

In effect, the bank is burdening you first with an unnecessary burden of 10% nominal interest for its own benefit. Then the bank is telling you that it helped you to save tax!

Even after the tax saving, you end up with a net loss to the equivalent of 8.8% nominal interest per year. In 30 years, your net loss will be 11.7x times the value of the mortgage loan the bank thrust upon you. The bank will be the sole and entire beneficiary of your loss.

## 8.2 IF YOU USE YOUR OWN DEPOSIT MONEY INSTEAD OF TAKING A MORTGAGE LOAN

If you use your own money, your net saving will be the annual interest payment of 8.8% nominal for 30 years. **In 30 years, your net benefit will be 11.7x times the value of the mortgage loan you avoided.**

You may be wondering: How about the tax-saving that I would lose!? True, without a mortgage loan, there will be no tax savings. But with a mortgage loan, even after availing of tax savings, your net loss would have been 8.8% per year or 11.7x times the value of your house in 30 years.

Without tax saving, your gross loss would have been 10% per year or 16.7x times the value of your house in 30 years. Did you incur this loss consciously so that you can recover 30% of it from the government? It is like paying $100 to get $30 free, gratis, incurring a net loss of $70.

If you use your own money from the Term Deposit to pay for the house, you will not get tax benefits. You will not get your free $30 from the government. But you will not also spend $100 from your own pocket, giving you a net saving of $70. In the case of your house, your net saving will be the equivalent of 8.8% nominal interest or 11.7x times the value of your home over a period of 30 years.

## 8.3 A FINAL ADVICE ON TAKING MORTGAGE LOAN WITH FIXED DEPOSIT AS SECURITY

**It is seldom a good idea to take a mortgage loan from a bank for the sake of tax deduction** when you have the needed money lying in a Fixed Deposit at an interest rate that is lower than the mortgage rate. Proper legal structuring of your own money as a mortgage loan, instead of a loan from a bank, may also help you to save taxes with you yourself, instead of the bank, as the ultimate beneficiary of the tax saving.

**Making extra costs to be able to avail of tax benefits is an equally bad idea.** If there is anyone who ultimately benefits at the expense of the Treasury, it will not be you, i.e., the person making extra costs, but a third person like a bank or intermediary.

If there is money to be earned with your money, the sequence of beneficiaries must be you yourself first and second, then the Treasury and then only the bank, as last. Let the bank not turn it around, misleading you. Get educated in financial mathematics so that no one can fool you around, as my mortgage advisor tried with me long ago.

\* \* \* \*

# Chapter 9:

# The Dirty Secret: How banks make more money for themselves than for you using your deposit

## See how banks make more money for themselves using your deposit than they make for yourself.

We all know that a higher interest rate gives a higher yield. The banks borrow from us depositors at a specific interest rate, and then they lend out the same money to borrowers at a higher interest rate. That way, the banks cover the operational costs and make a profit for themselves, as we all know. But that is only part of the story, the part that is visible to the naked eye, like the top one-tenth of an iceberg.

But banks also make use of what we just learned in the previous four chapters. Let us take a short review.

## 9.1       REVIEW OF WHAT WE LEARNED

1. We have seen in chapter 7 that, for an equal increase in the nominal interest rate, for example, an increase of 1% from 6% to 7% and 16% to 17%, the increase in yield amount will not be equal for any time period, except the first year. The value of an additional 1% yield rate can vary wildly and can be huge. For example, in a **30-year investment**, the value of the 1% difference in yield rate between **16% & 17%** is **13.5x times** the value of the 1% difference between **6% & 7%.** How much the difference is, depends on the height of the yield rates involved and the time-period or duration of the investment. The higher the yield rates involved or, the longer the investment period, the higher will be the difference.

2. A derivative of what we have seen in chapter 7 as stated above and elaborated further in chapter 8 is that, for any particular time period, the cumulative yield amount, for example, for the 3% yield rate that lies between **9% & 12%** will be larger than the cumulative yield amount for the 3% that lies between **0% and 3%.** For a **30-year investment** period, the respective Compound Yield Factors (CYF) are 16.7 and 1.43, giving a **ratio of 11.7**.

3. Likewise, we have seen in chapter 6 that in the world of compounding, simple arithmetic does not apply to yield rates. For example, yield rates of **9% + 3%** do not add up to 12% yield, but only to **9.84**% for a 30-year investment. Or that **9% + 9% + 4.2** % do not add up to **22.2% yield**, but only to **12%** for a **30-year investment**. Here again, how much the difference is, depends on the

height of the yield rates involved and the time-period or duration of the investment. Here also, the higher the yield rates involved or, the longer the investment period, the higher will be the difference.

4. In chapter 5, we have seen that, when the investment **period is doubled**, the Growth Ratio of the final amount or the **CAF value increases by the square** of its original value, and when the time-period is tripled, the Growth Factor of the final amount or CAF value increases by the 3rd power, etc.

5. In chapter 5, we have also seen that for any **equal time-interval, the Ratio of final amounts will be exactly the same** irrespective of where the time-interval lies so long as the yield rate remains unchanged. For example, for a 10% yield rate, the ratio of final amounts with a time interval of 5 years between 4 and 9 years will be exactly the same as the ratio of final amounts between 14 and 19 years or between 35 and 40 years.

It is the above hidden mathematical secrets that banks use as instruments to make enormous profits for themselves out of sight of the depositor.

## 9.2     EXAMPLE: TAKING A 10-YEAR DEPOSIT AT 6% INTEREST AND LENDING IT AT 12% INTEREST

A practical example will make it easier to understand how the banks make huge profits from your deposit. By understanding how the banks do it, hopefully, you can earn more for yourself too. That is why this topic is also discussed here.

At the time of writing this book (November 2020), the effective interest rate that banks give to depositors in a major developing country is, on average, no more than 6% p.a.

On the other hand, the effective interest rate that the banks charge from borrowers is on average 12%, if not more. The range of lending rates is very wide, from about 8.5 % to 20% nominal, and the effective interest rate varies from about 10% to 22%. Let us assume that the average lending rate is 12% only.

If someone deposits $100 in a 10-year FD at 6% interest, after 10 years, he gets a total of $179.08. His yield amount is $79.08.

One would think that the bank lends it out for 12% p.a. and therefore, the bank also earns 6% or $79.08, just like the depositor. You may even think that the bank also makes costs, and consequently, the bank makes, net, less than the depositor.

But wait! The bank lends out the money against 12% interest p.a. At the end of the 10-year period, the borrower pays back $310.58, of which $100 is the principal amount, and $210.58 is the interest the bank earned.

For the sake of simplification, we assume here that the borrower pays back in a lump sum amount at the end of the 10-year borrowing period. But in practice, it may be monthly or yearly, which may be of some advantage to the borrower without it being of disadvantage to the bank because of the continuum of inflows and outflows of money in which a bank typically operates.

Of this $210.58, the bank has given the depositor his interest, which is $79.08. The bank's profit is, therefore, $131.50 gross.

In this example, the bank earned a total of $210.58 using the deposit, paid the depositor $79.08, and kept for itself $131.50. Bank earned thus 1.66x times what the depositor earned.

At first sight, the bank earned 6%, and the depositor also earned 6%, equal amounts you would think. But the banker's 6% is 66% bigger than the depositor's 6%.

## 9.2.1    If deposit and lending periods were 5 years

If the deposit period were only 5 years instead of 10, the depositor would have earned $33.82 instead of $79.08, and the bank would have made $42.41 only instead of $131.50. Still, the bank's earnings would be 1.25x times higher than the earnings of the depositor. The 6% interest earned here by the banker is 25% bigger than the 6% interest earned by the depositor. The equivalent effective interest rate for the banker's 6% would be 7.33% while that of the depositor's 6% is only 6% p.a. The equivalent Simple Annual Yield that the bank receives is 8.48% (= 42.41/ 5) while that for the depositor is only 6.76% p.a. (= 33.82/ 5).

## 9.2.2    If deposit and lending periods were one year

In this example, we assumed that the deposit is made for 10 years and the loan is made for 10 years. But suppose the deposit and loan are made just for one year only, after which the deposit is withdrawn, and the loan is repaid. And you repeat this process every year. In such a case, there would be no compounding of interest either on the deposit side or on the lending side. The bank will collect an interest amount of 12% for one year, give 6% to the de depositor and keep 6% for itself. The interest received from the borrower is divided equally in this case.

But even in this case, the bank would lend out also the 6% interest it received and receive the entire 12% interest for itself from another borrower. This process will repeat year after year. On the other side, the bank would also be receiving fresh deposits, even if they are for one year-periods. Therefore, even in this case of average one-year deposits and lending, the money inflows and outflows will be a continuum with only a bit more fluctuating balance sheet than if the average period was 10 years. The profit will be practically the same.

Due to the continuum of inflow and outflow of money, the profit that the bank earns by taking deposits and lending them out will practically be the same irrespective of whether the average deposit period is one year or ten years or more.

We had seen that if it is done every 10 years instead of every year, the bank would be earning $131.50 and the depositor only $79.08. The bank made 66% more than the depositor. If the time-period were 20 years instead of 10 years, the difference between the earning of the **same** depositor and bank would have been considerably bigger. But the bank's total earnings, in dollar terms, remain practically the same whether the deposit came from one single depositor with a 20-year deposit or 20 different depositors in 20 years with a 1-year deposit each.

### 9.2.3     For the bank, all lending periods are virtually perpetual

Wait again! We considered only 10 years. But the inflow and outflow of money is a continual process in the bank, year after year, non-stop, and this process can be interpolated to 20, 30, or 100 years or so long as the bank would exist. At any given point in time, the total of all the deposits the bank has received can be treated as one large sum on which it owes 6% interest, and 95% of it lent out at 12%.

From the money lent out, the bank generally receives due interest monthly, which in turn is lent out again, and so on. Therefore, it does not matter whether the money lent out is short-term or long-term. For the bank, it is as if the interest it receives is compounding perpetually.

In this continual process, the bank would get richer and richer every day, and at some point in time, the money it lends out can be more of its own money than depositors' money. The share of banks profit would therefore increase still more as it can keep the whole 12% interest earned with its own money for itself. The earning has a snowball effect.

### 9.2.4     A minimum deposit and lending period of 10 years can be assumed instead of a continuum

But because the bank also makes costs, pays out a part or whole of the profit as a dividend to the owners of the bank, pays itself remarkably high salaries and perks and bonuses, sometimes makes bad irrecoverable loans, and sometimes gets looted from inside or outside in other ways, the wealth of the bank does not get infinitely large. Banking regulations in most countries also limit the size of the banks.

All in all, though the inflows and outflows of money are continuous processes with nearly infinite profit on the horizon, due to the reasons given above, we have to consider a more practical average deposit and lending period for calculating the profit that a bank makes.

A period of 10 years needs to be considered as a minimum. A 30-year period may be more realistic.

If it is 10 years and the interest rates are 6% for deposit and 12% for lending, the bank earns $131,50 in 10 years for every $100 deposit. That is equivalent to a nominal interest rate of 8.75% per annum compounded annually, giving a Simple Annual Yield of 13.15% p.a. to the bank.

### 9.3     INSIGHT

### 9.3.1     In a 10-year period

In summary, the depositor gets a nominal interest rate of 6% p.a. and the equivalent of the bank's profit is 8.75%. The Simple Annual yield is 7.19% for the depositor and 13.15% for the bank.

## 9.3.2      In a 30-year period

When you deposit an amount in the bank for 6% annual interest and keep it there for 30 years, and the bank lends it out against 12% interest, you get only 16.4% of what the bank receives as interest from the borrower, and the bank keeps 83.6% for itself. Bank's differential earning of 6% (= 12 – 6) is 5.1x times as valuable as your nominal 6% interest.

The Bank's share of earnings, in this case, is equivalent to an 11.36% nominal interest rate. Your earning is a 6% nominal interest rate.

> ✓   Your nominal 6% interest rate is therefore equivalent to the differential interest rate of only 0.64% that lies between 11.36% and 12.0%.

## 9.3.3      Other people's money

This 11.36% nominal interest that the bank earns is on the money that you deposited with the bank and NOT on the bank's own capital. Because of the 11.36% p.a. rate of return on the deposits the bank holds, its rate of return on its own much smaller capital will be extremely high. It can be fabulous. It is by using other peoples' money, the depositors' money, that banks make a lot of money for themselves and their owners.

Rich people own the bank, and therefore it is rich people who make more money with the bank using other people's money. The enormous competition in most countries for getting a banking license is understandable, especially in countries with relatively weak banking regulations, little control, lacking discipline, and high corruption.

## 9.4      HOW CAN WE BENEFIT FROM THIS INSIGHT?

A fixed deposit in a bank is not a serious investment vehicle to build wealth. Banks make more money with your money than you yourself can make from a Term Deposit.

Use it only as a saving instrument for a small part of your wealth in order to meet short-term expenses.

**If you still decide to put some money in a CD or TD or FD, keep the following in mind:**

1.   Search for a rock-solid bank with the highest yield rate without compromising safety. We have seen that even a marginally higher interest rate can make a considerable difference in your net worth in the long term.

2.   Choose a reputed big bank. Certainly, avoid small private banks and co-operative banks.

3. Avoid online-only banks for CDs, TDs, or FDs irrespective of where they are located, even if it is in your backyard under your visual supervision. Online banks are good enough for Debit cards and online shopping, but not for entrusting your savings.

4. Avoid co-operative banks, especially in developing countries. Often, they are not adequately regulated and supervised, and the deposits are not guaranteed by the central bank or government.

5. Avoid banks in foreign countries except in developed countries with a rock-solid banking system.

6. Do not put more money in CD, TD, or FD than what is covered by the respective national deposit insurance schemes. Be aware that, in many developing countries, the limits protected by such insurance schemes are negligibly low.

There are several other investment vehicles that will give you at least double or more nominal rate of return than FD and which may also be tax-sheltered at the same time, unlike FD.

**Even without any tax planning or tax shelter, if you can get a double of the 8% yield rate that you get on an FD with 20% tax rate, over a 40-year period, by the time you retire, your final amount or (after-tax) net worth can be 10.3x times higher than your net worth with the FD.**

**But with proper tax planning (not tax evasion, but choosing the appropriate investment with Deferred tax of 20%), your net worth can be 25.4x times higher than your net worth with the FD.**

See chapter 21 for a summary of investment vehicles that are much more attractive for wealth-building than FD. Stock market and real estate are much better choices than FD, also from a tax perspective.

For insight into TAX DRAG and other tax-related matters and calculations, and the shock that you are sure to feel when you get the insight, see Volume II of this series of books, which will be published shortly.

For all automatic calculations, including Tax Drag and other tax-related figures, you can procure the software program which I have developed and will be made available soon.

## 9.5 BEWARE

Do not rely blindly on percentages only to make financial decisions. Look at also and compare the absolute values always.

As we have just seen in this book so far, especially in chapters 7, 8 & 9, percentages alone can be extremely misleading.

* * * *

# Chapter 10:

# How Borrowing to Invest can airlift you to super-wealth

In section 9.1 of the previous chapter, we had summarized 5 items that we had learned so far and which form the secret basis for banks to use depositors' money to make more money for themselves than for the depositors. When a bank takes a deposit, what it does, in fact, is borrowing money from the depositor.

Why shouldn't we apply the same method for ourselves if we do not have money readily available for investment?

Even if we do have some money readily available to invest, why shouldn't we also borrow some money to increase our investment and ultimately increase our earnings as the banks do?

Why shouldn't we borrow the depositors' money from the bank and use it for an investment with a higher yield rate? Let us use an example.

## 10.1    EXAMPLE

If a client deposited **$20,000** at a **9%** interest rate, in **30 years**, his total yield, as can be seen in the CYF table, would be **12.3x** times the deposited amount.

Lending out the same amount at a **12%** interest rate, the bank would have received a total yield of **29.0x** times the deposited amount. After deducting the depositor's due share, the Bank's own share of the total yield would be **16.7x** times the deposited amount (=29.0 – 12.3). The Bank has earned even more than the depositor with a mere **3% margin** in interest rate.

Let us assume that we are the borrower from the bank at a 12% interest rate. We have an attractive long-term investment opportunity that would yield **18%** p.a. but we do not have any own money to invest. That is why we borrow **$20,000** from the bank at a relatively high interest rate of 12%.

But all our well-wishers advised against it. They opined that the 6% margin (= 18% - 12%) was not attractive enough to borrow at such a high rate of interest. They had even done the math. At the **marginal 6%** interest rate, we would be earning only **4.7x times** the investment, or a total of only **$94,000** (= 4.7 x 20,000) in 30 years. 4.7 is, indeed, the CYF value corresponding to a 6% yield rate for 30 years.

But we know the math better. At an 18% yield rate, our total yield would be 142.4x times the investment and not 4.7x times. After deducting all the interest payments to the bank, our net yield would be 113.4x times (= 142.4 – 29) the invested amount or $2.27 Million (= 113.4 x 20,000). That is a 24x times bigger profit than the $94,000 that our concerned well-wishers had calculated.

Even if we had borrowed only $10,000 instead of $20,000, we would have reached millionairedom with a net yield of $1.14 Million.

## 10.2    INSIGHT

As you will realize by the time you finish reading this book, it is not the amount of money that you have available to invest that will determine the speed at which you will reach your targeted net worth of, for example, $1 million, but it is the yield rate and the tax treatment of your investment that will have the maximum impact on the growth rate of your net worth.

As we have already seen in chapter 5, the time-period or duration of investment is the ultimate maximizer of wealth. Sky will be the limit for your wealth to reach if you let the initial investment with a high yield rate and favorable tax treatment grow for an unlimited time period, even if the initial investment is a modest amount.

The amount of initial investment is the one parameter with the least influence on the growth rate and time needed to reach a target amount of net worth. If you double your initial investment, your net worth will be double at any given moment.

But you do need an initial investment to build wealth, just as much as you need a seed to grow a tree.

Therefore, if you do not have the seed money, borrow.

And even if you do have the seed money but can make multiples of it by borrowing, by all means, borrow and invest. Play the same game that the banks play in your own mini playground.

There is nothing wrong if you embrace the slogan "Borrow and multiply." You will be on the same highway to riches that almost all the Billionaires in the world have taken before you.

See chapter 12 for more information about the effects of initial investment on wealth-building.

All in all, even with a small amount of start capital, even if it is entirely borrowed, you can achieve incredible wealth.

## 10.3      THE TAKEAWAY

1.  Do not be held back by a lack of money to invest. Borrowing can also be a great way to get an airlift to millionairedom instead of riding a donkey-cart reaching nowhere.

2.  Do the complete math using the actual amounts and numbers involved before making investment decisions. Using percentages alone or ratios alone can be totally misleading.

3.  Do not be misguided to think that you need a huge start capital to become a millionaire. Long-term investment with a high yield rate and favorable tax treatment is far more important than the amount of investment. Therefore, start early, even with a small amount, even borrowed or begged.

4.  Remember, all the giant companies of today, and almost all the super-wealthy people, created their massive wealth by using other people's money. Do not insist on being an exception.

## 10.4      A NOTE OF CAUTION

When borrowing money, there is always an inherent risk that your investment project does not progress as expected or even fails, and you fall into default on servicing or repayment of your debt. Make sure that, if such a situation arises, you will be able to survive it financially. Legal advice and proper legal structuring of the debt can be essential parts of the precautionary measures you should take in advance.

\* \* \* \*

# Chapter 11:

# What will it take to reach $1 million in Net Worth?

In this chapter, we will consider various combinations of initial investment and yield rate and see how long it will take to accumulate a net worth of $1 million.

We will analyze how the needed time to reach a net worth of $ 1 million behaves when initial investments and yield rates are changed.

## 11.1    THE INGREDIENTS: INITIAL INVESTMENT, YIELD RATE, AND TIME-PERIOD

Our target is to build wealth in the biggest, quickest, and easiest ways possible and with the minimum possible initial investment. It is no different than building your dream house.

In any investment program, there are mainly 5 variables. They are:

1. **Initial investment or principal** (P)
2. **Time-period or number of years** (N)
3. **Yield rate** (R)
4. **Tax rate** (T)
5. **Final amount or net worth** (NW)

We had already fixed our target for net worth at $1 million. This variable is therefore eliminated.

We are not considering tax and tax drag in detail in this volume of the book as they are treated in detail in volume 2 of the series. In this chapter, we assume the tax to be zero.

Therefore, we need to consider only 3 variables, namely, initial investment, time-period, and yield rate.

In this chapter, we will take a global look at the mutual interaction of initial investment, yield rate, and time-period when the common goal of $1 million net worth is superimposed on them.

In chapter 12, we will go in-depth into the behavior of initial investment.

In chapter 13, we will go in-depth into the behavior of yield rate.

In the previous chapters, we had analyzed them also, but without this common target of $1 million net worth imposed on them, thereby letting each of the 3 ingredients fly free and hunt for maximum net worth.

Therefore, in this chapter, and in chapters 12 & 13, we will be looking at these 3 variables from a different perspective, which will lead us to further and broader insights.

## 11.2 WHAT MIX OF INITIAL INVESTMENT, YIELD RATE & TIME-PERIOD SHOULD WE CHOOSE?

**How long it will take for you to accumulate $1 million net worth** depends on the cocktail you choose to mix: the mix of initial investment and yield rate.

If you have a **specific time period** in mind, for example, 20 years, you can try different mixes of yield rates and initial investments.

If you have a **specific and achievable yield rate** in mind, for example, 18% p.a., you can try different mixes of time -periods and initial investments.

If you have a specific **initial investment** in mind, for example, $5,000, you can try different mixes of time -periods and feasible yield rates.

So, let us consider the criteria that we will use for the 3 ingredients.

### 11.2.1 Initial Investment

With respect to the $1million net worth you are targeting, it may be a relatively tiny amount that you have readily available or can raise easily. Even if it is only 0.5% of your targeted $1 million ($5,000 to get 1 million), we will analyze how much of the other two ingredients you will need in order to reach your target of $1 million.

We will then raise this initial investment to higher amounts and see how faster we can reach millionairedom or how much higher our net worth can reach in the same time period.

### 11.2.2 Yield rate

At this stage, before you have been equipped with the information and insight needed to make a choice of the investment vehicle, we will consider a realistic range of yield rates, from 5% p.a. to 40% p.a. Further down in this book, in chapter 21, we will see which percentage can come from which investment vehicle.

We will start with a 5% yield rate and then raise it to higher values and see how faster we reach millionairedom or how much higher our net worth can reach in the same time period.

## 11.2.3     Time-period

We are planning to have a $1 million net worth, but we must have it also within a reasonable time period. We will consider a wide range of time-periods and will consider subsequently what amount of initial investment needs to be combined with which yield rate in order to reach our target within the chosen time period.

## 11.3      INVESTMENT MATRIX FOR TIME-PERIOD

Taking all the above into account, we have created a matrix of the above three ingredients, namely initial investment, yield rate, and time period, so that you can determine which combination suits you best.

In the tables and graphs that follow, you will see a seemingly unrealistic number of years and yield rates, but they are included here consciously to demonstrate their effects on the total return of an investment.

This matrix is embedded, indirectly, in the Compound Amount Factor table (CAF table) given in Appendix-A, but that may be a bit hard for you to read and understand at this stage. In chapter 14, you can learn how to use the Compound Amount Factor table to make your choice of entry point on the highway to millionairedom.

This separate matrix here should make it easier.

In table 11.1, note that the values drop in the horizontal direction at a fast rate, but the drop in the vertical direction is relatively quite slow.

That means that increasing the yield rate will take you to your target of $1 million a lot faster than a proportional increase in initial investment.

That also means, contrary to popular belief, that the secret to building huge wealth lies not in having an abundance of money to invest but in investing whatever amount you have for the highest possible yield rate and the longest possible time period.

| Number of Years needed to reach $1 MILLION Net Worth | | | | | | | | |
|---|---|---|---|---|---|---|---|---|
| Initial Investment, $ | Yield Rate | | | | | | | |
| | 5% | 10% | 15% | 20% | 25% | 30% | 35% | 40% |
| 5,000 | 108.6 | 55.6 | 37.9 | 29.1 | 23.7 | 20.2 | 17.7 | 15.7 |
| 10,000 | 94.4 | 48.3 | 33.0 | 25.3 | 20.6 | 17.6 | 15.3 | 13.7 |
| 15,000 | 86.1 | 44.1 | 30.0 | 23.0 | 18.8 | 16.0 | 14.0 | 12.5 |
| 20,000 | 80.2 | 41.0 | 28.0 | 21.5 | 17.5 | 14.9 | 13.0 | 11.6 |
| 25,000 | 75.6 | 38.7 | 26.4 | 20.2 | 16.5 | 14.1 | 12.3 | 11.0 |
| 30,000 | 71.9 | 36.8 | 25.1 | 19.2 | 15.7 | 13.4 | 11.7 | 10.4 |
| 35,000 | 68.7 | 35.2 | 24.0 | 18.4 | 15.0 | 12.8 | 11.2 | 10.0 |
| 40,000 | 66.0 | 33.8 | 23.0 | 17.7 | 14.4 | 12.3 | 10.7 | 9.6 |
| 45,000 | 63.6 | 32.5 | 22.2 | 17.0 | 13.9 | 11.8 | 10.3 | 9.2 |
| 50,000 | 61.4 | 31.4 | 21.4 | 16.4 | 13.4 | 11.4 | 10.0 | 8.9 |
| 55,000 | 59.4 | 30.4 | 20.8 | 15.9 | 13.0 | 11.1 | 9.7 | 8.6 |
| 60,000 | 57.7 | 29.5 | 20.1 | 15.4 | 12.6 | 10.7 | 9.4 | 8.4 |
| 65,000 | 56.0 | 28.7 | 19.6 | 15.0 | 12.2 | 10.4 | 9.1 | 8.1 |
| 70,000 | 54.5 | 27.9 | 19.0 | 14.6 | 11.9 | 10.1 | 8.9 | 7.9 |
| 75,000 | 53.1 | 27.2 | 18.5 | 14.2 | 11.6 | 9.9 | 8.6 | 7.7 |
| 80,000 | 51.8 | 26.5 | 18.1 | 13.9 | 11.3 | 9.6 | 8.4 | 7.5 |

Table 11.1: investment Matrix for the number of years: **Combinations of initial investment, yield rate, and number of years that will be needed to reach $1 million net worth.**

This table is the same as **Table 12.1** in chapter 12 and **Table 13.1** in chapter 13.

Figure 11.1 and Figure 11.2 show the values in this table in a graphical form together with the relevant observations.

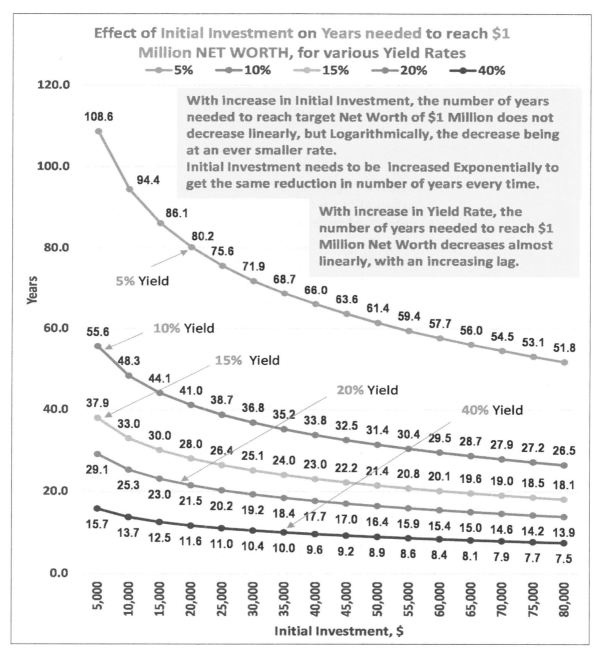

Figure 11.1: **Effect of** initial investment **on the** number of years **needed to reach** $1 million net worth **for various yield rates, with initial investment on standard LINEAR scale.**

This figure is the same as **Fig. 12.1** in chapter 12 and **Fig. 13.1** in chapter 13.

All the values in this graph are taken from Table 11.1.

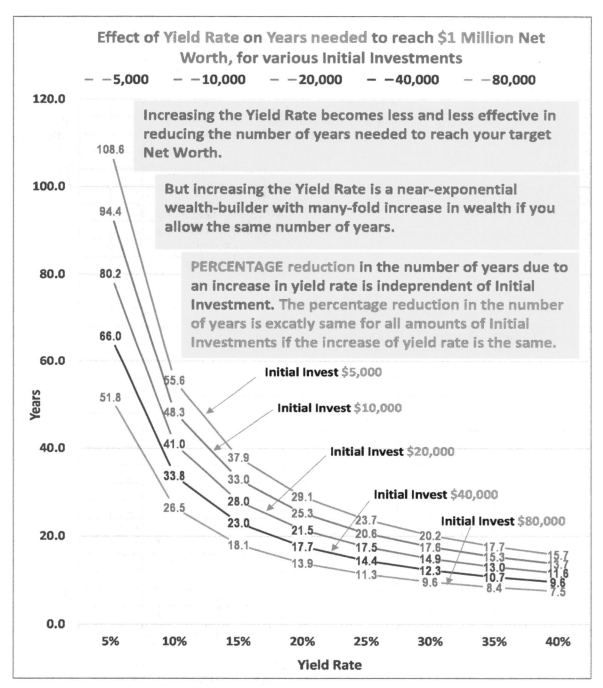

**Figure 11.2: Effect** of yield rate **on the** number of years **needed to reach** $1 million net worth **for various amounts of the initial investment.**

This figure is the same as **Figure 13.2** in chapter 13.

All the values in this graph are taken from Table 11.1.

## 11.4      INFLUENCE OF TIME-PERIOD

In chapter 5, we had seen that the number of years or the time-period is of supreme influence in wealth-building. For every doubling of time-period, the Compound Amount Factor (CAF) or Growth Factor of principal increases by its square.

**Doubling of time-period** from 5 to 10 years means: CAF value for 10 years is the **square of CAF value** for 5 years.

**Tripling of time-period** from 5 to 15 years means: CAF value for 15 years is the **3rd power of CAF value** for 5 years.

**Quadrupling of time-period** from 5 to 20 years means: CAF value for 20 years is the **4th power of CAF value** for 5 years, or the square of CAF value for 10 years.

Put it differently, the ratio of the final amount or CAF value between two time-periods will be the same for any other equal time-period. The ratio of CAF values **between 5 & 10 years** will be precisely the same as the ratio **between years 25 & 30 years.**

## 11.5      ANALYSIS OF TABLE 11.1 AND FIGURES 11.1 & 11.2

These figures and the table show the effects of **initial investment** and **yield rate** on time needed to reach $1 million net worth.

Table 11.1 is a matrix that shows the number of years that would be needed to reach a final amount of **$1 million** for various combinations of yield rates and initial investments.

The values in Table 11.1 are valid for any kind of investment, be it FD in a bank account at a **5%** interest rate or investment in the stock market with a **40%** annual return. Likewise, the initial investment in the table varies from **$5,000** to **$80,000**.

Our target is to have a net worth or final amount of $1 million in the shortest possible time. From the table or graphs, you can choose a combination of initial investment and yield rate that is feasible in your situation and see how many years it would take to have $1 million in your account.

## 11.5.1      Effect of initial investment

Assume that you can get a yield rate of **20%** p.a. in the stock market, and you have **$20,000** available to invest in it. From the table, you can see that it would take **21.5** years to reach **$1 million**.

Is a time span of 21.5 years too long a waiting period to become a millionaire?

Is a net worth of $1 million not big enough to justify that long a wait?

In the table and graphs, you can see what happens if you double your initial investment from **$20,000 to $40,000**. Instead of **21.5 years**, you would reach your goal in **17.7 years**. You might be disappointed with a gain of only **3.8 years** out of 21.5. But if you could wait out the entire 21.5 years, you would have $2 million instead of just $1 million.

**By doubling the initial investment, you double your final amount in the same time period.**

**By doubling the initial investment, you gain only a fraction (3.8 out of 21.5 years) of the original time-period to reach your specific target of $1 million.**

In chapter 12, we will go in-depth into the behavior of **initial investment**.

## 11.5.2    Effect of yield rate

If you can find an investment opportunity that can give you an annual yield rate of **25% instead of 20%**, you will reach your $1 million net worth in **17.5 years instead of 21.5 years,** a gain of **4 years,** but without having to double your initial investment from $20,000 to $40,000.

But, as you will see later, if you could wait another 4 years to reach the original period of 21.5 years, your net worth would increase to **about $2.5 million** without having increased your initial investment of $20,000.

That is 2.5x times the net worth you would have reached with your initial investment of $20,000 and a 20% yield rate.

That is also $0.5 million more than the $2 million you would have reached by doubling your initial investment from $20,000 to $40,000 at a 20% yield rate.

This also shows how powerful the **5% Differential yield rate** is, i.e., the 5% that lies between 20% and 25%. See chapter 7 for more about the value of differential yield rates.

In chapter 13, we will go in-depth into the behavior of **yield rate.**

* * * *

# Chapter 12:

# Effect of Initial Investment on Time needed to reach $1 million Net Worth

## Effect of Increasing the initial investment on time needed to reach $1 million net worth.

Please read chapter 11 for an overview of what we are discussing here before immersing deeper into this chapter.

In this chapter, we will analyze the influence of initial investment on time needed to reach our targeted net worth of $1 million.

### 12.1    INVESTMENT MATRIX FOR TIME-PERIOD

Table 11.1 from chapter 11 is copied into this chapter for ease of reference and relabeled as Table 12.1.

It is the investment matrix that shows the number of years that would be needed to reach a final amount of $1 million for various combinations of yield rates and initial investments.

For the same reason, Figure 11.1 from chapter 11 is also copied into this chapter and relabeled as Figure 12.1.

| Number of Years needed to reach $1 MILLION Net Worth | | | | | | | | |
|---|---|---|---|---|---|---|---|---|
| **Initial Investment, $** | **Yield Rate** | | | | | | | |
| | **5%** | **10%** | **15%** | **20%** | **25%** | **30%** | **35%** | **40%** |
| 5,000 | 108.6 | 55.6 | 37.9 | 29.1 | 23.7 | 20.2 | 17.7 | 15.7 |
| 10,000 | 94.4 | 48.3 | 33.0 | 25.3 | 20.6 | 17.6 | 15.3 | 13.7 |
| 15,000 | 86.1 | 44.1 | 30.0 | 23.0 | 18.8 | 16.0 | 14.0 | 12.5 |
| 20,000 | 80.2 | 41.0 | 28.0 | 21.5 | 17.5 | 14.9 | 13.0 | 11.6 |
| 25,000 | 75.6 | 38.7 | 26.4 | 20.2 | 16.5 | 14.1 | 12.3 | 11.0 |
| 30,000 | 71.9 | 36.8 | 25.1 | 19.2 | 15.7 | 13.4 | 11.7 | 10.4 |
| 35,000 | 68.7 | 35.2 | 24.0 | 18.4 | 15.0 | 12.8 | 11.2 | 10.0 |
| 40,000 | 66.0 | 33.8 | 23.0 | 17.7 | 14.4 | 12.3 | 10.7 | 9.6 |
| 45,000 | 63.6 | 32.5 | 22.2 | 17.0 | 13.9 | 11.8 | 10.3 | 9.2 |
| 50,000 | 61.4 | 31.4 | 21.4 | 16.4 | 13.4 | 11.4 | 10.0 | 8.9 |
| 55,000 | 59.4 | 30.4 | 20.8 | 15.9 | 13.0 | 11.1 | 9.7 | 8.6 |
| 60,000 | 57.7 | 29.5 | 20.1 | 15.4 | 12.6 | 10.7 | 9.4 | 8.4 |
| 65,000 | 56.0 | 28.7 | 19.6 | 15.0 | 12.2 | 10.4 | 9.1 | 8.1 |
| 70,000 | 54.5 | 27.9 | 19.0 | 14.6 | 11.9 | 10.1 | 8.9 | 7.9 |
| 75,000 | 53.1 | 27.2 | 18.5 | 14.2 | 11.6 | 9.9 | 8.6 | 7.7 |
| 80,000 | 51.8 | 26.5 | 18.1 | 13.9 | 11.3 | 9.6 | 8.4 | 7.5 |

Table 12.1: investment Matrix for the number of years: **Combinations of initial investment, yield rate, and the number of years that will be needed to reach $1 million net worth.**

This table is the same as **Table 11.1** in chapter 11 and **Table 13.1** in chapter 13.

Figures 12.1 & 12.2 show the values in this table in a graphical form together with the relevant observations.

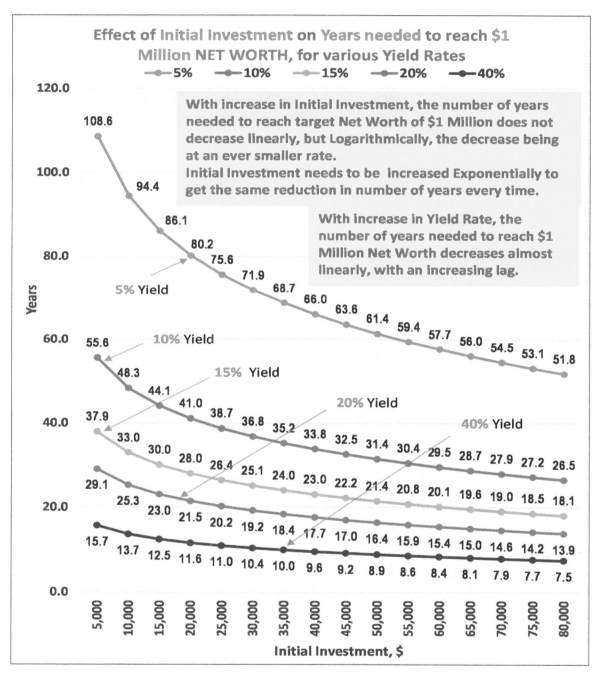

**Figure 12.1:** **Effect of** initial investment **on the** number of years **needed to reach** $1 million net worth **for various yield rates, with initial investment on standard LINEAR scale.**

This figure is the same as **Fig. 11.1** in chapter 11 and **Fig. 13.1** in chapter 13.

All the values in this graph are taken from Table 12.1.

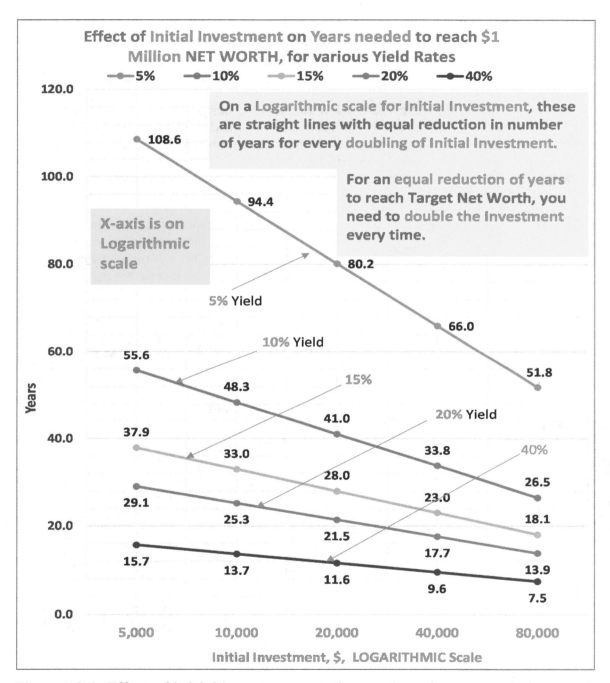

**Figure 12.2: Effect of** initial investment **on the** number of years **needed to reach** $1 million net worth **for various yield rates, with initial investment on** LOGARITHMIC **scale.**

All the values in this graph are taken from Table 12.1.

The data in Figure 12.2 are the same as the data in Figure 12.1, with the only difference that Figure 12.2 has the X-axis for the initial investment in Logarithmic scale while Figure 12.1 has the X-axis in regular Linear scale. As a result, the graph lines in Figure 12.2 are perfectly straight lines, while the graph lines in Figure 12.1 are Logarithmic curves.

*For nerds only*: Logarithmic curves on a linear axis become straight lines on a logarithmic axis, and vice versa.

## 12.2    COMPARATIVE INVESTMENT MATRIX FOR TIME-PERIOD WITH 0.5% INITIAL INVESTMENT AS REFERENCE BASE

See table 12.2 and figures 12.3, 12.4 & 12.5.

The Reference Base in this table (Table 12.2) is 0.5%. That means, the initial investment of $5,000 that serves as the reference base for comparison, has a value of only 0.5% of the targeted net worth (0.5% = 5,000/ 1,000,000).

**If the reference base changes, for example, $10,000 instead of $5,000, the values in the table will change, as you can see in the 2nd and 3rd graph lines in** Figures 12.3 & 12.4.

Note that all horizontal values in this table are the same. That means the percentage change in time needed to reach a targeted net worth due to a change in initial investment is the same for all yield rates. In other words, if you win a 13.1% (= 100 - 86.9) gain in time by doubling your initial investment from $5,000 to $10,000, the gain will be the same for all yield rates.

In other words, when initial investment changes, its effect on the time period will be the same regardless of yield rates.

This Table (Table 12.2) and the values in it apply equally to the total yield amount (i.e., excluding principal) as well as the total final amount or net worth (i.e., including principal).

| Percentage of Years needed to reach $1 MILLION Net Worth with $5,000 Initial Investment as Base | | | | | | | | |
|---|---|---|---|---|---|---|---|---|
| Initial Investment, $ | Yield Rate | | | | | | | |
| | 5% | 10% | 15% | 20% | 25% | 30% | 35% | 40% |
| 5,000 | 100.0% | 100.0% | 100.0% | 100.0% | 100.0% | 100.0% | 100.0% | 100.0% |
| 10,000 | | | | 86.9% | | | | |
| 15,000 | | | | 79.3% | | | | |
| 20,000 | | | | 73.8% | | | | |
| 25,000 | | | | 69.6% | | | | |
| 30,000 | | | | 66.2% | | | | |
| 35,000 | | | | 63.3% | | | | |
| 40,000 | | | | 60.8% | | | | |
| 45,000 | | | | 58.5% | | | | |
| 50,000 | | | | 56.5% | | | | |
| 55,000 | | | | 54.7% | | | | |
| 60,000 | | | | 53.1% | | | | |
| 65,000 | | | | 51.6% | | | | |
| 70,000 | | | | 50.2% | | | | |
| 75,000 | | | | 48.9% | | | | |
| 80,000 | | | | 47.7% | | | | |

Table 12.2: Percentage of Years needed to reach $1 million net worth with $5,000 initial investment as the Reference Base.

Figures 12.3 & 12.4 show the values in this table in a graphical form together with the relevant observations.

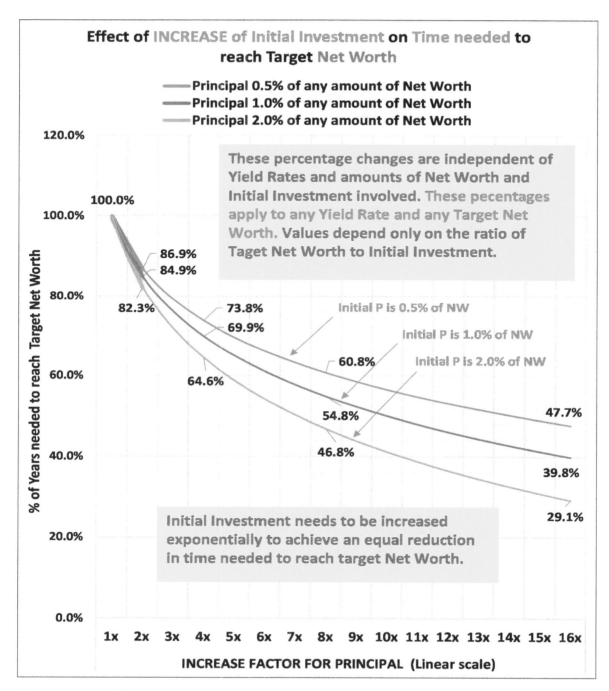

**Figure 12.3: Effect of INCREASE of initial investment on the Percentage of Years needed to reach $1 million net worth with initial investment on regular LINEAR scale.**

The values in the uppermost graph-line are taken from Table 12.2. Values for the other two graph lines are not shown in any table in this book.

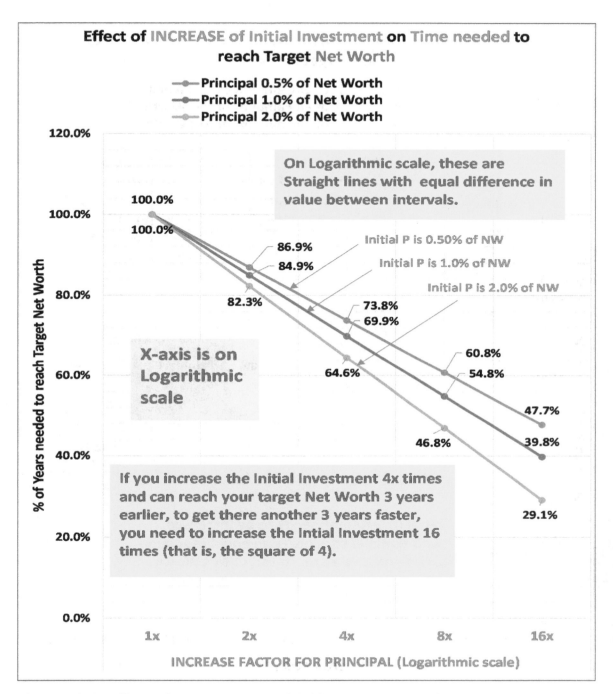

**Figure 12.4: Effect of** INCREASE of initial investment **on the** Percentage of Years **needed to reach** $1 million net worth **with initial investment on a** LOGARITHMIC scale.

The values in the uppermost graph line are taken from Table 12.2. Values for the other two graph lines are not shown in any table in this book.

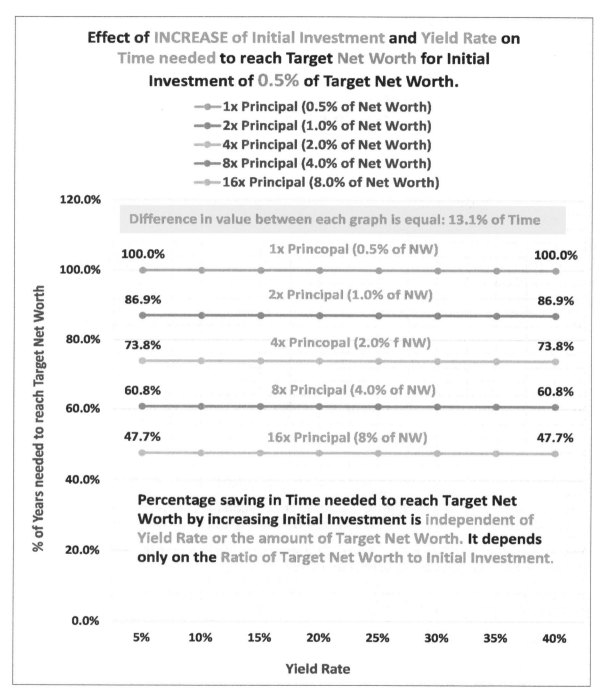

Figure 12.5: **Effect of** INCREASE **of initial investment** on Time **needed to reach $1 million net worth** **with initial investment of** 0.5% **of net worth as the** Reference Base.

All the values in this graph are taken from <u>Table 12.2.</u>

## 12.3     ANALYSIS OF FIGURES 12.1 TO 12.5

### 12.3.1     Figure 12.1

This is a graphical presentation of some of the values in the investment matrix in Table 12.1. See chapter 11 for an explanation of the investment matrix table.

Figure 12.1 shows the number of years needed to reach **$1 million** net worth when plotted against increasing values of initial investment, from **$5,000 to $80.000**.

The graphs are plotted for yield rates of 5%, 10%, 15%, 20% & 40%. Other yield rates shown in the investment matrix are not included in the figure to avoid overcrowding at the cost of readability.

As you can see, the graph lines are not straight lines but become more and more horizontal with the increase of initial investment. That means the relationship is **not linear**. If you double the initial investment, the time needed to reach your targeted net worth does not reduce by half. The reduction in time is much smaller.

The **time reduces only logarithmically** due to an increase of initial investment.

In other words, the **initial investment needs to be increased exponentially** in order to get an equal reduction in time.

This conclusion can also be drawn by looking at Figure 12.2, in which the graph lines are straight when initial investment on the X-axis is plotted on a Logarithmic scale.

### 12.3.2     Figure 12.2

The data in Figure 12.2 are the same as the data in Figure 12.1.

The only difference is that Figure 12.2 has the X-axis for the initial investment in the **Logarithmic scale** while Figure 12.1 has the X-axis in the normal **Linear scale.**

As a result, the graph lines in Figure 12.2 are perfectly straight lines, while the graph lines in Figure 12.1 have Logarithmic curves.

You can see in figure 12.2 that, in order to achieve an equal reduction in time, you need to double the initial investment every time.

**That also means the following:**

**The initial investment needs to be increased exponentially to achieve an equal reduction in time-period.**

**In other words, the principal amount must be doubled every time to achieve the same reduction in the number of years.**

If you doubled the principal and got 3 years reduction in the number of years needed, in order to get another 3 years reduction (total 6 years including the first reduction), you need to double the principal again. This second doubling means your principal needs to be multiplied 4 times with respect to the original amount.

To achieve another 3 years reduction in time-period (total 9 years thus), you need to double the principal again. That means increasing the principal from 4 times to 8 times the original amount. And so on.

### 12.3.3      Figures 12.3 & 12.4

Figure 12.3 shows the percentage of the number of years needed to reach our targeted net worth of $1 million plotted against increasing initial investment. The X-axis showing the initial investment is **linear.**

As you can see, the graph lines flatten out more and more as the initial investment increases. To get a quantitatively equal reduction in time-period every time, the needed multiple of the initial investment will be 2x, 4x, 8x, 16x, etc.

The graph lines show a **logarithmic decrease of time-period on a linear x-axis with the initial investment.**

Figure 12.4 shows the same data as in Figure 12.3. The difference is that the horizontal axis is not linear, but logarithmic with each step doubling in value. As a result, the graph lines are all straight lines.

The conclusion from these two figures is the same as our conclusion from Figures 12.1 & 12.2, namely, that the **initial investment** needs to be **increased exponentially** in order to achieve an equal reduction in time-period.

### 12.3.4      Figure 12.5

The graph in Figure 12.5 reveals the following when the initial investment is **0.5%** of the targeted net worth.

In our example, the initial investment is $5,000 to reach $1 million net worth.

If you double the principal to **1%** of the targeted net worth, the years needed will be **13.1%** less (= 100 – 86.9).

If you double the principal again, total **4x times** (= 2^2) thus, to **2%** of the targeted final amount, the years needed will be reduced by another **13.1%** of the original number of years.

If you want another 13.1% of the time reduced, thus for a third time, thus reach your target amount in **60.8%** of the original time, you need to double your investment again to **8x times** the original (= 2^3).

For another 13.1% off, thus, for a fourth time, you need **16x** times (= 2^4) the original investment, and you can reach your target in **47.7%** of the original time.

### 12.3.4.1 Conclusion 1

Putting it more technically, you can see in Figure 12.5 that you need to increase the investment **exponentially** to achieve an equal saving in time.

This is a conclusion we had already drawn also in the foregoing sections of this chapter.

That means increasing the principal amount alone to reach your $1 million faster becomes increasingly and rapidly less effective.

Increasing the initial investment is, therefore, not the most efficient way to become a millionaire quickly.

That also means that you do not necessarily have to have a significant start capital to become a millionaire over a period of time.

Increasing the yield rate is a much faster way to reach the target of $1 million net worth, as you can see in Figure 12.1 and elaborated further in chapter 13.

### 12.3.4.2 Conclusion 2

A second observation you can make easily from Figure 12.5 is that the yield rate does not change this relationship of 13.1% reduction in time due to every doubling of the initial investment. The line representing this 13.1% change is flat and horizontal across all yield rates.

The **yield rate** has no influence on the change in time-period due to any change in initial investment. The percentage change in time-period applies equally to the yield rate of 5% as well as 30% or 40%.

We had drawn this conclusion earlier also by looking at Table 12.2 in section 12.2.

### 12.3.4.3 Conclusion 3

A third observation you can make easily from Figure 12.5 is that the distance between each horizontal line is equal at 13.1% each. Each horizontal line represents a principal amount that is exactly double the line just above it.

This is a visual confirmation of conclusion-1 made above that you will need an exponential increase of initial investment to get an equal reduction in time to reach your targeted net worth.

This means that the decrease in time to reach your targeted net worth due to an increase of initial investment is a logarithmic decrease.

Conversely, this means also that the initial investment needs to be increased exponentially to achieve an equal reduction in time-period.

We had drawn these conclusions earlier also from the other tables and figures.

*For nerds only*: Logarithmic decrease or decline means just the inverse of exponential decrease. The time keeps on reducing **ever slower in a logarithmic decrease** instead of keeping on reducing **ever faster in** an exponential decrease.

### Note

Though the percentage of reduction in time is the same for all interest rates as represented by the horizontal lines in Figure 12.5, the actual length of time, in years, needed to reach your targeted net worth of $1 million will be considerably shorter with every increase of interest rate. It is only the *Percentage* change that is constant and horizontal, but not the absolute or actual number of years.

## 12.4      HOW MANY PERCENT IS THE REDUCTION IN TIME-PERIOD WITH EVERY DOUBLING OF INITIAL INVESTMENT?

It depends on how much percentage of the targeted final amount you want to invest initially. If you have a relatively high amount of initial investment, doubling it will result in a higher percentual reduction in time-period. And vice versa.

In our example, if the principal ($5,000) is 0.5% of the targeted final amount, and if that is doubled to 1% of the targeted final amount, the time-period needed will reduce by 13.1% (= 100 – 86.9). This situation is depicted by the uppermost graph line in Figures 12.3 & 12.4 and also by all the lines in Figure 12.5.

But if the principal were 1% ($10,000) of the targeted final amount, upon doubling it to 2%, the time-period needed would reduce by 15.1% (= 100 – 84.9). This situation is depicted by the second graph line in Figures 12.3 & 12.4.

If the principal were 2% ($20,000) of the targeted final amount, upon doubling it to 4%, the time-period needed would reduce by 17.7% (= 100 – 82.3). This situation is depicted by the bottom graph line in Figures 12.3 & 12.4.

As a general rule, we can state the following:

**The bigger the initial investment relative to the targeted final amount, the bigger its influence on the time-period when it changes.**

## 12.5      EFFECT OF INCREASE OF INITIAL INVESTMENT ON NET WORTH IN A GIVEN TIME-PERIOD

Let us take an **example:**

If you invest $10,000 at a 20% yield rate, you will have a net worth of $1 million in 25.3 years, as you can see in Table 12.1.

**The question**: What will be the net worth in the same time period of 25.3 years if you invest $20,000 now instead of $10,000?

**The answer**: It is simple. The final amount, yield amount, and net worth will simply double.

If you double the initial investment, everything will double if the time-period remains the same.

If you increase the initial investment 100x times, your net worth will also be 100x bigger in the same time period.

As a general rule, we can state the following:

If the time period is fixed, the final amount, net worth, and cumulative yield will change proportionately to the initial investment. The relationship is linear.

## 12.6    THE FASTEST WAY TO BUILD WEALTH

### 12.6.1    What we have learned so far

1). Increasing the time-period has the maximum effect on the final amount and net worth than a proportionate increase of yield rate.

2). Increasing the yield rate has the second maximum effect on the final amount and net worth when compared with a proportionate increase of time-period.

3). Increasing the initial investment has the least effect on the final amount and net worth compared to a proportionate increase of time-period or yield rate.

Ideally, we should make maximum use of all three instruments above, simultaneously, to build wealth to the maximum height and at the fastest speed.

### 12.6.2    Time-period and net worth

Time-period is the biggest wealth- builder of all, as we have seen in earlier chapters. And it is available to all of us, gratis. Therefore, we must make maximum use of it to maximize wealth.

But still, it is not an increase of time-period that we want initially, but a maximum decrease and still get the same net worth.

Therefore, increasing the time-period of an investment will be the last of the 3 variables we should use to maximize our wealth. We will use it only after maximizing the other 2 variables, namely yield rate, and initial investment.

## 12.6.3 Yield rate and net worth

As we will see in chapter 13, **maximizing the yield rate** is the **most efficient** instrument we can use to maximize our net worth in any given time period.

But the problem with a high yield rate is that its availability is always very much limited, and as investors, we have little or no control over it after investment.

## 12.6.4 Initial investment is the least efficient but the fastest and most powerful wealth builder

The **initial investment** is the **least efficient** in building wealth in the long term, but having maximized the yield rate and put a time limit to maximize our net worth, increasing the initial investment is the only instrument we have available to maximize our net worth.

The initial investment, aside from being the only practical instrument we have at our disposal after fixing yield rate and time-period, has the added benefit that we have complete control over it. We can decide whether we will invest $1 thousand or $1 million.

We have seen that if you double your initial investment, it will double your total return and net worth, **and if you increase your initial investment 100-fold, it will increase your total return and net worth 100-fold.**

We will see below, through an example, that the amount of initial investment, though less efficient than time-period or yield rate, is the only ingredient with the mega-power to build massive wealth in the shortest possible time.

### 12.6.4.1 Example

Assume you invested $10,000 in a project or stock market with an average of 21.6% yield rate.

In 20 years, ignoring tax, your net worth would have grown 50x times to $0.5 million.

If you had invested $1 million instead of $10,000, your net worth in 20 years would have grown to $50 million instead of only $0.5 million.

The difference between a net worth of $0.5 million and $50 million is a huge $49.5 million.

All that it took was an additional investment of $0.99 million (= 1,000,000 − 10,000). Your additional investment grew also 50x times higher (= 49.5/ 0.99).

If you continued the investments for another 20 years (total 40 years thus), your net worth would have grown again by a factor of 50x, and the amounts would have been as follows:

$25 million with $10,000 initial investment. (= 0.5 x 50).

$2,500 million with $1 million initial investment. (= 50 x 50).

The difference is a colossal $2,475 million. All that it took was an extra investment of $0.99 million over a time span of your active working life of 40 years.

If you could foresee in advance that you could earn an additional $2,475 million by investing an additional $0.99 million, wouldn't you have moved heaven and earth to raise that $0.99 million?

Therefore, you should always make maximum use of the leverage you can get by maximizing your initial investment.

## 12.7    INSIGHT

The initial investment has a massive power to build colossal wealth if it is available abundantly. For example, Jeff Bezos can easily make an additional $200 Billion in 4 or 5 years as a return on his massive investment in Amazon worth about $200 Billion as in December 2020.

However, a doubling of initial investment will deliver only a relatively small reduction in the time period needed to reach your targeted final amount.

If your target is to reach a specific amount of net worth in the shortest possible time period, for example, $1 million, then the Initial investment must be doubled every time to get equal years of reduction in time-period.

The relationship of time-period with initial investment is one of a logarithmic decrease of time-period for equal increases of the initial investment.

Put it differently, the relationship of time-period with initial investment is one of an exponential increase of initial investment for equal decreases of time-period.

If your target is to maximize wealth in a specific time period, and if the initial investment is doubled, the final amount will double in the same time period. If it is tripled, the final amount will be tripled. The relationship between initial investment and final amount is linear.

For example, if your Amazon shares worth $2,000 would double to $4,000 in 3 years (with a rate of return of 26.0%), your neighbor's $2 million would double to $4 million also in 3 years, and Jeff Bezos' $200 Billion would also double to $400 Billion in 3 years.

While you would have earned $2,000 in 3 years, Jeff Bezos would have earned $200 Billion using the very same instrument. The factor of difference is 100 million.

The only reason for Jeff Bezos' 100 million times higher gain is his 100 million times higher Initial investment.

Mathematics does not discriminate. It just gave you $2,000 and gave Jeff Bezos $200 Billion in what is mathematically equal treatment! Give it another 3 years, and it would all double again. Your $4,000 would become $8,000, and Jeff Bezos' $400 Billion would become $800 Billion.

**It shows that the power of initial investment to accumulate wealth is tremendous.**

As increasing the initial investment, after maximizing the yield rate, is the only instrument available to you to build huge wealth in a given time period, you should always maximize your initial input.

Borrow and invest if you can but borrow sensibly. See chapter 10 for details on borrowing for investment.

* * * *

# Chapter 13:

# Effect of Yield Rate on Time needed to reach $1 million Net Worth

## Effect of change of yield rate on time needed to reach $1 million net worth.

Please read chapter 11 for an overview of what we are discussing here before immersing deeper into this chapter.

In this chapter, we will analyze the influence of yield rate on time needed to reach our targeted net worth of $1 million.

## 13.1     REVIEW

As summarized in chapter 11, the 5 variables in any investment program are:

1. **Initial investment or principal** (P)
2. **Time-period or number of years** (N)
3. **Yield rate** (R)
4. **Tax rate** (T)
5. **Final amount or net worth** (NW)

As we are assuming the tax rate to be zero in this chapter, we have only 4 variables to consider.

We had already analyzed the impact of **time-period** on net worth and other parameters in chapter 5 and the impact of **yield rate** in chapter 6. We had also examined the effect of **initial investment** on **net worth** in chapter 12.

We had also analyzed the effect of **initial investment** on the **time-period** needed to reach a targeted net worth of $1 million in chapter 12.

In this chapter, we will look specifically at the effect of **yield rate** on the **time-period** needed to reach a targeted net worth of $1 million.

## 13.2     INVESTMENT MATRIX FOR TIME-PERIOD

Table 11.1 from chapter 11 is copied into this chapter for ease of reference and is relabeled as Table 13.1.

It is the investment matrix that shows the number of years that would be needed to reach a final amount of **$1 million** for various combinations of yield rates and initial investments.

For ease of reference, Figures 11.1 & 11.2 from chapter 11 are also copied into this chapter and relabeled as Figures 13.1 & 13.2, respectively.

| Number of Years **needed to reach $1 MILLION** Net Worth | | | | | | | | |
|---|---|---|---|---|---|---|---|---|
| **Initial Investment, $** | **Yield Rate** | | | | | | | |
| | **5%** | **10%** | **15%** | **20%** | **25%** | **30%** | **35%** | **40%** |
| 5,000 | 108.6 | 55.6 | 37.9 | 29.1 | 23.7 | 20.2 | 17.7 | 15.7 |
| 10,000 | 94.4 | 48.3 | 33.0 | 25.3 | 20.6 | 17.6 | 15.3 | 13.7 |
| 15,000 | 86.1 | 44.1 | 30.0 | 23.0 | 18.8 | 16.0 | 14.0 | 12.5 |
| 20,000 | 80.2 | 41.0 | 28.0 | 21.5 | 17.5 | 14.9 | 13.0 | 11.6 |
| 25,000 | 75.6 | 38.7 | 26.4 | 20.2 | 16.5 | 14.1 | 12.3 | 11.0 |
| 30,000 | 71.9 | 36.8 | 25.1 | 19.2 | 15.7 | 13.4 | 11.7 | 10.4 |
| 35,000 | 68.7 | 35.2 | 24.0 | 18.4 | 15.0 | 12.8 | 11.2 | 10.0 |
| 40,000 | 66.0 | 33.8 | 23.0 | 17.7 | 14.4 | 12.3 | 10.7 | 9.6 |
| 45,000 | 63.6 | 32.5 | 22.2 | 17.0 | 13.9 | 11.8 | 10.3 | 9.2 |
| 50,000 | 61.4 | 31.4 | 21.4 | 16.4 | 13.4 | 11.4 | 10.0 | 8.9 |
| 55,000 | 59.4 | 30.4 | 20.8 | 15.9 | 13.0 | 11.1 | 9.7 | 8.6 |
| 60,000 | 57.7 | 29.5 | 20.1 | 15.4 | 12.6 | 10.7 | 9.4 | 8.4 |
| 65,000 | 56.0 | 28.7 | 19.6 | 15.0 | 12.2 | 10.4 | 9.1 | 8.1 |
| 70,000 | 54.5 | 27.9 | 19.0 | 14.6 | 11.9 | 10.1 | 8.9 | 7.9 |
| 75,000 | 53.1 | 27.2 | 18.5 | 14.2 | 11.6 | 9.9 | 8.6 | 7.7 |
| 80,000 | 51.8 | 26.5 | 18.1 | 13.9 | 11.3 | 9.6 | 8.4 | 7.5 |

Table 13.1: investment Matrix for the number of years: **Combinations of initial investment, yield rate, and the number of years that will be needed to reach $1 million net worth.**

This table is the same as **Table 11.1** in chapter 11 and **Table 12.1** in chapter 12.

Figures 13.1 & 13.2 show the values in this table in a graphical form together with the relevant observations.

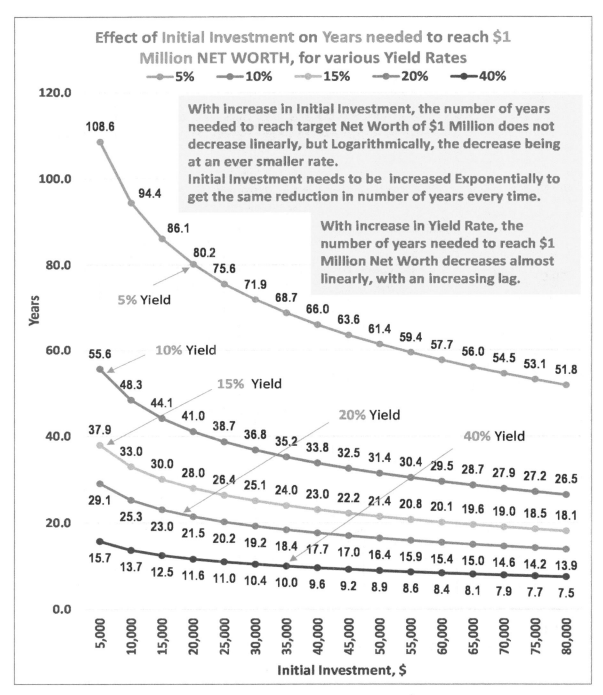

Figure 13.1: **The number of years needed to reach** $1 million net worth **for various yield rates and initial investments.**

This figure is the same as **Fig. 11.1** in chapter 11 and **Fig. 12.1** in chapter 12.

All the values in this graph are taken from Table 13.1.

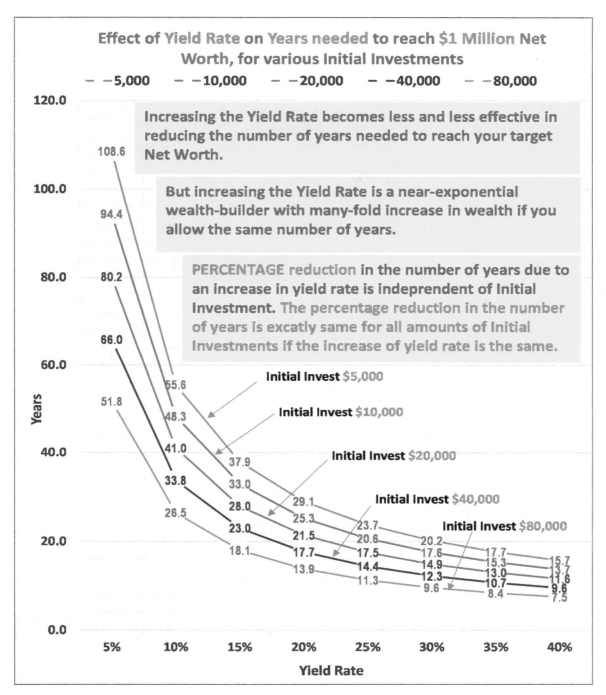

Figure 13.2: **Effect of yield rate on the number of years needed to reach $1 million net worth for various amounts of initial investments.**

This figure is the same as **Figure 11.2** in chapter 11.

All the values in this graph are taken from Table 13.1.

**13.3**     **COMPARATIVE INVESTMENT MATRIX FOR TIME-PERIOD WITH 5% YIELD RATE AS REFERENCE BASE**

Percentage of Years **needed to reach** $1 MILLION Net Worth with 5% Yield Rate as Base

| Initial Investment, $ | Yield Rate | | | | | | | |
|---|---|---|---|---|---|---|---|---|
| | 5% | 10% | 15% | 20% | 25% | 30% | 35% | 40% |
| Proportionate % of years | 100.0% | 50.0% | 33.3% | 25.0% | 20.0% | 16.7% | 14.3% | 12.5% |
| 5,000 | 100.0% | | | | | | | |
| 10,000 | 100.0% | | | | | | | |
| 15,000 | 100.0% | | | | | | | |
| 20,000 | 100.0% | | | | | | | |
| 25,000 | 100.0% | | | | | | | |
| 30,000 | 100.0% | | | | | | | |
| 35,000 | 100.0% | | | | | | | |
| 40,000 | 100.0% | 51.2% | 34.9% | 26.8% | 21.9% | 18.6% | 16.3% | 14.5% |
| 45,000 | 100.0% | | | | | | | |
| 50,000 | 100.0% | | | | | | | |
| 55,000 | 100.0% | | | | | | | |
| 60,000 | 100.0% | | | | | | | |
| 65,000 | 100.0% | | | | | | | |
| 70,000 | 100.0% | | | | | | | |
| 75,000 | 100.0% | | | | | | | |
| 80,000 | 100.0% | | | | | | | |

Table 13.2: **Percentage of Years needed to reach** $1 million net worth **with** 5% yield rate **as the** Reference Base.

Figure 13.3 shows the values in this table in a graphical form together with the relevant observations.

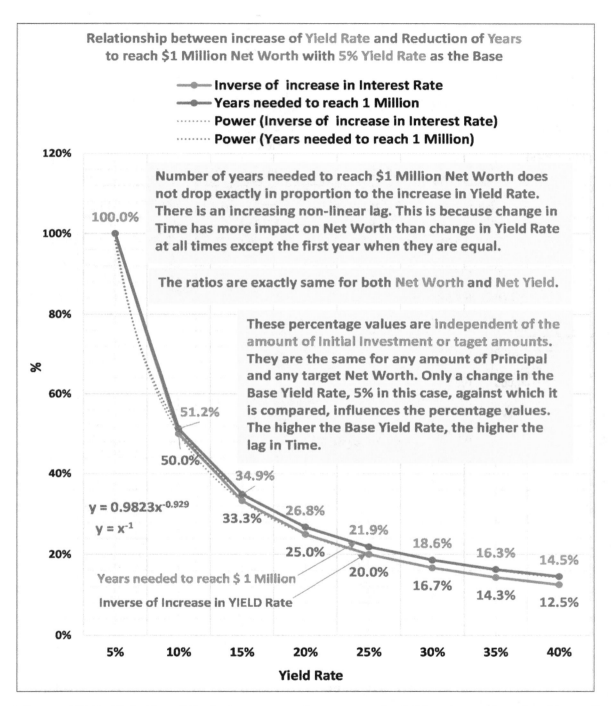

**Relationship between increase of** Yield Rate **and Reduction of** Years **to reach $1 Million Net Worth with** 5% Yield Rate **as the Base**

- ●— Inverse of increase in Interest Rate
- ●— Years needed to reach 1 Million
- ········ Power (Inverse of increase in Interest Rate)
- ········ Power (Years needed to reach 1 Million)

Number of years needed to reach $1 Million Net Worth does not drop exactly in proportion to the increase in Yield Rate. There is an increasing non-linear lag. This is because change in Time has more impact on Net Worth than change in Yield Rate at all times except the first year when they are equal.

The ratios are exactly same for both Net Worth and Net Yield.

These percentage values are independent of the amount of Initial Investment or taget amounts. They are the same for any amount of Principal and any target Net Worth. Only a change in the Base Yield Rate, 5% in this case, against which it is compared, influences the percentage values. The higher the Base Yield Rate, the higher the lag in Time.

$y = 0.9823x^{-0.929}$

$y = x^{-1}$

Years needed to reach $ 1 Million

Inverse of Increase in YIELD Rate

**Figure 13.3: Relationship between an** increase of yield rate **and** reduction of Years **needed to reach** $1 million net worth **with** 5% yield rate **as the** Reference Base.

All the values in this graph are taken from Table 13.2.

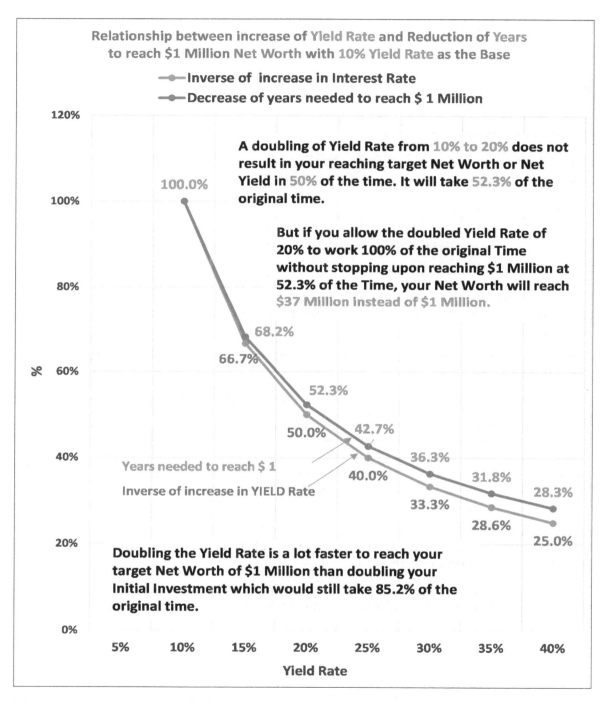

Figure 13.4: **Relationship between an** increase of yield rate **and** reduction of Years **needed to reach** $1 million net worth **with** 10% yield rate **as the** Reference Base.

Values for this graph are not taken up as a table in this book.

## 13.4    ANALYSIS OF TABLES & FIGURES

Note that all **vertical values in a column in Table 13.2 are the same**. That means the percentage change in time needed to reach a targeted net worth due to a change in **yield rate** is the same for all amounts of the **initial investment**.

**In other words, when the yield rate changes, its effect on the time period expressed in percentage, is the same for all amounts of the initial investment.**

Table 13.2 and the values in it apply equally also to the total **yield amount** (excluding principal) as well as the total **final amount** (including principal).

In Table 13.2 and Figures 13.2, 13.3 & 13.4, the following can also be observed.

### 13.4.1    Time-period does not drop fully proportional to increase in yield rate

If the **5%** yield rate is increased **2-fold** from **5% to 10%**, the time needed to reach our target of $1 million does not drop fully to the proportional **50%**, but only to **51.2%** (see Figure 13.3).

If the **10%** yield rate is taken as the basis, the time needed will drop only to **52.3%** (see Figure 13.4).

If a **20%** yield rate is taken as the basis, the time needed will drop only to **54.1%** (not shown in this book in table or figure).


If the **5%** yield rate is increased **4-fold** from **5% to 20%**, the time needed to reach $1 Million does not drop fully to the proportional **25%**, but only to **26.8%** (see Figure 13.3).

If the **10%** yield rate is taken as the basis, and it is increased **4-fold** from **10% to 40%**, the time needed to reach $1 Million does not drop fully to the proportional **25%**, but only to **28.3%** (see Figure 13.4).

You can see this close relationship clearly in the graphs in Figures 13.3 & 13.4, which are made with 5% & 10% yield rates respectively as the basis for comparison.

### 13.4.2    The above ratios remain the same for any initial investment

This relationship or ratio between a change in yield rate and time-period is the same **irrespective of the amount of initial investment.**

In other words, when the yield rate changes, its effect on the time period is the same for any amount of initial investment.

### 13.4.3    The above ratios remain the same for any targeted net worth

This relationship or ratio is also exactly the same irrespective of the amount of targeted final amount. It is the same if your targeted net worth is $1 million or $100 million.

### 13.4.4    The higher the yield rate, the smaller the effect of its change on time-period

If the 5% yield rate is the Reference Base, doubling it to 10% will reduce the time-period to 51.2% instead of the proportionate 50.0%. The reduction in time-period is only 48.8% instead of the proportionate 50%.

If the 10% yield rate is the Reference Base, doubling it to 20% will reduce the time-period to 52.3% instead of the proportionate 50.0%. The reduction in time-period is only 47.7% instead of the proportionate 50%.

If the 20% yield rate is the Reference Base, doubling it to 40% will reduce the time-period to 54.1% instead of the proportionate 50.0%. The reduction in time-period is only 45.9% instead of the proportionate 50%.

If the 40% yield rate is the Reference Base, doubling it to 80% will reduce the time-period to 57.3% instead of the proportionate 50.0%. The reduction in time-period is only 42.7% instead of the proportionate 50%.

If the 50% yield rate is the Reference Base, doubling it to 100% will reduce the time-period to 58.5% instead of the proportionate 50.0%. The reduction in time-period is only 41.5% instead of the proportionate 50%.

If the 100% yield rate is the Reference Base, doubling it to 200% will reduce the time-period to 63.1% instead of the proportionate 50.0%. The reduction in time-period is only 36.9% instead of the proportionate 50%.

### 13.4.4.1    As a rule, we can state the following

When the yield rate is increased, the time needed to reach a targeted net worth does not reduce in equal proportion. The reduction or saving in time is less than the proportionate linear reduction.

The higher the increase in yield rate, the more the deviation of reduction of time from linear reduction. By a 2-fold increase of yield rate from 5% to 10%, the relative deviation is 2.4%, while by a 4-fold increase of yield rate from 5% to 20%, the relative deviation is 7.2%.

The higher the yield rate, the smaller the reduction or saving in time achieved by increasing the yield rate. By a 2-fold increase of yield rate from 5% to 10%, the relative deviation is 2.4%, while by a 2-fold increase of yield rate from 20% to 40%, the relative deviation is 8.2%.

### 13.4.4.2    Easiest rule to remember

Easiest to remember, though not precise to the percent, is the following:

Doubling of yield rate will give you the same final amount in a little more than half the time.

3x increase of yield rate will give you the same final amount in a little more than one-third of the time.

4x increase of yield rate will give you the same final amount in a little more than one-fourth of the time.

*For nerds only*: In mathematical jargon, the relationship between yield rate and the time needed to reach a targeted net worth is not linear or exponential or logarithmic but polynomial. That means an equation defining the relationship will be complex with several components added together.

### Note

Please keep the distinction between net worth and net yield in mind when you are comparing figures. Net worth will always give a different percentage difference with each other than what the corresponding net yield will give because net worth also includes the initial investment while net yield does not have it.

\* \* \* \*

# Chapter 14:

# How to use the **CAF table** to make investment calculations

In the previous chapters, we had chosen a targeted net worth of $1 million and analyzed how your initial investment, time-period, yield rate, and net worth itself would be impacted if any one of these four investment parameters changed.

Calculations in the previous chapters involved quite some calculations as we wanted the final amount or net worth to be exactly $1 million and wanted to know how the other parameters interacted to changes in them. It was needed to get a good understanding of the mutual relationships among the four investment parameters.

But there is a much simpler way, without complicated calculations, to plan your path to the millions, and that is by using the CAF table.

Let us take an example to make it easier.

## 14.1      EXAMPLE

Suppose you have $25,000 in a Fixed Deposit in your bank account, and it is earning a meager **7% p.a.** for yourself and an additional 8% effective for the bank, as explained in chapter 9. You know that the stock markets are doing very well in the long term and that you can make **21% p.a.**, net, after deducting costs. By reading this book so far, and especially from chapter 7, you also know that the 21% yield rate is a lot more than 3x times the 7% yield rate.

**21% yield rate is not equal to 3x times 7%** yield rate in wealth-building. It may be 40x times or 137x times 7%, as we will see below.

You also have the possibility to raise an extra $25,000 by selling part of your gold jewelry lying unused in the locker and use it to invest in the stock market. After all, Gold is not expected to appreciate as much as the stock market in the coming years. You now have a total of $50,000 to invest.

Let us **calculate, using the CAF table**, what your net worth will be in 20, 25, or 30 years or upon retirement in 40 years.

**20 years**

In the CAF table, at the cross-section of **20 years and 21%**, you see the value **45.26**, and against **20 years and 7%**, you see the value **3.87**.

The final amount after **20 years** will be **$2,263,000** (= 45.26 x 50,000). But if you keep it in FD in the bank at 7%, you would have only **$193,500** (= 3.87 x 50,000). The difference is **11.7x times**.

**25 years**

In the CAF table, at the cross-section of **25 years and 21%**, you see the value **117.4,** and against **7%,** you see the value **5.43.**

The final amount after **25 years** will be **$5,870,000** (= 117.4 x 50,000). But if you keep it in FD in the bank at 7%, you would have only **$271,500** (= 5.43 x 50,000). The difference is **21.6x times**.

**30 years**

In the CAF table, at the cross-section of **30 years and 21%**, you see the value **304.5,** and against **7%,** you see the value **7.61.**

The final amount after **30 years** will be **$15,225,000** (= 304.5 x 50,000). But if you keep it in FD in the bank at 7%, you would have only **$380,500** (7.61 x 50,000). The difference is **40x times**.

**40 years**

In the CAF table, at the cross-section of **40 years and 21%**, you see the value **2,048,** and against **7%,** you see the value **14.97.**

The final amount after **40 years** will be **$102,400,000** (= 2,048 x 50,000). But if you keep it in FD in the bank at 7%, you would have only **$748,500** (14.97 x 50,000). The difference is **137x times**.

**Summary**

Summarizing the effect of our switch from Fixed Deposit in a bank to investing in the Stock Market, we can note the following.

> **21% yield is equal to** 11.7x TIMES **7% yield in 20 years instead of the linear 3x times!**

> **21% yield is equal to** 21.6x TIMES **7% yield in 25 years instead of the linear 3x times!**

> **21% yield is equal to** 40x TIMES **7% yield in 30 years instead of the linear 3x times!**

> **21% yield is equal to** 137x TIMES **7% yield in 40 years instead of the linear 3x times!**

## 14.2 USE OF CAF TABLE

In the above example, we used the CAF table to find the CAF value (or Growth Factor) and had to do only one straightforward multiplication to get the final amount.

To get the final amount, you only need to find the CAF value in the table at the cross-section of the desired interest rate and the number of years and multiply that with your initial investment. It is that simple!

If you want another combination of interest rate and the number of years, but the same initial investment and final amount, go to the cross-section of interest rate and the number of years where the same CAF value appears.

For example, with reference to the values in the example above with a 21% yield rate and 20 years, if you want to know how long it will take to reach $2,263,000 net worth if the annual yield was 25% instead of 21%, you follow the 25% column and come across a CAF value 44.41 at 17 years which is very close to the previous 45.26. Now you know right away, without any further calculation, that you will have the same amount in about 17 years instead of 20 years.

For anyone aspiring to become a millionaire in the shortest possible time, the CAF table is the virtual chessboard for him or her to play. It is the single most indispensable tool one should have in addition to the calculation software **YIELDOMETER,** which we will discuss in chapter 22 of this book.

## 14.3 GROWTH OF WEALTH IS LIKE GROWTH OF A TREE

In the above example, we have seen that, with a $50,000 initial investment, in the first 20 years, we added $2.213 Million (= 2,263,000 - 50,000) to our net worth (excluding the initial investment).

But in just 10 years after that, we could add another amount as high as $12.962 Million (= 15,225,000 – 2,263,000) to our net worth.

But in another 10 years again after that, we could add a staggering amount of $87.175 Million (= 102,400,000 - 15,225,000) to our net worth.

Money and wealth grow exponentially, like a tree. You will see a couple of green leaves after one year, tens of them after the second year, hundreds after 3 years, thousands after 4 years, and a giant tree after 20 years.

Likewise, you can plant a money-tree. Plant a tree that grows extremely fast. Plant it on fertile ground. And plant it when you are young so that it would have grown into a big tree, and you can enjoy the fruit and the shade of it when you are tired of working for a living.

This book is all about planting a fast-growing money tree on fertile ground and making it grow fast. In chapter 21, we will go deeper into the different types of soils, different kinds of trees, their growth rates, and the quantity and quality of fruit each will deliver.

\* \* \* \*

# Chapter 15:

# Make a route plan to reach $1 Million or more Net Worth using CAF or CYF table

In the previous chapter, chapter 14, we had used the Compound Amount Factor (CAF) table to calculate the net worth of an investment. The CAF table is given in Appendix-A and described in chapter 4 of this book.

In this chapter, we will be using the Compound yield Factor (CYF) table as we will be calculating the **net yield** or total return of an investment first before calculating the **net worth**. The CYF table is given in Appendix-B and described in chapter 4 of this book.

## 15.1    WHICH TABLE TO USE: CAF TABLE OR CYF TABLE?

The most straightforward table to use to calculate the final amount or net worth of an investment is the CAF table.

The most straightforward table to use to calculate the total yield of an investment is the CYF table.

However, both the tables can be used interchangeably for calculating the final amount or total yield if you take the difference between the two tables into account.

## 15.1.1    Difference between CAF & CYF tables

The difference between the two is described in detail in chapter 4. The essence of the difference is the following.

For any combination of yield rate and time-period, **CYF = CAF – 1.00**.

Put it differently, **CAF = CYF + 1.00.**

The CAF value is thus higher than the corresponding CYF value by 1.00.

If you are using only one table for all calculations and that is the **CAF** table, calculate as below for any combination of yield rate and time-period:

**Net worth = CAF value x initial investment.**

**Net yield = (CAF value – 1.00) x initial investment.**

If you are using only one table for all calculations and that is the CYF table, calculate as below for any combination of yield rate and time-period:

Net worth = (CYF value + 1.00) x initial investment.

Net yield = CYF value x initial investment.

## 15.2    THE CALCULATIONS WE WILL MAKE

Assimilating all the insights we have gained so far, let us make some calculations to add one or more million dollars EXTRA to your net worth even if you are a starter with only one month's salary as your present net worth.

Aside from the type of investment you may choose, for any investment, there are five primary variables that you must decide upon and fix to enable you to make the calculations. Those variables, as also described in section 11.1, are:

1.  The initial investment or principal (P), the amount you plan to invest.

2.  The number of years (N), the period within which you want to reach your target of an additional net worth of one million dollars or more.

3.  Yield rate (R), the rate of return on your investment.

4.  Tax rate (T), your tax rate for the income or capital gains from this investment.

5.  Net yield (NY) or net worth (NW) that you want to add to your current (positive or negative) wealth.

**Let us fix 4 of these 5 variables at the desired level first, and then see what the value of the fifth variable needs to be in order to meet the pre-set levels of the first 4 variables.**

**We will do this in turn for all 5 variables.**

## 15.3    CALCULATING THE NET YIELD (NY) AND NET WORTH (NW) FOR ANY GIVEN SET OF INVESTMENT PARAMETERS

### 15.3.1    Example 15.3.1

1.  Initial investment (P): $25,000.
2.  Number of years (N): 25.
3.  Yield rate (R): 20% p.a.
4.  Tax rate (T): 0%.
5.  Net yield (NY): xx?
6.  Net worth (NW): xx?

In the CYF table, we follow the 25-year row and the 20% yield column, and at the intersection, we get the CYF value of 94.40.

The corresponding **CAF** value is **95.40** (= 94.40 + 1.00).

That means, with no tax due, $1 invested gives a net yield of $94.40 and a net worth of $95.40 at the end of 25 years.

Therefore, $25,000 invested delivers a net yield of $**2,360,000** (= 94.40 x 25,000).

Net worth of the same investment is $**2,385,000** (= 95.40 x 25,000).

## 15.4      CALCULATING THE INITIAL INVESTMENT (P) NEEDED TO REACH $1 MILLION NET YIELD OR NET WORTH IN A GIVEN NUMBER OF YEARS

### 15.4.1      Example 15.4.1

1. Initial investment (P): **xx?**
2. Number of years (N): **25**.
3. Yield rate (R): **20%** p.a.
4. Tax rate (T): **0%**.
5. Target net yield (NY): **$1 million**.
6. Target net worth (NW): **$1 million**.

Using the CYF table, for 25 years and 20% yield rate, the **CYF** value is **94.40.**

The corresponding **CAF** value is **95.40** (= 94.40 + 1.00).

That means, with no tax due, $1 invested gives a net yield of $94.40 and a net worth of $95.40 at the end of 25 years.

Investment (P) needed to get $1 million net yield = $**10,594** (= 1,000,000/ 94.40).

Investment (P) needed to get $1 million net worth = $**10,483** (= 1,000,000/ 95.40).


If it is $**10 million** that you target instead of $1 million, all that you need to do is divide 10 million, instead of 1 million, by the corresponding CYF or CAF value.

The needed investment for $10 million net yield will thus be exactly 10x times the investment needed to get a $1 million net yield. The same also applies to net worth.

Similarly, for a $**100** million net yield, the needed investment will be 100 times more. The same also applies to net worth.

**Therefore, we get the following results.**

Initial investment needed for $1 million net yield: $10,594.

Initial investment needed for $10 million net yield: $105,940.

Initial investment needed for $100 million net yield: $1,059,400.

If it is a reference to the **net worth** we want instead of **net yield**, we get the following.

Initial investment needed for $1 million net worth: $10,483.

Initial investment needed for $10 million net worth: $104,830.

Initial investment needed for $100 million net worth: $1,048,300.

### 15.4.2    Conclusion

The needed initial investment is directly proportional to the desired total net yield or net worth, provided the time-period and other investment parameters stay unchanged.

## 15.5    CALCULATING THE NUMBER OF YEARS (N) NEEDED TO REACH $1 MILLION NET YIELD OR NET WORTH

### 15.5.1    Example 15.5.1

1. Initial investment (P): $25,000.
2. Number of years (N): xx?
3. Yield rate (R): 20% p.a.
4. Tax rate (T): 0%.
5. Target net yield (NY): $1 million.
6. Target net worth (NW): $1 million.

With no tax due, for a $25,000 investment to deliver a net yield of $1 million, we need a CYF of 40 (= 1,000.000/ 25,000).

Similarly, to get a net worth of $1 million, we need a CAF of 40. The corresponding CYF value in the CYF table is 39 (= 40 - 1), as explained at the beginning of this chapter in section 15.1.1.

In the CYF table, if we go down the 20% yield column and find the row with a CYF value of 40, that row would tell us the number of years that we seek to get a $1 million net **yield.**

But in the CYF table, a CYF value of exactly 40 does not appear, but we find a CYF value of 37.34 against 20 years and a CYF value of 45.01 against 21 years. Therefore, the number of years that we seek lies between 20 and 21 years. By interpolating, we can conclude that it will take roughly 20.4 years (the exact value is 20.37 years, using the calculation software Yieldometer) for the net **yield** to reach $1 Million.

In a similar way, for the net worth of $1 million, we follow the CYF value of 39 and get the number of years to be approximately 20.2 years.

If it is a **$10 million** net yield that you target instead of $1 million, you need to calculate the corresponding CYF value first and then determine the required years from the CYF table.

The CYF value corresponding to $25,000 initial investment and net yield of $10 million is 400 (= 10,000,000/ 25,000).

Following the 20% yield column in the CYF table, we can conclude that we need approximately **32.9** years to reach the CYF value of 400, corresponding to a $10 million net yield.

In a similar way, we can find the time-period needed to reach any amount of net yield or net worth.

## Time-distance to net yield

**20.4** years needed to reach $1 million net yield.

**32.9** years needed to reach $10 million net yield.

**36.7** years needed to reach $20 million net yield.

**41.7** years needed to reach $50 million net yield.

**45..5** years needed to reach $100 million net yield.

**54.3** years needed to reach $500 million net yield.

**58.1** years needed to reach $1,000 million net yield.

## Time-distance to net worth

**20.2** years needed to reach $1 million net worth.

**32.9** years needed to reach $10 million net worth.

**36.7** years needed to reach $20 million net worth.

**41.7** years needed to reach $50 million net worth.

**45.5** years needed to reach $100 million net worth

**54.3** years needed to reach $500 million net worth.

**58.1** years needed to reach $1,000 million net worth.

## 15.5.2     Observations

### 15.5.2.1     Exponential growth with time

In the above list, you can see the tremendous influence of time-period on net worth. The effect is not linear like the influence of investment amount, but exponential in which every increase in time is a lot more powerful than an equal increase just before it.

In chapter 5, we had already seen that, for net worth, the following applies.

**For equal time-periods, the growth ratios of net worth, or ratios of CAF values, are equal.**

**That means, if the net worth grew 10-fold from $1 million to $10 million in a time period of 8 years, it would also take 8 years for net worth to grow 10-fold from 100 million to 1,000 million or from 1 Billion to 10 Billion.**

**That also means that for every doubling of time-period, the CAF value increases by its square; for a tripling of time-period, the CAF value increases by its 3rd power; for N-fold increase in time-period, the CAF value increases by its Nth power, etc.**

The above relationship applies strictly only to CAF value, net worth, and the annual yield amount, but not to CYF value, net yield, or cumulative yield amount, as we had seen earlier in chapter 5.

In this example, we can see that it takes 12.63 years for the net worth to grow 10-fold anywhere across the whole spectrum of growth.

### 15.5.2.2     The gap between the time-periods needed to reach net worth and net yield

We can see further that, in the rounded-off numbers, there is no clearly visible difference in the time period needed to reach $10 million net yield or $10 million net worth even though there is a difference of 1.00 between the CAF and CYF values. This is because, at higher values of CAF and CYF, the difference of just 1.00 gets relatively too small to show up in the number of years that are rounded off. You can see the difference only if you zoom in on the decimal points.

But when the CAF and CYF values are relatively small, the difference of 1.00 between the values gets more relevant, and the difference in the number of years gets considerably bigger, as shown below.

20.4 is the number of years needed to reach a $1 million net yield, but only 20.2 years needed to reach $1 million net worth (CYF and CAF values of 40).

8.8 years needed to reach $100,000 net yield, but only 7.6 years needed to reach $100,000 net worth (CYF and CAF values of 4.00).

6.0 years needed to reach $50,000 net yield, but only 3.8 years needed to reach $50,000 net worth (CYF and CAF values of 2.00).

On the extreme end, we also get the following:

3.8 years needed to reach $25,000 net yield, but only 0.0 years needed to reach $25,000 net worth (CYF and CAF values of 1.00). You already have a net worth of $25,000 in the form of the initial investment when you start the investment, and therefore, the time period needed to reach that amount is zero.

See chapter 5 for more information about the influence of time-period on the results of an investment.

## 15.6 CALCULATING THE NUMBER OF YEARS (N) NEEDED FOR NET YIELD (NY) OR NET WORTH (NW) TO REACH A DESIRED MULTIPLE OF INVESTMENT (CYF OR CAF)

### 15.6.1 Example 15.6.1

Let us see how many years (N) it will take to have a net yield or net worth of 40 times the initial investment if the other parameters are as below.

1. Initial investment (P): $25,000.
2. Number of years (N): xx?
3. Yield rate (R): 20% p.a.
4. Tax rate (T): 0%.
5. Targeted growth of net yield (CYF): 40 times the investment.
6. Targeted growth of net worth (CAF): 40 times the investment.

Here, the CYF and CAF values are given directly instead of them having to be calculated. The net yield of 40 times the investment means CYF value is 40, and the net worth of 40 times investment means CAF value is 40.

If it is 400x times the initial investment that we seek as the net return, the CYF value would be 400, and it corresponds to a net return of $10 million (= 25,000 x 400).

The rest of the calculation is exactly the same as in example 15.5.1 above.

As we had seen, the number of years needed to reach a net yield of 40 times the investment is 20.4 years, and for a net worth of 40 times the investment, it is 20.2 years.

**For net yield, we get the following results**, exactly as in <u>example 15.5.1</u> above.

**20.4** years to reach a net yield of **40** times initial investment (= $**1** million).

**32.9** years to reach a net yield of **400** times initial investment (= $**10** million).

**36.7** years to reach a net yield of **800** times initial investment (= $**20** million).

**41.7** years to reach a net yield of **2,000** times initial investment (= $**50** million).

**54.3** years to reach a net yield of **20,000** times initial investment (= $**500** million).

**58.1** years to reach a net yield of **40,000** times initial investment (= $**1,000** million).

The number of years needed for **net worth** is also exactly the same as in <u>example 15.5.1</u> above.

## 15.7 CALCULATING THE YIELD RATE (R) NEEDED TO REACH $1 MILLION NET YIELD OR NET WORTH

### 15.7.1 Example 15.7.1

1. Initial investment (P): $**25,000**.
2. Number of years (N): **25.**
3. Yield rate (R): **xx?** p.a.
4. Tax rate (T): **0%.**
5. Target net yield (NY): **$1 million**.
6. Targeted net worth (NW): **$1 million**.

Investment of $25,000 delivers $1 million net yield in 25 years.

Therefore, the CYF value is 40 (= 1,000,000/ 25,000).

In the CYF table, following the row for 25 years, we can see that approximately **16% yield** rate delivers a CYF value of almost 40. This is the yield rate that we sought.

If the targeted net return was **$2 million** instead of $1 million, The CYF value would be 80 instead of 40, and the needed yield rate would be **19.2%.**

If the targeted net return was **$3 million** instead of $1 million, the CYF value would be 120 instead of 40, and the needed yield rate would be **21.2%.**

Given below is the result of similar calculations. These calculations were done using software **Yieldometer** as using the CAF or CYF tables would not have given the precision that is desired for this book.

**Yield rates needed to reach** net yield amount or net return

16.01% yield rate would deliver $1 million net yield in 25 years.

19.22% yield rate would deliver $2 million net yield in 25 years.

21.15% yield rate would deliver $3 million net yield in 25 years.

23.63% yield rate would deliver $5 million net yield in 25 years.

27.09% yield rate would deliver $10 million net yield in 25 years.

30.66% yield rate would deliver $20 million net yield in 25 years.

The yield rates needed to deliver corresponding amounts of net worth are as below. As you can see, the difference in yield rates required to reach the net target yield is minimal.

**Yield rates needed to reach the** net worth

15.90% yield rate would deliver $1 million net worth in 25 years.

19.16% yield rate would deliver $2 million net worth in 25 years.

21.11% yield rate would deliver $3 million net worth in 25 years.

23.61% yield rate would deliver $5 million net worth in 25 years.

27.08% yield rate would deliver $10 million net worth in 25 years.

30.65% yield rate would deliver $20 million net worth in 25 years.

## 15.7.2    Observations

### 15.7.2.1    Near-Exponential growth of wealth with the yield rate

In the above list, you can see the tremendous influence of yield rate on the net yield and net worth.

The influence on net worth is not linear like the influence of investment amount, and not fully exponential like the time period of investment, but it is near-exponential in which every percent increase is a lot more potent than the same increase just below it.

See chapter 6 for more information about the influence of yield rate on the results of an investment.

## 15.8 CALCULATING NET YIELD (NY) AND NET WORTH (NW) AS A MULTIPLE OF INITIAL INVESTMENT (CYF & CAF)

### 15.8.1 Example 15.8.1

1. Initial investment (P): $25,000.
2. Number of years (N): 25.
3. Yield rate (R): 20% p.a.
4. Tax rate: 0%.
5. Net yield (NY) as a multiple of the initial investment (CYF): xx?
6. Net worth (NW) as a multiple of the initial investment (CAF): xx?

Here, what we actually need to find out is the net CYF value. Net CYF is, by definition, the factor by which the investment needs to be multiplied in order to get the net yield.

In the CYF table, we follow the 25-year row and the 20% yield column, and at the intersection, we get the CYF value of 94.40.

That means, with this investment, we get a net yield that is 94.40 times the initial investment.

The corresponding net yield amount will be: $2,360,000 (= 94.40 x 25,000).

Similarly, in the CAF table, we follow the 25-year row and the 20% yield column, and at the intersection, we get the CAF value of 95.40.

If you are using only the CYF table and not the CAF table, you could also arrive at this CAF value by merely adding 1.00 to the CYF value as described at the beginning of this chapter in section 15.1.1.

That means, with this investment, we get a net worth that is 95.40 times the initial investment.

The corresponding net worth amount will be: $2,385,000 (= 95.40 x 25,000).

\* \* \* \*

# Chapter 16:

# Why you should aim for $10 or 100 Million instead of only 1 Million

In this chapter, we have made several investment matrixes for various combinations of initial investments, yield rates, and years needed to reach net worth varying from $0.1 million to $1,000 Billion.

## 16.1 TABLES WITH RESULTS OF INVESTMENT

See tables 16.1 to 16.5.

<u>Table 16.1</u> shows, for an investment of $10,000 and various yield rates, which amount it would grow to with the passing of years.

<u>Table 16.2</u> shows the same for an investment of $100,000.

You can see that all the values in table 16.2 are exactly 10x times higher than the values in table 16.1. In any given time period, the final amount reached is directly proportional to the amount invested.

<u>Table 16.3</u> shows, for an investment of $10,000 and various yield rates, how many years it would take to reach a targeted final amount or net worth (with zero tax).

<u>Tables 16.4</u> & <u>16.5</u> show the same for investment amounts of $0.1 million and $1 million, respectively.

These tables are fascinating, and to those who take a closer look, they reveal how immense wealth is built.

These tables also reveal all the inter-relationships between investment amount, time-period, yield rate, and growth rate.

If you take a closer look at these tables with a calculator in hand, you can see that everything that we have learned so far in this book is hidden in the values in these tables.

I would certainly recommend spending some time with these tables as the key to the millionaires- club is hidden in them.

## 16.2 HOW TO REACH $100 MILLION NET WORTH

In table 16.3, you can see that if you invest $10,000 against a 20% yield rate, it will multiply 10x times to reach $0.1 million in 12.6 years.

It will multiply 100x times to reach $1 million in 25.3 years.

This is exactly in line with what we had learned earlier, i.e., equal multiples of net worth will always take the exact same time. In this case of a 20% yield rate, it takes 12.6 years for a 10-fold increase, another 12.6 years for another 10-fold increase to 100x times the invested amount, and another 12.6 years to reach a total of 1,000x times the invested amount.

**In summary:**

We reach $0.1 million in 12.6 years.

We reach $1 million in another 12.6 years or a total of 25.3 years.

We reach $10 million in another 12.6 years or a total of 37.9 years.

We reach $100 million in another 12.6 years or a total of 50.5 years.

**Let us see what we earned in each period:**

$0.09 million in the first period of 12.6 years (= 100,000 – 10,000).

$0.9 million in the second period of 12.6 years (= 1M – 0.1M).

$9 million in the third period of 12.6 years (= 10M – 1M).

$90 million in the fourth period of 12.6 years (100M – 10M).

We can see that our earnings also increase by a factor of 10 in each period.

If we have only one period of 12.6 years available, we would like to skip the first 3 periods and embrace only the 4th period. This period alone will give us a return of $90 million, while the other 3 periods together will earn hardly 10 million.

## 16.3 HOW TO SKIP THE FIRST 3 SLOW PERIODS AND EARN $90 MILLION IN JUST ONE FAST PERIOD OF 12.6 YEARS?

The answer is simple: If we have $10 million available to invest, we can skip the low-yielding first, second, and third periods altogether. That way, we can earn $90 million in 12.6 years instead of only $0.09 million. That is an increase in earnings by a factor of 1,000, but also an increase in initial investment by a factor of 1,000 (10 thousand to 10 million).

## 16.4      WHAT IF WE DO NOT HAVE THE $10 MILLION TO INVEST

To earn $90 million in 12.6 years, we need to invest $10 million. That is one-ninth or 11.1 % of the return on investment (= 10/ 90).

With only a $10,000 investment, the investment-to-yield ratio will also be exactly the same, 11.1%.

The only difference is that we would invest an amount that is 1,000x times bigger than the original amount (= 10M/ 0.01M), and the return would also be 1000x times higher, but all in the same time span.

With a limited number of years in our lives to reach our target of millionairedom, we do not have 50.3 years to wait to have $100 million but want it in 12.6 years.

Moreover, if we can realize it this way, it is possible that we could also reach Billionairedom in the very same 50.3 years.

Therefore, it is worth scraping all the money available and making this investment.

### 16.4.1      Borrowing is an option

As we had analyzed in chapter 10, borrowing to invest can be an incredibly attractive option.

If we can borrow $10 million for 12.6 years at a 12% interest rate, the total cost to us in interest would be approximately $32 million. At the end of the investment period of 12.6 years, our net gain from this investment with a 20% yield rate would be $58 million (= 90 – 32).

If the borrowing is against a 14% interest rate instead of 12%, the borrowing cost would be $42 million, and our net gain $48 million (= 90 – 42).

If the borrowing is against a 10% interest rate instead of 12%, the borrowing cost would be $23 million, and our net gain $67 million (= 90 – 23).

## 16.5      WHAT IF WE HAVE JUST $1 MILLION TO INVEST INSTEAD OF $10 THOUSAND OR $10 MILLION

We have seen earlier in this chapter that at a 20% yield rate, the growth factor (CAF value) of an investment is 10x times in every 12.6 years.

With $1 million invested, we will hit the $10 million mark in the first 12.6 years and hit the $100 million mark in the second 12.6 years. It would take us a total of 25.3 years instead of the 50.6 years that it would have taken with only a $10,000 initial investment.

In effect, with this, we are merely skipping the first two periods of 12.6 years each by bringing in our own money to invest instead of waiting 25.3 years to earn it first.

See Table 16.5 for this and many other investment situations with an initial investment of $1 Million.

## 16.6 WHAT IF WE HAVE JUST $100 THOUSAND TO INVEST INSTEAD OF $10 THOUSAND OR $1 MILLION OR $10 MILLION

See Table 16.4 for various investment situations with an initial investment of $100,000.

See also Table 16.2 to see how this investment grows with years.

You can see that we saved the first period of 12.6 years and could reach the $100 million target in 37.9 years.

If we had a yield rate of 40% instead of 20%, we would have reached the target in 20.5 years, only a little more than half of the 37.9 years needed with a 20% yield rate.

## 16.7 INSIGHT

Maximize the amount of your investment, even by borrowing with low and affordable risk.

With a 25.9% yield rate, your investment will grow 10x times in 10 years, 100x times in 20 years, and 1,000x times in 30 years.

If you invest $10,000 today, in 20 years, you will have a $1 million net worth. Invest $1 million today and have $100 million in 20 years.

Time-distance for a 100-fold increase in your wealth from $1 million to destination $100 million is the same as the time-distance from $10,000 to destination $1 million. Therefore, always choose the highest achievable target and the maximum possible initial investment!

If you do not have money to invest, and the investment is a safe one, borrowing to invest can be your Ferrari on the highway to millionairedom. See chapter 10 for details about borrowing to invest.

Almost all super-wealthy individuals and companies have grown so big, mostly with other people's money. With only your own money from an average job, the chance of becoming a multi-millionaire is quite tiny.

| Investment Matrix for Net Worth in $ Millions | | | | | | | | | |
|---|---|---|---|---|---|---|---|---|---|
| Initial Investment, $ | | | 10,000 | | | | | | |

| Years | Yield Rate | | | | | | | | | |
|---|---|---|---|---|---|---|---|---|---|---|
| | 5% | 10% | 15% | 20% | 25% | 30% | 35% | 40% | 45% | 50% |
| | Net Worth in $ Millions | | | | | | | | | |
| 0 | 0.010 | 0.010 | 0.010 | 0.010 | 0.010 | 0.010 | 0.010 | 0.010 | 0.010 | 0.010 |
| 5 | 0.013 | 0.016 | 0.020 | 0.025 | 0.031 | 0.037 | 0.045 | 0.054 | 0.064 | 0.076 |
| 10 | 0.016 | 0.026 | 0.040 | 0.062 | 0.093 | 0.138 | 0.201 | 0.289 | 0.411 | 0.577 |
| 15 | 0.021 | 0.042 | 0.081 | 0.154 | 0.284 | 0.512 | 0.902 | 1.56 | 2.63 | 4.38 |
| 20 | 0.027 | 0.067 | 0.164 | 0.383 | 0.867 | 1.90 | 4.04 | 8.37 | 16.9 | 33.3 |
| 25 | 0.034 | 0.108 | 0.329 | 0.954 | 2.65 | 7.06 | 18.1 | 45.0 | 108 | 253 |
| 30 | 0.043 | 0.174 | 0.662 | 2.37 | 8.08 | 26.2 | 81.3 | 242 | 693 | 1,918 |
| 35 | 0.055 | 0.281 | 1.33 | 5.91 | 24.7 | 97.3 | 364 | 1,302 | 4,445 | 14,561 |
| 40 | 0.070 | 0.453 | 2.68 | 14.7 | 75.2 | 361 | 1,634 | 7,000 | 28,492 | 110,573 |
| 45 | 0.090 | 0.729 | 5.39 | 36.6 | 230 | 1,341 | 7,329 | 37,650 | 182,625 | 839,666 |
| 50 | 0.115 | 1.17 | 10.8 | 91.0 | 701 | 4,979 | 32,862 | 202,489 | 1,170,577 | 6,376,215 |
| 55 | 0.146 | 1.89 | 21.8 | 226 | 2,138 | 18,488 | 147,352 | | | |
| 60 | 0.187 | 3.04 | 43.8 | 563 | 6,525 | 68,644 | 660,733 | | | |
| 65 | 0.238 | 4.90 | 88.2 | 1,402 | 19,914 | 254,870 | | | | |
| 70 | 0.304 | 7.90 | 177 | 3,489 | 60,772 | 946,313 | | | | |
| 75 | 0.388 | 12.7 | 357 | 8,681 | 185,460 | | | | | |
| 80 | 0.496 | 20.5 | 718 | 21,602 | 565,980 | | | | | |
| 85 | 0.633 | 33.0 | 1,443 | 53,753 | | Values here are above $1,000 BILLION | | | | |
| 90 | 0.807 | 53.1 | 2,903 | 133,756 | | | | | | |
| 95 | 1.03 | 85.6 | 5,838 | 332,827 | | | | | | |
| 100 | 1.32 | 138 | 11,743 | 828,180 | | | | | | |

Table 16.1: Net worth **of an initial investment of** $10,000 **and zero tax for various time-periods and** yield rates. **All values are in** Millions of Dollars.

| | Investment Matrix for Net Worth in Millions $ | | | | | | | | | |
|---|---|---|---|---|---|---|---|---|---|---|
| Initial Investment, $ | | | 100,000 | | | | | | | |
| | Yield Rate | | | | | | | | | |
| Years | 5% | 10% | 15% | 20% | 25% | 30% | 35% | 40% | 45% | 50% |
| | Net Worth in $ Millions | | | | | | | | | |
| 0 | 0.100 | 0.100 | 0.100 | 0.100 | 0.100 | 0.100 | 0.100 | 0.100 | 0.100 | 0.100 |
| 5 | 0.128 | 0.161 | 0.201 | 0.249 | 0.305 | 0.371 | 0.448 | 0.538 | 0.641 | 0.759 |
| 10 | 0.163 | 0.259 | 0.405 | 0.619 | 0.931 | 1.379 | 2.011 | 2.893 | 4.108 | 5.767 |
| 15 | 0.208 | 0.418 | 0.814 | 1.541 | 2.842 | 5.119 | 9.016 | 15.56 | 26.33 | 43.79 |
| 20 | 0.265 | 0.673 | 1.637 | 3.834 | 8.674 | 19.00 | 40.43 | 83.67 | 168.8 | 332.5 |
| 25 | 0.339 | 1.083 | 3.292 | 9.540 | 26.47 | 70.56 | 181.3 | 450.0 | 1,082 | 2,525 |
| 30 | 0.432 | 1.745 | 6.621 | 23.74 | 80.78 | 262.0 | 812.9 | 2,420 | 6,935 | 19,175 |
| 35 | 0.552 | 2.810 | 13.32 | 59.07 | 246.5 | 972.8 | 3,645 | 13,016 | 44,451 | 145,611 |
| 40 | 0.704 | 4.526 | 26.79 | 147.0 | 752.3 | 3,612 | 16,344 | 70,004 | 284,918 | 1,105,733 |
| 45 | 0.899 | 7.289 | 53.88 | 365.7 | 2,296 | 13,411 | 73,286 | 376,497 | 1,826,249 | 8,396,662 |
| 50 | 1.147 | 11.74 | 108.4 | 910.0 | 7,006 | 49,793 | 328,616 | 2,024,892 | 11,705,773 | 63,762,150 |
| 55 | 1.464 | 18.91 | 218.0 | 2,264 | 21,382 | 184,878 | 1,473,524 | | | |
| 60 | 1.868 | 30.45 | 438.4 | 5,635 | 65,253 | 686,438 | 6,607,332 | | | |
| 65 | 2.384 | 49.04 | 881.8 | 14,021 | 199,136 | 2,548,695 | | | | |
| 70 | 3.043 | 78.97 | 1,774 | 34,889 | 607,716 | 9,463,127 | | | | |
| 75 | 3.883 | 127.2 | 3,567 | 86,815 | 1,854,603 | | | | | |
| 80 | 4.956 | 204.8 | 7,175 | 216,023 | 5,659,799 | Values here are above $1,000 BILLION | | | | |
| 85 | 6.325 | 329.9 | 14,432 | 537,534 | | | | | | |
| 90 | 8.073 | 531.3 | 29,027 | 1,337,557 | | All values in this table are 10x times the values in table for $10,000 investment | | | | |
| 95 | 10.30 | 855.7 | 58,384 | 3,328,269 | | | | | | |
| 100 | 13.15 | 1,378 | 117,431 | 8,281,797 | | | | | | |

Table 16.2: Net worth of an initial investment of $100,000 and zero tax for various time-periods and yield rates. All values are in Millions of Dollars.

| Investment Matrix for Time-period in Years | | | | | | | | | | | |
|---|---|---|---|---|---|---|---|---|---|---|---|
| **Initial Investment, $** | | | | 10,000 | | | | | | | |
| **Target Net Worth** | | **Yield Rate** | | | | | | | | | |
| Million or Billion | Million $ | 5% | 10% | 15% | 20% | 25% | 30% | 35% | 40% | 45% | 50% |
| | | Years needed | | | | | | | | | |
| 0.1 M | 0.1 | 47.2 | 24.2 | 16.5 | 12.6 | 10.3 | 8.8 | 7.7 | 6.8 | 6.2 | 5.7 |
| 1 M | 1 | 94.4 | 48.3 | 33.0 | 25.3 | 20.6 | 17.6 | 15.3 | 13.7 | 12.4 | 11.4 |
| 2 M | 2 | 108.6 | 55.6 | 37.9 | 29.1 | 23.7 | 20.2 | 17.7 | 15.7 | 14.3 | 13.1 |
| 5 M | 5 | 127.4 | 65.2 | 44.5 | 34.1 | 27.9 | 23.7 | 20.7 | 18.5 | 16.7 | 15.3 |
| 10 M | 10 | 141.6 | 72.5 | 49.4 | 37.9 | 31.0 | 26.3 | 23.0 | 20.5 | 18.6 | 17.0 |
| 20 M | 20 | 155.8 | 79.7 | 54.4 | 41.7 | 34.1 | 29.0 | 25.3 | 22.6 | 20.5 | 18.7 |
| 50 M | 50 | 174.6 | 89.4 | 60.9 | 46.7 | 38.2 | 32.5 | 28.4 | 25.3 | 22.9 | 21.0 |
| 100 M | 100 | 188.8 | 96.6 | 65.9 | 50.5 | 41.3 | 35.1 | 30.7 | 27.4 | 24.8 | 22.7 |
| 200 M | 200 | 203.0 | 103.9 | 70.9 | 54.3 | 44.4 | 37.7 | 33.0 | 29.4 | 26.7 | 24.4 |
| 500 M | 500 | 221.8 | 113.5 | 77.4 | 59.3 | 48.5 | 41.2 | 36.1 | 32.2 | 29.1 | 26.7 |
| 1 B | 1,000 | 236.0 | 120.8 | 82.4 | 63.1 | 51.6 | 43.9 | 38.4 | 34.2 | 31.0 | 28.4 |
| 2 B | 2,000 | 250.2 | 128.1 | 87.3 | 66.9 | 54.7 | 46.5 | 40.7 | 36.3 | 32.9 | 30.1 |
| 5 B | 5,000 | 269.0 | 137.7 | 93.9 | 72.0 | 58.8 | 50.0 | 43.7 | 39.0 | 35.3 | 32.4 |
| 10 B | 10,000 | 283.2 | 145.0 | 98.9 | 75.8 | 61.9 | 52.7 | 46.0 | 41.1 | 37.2 | 34.1 |
| 20 B | 20,000 | 297.4 | 152.2 | 103.8 | 79.6 | 65.0 | 55.3 | 48.3 | 43.1 | 39.0 | 35.8 |
| 50 B | 50,000 | 316.1 | 161.8 | 110.4 | 84.6 | 69.1 | 58.8 | 51.4 | 45.8 | 41.5 | 38.0 |
| 100 B | 100,000 | 330.4 | 169.1 | 115.3 | 88.4 | 72.2 | 61.4 | 53.7 | 47.9 | 43.4 | 39.8 |
| 200 B | 200,000 | 344.6 | 176.4 | 120.3 | 92.2 | 75.3 | 64.1 | 56.0 | 50.0 | 45.2 | 41.5 |
| 500 B | 500,000 | 363.3 | 186.0 | 126.8 | 97.2 | 79.4 | 67.6 | 59.1 | 52.7 | 47.7 | 43.7 |
| 1,000 B | 1,000,000 | 377.5 | 193.3 | 131.8 | 101.0 | 82.6 | 70.2 | 61.4 | 54.7 | 49.6 | 45.4 |

Table 16.3: **Number of years needed to reach a Targeted net worth of $0.1 Million to $1,000 Billion with an initial investment of $10,000 and zero tax.**

| Investment Matrix for Time-period in Years | | | | | | | | | | | |
|---|---|---|---|---|---|---|---|---|---|---|---|
| **Initial Investment, $** | | 100,000 | | | | | | | | | |
| **Target Net Worth** | | **Yield Rate** | | | | | | | | | |
| Million / Billion | Million $ | 5% | 10% | 15% | 20% | 25% | 30% | 35% | 40% | 45% | 50% |
| | | Years needed | | | | | | | | | |
| 0.1 M | 0.1 | 0.0 | 0.0 | 0.0 | 0.0 | 0.0 | 0.0 | 0.0 | 0.0 | 0.0 | 0.0 |
| 1 M | 1 | 47.2 | 24.2 | 16.5 | 12.6 | 10.3 | 8.8 | 7.7 | 6.8 | 6.2 | 5.7 |
| 2 M | 2 | 61.4 | 31.4 | 21.4 | 16.4 | 13.4 | 11.4 | 10.0 | 8.9 | 8.1 | 7.4 |
| 5 M | 5 | 80.2 | 41.0 | 28.0 | 21.5 | 17.5 | 14.9 | 13.0 | 11.6 | 10.5 | 9.6 |
| 10 M | 10 | 94.4 | 48.3 | 33.0 | 25.3 | 20.6 | 17.6 | 15.3 | 13.7 | 12.4 | 11.4 |
| 20 M | 20 | 108.6 | 55.6 | 37.9 | 29.1 | 23.7 | 20.2 | 17.7 | 15.7 | 14.3 | 13.1 |
| 50 M | 50 | 127.4 | 65.2 | 44.5 | 34.1 | 27.9 | 23.7 | 20.7 | 18.5 | 16.7 | 15.3 |
| 100 M | 100 | 141.6 | 72.5 | 49.4 | 37.9 | 31.0 | 26.3 | 23.0 | 20.5 | 18.6 | 17.0 |
| 200 M | 200 | 155.8 | 79.7 | 54.4 | 41.7 | 34.1 | 29.0 | 25.3 | 22.6 | 20.5 | 18.7 |
| 500 M | 500 | 174.6 | 89.4 | 60.9 | 46.7 | 38.2 | 32.5 | 28.4 | 25.3 | 22.9 | 21.0 |
| 1 B | 1,000 | 188.8 | 96.6 | 65.9 | 50.5 | 41.3 | 35.1 | 30.7 | 27.4 | 24.8 | 22.7 |
| 2 B | 2,000 | 203.0 | 103.9 | 70.9 | 54.3 | 44.4 | 37.7 | 33.0 | 29.4 | 26.7 | 24.4 |
| 5 B | 5,000 | 221.8 | 113.5 | 77.4 | 59.3 | 48.5 | 41.2 | 36.1 | 32.2 | 29.1 | 26.7 |
| 10 B | 10,000 | 236.0 | 120.8 | 82.4 | 63.1 | 51.6 | 43.9 | 38.4 | 34.2 | 31.0 | 28.4 |
| 20 B | 20,000 | 250.2 | 128.1 | 87.3 | 66.9 | 54.7 | 46.5 | 40.7 | 36.3 | 32.9 | 30.1 |
| 50 B | 50,000 | 269.0 | 137.7 | 93.9 | 72.0 | 58.8 | 50.0 | 43.7 | 39.0 | 35.3 | 32.4 |
| 100 B | 100,000 | 283.2 | 145.0 | 98.9 | 75.8 | 61.9 | 52.7 | 46.0 | 41.1 | 37.2 | 34.1 |
| 200 B | 200,000 | 297.4 | 152.2 | 103.8 | 79.6 | 65.0 | 55.3 | 48.3 | 43.1 | 39.0 | 35.8 |
| 500 B | 500,000 | 316.1 | 161.8 | 110.4 | 84.6 | 69.1 | 58.8 | 51.4 | 45.8 | 41.5 | 38.0 |
| 1,000 B | 1,000,000 | 330.4 | 169.1 | 115.3 | 88.4 | 72.2 | 61.4 | 53.7 | 47.9 | 43.4 | 39.8 |

Table 16.4: Number of years needed to reach a Targeted net worth of $0.1 Million to $1,000 Billion with an initial investment of $100,000 and zero tax.

| Investment Matrix for Time-period in Years | | | | | | | | | | | |
|---|---|---|---|---|---|---|---|---|---|---|---|
| Initial Investment, $ | | 1,000,000 | | | | | | | | | |
| Target Net Worth | | Yield Rate | | | | | | | | | |
| Million / Billion | Million $ | 5% | 10% | 15% | 20% | 25% | 30% | 35% | 40% | 45% | 50% |
| | | Years needed | | | | | | | | | |
| 0.1 M | 0.1 | Not Applicable | | | | | | | | | |
| 1 M | 1 | 0.0 | 0.0 | 0.0 | 0.0 | 0.0 | 0.0 | 0.0 | 0.0 | 0.0 | 0.0 |
| 2 M | 2 | 14.2 | 7.3 | 5.0 | 3.8 | 3.1 | 2.6 | 2.3 | 2.1 | 1.9 | 1.7 |
| 5 M | 5 | 33.0 | 16.9 | 11.5 | 8.8 | 7.2 | 6.1 | 5.4 | 4.8 | 4.3 | 4.0 |
| 10 M | 10 | 47.2 | 24.2 | 16.5 | 12.6 | 10.3 | 8.8 | 7.7 | 6.8 | 6.2 | 5.7 |
| 20 M | 20 | 61.4 | 31.4 | 21.4 | 16.4 | 13.4 | 11.4 | 10.0 | 8.9 | 8.1 | 7.4 |
| 50 M | 50 | 80.2 | 41.0 | 28.0 | 21.5 | 17.5 | 14.9 | 13.0 | 11.6 | 10.5 | 9.6 |
| 100 M | 100 | 94.4 | 48.3 | 33.0 | 25.3 | 20.6 | 17.6 | 15.3 | 13.7 | 12.4 | 11.4 |
| 200 M | 200 | 108.6 | 55.6 | 37.9 | 29.1 | 23.7 | 20.2 | 17.7 | 15.7 | 14.3 | 13.1 |
| 500 M | 500 | 127.4 | 65.2 | 44.5 | 34.1 | 27.9 | 23.7 | 20.7 | 18.5 | 16.7 | 15.3 |
| 1 B | 1,000 | 141.6 | 72.5 | 49.4 | 37.9 | 31.0 | 26.3 | 23.0 | 20.5 | 18.6 | 17.0 |
| 2 B | 2,000 | 155.8 | 79.7 | 54.4 | 41.7 | 34.1 | 29.0 | 25.3 | 22.6 | 20.5 | 18.7 |
| 5 B | 5,000 | 174.6 | 89.4 | 60.9 | 46.7 | 38.2 | 32.5 | 28.4 | 25.3 | 22.9 | 21.0 |
| 10 B | 10,000 | 188.8 | 96.6 | 65.9 | 50.5 | 41.3 | 35.1 | 30.7 | 27.4 | 24.8 | 22.7 |
| 20 B | 20,000 | 203.0 | 103.9 | 70.9 | 54.3 | 44.4 | 37.7 | 33.0 | 29.4 | 26.7 | 24.4 |
| 50 B | 50,000 | 221.8 | 113.5 | 77.4 | 59.3 | 48.5 | 41.2 | 36.1 | 32.2 | 29.1 | 26.7 |
| 100 B | 100,000 | 236.0 | 120.8 | 82.4 | 63.1 | 51.6 | 43.9 | 38.4 | 34.2 | 31.0 | 28.4 |
| 200 B | 200,000 | 250.2 | 128.1 | 87.3 | 66.9 | 54.7 | 46.5 | 40.7 | 36.3 | 32.9 | 30.1 |
| 500 B | 500,000 | 269.0 | 137.7 | 93.9 | 72.0 | 58.8 | 50.0 | 43.7 | 39.0 | 35.3 | 32.4 |
| 1,000 B | 1,000,000 | 283.2 | 145.0 | 98.9 | 75.8 | 61.9 | 52.7 | 46.0 | 41.1 | 37.2 | 34.1 |

Table 16.5: Number of years needed to reach a Targeted net worth of $0.1 Million to $1,000 Billion with an initial investment of $1,000,000 and zero tax.

# Chapter 17:

# An Uncomfortable Truth: How mathematical laws will always make the Wealth-Gap between Rich & Poor grow exponentially

## 17.1    INTRODUCTION

*The natural flow of Water is always from top to bottom. It is the law of Physics.*

*The natural flow of Wealth is always from bottom to top. It is the law of Mathematics.*

The explanation for this characteristic of the flow of wealth lies, in part, also veiled in Tables 16.1 to 16.5 in chapter 16.

The mathematical reasoning given in the previous chapter 16 in support of the call to maximize initial investment in order to maximize wealth goes equally to explain why wealthy people are able to amass wealth at a much faster rate than ordinary people. Reason number 1 in the list below, i.e., mathematical laws, is the fundamental cause of good things like maximizing wealth through maximizing investment, but at the same time also of bad things like the widening wealth gap between rich and poor.

## 17.2    REASONS FOR THE WIDENING WEALTH-GAP

1. **The unbreakable laws of mathematics. This is by far the most important reason.**

2. **Leveraging through borrowing to invest is available only to the rich, not the poor.**

3. **High investment thresholds for some high-yielding investments, which make them accessible only to the rich, not the poor.**

4. **Unaffordability of any financial risk inherently reduces the chances for the poor to generate the maximum return from investments.**

5. **Wealth makes it possible to create own businesses or products, which generally form the class of investments with the highest return.**

6. **Wealthy people have more possibilities to avoid or reduce tax and tax drag than the poor.**

## 17.3      EXAMPLE 17.3

We will use an example again to demonstrate the points easily.

Let us assume that you are an average young person with an average job and average salary and a saving of $10,000 in a Fixed Deposit in a bank.

Your neighbor and friend, Joe, is also young and has an average job and average income, just like you. Even your houses and cars are identical. The only difference is that he had received an inheritance and therefore has a bank balance of $1 million.

Your other assets, like the house, are worth $2 million each. So, your total asset is $2.01 million and that of Joe $3.0 million.

In dollar terms, the difference in net worth is $0.99 million (= 3.00 – 2.01).

In this example, let us leave the value of the house out of consideration because the value of the house is not being utilized by either of you for investment or building wealth. Each of you is investing only the bank balance you have.

Let us consider the various investment options and see how the net worth develops further over the years.

**The starting position is this:**

Your net worth: **$0.01 million (10,000).**

Joe's net worth: **$1.0 million.**

**Wealth Gap** or the difference in net worth between you and Joe: **$0.99 million** (= 1.00 – 0.01).

The ratio of Joe's net worth to yours: **100x** (= 1.00/ 0.01).

Let us assume that you both decided to get on the highway to riches and decided to use the stock market as your Ferrari to reach the millions fast.

You invest your bank balance of **$10,000,** and Joe does the same with his **$1 million.** You both expect an average yield rate of **20%** p.a. We assume that tax does not play a role.

As can be seen in Tables 16.3 & 16.5, and as discussed in chapter 16, at a **20%** yield rate, your net worth would grow **10x times** every **12.6 years.**

**That means your net worth would grow as follows:**

10x times in 12.6 years (rounded off).

100x times in 25.3 years.

1,000x times in 37.9 years.

10,000x times in 50.5 years.

## 17.3.1    First period of 12.6 years

In this period, your investment has grown 10x times from $10,000 to $100,000.

In this period, Joe's investment has grown 10x times from $1.0 million to $10 million.

Increase of your net worth in this period: $90,000 (= 100,000 – 10,000).

Increase of Joe's net worth in this period: $9 million (= 10 – 1).

The ratio of Joe's earnings to yours: 100x (= 9.00/ 0.09).

Additional wealth Gap or difference in earnings between you and Joe that arose in the first period: $8.91 million (= 9.0 – 0.09).

Total Wealth Gap between you and Joe at the end of the first period: $9.90 million (= 8.91 + 0.99). This is 10x times more than the wealth-gap at the start.

## 17.3.2    Second period of 12.6 years (25.3 years from the start)

In this period, your investment has grown 10x times from $0.10 million to $1,00 million.

In this period, Joe's investment has grown 10x times from $10 million to $100 million.

Increase of your net worth in this period: $0.9 million (= 1.00 – 0.10).

Increase of Joe's net worth in this period: $90 million (= 100 – 10).

Ratio of Joe's earnings to yours: 100x (= 90.0/ 0.9).

Additional wealth Gap or difference in earnings between you and Joe that arose in the second period: $89.1 million (= 90.0 – 0.9).

Total Wealth Gap between you and Joe at the end of the second period: $99 million (= 89.10 + 9.90). This is 10x times more than the wealth gap at the end of the first period and 100x times more than the wealth gap at the start.

### 17.3.3    Third period of 12.6 years (37.9 years from the start)

In this period, your investment has grown 10x times from $1 million to $10 million.

In this period, Joe's investment has grown 10x times from $100 million to $1,000 million.

Increase of your net worth in this period: $9 million (= 10 – 1).

Increase of Joe's net worth in this period: $900 million (= 1,000 – 100).

The ratio of Joe's earnings to yours: 100x (= 900/ 9).

Additional wealth Gap or difference in earnings between you and Joe that arose in the third period: $891 million (= 900 – 9).

Total Wealth Gap between you and Joe at the end of the third period: $990 million (= 891 + 99). This is 10x times more than the wealth gap at the end of the second period, 100x times more than the wealth gap at the end of the first period, and 1,000x times more than the wealth gap at the start.

### 17.3.4    Fourth period of 12.6 years (50.5 years from the start)

In this period, your investment has grown 10x times from $10 million to $100 million.

In this period, Joe's investment has grown 10x times from $1,000 million to $10,000 million.

Increase of your net worth in this period: $90 million (= 100 – 10).

Increase of Joe's net worth in this period: $9,000 million (= 10,000 – 1,000).

The ratio of Joe's earnings to yours: 100x (= 9,000/ 90).

Additional wealth Gap or difference in earnings between you and Joe that arose in the fourth period: $8,910 million (= 9,000 – 90).

Total Wealth Gap between you and Joe at the end of the fourth period: $9,900 million (= 8,910 + 990).

This wealth-gap is 10x times more than the wealth gap at the end of the third period, 100x times more than the wealth gap at the end of the second period, 1,000x times more than the wealth gap at the end of the first period, and 10,000x times more than the wealth gap at start.

### 17.3.5    Let us summarize the results

After 50.5 years, you and your neighbor Joe may be just retiring. Let us compare the start positions of your wealth with the end positions.

## You

At the start, you had a net worth of **$0.01** million.

Your total earnings in 50.5 years: **$99.99 million** (= 0.09 + 0.90 + 9.00 + 90.00).

Now you have a net worth of **$100** million (= 99.99 + 0.01).

In 50.5 years, your net worth increased by a factor of **10,000x** (= 100/ 0.01).

## Joe

At the start, Joe had a net worth of **$1.00** million.

Joe's total earnings in 50.5 years: **$9,999 million** (= 9 + 90 + 900 + 9,000).

Now Joe has a net worth of **$10,000** million (= 9,999 + 1).

In 50.5 years, Joe's net worth increased by a factor of **10,000x** (= 10,000/ 1).

### 17.3.6    Comparing you and Joe

### Earnings

Your net worth increased by **$99.99 million** in 50.5 years, while Joe's increased by **$9,999 million**.

**The ratio of INCREASE of net worth, or ratio of EARNINGS between you and Joe: 100x** (= 9,999/ 99.99).

Joe's EARNINGS, or INCREASE of net worth, is 100x times more than that of yours, while both yourself and Joe had invested in the same program and got the same yield rate of 20%.

**The only reason for this 100x times difference in earning is that Joe had 100x times more money to invest than you had.**

### Net worth

The ratio of the net worth of you and Joe, in the beginning, was **100x** (= 1.0/ 0.01).

The ratio of net worth after 50.5 years is **100x** (= 10,00/ 100).

**The ratio of net worth remains constant though the net worth of you and Joe has increased by a factor of 10,000x.**

### The Wealth Gap between you and Joe

The wealth gap between you and Joe at the start: **$0.99 million** (= 1.00 – 0.01).

The wealth gap between you and Joe after 50.5 years: **$9,900 million** (= 10,000 – 100).

The ratio of Wealth Gap at the finish to Wealth Gap at the start: **10,000x** (= 9,900/0.99).

That means the wealth gap increased by a factor of 10,000x, which is equal to the factor by which also the net worth increased.

Looking at the individual periods of 12.6 years, we can see that **every time the net worth grew by a factor of 10x, the wealth gap also grew by a factor of 10x.**

Wealth Gap at the start: $0.99 million.

Wealth Gap at the end of the first period: $9.9 million.

Wealth Gap at the end of the second period: $99 million.

Wealth Gap at the end of the third period: $990 million.

Wealth Gap at the end of the fourth period: $9,900 million.

**The above example and observations lead us to formulate two laws of mathematics that will always apply to investments and the growth of wealth.**

## 17.4 MATHEMATICAL LAWS PERTAINING TO INVESTMENT AND GROWTH OF WEALTH

From example 17.3, we can derive two fundamental and mathematically absolute laws that govern the growth of wealth.

### 17.4.1 Mathematical Law 1 related to the growth of wealth

#### 17.4.1.1 Law 1, Equation

**For any two investments with equal yield rates and duration:**

RATIO of final amounts = RATIO of initial investments

##### 17.4.1.1.1 Example 17.4.1.1.1

In our example of the investment with you and Joe, the **ratio of investment** amounts at the start was **100x**. After an increase of **10,000x** times in value in 50.5 years, the ratio of the final amounts was still **100x** though the **wealth gap** increased **10,000x** times.

A pair of investments of **$2 million** and **$8 million** have a ratio of **4x**. If they grow **50x** times in value in any number of years, the respective final amounts will be **$100** million and $400 million. The ratio of these final amounts is also 4x as it was initially.

However, the wealth gap of $6 million at the start would grow 50x times too and would become $300 million, which also corresponds exactly with the difference in the final amounts (= 400 – 100).

## 17.4.1.2    Law 1, Statement

Law 1 can also be reframed into the following statement:

If everything else is equal, the *rate of increase of wealth*, expressed in dollars per year, will be directly proportional to the amount of wealth one already possesses.

### 17.4.1.2.1    Example 17.4.1.2.1

Take a look at Table 16.5. With a 25% yield rate, it takes only 3.1 years to double your investment.

That means, if you have $1 million to invest, you could double it and get an additional $1 million in 3.1 years.

But if your name is Warren Buffett and you have $1 Billion to invest, you could double it too and get an additional $1 Billion in 3.1 years.

You will be making 1,000x more dollars per year in this case because you have 1,000x times more money to invest. The ratio is linear.

This is simply the main reason why rich people get super-rich much faster.

This is also one of the reasons why borrowing money for investment can be a good idea, as discussed in chapter 10.

## 17.4.2    Mathematical Law 2 related to the growth of wealth

## 17.4.2.1    Law 2, Equations

For any two investments with equal yield rates and duration:

## Equation 1

Final Wealth Gap in dollars = Initial Wealth Gap in dollars x Growth Factor of Investment.

**Equation 2** (it is a derivative of Equation 1)

**The ratio of Final Wealth Gap in dollars to Initial Wealth Gap in dollars = Growth Factor of Initial Investment**

Applying these equations to investments by yourself and Joe, we get the following:

**Equation 1**

Final wealth gap $9,900 = Initial wealth gap $0.99 x Growth Factor 10,000.

**Equation 2**

Final wealth gap $9,900 / Initial wealth gap $0.99 = Growth Factor 10,000.

### 17.4.2.1.1    Example 17.4.2.1.1

Two investments of $1 million and $5 million have a wealth gap of $4 million. If those investments grow 6-fold in the course of time to $6 million and $30 million respectively, the original wealth gap of $4 million would also increase 6-fold to $24 million, which is also exactly the difference between the final amounts of $30 million and $6 million.

If two investments with a gap of $3 million between them increase 10-fold in value, the wealth gap will also increase 10-fold to $30 million irrespective of the amounts or time-period of investment. It could be a pair of investments of $2 million & $5 million or a pair of $50 million & $53 million.

### 17.4.2.2    Law 2, Statement

Law 2 can also be framed into the following statements.

### Statement 1

**For any two investments with equal yield rates, the Wealth Gap in dollars will grow at the same rate as the growth rate of the investments.**

### Statement 2

**If everything else is equal, rich people will get richer, in dollar terms, at an *exponentially faster rate* than people who are less wealthy.**

Mathematics is irrefutable, and so are these two laws, formulas, and statements.

## 17.5        INSIGHT

Law 2 above and the example of investments by yourself and Joe show that if you have more money to invest than someone else, the wealth gap will increase over time at exactly the same rate as the growth rate of the investments.

As the growth rate of the invested amount is exponential with time, thus speeding up ever more quickly as we have seen in the previous chapters, **the growth of the wealth gap is also exponential with time, speeding up ever more quickly**.

**A relatively small difference in wealth can become a vast gulf in the course of time, as we have seen in the example of yourself and Joe.**

The ratio of net worth will remain constant while the gap in net worth will keep on widening.

It is like the pair of numbers 2 & 6 increasing a 1,000-fold in value to 2,000 & 6,000, respectively. The ratio remains constant at 3, but the value gap increased from 4 to 4,000. If it increases another 10-fold to 20,000 & 60,000 respectively, the value gap would also increase 10-fold to 40,000.

This is what happens in building wealth. The wealth of richer people with more money available to invest, and their wealth-gap with poorer people, will always grow exponentially with time at an ever-increasing speed unless there is external intervention like progressive wealth tax and progressive income tax.

**This exponential growth of the wealth gap between the rich and poor is inevitable because the growth occurs according to the irrefutable laws of mathematics as explained above.**

## 17.6        REASON 1: MATHEMATICAL LAWS RELATED TO GROWTH OF WEALTH

The two mathematical laws pertaining to investment and growth of wealth, as discussed in sections 17.1 to 17.5 above, are re-stated here for ease of reference.

**Law 1: If everything else is equal, the _rate of increase of wealth_, expressed in dollars per year, will be directly proportional to the amount of wealth one already possesses.**

**Law 2: If everything else is equal, rich people will get richer, in dollar terms, at an _exponentially faster rate_ than people who are less wealthy.**

From the discussions in sections 17.1 to 17.5, it is clear that these two mathematical laws constitute the main reason for the wealth gap between rich and poor to grow exponentially.

## 17.7      REASON 2: LEVERAGING THROUGH BORROWING FOR INVESTMENT

Please refer to chapter 10 for details and analysis of investment with borrowed money.

Borrowing to invest is one of the most universally applied methods to build immense wealth. Jeff Bezos, Bill Gates, and most other multibillionaires got there using other people's money for the most part.

Borrowing to invest in any substantial way, however, is feasible only to those who have enough wealth to offer as collateral to secure the loan.

Let us use an example to illustrate.

### 17.7.1     Example 17.7.1

Please refer to example 17-1 at the beginning of this chapter, in which you invested $10,000 at a 20% yield rate and your neighbor Joe invested $1 million in the same scheme. After 50.5 years, your investments had grown by a factor of 10,000x, leaving you with a net worth of $100 million and Joe with a net worth of $10 Billion.

The ratio of Joe's net worth with yours remained constant at 100x, but the wealth gap between you and Joe had grown by a factor of 10,000x, from $0.99 million at the start to $9,900 million in the end.

Let us assume that, foreseeing such a gigantic wealth gap with your neighbor in the future and not wanting to live like a mouse next to an elephant, you decide to borrow and invest in order to keep the wealth gap as small as possible.

### 17.7.2     Borrowing $1.5 million against 12% interest rate to invest for 20% yield rate

Based on the value of your house worth $2 million, you could borrow up to $1.5 million against an interest rate of 12%. You do the math and decide to borrow $1.5 million and invest that whole amount in the project.

Let us look at your investment results at the end of 50.5 years.

Your investment: $1.5 Million (to keep it simple, we ignore your own $10,000).

Your final amount or Gross worth: $15.0 Billion (= 10,000x times 1.5 Million).

Total payment to the lending bank including interest and return of principal: $470 million (rounded off).

**Your net worth: $14.53 Billion** (= 15.00 – 0.47).

Your net worth would be $4.53 Billion more than that of Joe, and that too, all with borrowed money!

### 17.7.3 Borrowing $1.5 million against 19% interest rate to invest for 20% yield rate

Let us look at the results if you had been declared "crazy" by your family and friends because you decided to borrow at an interest rate of 19% to invest at a yield rate of only 20%.

Your final amount or Gross worth: $15.0 Billion (= 10,000x times 1.5 Million).

Total payment to the lending bank, including interest and principal: $9.83 Billion (rounded off).

Your net worth: $5.17 Billion.

### 17.7.4 Borrowing $1.5 million against 17% interest rate to invest for 20% yield rate

Total payment to the lending bank, including interest and principal: $4.18 Billion (rounded off).

Your net worth: $10.82 Billion.

Even with borrowed money and a differential yield rate of only 3% (= 20% - 17%), your net worth would be higher than Joe's $10 Billion.

### 17.7.5 Conclusion

In the above examples, borrowing $1.5 million was feasible to you only because you had an asset worth $2 million to offer as collateral.

This possibility that is available only to wealthy people to create extra wealth with borrowed money increases the wealth gap between the rich and the poor.

### 17.8 REASON 3: SOME INVESTMENTS WITH HIGHER YIELD RATES ARE AVAILABLE ONLY TO LARGE INVESTORS

There are many investment opportunities that have high thresholds and therefore are available or feasible only to investors with a substantial amount of money to invest. Examples are:

- Venture capital investment.
- Seed capital investment in promising new ventures.
- Participation in Private Equity funds or Hedge funds.
- Take-over of companies.

For example, we can see from the CYF table in Appendix-B that if you can find an investment opportunity with a 30% yield rate instead of 20% for a 30-year period, your earnings will be higher by a factor of 11x.

## 17.9    REASON 4: WEALTHY PEOPLE CAN AFFORD MORE RISK AND GO FOR HIGHER YIELD

If you are wealthy and have money earmarked for investment, and you are not dependent on that money for a living, you can afford more risk and would be more inclined to invest in opportunities with higher yield rates though with higher risk.

As a result, wealthy people will be able to earn more than the average investor. This applies to all forms of direct and indirect investments, including investments through stock markets.

## 17.10    REASON 5: WITH WEALTH, YOU WILL BE ABLE TO CREATE YOUR OWN PRODUCT OR BUSINESS GENERATING HIGHER RETURN

Creating your own business is at the top of all lists as the ultimate way to create immense wealth. See chapter 21 for details. Investing in businesses of other people, directly or indirectly through stock markets, is only the second-best option to create immense wealth.

Almost all the hyper-rich people on earth have got there by creating their own businesses.

This option is feasible only to those who have the needed capital to invest in new ventures or could get other people's money to invest in their new businesses.

## 17.11    REASON 6: WEALTHY PEOPLE HAVE MORE POSSIBILITIES TO AVOID OR REDUCE TAX AND TAX DRAG THAN THE LESS WEALTHY

This is also a major factor contributing to the exponential growth of the wealth gap between rich and poor.

Tax is a wealth pump that also serves to reverse a part of the natural flow of wealth from the bottom to the top caused by the convoluted laws of mathematics, as seen in sections 17.1 to 17.6 above. But trying to avoid or minimize tax is probably the most widely practiced sport in the world.

With 200 countries and 200 tax systems in the world, and taxes ranging from zero percent to more than 50% of your income, you can play with the tax like playing chess on a chessboard with 200 squares spread over the entire surface of the globe.

Most of the people, especially the low-income salaried employees, are glued to one square on the chessboard, the square with their country's name on it. But that does not apply to very wealthy individuals and corporations. They can move around the globe and settle on places where tax is the lowest. Only the rich have this financial and logistical capability to seek and settle for the lowest tax rates in the world.

a separate volume, Volume II, of this series of books and titled "**Tax Drag, de Dragon that eats up your wealth.**"

However, to give you a taste of Tax Drag, a fragment from that book in the form of an example is reproduced below.

It is sure to shock you! And enlighten you! And shake you awaken!

## 18.2    EXAMPLE 18.2 TO SHOW THE EFFECT OF TAX DRAG

Let us consider the financial situation of a well-settled young couple, Tom and Lisa, in their early thirties and living in New York City. He is a doctor, and she is a nurse. Both have been working for some years, and they have a combined saving of **$1 million**. They are planning to get children, and as part of that planning, they have decided that Lisa would stop working altogether and devote full time to bringing up the children.

### 18.2.1    The financial plan

But not wanting to be wholly dependent financially on her husband in the long run, Lisa made the following arrangement with Tom.

- Tom would have the entire saving of **$1 million** solely in his name, and he would invest it in a tax-exempt scheme generating an average **yield of 20%** per year.

- Of the 20% tax-exempt yield that Tom receives every year, he would transfer **30% of it to Lisa's own account**. After all, Tom does not have to pay any tax on this income, and he sees giving 30% of it to Lisa only as an equivalent tax.

- Lisa would invest whatever amount she gets annually from Tom in the same investment scheme that Tom is also participating in, and she would also get the same 20% tax-exempt yield every year.

- Both Tom and Lisa would participate in the investment scheme on a compounding basis. That means they would not withdraw any of the yield amounts but would reinvest their total annual yield in the same scheme in order to build up retirement capital.

- Tom's regular income from his job is high enough to have a comfortable living for the entire family. So, their investment can quietly grow as they get older.

Is this now a fair deal? What do you think? Tom gets their combined saving of $1 million in his own name, and Lisa gets nothing. Worse still, Lisa gets only 30% of the yield that Tom receives every year, and Tom gets to keep 70%. It looks like a very unfair deal because Lisa seems to be at an enormous disadvantage here!

## 18.2.2     35 years later

Fast forward to 35 years from now when Tom and Lisa are at retirement age. They go to the bank, and the bank manager tells them that in one account, there is $98.1 million, and in the other, $492.568 million. For convenience, let us round it off to 98 and 493 million.

Both Tom and Lisa are happily surprised because the final amounts in both their accounts far exceed their expectations. They had invested only $1 million 35 years ago, and now they have together $591 million!

Tom and Lisa assume, naturally, that Tom's account has delivered $493 million and Lisa's 98 million. After all, Tom started out with $1 million and Lisa with nothing, and moreover, Tom kept 70% of the yearly yield, and all that Lisa got was 30%. No one likes to ask dumb questions, especially not a doctor and nurse, and especially not about such an obvious matter. When you know something with absolute certainty, and there is no trace of doubt about it, there is no need to ask. So, they do not ask the bank manager for further details, also because they are intoxicated with joy at the unexpectedly high amounts each of them has.

## 18.2.3     The confusion

Then the bank manager turns to Lisa and asks her what she is planning to do with the nearly half a Billion dollar she has. Utter confusion follows. Lisa tries to correct the bank manager by telling him that she has only 98 million and that it should be to her husband that he should be asking about the 493 million he has.

This is the moment that the bank manager realizes that Tom and Lisa are confused. So, he tells them that Lisa has the bigger amount of $493 million and Tom the smaller amount of 98 million. Tom and Lisa are convinced that the bank has made a mistake and interchanged their accounts. No verbal explanation by the bank manager would convince them that Lisa has a net worth 5 times bigger than that of Tom. So, the bank manager prints out the calculation sheet and explains how the amounts have been built up over time. (The table and further details are covered in Volume II of the book series).

## 18.3     EXPLANATION

From the year-by-year build-up of the individual accounts of Tom and Lisa, it becomes clear that the bank manager did not interchange their accounts. It is also clear that, at the end of 35 years, Lisa has indeed a net worth that is 5 times bigger than that of Tom.

You can also see that, though Tom started out with $1 million and Lisa with NULL capital, Lisa's net worth had already exceeded that of Tom at the end of 14 years.

### 18.3.1 The reason why Tom ended up with only one-sixth of the total net worth

There is only one reason, and that is the effect of "**Tax Drag**" on Tom.

Though Tom was not paying any tax as such, he was paying 30% of his yield to Lisa. In that respect, from Tom's perspective, we can consider Lisa to be the equivalent of the tax collector!

Tom was, in effect, paying the equivalent of 30% tax on his annual income of 100%.

Lisa, the receiver of that 30%, was paying no tax at all on her annual income of 30%.

It is only this 30% tax that made their fortunes reverse despite Lisa's start with zero capital and Tom's start with a million dollar!

This is what Tax Drag does. An enormous drag on your speed to reach your target wealth. It is like you climbing an escalator that is coming down in order to get to an upper floor, a devilish escalator with Artificial Intelligence that also increases its speed every time you climb a step!

### 18.4 RELEASE OF VOLUME 2 OF THIS BOOK-SERIES AND THE CALCULATION SOFTWARE YIELDOMETER

Volume II of the book series **Highway to Riches** that covers tax drag in detail and analyzes methods to reduce tax drag considerably, though already written, is expected to be published within three months of publication of this first volume of the series.

So also, the Software program, titled **YIELDOMETER**, that can calculate all the results of investment, including tax and tax drag, though already developed and was used by me for calculations involving this series of books, will also be released within three months of publication of this first volume of the series. See chapter 22 for more details about the software program.

If you wish to be notified when Volume II of the book series or the software program becomes available for purchase, please send a note per email to info@dekkaan.com or jacobsebastian@highwaytoriches.info. If you just mention NOTIFY ME or anything similar, that will suffice.

* * * *

# Chapter 19:

# A Fool's Paradise: How Mathematics make Tax Evaders end up with less wealth instead of more

On the face of it, no one on earth wants to lose money, be it 40%, 10%, or even 5% of what we have earned the hard way. But the tax is an inevitable part of life, and we will all lose some money to tax.

To make it worse, earlier in this book, in section 3.4 and chapter 18, we have seen the devastating effect of tax drag on our wealth in the long term. In an active wealth-building lifespan of 50 years, if we honestly and blindly pay income tax without intelligent planning, we may end up with only 5% or 10% or 15% of the potential net worth we might have accumulated without the burden of tax drag.

## 19.1 LOSS DUE TO TAX DRAG: YOU CAN REDUCE IT SUBSTANTIALLY THROUGH SOUND PLANNING

But such huge losses due to tax drag are only for those who lack the knowledge and the financial and mathematical insights to do proper tax planning.

Plan wealth-building wisely and in such a way that the tax burden is reduced to the minimum by investing in the tax-exempt or tax-deferred arenas instead of the arena of cascading income tax.

We have seen earlier in section 3.4 and chapter 18 that, for long-term investments, a deferred tax, which is generally applied as long-term capital gains tax in most countries, can reduce the tax drag enormously.

That is mainly because, with capital gains tax, the tax drag is generally equal to the nominal tax. Moreover, various deductions and cost indexing are typically allowed in most countries, which can further suppress the total tax burden to a level considerably below the nominal tax rate.

All in all, by choosing the investment venues wisely and by availing of tax exemptions, tax deferrals, cost deductions, and especially avoiding recurring income tax on your investments, you can reduce the tax drag to a much lower proportion than it would be with annually payable income tax.

That means, with proper planning and choice, you can considerably reduce the tax burden instead of blindly evading it.

A tax evader might still think that, by evading even the reduced tax burden as sketched here, he might still be saving a lot of money by not paying any tax at all.

But he is likely to be utterly wrong most of the time, ending up losing a lot of money ultimately.

## 19.2    YOU CAN EARN A LOT MORE WITH WHITE MONEY THAN WITH BLACK MONEY

### 19.2.1    Your vault for storing wealth

In any wealth-building program, it is only the net after-tax earnings that ultimately count.

Let us imagine that your wealth-building program is a vault with a front door and a back door, and you use it to store all your wealth in stacks of dollars.

The front door is exclusively for the inflow of wealth. It is here that all the pre-tax earnings flow in.

The back door is exclusively for the outflow of wealth that is due to tax.

The difference between the inflow and outflow is your net earnings.

### 19.2.2    How do tax evaders lose money?

It is on the earning side that tax evaders are generally blind and really lose money, sometimes a lot of money. In fact, the majority of them may be losing more money on the front side, the earning side, than they save on the backside, the tax side.

Tax evaders are driving through the financial landscape of life with their eyes constantly on the rear-view mirror and therefore miss to see, and benefit from, the opportunities that lie ahead of them.

The sum of the loss of earnings on the front side and the gain on the tax-evading backside is probably negative for most tax evaders.

Black money is hidden money. If you hide that money in a back-room bank account somewhere, the **interest that you can earn on it may be negligible**.

Even if you invest that hidden money somewhere, **the return you can get on such investments will always be lower than what is possible with white money**, assuming that the tax evader is not engaged in criminal activities for higher returns.

We have seen throughout this book, especially in chapter 7, that a 1% or 2% higher or lower rate of return can make an enormous difference in the height of your net worth in the long term. It is the power of the **Differential yield rate** that tax evaders gravely miscalculate and lose money ultimately.

See chapter 7 to learn more about Differential yield rates.

Another way that tax evaders lose heavily, but unnoticed, is the convoluted way that money managers in tax havens calculate their **service charge or management fee or commission.** Often it comes down to something like this: "we will earn 12% return for you; our service charge will be 3%; you will get 9% net per year".

Hardly anyone knows that the Differential yield rate is at play here and that the **value of the 3% differential yield rate can even be more than the value of the 9% nominal yield rate that the tax evader is offered.**

Over a **40-year period**, the value of the **3% Differential yield rate** that lies between the nominal yield rates of 9% and 12% is **2x times the value of the 9%** nominal yield rate. Its value is equivalent to a nominal yield rate of **10.9%.**

Let us see, through an example, how tax evaders lose money ultimately.

## 19.3     EXAMPLE

Charles has **$1 million** to invest and is keen on saving tax on any return he can get. He can invest it openly in his own country for a 15% p.a. gross return. His tax bracket is 30%. With a time horizon of **40 years** till retirement age in mind, he is keen not to lose any money on tax.

He could also have invested it openly in his own country also on a tax-deferred basis with the exact 15% yield and 30% tax rate. But 30% tax? No way for Charles! He is enamored with having it all tax-free. He is tax phobic.

He somehow manages to move the money off to some tax haven where it goes into an obscure account and finally to an investment at 12% p.a., 3% management fee (hiding fee, actually), leaving Charles with a net yield of 9% p.a., tax-free! And Charles is content! He saved 30% tax on $1 million for 40 years! No small feat, to his pride!

Charles' net, tax-free earning is 9.0% p.a. after deducting the management fee, which he believes is equal to **3% yield** annually (= 12 – 9).

Over 40 years, by the time Charles retires, this investment would yield him a net return of **$30** million.

But if he had invested it openly in his own country at a **15% yield** rate and **30% deferred tax**, his net return would have been **$187** million!

Even if the tax were not deferred, but the annual tax was due, his net return would have been **$53** million.

In fact, what Charles did was converting white money into black money with the sole aim of saving tax and ended up having only **$30** million difficult-to-spend black money instead of **$187** million clean white money! Brilliant idiocy!

The ones who profited most were his money managers in the tax haven. In 40 years, the total return at a **12%** nominal yield rate was **$92 million**. They gave **$30 million** to Charles, representing a 9% nominal yield rate, and secretly pocketed **$60 million** representing the **3% Differential yield rate** lying between 9% & 12%. Charles thinks the money managers earned only $2.3 million, corresponding to a 3% nominal yield rate.

Please see chapter 7 to learn more about Differential yield rates.

Charles cannot even spend his $30 million with peace of mind because it is hidden money, black money! If he gets caught, he might very well lose half, if not more, of his $30 million and risks jail term. They are certainly not the proper ingredients for a comfortable and relaxed retired life.

## 19.4 TAX EVASION WILL ULTIMATELY COST YOU MORE MONEY THAN THE TAX YOU SAVE

From the above example, we can see that evading tax cost Charles $187 million of clean white money in return for $30 million black money.

If he had invested in his own country at a 15% yield rate and 30% capital gains tax, the inflow to his vault would have been $267 million, outflow $80 million, leaving $187 million clean white money inside.

Charles is not the only loser with his tax phobia. The government of his country also lost $80 million in tax income.

In his zest for saving on tax, he guarded only the backdoor of his vault and left the front door unattended, letting the money managers loot him.

This is probably the case with most tax evaders! All are probably losers in the game!

It sounds and feels triumphant to them to have the full 100% instead of only 70%, no matter 100% or 70% of what. 100% is always bigger than 70% to them! Charles got 100% of $30 million at the cost of missing 70% of $267 million.

Those who educate themselves and do the math will never become tax evaders. Who wants to lose money, pay dearly for help in losing it, convert such a depleted sum of money from white money to hard-to-spend black money and, at the end of the day, risk losing it all and going to prison!

\* \* \* \*

# Chapter 20:

# Dig the Gold Mine: Investing in Foreign stock markets instead of Domestic can generate many-fold higher returns

## 20.1    INTRODUCTION

This chapter looks at the performance of some of the major stock indices in the world and compares some of them with each other after converting the performance values to the same currency.

The aim of the comparison is to help us determine which country or which stock market would give us the highest rate of return. A typical question we will answer is this: **is it better for someone living in London to invest in the stock market in the USA than investing in the domestic stock market in London?**

The performance values are Annualized Rate of Return (ROR) and are calculated here as CAGR in order to eliminate any ambiguity.

**CAGR** stands for Compound Annual Growth Rate. It is the **Annualized Rate of Return (ROR).**

The CAGR was calculated from the respective index values.

**A 2% p.a. dividend yield rate** is **assumed across the board and added to the index growth rate.** All CAGR values in this chapter are therefore 2% higher than the respective index growth rates.

**The essence of the topic covered is that by investing in a different stock market and currency than your domestic market and currency, sometimes huge gains can be realized, especially if your native currency is losing value with respect to other major currencies.**

**The total return that can be realized by migrating your stock market investments can sometimes be many folds or hundreds of percentages higher than the return that can be realized in your domestic market.**

In this chapter, we will look at the results of stock markets of **USA, UK, Germany, and India.**

**Then we will look at two scenarios:**

1. What would be the return if the residents of these countries invested in the stock market in USA instead of in their domestic market. The results are compared in the domestic currency of the investor, i.e., GBP, Euro, and Indian Rupee, respectively.

2. What would be the return if the residents of USA invested in the stock market in these countries instead of in USA itself. The results are compared in USD.

## 20.2  FORMULA FOR CONVERSION OF CURRENCIES FOR STOCK MARKET RETURNS

In order to compare the performance of stock markets with each other, the performance values need to be in the same currencies. If the native currencies of two stock markets are different, for example, GBP for FTSE 100 and USD for Dow Jones, their performance values need to be converted to the other currency first to enable comparison.

The conversion is complicated by the fact that the relative values of the currencies may have changed over time, one devaluating with respect to the other, and that change needs to be incorporated in the conversion.

### 20.2.1  Example 20.2.1

The average rate of return for FTSE 100 in the 10-year period 2010-2019 was 5.8% p.a., measured in GBP (see list of results below).

The average rate of return for the three major US stocks in the same 10-year period 2010-2019 was 14.2% p.a., measured in USD (see list of results below).

UK residents also could have achieved the same 14.2% p.a. return if they had invested in USA. For that, their GBP had to be converted to USD first. When the investment period in USA was finished, 10 years later in our example, the USD had to be converted back to GBP for repatriation to the UK.

If the exchange rate between GBP and USD had remained the same in this 10-year period, the result would have also been 14.2% p.a. measured in GBP.

But in this case, between 1 January 2010 and 1 January 2020, GBP had devalued with respect to USD. The value changed from 0.619 GBP per USD to 0.765 GBP per USD, a total decline of 24% in the value of GBP. This works out to be an annualized CAGR of 2.14% p.a. for the conversion rate of USD to GBP.

That means, when you converted USD back to GBP at the end of the investment period, in addition to the 14.2% return you had already got in the stock market in USA, you also got 2.14% p.a. more GBP over and above the 14.2% you had already got.

Therefore, your 14.2% p.a. gain and principal in USD increases by an additional 2.14% when converted back to GBP. The 114.2%, when increased by 2.14%, becomes 116.64% (= 1.142 x 1.0214).

Therefore, the effective rate of return in GBP becomes 16.64%. (= 1.142 x 1.0214 – 1). It is rounded off to 16.6% p.a. in the list below.

## 20.2.2    Notional formula for conversion of currency

The notional formula for converting the ROR for investment in a foreign currency to ROR in domestic currency can be expressed as below:

**ROR in domestic currency = (ROR in foreign market in foreign currency) x (CAGR for change in the exchange rate).**

**ROR in GBP = (ROR in US stock market in USD) x (CAGR for change in the exchange rate in GBP to USD).**

Or

**ROR in GBP = (ROR in US stock market in USD) / (CAGR for change in the exchange rate in USD to GBP).**

## 20.2.3    Mathematical formula for conversion of currency

The mathematical formula for converting the ROR for investment in a foreign currency to ROR in domestic currency can be expressed as below:

**ROR in domestic currency = {(1 + ROR in foreign market in foreign currency) x (1+ CAGR for change in exchange rate of domestic currency to foreign currency) – 1}.**

Or

**ROR in domestic currency = {(1 + ROR in foreign market in foreign currency) / (1+ CAGR for change in exchange rate of foreign currency to domestic currency) – 1}.**

Whichever of the above two formulas you use, the results will be the same.

**Beware**: There is a common mistake that many people make! The ROR in the stock market and the percentage change in exchange rates between the two currencies cannot simply be added together arithmetically. They must be multiplied or divided mathematically according to any one of the two mathematical formulas above.

Note: The calculation of CAGR and the ROR is rather complex. The easiest way to calculate both is to use a suitable software program.

The software program **Yieldometer**, also developed by the author of this book, has all these features also built-in. You feed in the basic raw numbers, and the program will show you all the results instantly.

Please see chapter 22 for more information about Yieldometer.

## 20.3     THE RESULTS

The 2000-20009 period in the list below covers three major downturns caused by the dot com bubble, the 9/11 attacks on the World Trade Center, and the global financial crisis that started in 2008.

The term **CAGR** used here is the abbreviation for **Compound Annual Growth Rate**. It is the annual growth rate in percentage, which, when compounded annually over the period considered, would yield the total results achieved in that period.

### 20.3.1     USA

**NASDAQ Composite Index**

CAGR for **10-year**-period, 1990-1999: 26.5% p.a.

CAGR for **10-year**-period, 2000-2009: (-) 3.7% p.a.

CAGR for **10-year**-period, 2010-2019: 16.8% p.a.

CAGR for **30-year**-period, 1990-2019: 12.5% p.a.

**Dow Jones 30 Industrial Average Index**

CAGR for **10-year**-period, 1990-1999: 17.5% p.a.

CAGR for **10-year**-period, 2000-2009: 2.9% p.a.

CAGR for **10-year**-period, 2010-2019: 12.5% p.a.

CAGR for **30-year**-period, 1990-2019: 10.1% p.a.

**S&P 500 Index**

CAGR for **10-year**-period, 1990-1999: 17.2% p.a.

CAGR for **10-year**-period, 2000-2009: (-) 0.6% p.a.

CAGR for **10-year**-period, 2010-2019: 13.2% p.a.

CAGR for **30-year**-period, 1990-2019: 9.8% p.a.

## Average of NASDAQ, DOW JONES, and S&P 500

CAGR for 10-year-period, 1990-1999: 20.4% p.a.

CAGR for 10-year-period, 2000-2009: (-) 0.5% p.a.

CAGR for 10-year-period, 2010-2019: 14.2% p.a.

CAGR for 30-year-period, 1990-2019: 10.8% p.a.

## 20.3.2    UK

### FTSE 100 (London): results for UK investors with GBP investing in FTSE 100

### Values are the original results based on British Pound (GBP)

CAGR for 10-year-period, 1990-1999: 13.4% p.a. in GBP.

CAGR for 10-year-period, 2000-2009: (-) 0.7% p.a. in GBP.

CAGR for 10-year-period, 2010-2019: 5.8% p.a. in GBP.

CAGR for 30-year-period, 1990-2019: 6.0% p.a. in GBP.

## 20.3.3    India

### BSE Sensex (Bombay Stock Exchange, India).

### Values are the original results based on Indian Rupee (INR)

CAGR for 10-year-period, 1990-1999: 22.5% p.a. in INR.

CAGR for 10-year-period, 2000-2009: 15.5% p.a. in INR.

CAGR for 10-year-period, 2010-2019: 11.0% p.a. in INR.

CAGR for 30-year-period, 1990-2019: 16.3% p.a. in INR.

## 20.3.4    Germany

### DAX 30 (Germany)

### Values are based on EURO (EUR)

CAGR for 10-year-period, 1990-1999: 16.1% p.a. in EUR.

CAGR for 10-year-period, 2000-2009: 0.0% p.a. in EUR.

CAGR for 10-year-period, 2010-2019: 11.2% p.a. in EUR.

CAGR for 30-year-period, 1990-2019: 8.9% p.a. in EUR.

## 20.3.5     Japan

**NIKKEI 225 Index (Japan)**

CAGR for the 10-year-period 2010-2019 was 10.4% p.a. in Japanese Yen (JPY).

CAGR for 10-year-period 2010-2019 was 8.6% p.a. in USD. Japanese Yen had lost value against USD in this period at a CAGR of (-)1.66% p.a.

## 20.4     COMPARING STOCK MARKET PERFORMANCE UK-USA

### 20.4.1     UK and USA Stock market performance in GBP

#### 20.4.1.1     FTSE 100 (London): results for UK investors with GBP investing in FTSE 100

**Values are the original results based on British Pound (GBP)**

CAGR for 10-year-period, 1990-1999: 13.4% p.a. in GBP.

CAGR for 10-year-period, 2000-2009: (-) 0.7% p.a. in GBP.

CAGR for 10-year-period, 2010-2019: 5.8% p.a. in GBP.

CAGR for 30-year-period, 1990-2019: 6.0% p.a. in GBP.

#### 20.4.1.2     US stock market average of NASDAQ, DOW JONES, and S&P 500, in GBP: results for UK investors with GBP investing in USA

**Values below are based on British Pound (GBP)**

If you are a UK-based investor investing in the US stock market, this would be your final results in GBP after exchange to USD and back to GBP. Exchange costs are not considered.

Your GBP was first converted to USD at the start of investment and converted back to GBP at the end of investment using the real-time exchange rates. The difference in exchange rates between the two conversions can affect the final results positively or negatively.

CAGR for 10-year-period, 1990-1999: 20.5% p.a. in GBP.

CAGR for 10-year-period, 2000-2009: (-) 0.4% p.a. in GBP.

CAGR for 10-year-period, 2010-2019: 16.6% p.a. in GBP.

CAGR for 30-year-period, 1990-2019: 11.7% p.a. in GBP.

## 20.4.2 UK and USA Stock market performance in USD

### 20.4.2.1 US stock market average of NASDAQ, DOW JONES, and S&P 500, in USD: Original results for US investors with USD investing in USA

CAGR for 10-year-period, 1990-1999: 20.4% p.a. in USD.

CAGR for 10-year-period, 2000-2009: (-) 0.5% p.a. in USD.

CAGR for 10-year-period, 2010-2019: 14.2% p.a. in USD.

CAGR for 30-year-period, 1990-2019: 10.8% p.a. in USD.

### 20.4.2.2 FTSE 100 (London): Results for US investors with USD investing in FTSE 100

## Values below are based on USD

If you are a USA-based investor investing in FTSE, this would be your results in USD after exchange to GBP and back to USD. Exchange costs are not considered.

Your USD was first converted to GBP at the start of investment and converted back to USD at the end of investment using the real-time exchange rates. The difference in exchange rates between the two conversions can affect the final results positively or negatively.

CAGR for 10-year-period, 1990-1999: 13.3% p.a. in USD.

CAGR for 10-year-period, 2000-2009: (-) 0.9% p.a. in USD.

CAGR for 10-year-period, 2010-2019: 3.6% p.a. in USD.

CAGR for 30-year-period, 1990-2019: 5.2% p.a. in USD.

### 20.4.3 Comparing UK and USA stock markets for the 10-year period 2010-2019

The average Rate of Return of NASDAQ, Dow Jones, and S&P 500 together for this period was 14.2% p.a.

The average Rate of Return of FTSE 100 for this period in US Dollar terms was 3.6% p.a. It was 5.8% p.a. in terms of GBP. This difference is caused by the depreciation of GBP with respect to USD. The CAGR for depreciation in this period was 2.14% p.a.

#### 20.4.3.1 US investors investing in UK

With a ROR of 14.2% p.a., the US stock market performed considerably better than the UK stock market with its 3.6% p.a., all measured in USD.

**If US residents had invested in the stock market in UK instead of in USA, they would have made huge losses in this period**. The total return in the 10-year period would have been only 42% instead of 277%. The total return would have been only 15% (= 42/ 277) of the total return in USA. The loss in total return would have been 85% (= 100 − 15).

The ratio of total return on investing in USA to investing in UK: 6.6x times, Loss (= 277/ 42). The loss comes from the decrease of ROR from 14.2% to 3.6% p.a. in USD.

#### 20.4.3.2 UK investors investing in USA

**Conversely, if UK investors had invested in the US stock market instead of in UK itself, they would have profited hugely**. Their ROR would have been 16.6% p.a. instead of 5.8% p.a. they got in the UK stock market, all measured in GBP.

The total return in the 10-year period would have been 364% instead of only 76%. The total return would have been 480% (= 364/ 76) of the total return they would have got in the UK stock market. The total return upon investing in UK itself would have been only 21% (= 76/ 364) of total return upon investing in USA. The loss in total return if invested in UK itself would have been 79% (= 100 - 21), measured in GBP.

The ratio of total return on investing in USA to investing in UK: 4.8x times, Gain (= 364/ 76). The gain comes from the increase of ROR from 5.8% to 16.6% p.a., in GBP.

### 20.4.4 Comparing UK and US stock markets for the 30-year period 1990-2019

The average Rate of Return of NASDAQ, Dow Jones, and S&P 500 together for this period was 10.8% p.a.

The average Rate of Return of FTSE 100 for this period in US Dollar terms was 5.2% p.a. It was 6.0% p.a. in terms of GBP. This difference is caused by the depreciation of GBP with respect to USD. The CAGR for depreciation in this period was 0.78% p.a.

### 20.4.4.1    US investors investing in UK

With a ROR of 10.8% p.a., the US stock market performed considerably better than the UK stock market with its 5.2% p.a., all measured in USD.

**If US residents had invested in the stock market in UK instead of in USA, they would have made huge losses in this period.** The total return in the 30-year period would have been only 358% instead of 2,070%. The total return would have been only 17% (= 358/ 2070) of the total return in USA. The loss in total return would have been 83% (= 100 – 17).

The ratio of total return on investing in USA to investing in UK: 5.8x times, Loss (= 2070/ 358). The loss comes from the decrease of ROR from 10.8% to 5.2% p.a. in USD.

### 20.4.4.2    UK investors investing in USA

**Conversely, if UK investors had invested in the US stock market instead of in UK itself, they would have profited hugely.** Their ROR would have been 11.7% p.a. instead of 6.0% p.a. they got in the UK stock market, all measured in GBP.

The total return in the 30-year period would have been 2,660% instead of only 474%. The total return would have been 560% (= 2660/ 474) of the total return they would have got in the UK stock market. The total return upon investing in UK itself would have been only 18% (= 474/ 2660) of total return upon investing in USA. The loss in total return if invested in UK itself would have been 82% (= 100 - 18), measured in GBP.

The ratio of total return on investing in USA to investing in UK: 5.6x times, Gain (= 2660/ 474). The gain comes from the increase of ROR from 6.0% to 11.7% p.a., in GBP.

### 20.4.5    Comparison of Return between NASDAQ and FTSE 100 indices for the 30-year period 1990-2019

12.5% p.a. rate of return for a 30-year period, as has been the case with Nasdaq Composite Index, amounts to a total return of 33.2x times the investment.

6.0% p.a. rate of return for a 30-year period, as has been the case with FTSE 100 Index, amounts to a total return of 4.7x times the investment.

That means Nasdaq returns 33.2x times the investment to its investor, and FTSE 100 returns 4.7x times the investment to its investor.

The ratio of nominal return between Nasdaq and FTSE 100 in the 30-year period is 7.0 (= 33.2/ 4.7).

In other words, if investors in Nasdaq got a total return of USD 7.00 for every USD 10 invested, FTSE 100 investors got a total return of only GBP 1.00 for every GBP 10 invested.

### 20.4.6    Conclusions from UK-USA comparison

By comparison, this shows that the Stock market in London performed remarkably lower than the stock markets in USA in the past 30 years.

Over and above this lower performance also came the additional losses due to the loss of value of GBP with respect to USD. This has further worsened the performance of FTSE when measured in USD.

Important: **For people residing in USA, it would have resulted in significant losses if they had invested in the stock market in London instead of the stock market in USA**. The FTSE 100 index grew much slower than all US indices. Additional losses would have been incurred due to the loss of value of GBP with respect to USD during all the periods considered. This is because when you reconvert GBP back to USD, you would also get a lower amount of USD due to the reduced value of GBP.

Important: **Conversely, this also means that for people living in the UK, it is a lot more attractive for them to invest in the US stock market than in London. In addition to the much higher performance of US stocks, they would also gain from the depreciation of GBP with respect to USD.**

### 20.5    COMPARING STOCK MARKET PERFORMANCE INDIA-USA

### 20.5.1    Indian and USA Stock market performance in INR

### 20.5.1.1    BSE Sensex (Bombay Stock Exchange, India)

**Values are the original results based on Indian Rupee (INR)**

CAGR for 10-year-period, 1990-1999: 22.5% p.a. in INR.

CAGR for 10-year-period, 2000-2009: 15.5% p.a. in INR.

CAGR for 10-year-period, 2010-2019: 11.0% p.a. in INR.

CAGR for 30-year-period, 1990-2019: 16.3% p.a. in INR.

**20.5.1.2    US stock market average of NASDAQ, DOW JONES, and S&P 500, in INR: Results for Indian investors with INR investing in USA**

## Values below are based on Indian Rupee (INR)

If you are an India-based investor investing in US stock market, this would be your final results in INR after exchange to USD and back to INR. Exchange costs are not considered.

Your INR was first converted to USD at the start of investment and converted back to INR at the end of investment using the real-time exchange rates. The difference in exchange rates between the two conversions can affect the final results positively or negatively.

CAGR for 10-year-period, 1990-1999: 32.3% p.a. in INR.

CAGR for 10-year-period, 2000-2009: (-) 0.4% p.a. in INR.

CAGR for 10-year-period, 2010-2019: 19.4% p.a. in INR.

CAGR for 30-year-period, 1990-2019: 16.1% p.a. in INR.

## 20.5.2    Indian and USA Stock market performance in USD

**20.5.2.1    US stock market average of NASDAQ, DOW JONES, and S&P 500, in USD: Original results for US investors with USD investing in USA**

CAGR for 10-year-period, 1990-1999: 20.4% p.a. in USD.

CAGR for 10-year-period, 2000-2009: (-) 0.5% p.a. in USD.

CAGR for 10-year-period, 2010-2019: 14.2% p.a. in USD.

CAGR for 30-year-period, 1990-2019: 10.8% p.a. in USD.

**20.5.2.2    BSE Sensex (Bombay Stock Exchange, India): Results for US investors with USD investing in BSE Sensex.**

## Values below are based on USD

If you are a USA-based investor investing in BSE Sensex, this would be your results in USD after exchange to INR and back to USD. Exchange costs are not considered.

Your USD was first converted to INR at the start of investment and converted back to USD at the end of investment using the real-time exchange rates. The difference in exchange rates between the two conversions can affect the final results positively or negatively.

CAGR for 10-year-period, 1990-1999: 11.5% p.a. in USD.

CAGR for 10-year-period, 2000-2009: 15.3% p.a. in USD.

CAGR for 10-year-period, 2010-2019: 6.2% p.a. in USD.

CAGR for 30-year-period, 1990-2019: 11.0% p.a. in USD.

### 20.5.3     Comparing Indian and US stock markets for the 10-year period 2010-2019

The average Rate of Return of NASDAQ, Dow Jones, and S&P 500 together for this period was 14.2% p.a.

The average Rate of Return of BSE Sensex for this period in US Dollar terms was 6.2% p.a. It was 11.0% p.a. in terms of Indian Rupee. This difference is caused by the depreciation of INR with respect to USD. The CAGR for depreciation in this period was 4.53% p.a.

#### 20.5.3.1     US investors investing in India

With a ROR of 14.2% p.a., the US stock market performed considerably better than the Indian stock market with its 6.2% p.a., all measured in USD.

**If US residents had invested in the stock market in India instead of in USA, they would have made huge** losses **in this period**. The total return in the 10-year period would have been only 83% instead of 277%. The total return would have been only 30% of the total return in USA. The loss in total return would have been 70%.

The ratio of total return on investing in USA to investing in India: 3.34x times, Loss (= 277/ 83). The loss comes from the decrease of ROR from 14.2% to 6.2% p.a. in USD.

#### 20.5.3.2     Indian investors investing in USA

**Conversely, if Indians had invested in the US stock market instead of in India, they would have** profited **hugely**. Their ROR would have been 19.4% p.a. instead of the 11.0% p.a. they got in the Indian stock market, all measured in INR.

The total return in the 10-year period would have been 489% instead of only 184%. The total return would have been 2.66x times (= 489/ 184) of the total return they would have got in the Indian stock market. The total return upon investing in India itself would have been only 38% (= 184/ 489) of total return upon investing in USA.

The loss in total return if invested in India itself would have been 62% (= 100 - 38), measured in INR.

The ratio of total return on investing in USA to investing in India: 2.66x times, Gain (= 489/ 184). The gain comes from the increase of ROR from 11.0% to 19.4% p.a. in INR.

### 20.5.4    Comparing Indian and US stock markets for the 10-year period 2000-2009

As a result of the dot com bubble of 2000, the 9/11 attacks of 2001, and the global financial crisis that started in 2008, the performance of the stock markets in this period is markedly different than the 10-year period before and after this.

The average Rate of Return of NASDAQ, Dow Jones, and S&P 500 together for this period was (-) 0.5% p.a. (negative).

The average Rate of Return of BSE Sensex for this period in US Dollar terms was 15.3% p.a. It was 15.5% p.a. in terms of Indian Rupee. This small difference is caused by the depreciation of INR with respect to USD. The CAGR for depreciation in this period was only 0.15% p.a.

#### 20.5.4.1    US investors investing in India

With ROR of (-) 0.5% p.a., the US stock market performed dismally compared to the Indian stock market with its 15.3% p.a., all measured in USD.

**If US investors had invested in the stock market in India instead of in USA, they would have made huge** gains **in this period**. The total return in the 10-year period would have been 315% instead of (-) 5%, negative. Instead of exiting the 10-year period with only 95% of your investment left in your account, you could have closed the period with 415% in your account.

The ratio of your net worth on investing in India to investing in USA: 4.37x times, Gain (= 415/ 95). The gain comes from the increase of ROR from (-) 0.5% to 15.3% p.a., in USD.

#### 20.5.4.2    Indian investors investing in USA

**Conversely, if Indians had invested in the US stock market instead of in India, they would have made huge** losses. Their ROR would have been (-) 0.5% p.a. instead of 15.5% p.a. they got in the Indian stock market, all measured in INR.

The total return in the 10-year period would have been (-) 5.0% instead of 322%. The net worth would have been 22.5% (= 95/ 422) of the net worth they would have got in the Indian stock market. The net worth upon investing in India itself would have been 444% (= 422/ 95) of the net worth upon investing in USA. The gain in net worth if invested in India itself would have been 344% (= 444 - 100), measured in INR.

The ratio of net worth upon investing in USA to investing in India: 0.225x times, Loss (= 95/ 422). The loss comes from the decrease of ROR from 15.5% to (-) 0.5% p.a., in INR.

### 20.5.5    Comparing Indian and US stock markets for the 10-year period 1990-1999

The average Rate of Return of NASDAQ, Dow Jones, and S&P 500 together for this period was 20.4% p.a.

The average Rate of Return of BSE Sensex for this period in US Dollar terms was 11.5% p.a. It was 22.5% p.a. in terms of Indian Rupee. This difference is caused by the depreciation of INR with respect to USD. The CAGR for depreciation in this period was 9.91% p.a.

#### 20.5.5.1    US investors investing in India

With a ROR of 20.4% p.a., the US stock market performed considerably better than the Indian stock market with its 11.5% p.a., all measured in USD.

**If US residents had invested in the stock market in India instead of in USA, they would have made huge losses in this period**. The total return in the 10-year period would have been only 197% instead of 540%. The total return would have been only 36.5% of the total return in USA. The loss in total return would have been 63.5%.

The ratio of total return on investing in USA to investing in India: 2.74x times, Loss (= 540/ 197). The loss comes from the decrease of ROR from 20.4% to 11.5% p.a. in USD.

#### 20.5.5.2    Indian investors investing in USA

**Conversely, if Indians had invested in the US stock market instead of in India, they would have profited hugely.** Their ROR would have been 32.3% p.a. instead of 22.5% p.a. they got in the Indian stock market, all measured in INR.

The total return in the 10-year period would have been 1,543% instead of only 661%. The total return would have been 233% (= 1543/ 661) of the total return they would have got in the Indian stock market. The total return upon investing in India itself would have been only 43% (= 661/ 1543) of total return upon investing in USA. The loss in total return if invested in India itself would have been 57% (= 100-43), measured in INR.

The ratio of total return on investing in USA to investing in India: 2.33x times, Gain (= 1543/ 661). The gain comes from the increase of ROR from 22.5% to 32.3% p.a. in INR.

### 20.5.6    Conclusions from India-USA comparison

## 20.5.6.1 Decade 2000-2009

In the 10-year period 2000-2009, the decade of financial catastrophe for the world and USA in particular, the stock market in India performed remarkably higher than the stock markets in USA. The stock market in USA had negative growth of average (-) 0.5% p.a. in this period while the Indian stock market achieved a ROR of 15.3% p.a., all measured in USD.

In this decade, it would have fetched huge gains for US investors who had invested in the Indian stock market. Instead of booking a loss of (-) 5% of the invested capital in the US stock market, they would have got a total return **of** 315% in India, all measured in USD.

However, with the dot com collapse in 2000, the 9/11 attacks in 2001, and the financial meltdown of 2008, the decade 2000-2009 must be considered as an exceptional one for the stock market of USA.

## 20.5.6.2 Decades 1990-1999 and 2010-2019

In the 10-year periods 1990-1999 and 2010-2019, the stock market in India performed remarkably lower than the stock markets in USA. That is the case when measured in USD and INR.

A part of this poor performance of the Indian stock market compared to the US market is caused by the erosion of the value of INR with respect to USD.

Important: **For people residing in USA, it would have resulted in significant losses if they had invested in the stock market in India instead of the stock market in USA.**

Though the BSE Sensex index, in INR, grew nominally at a comparable rate to that of the US stock indices, the depreciation of INR with respect to USD ate away much of the gains when US investors converted their INR back to USD.

Important: **Conversely, this also means that for people living in India, it was a lot more attractive for them to invest in the US stock market than in India**. Aside from the comparable performance of the stock markets, they would have gained from the depreciation of INR with respect to USD.

Measured in INR, the ratio of total return from investing in the US stock market to total return from investing in the Indian stock market would have been 2.33x times for the decade 1990-1999 and 2.66x times for the decade 2010-2019.

## 20.6 COMPARING STOCK MARKET PERFORMANCE GERMANY-USA

## 20.6.1 German and USA Stock market performance in EURO

### 20.6.1.1 DAX 30 (Germany): Results for German investors with EURO investing in DAX 30

**Values are the original results based on EURO (EUR)**

CAGR for 10-year-period, 1990-1999: 16.1% p.a. in EUR.

CAGR for 10-year-period, 2000-2009: 0.0% p.a. in EUR.

CAGR for 10-year-period, 2010-2019: 11.2% p.a. in EUR.

CAGR for 30-year-period, 1990-2019: 8.9% p.a. in EUR.

### 20.6.1.2 US stock market average of NASDAQ, DOW JONES, and S&P 500, in EURO: Results for German investors with EUR investing in USA

**Values below are based on EURO (EUR)**

If you are a Germany-based investor investing in US stock market, this would be your final results in EUR after exchange to USD and back to EUR. Exchange costs are not considered.

Your EUR was first converted to USD at the start of investment and converted back to EUR at the end of investment using the real-time exchange rates. The difference in exchange rates between the two conversions can affect the final results positively or negatively.

CAGR for 10-year-period, 1990-1999: 23.1% p.a. in EUR.

CAGR for 10-year-period, 2000-2009: (-) 4.0% p.a. in EUR.

CAGR for 10-year-period, 2010-2019: 16.8% p.a. in EUR.

CAGR for 30-year-period, 1990-2019: 11.1% p.a. in EUR.

## 20.6.2 German and USA stock market performance in USD

### 20.6.2.1 US stock market average of NASDAQ, DOW JONES, and S&P 500, in USD: Original results for US investors with USD investing in USA

CAGR for 10-year-period, 1990-1999: 20.4% p.a. in USD.

CAGR for 10-year-period, 2000-2009: (-) 0.5% p.a. in USD.

CAGR for 10-year-period, 2010-2019: 14.2% p.a. in USD.

CAGR for 30-year-period, 1990-2019: 10.8% p.a. in USD.

### 20.6.2.2 DAX 30 (Germany): Results for USA investors with USD investing in DAX 30

### Values below are based on USD

If you are a USA-based investor investing in DAX 30, this would be your results in USD after exchange to EUR and back to USD. Exchange costs are not considered.

Your USD was first converted to EUR at the start of investment and converted back to USD at the end of investment using the real-time exchange rates. The difference in exchange rates between the two conversions can affect the final results positively or negatively.

CAGR for 10-year-period, 1990-1999: 13.6% p.a. in USD.

CAGR for 10-year-period, 2000-2009: 3.6% p.a. in USD.

CAGR for 10-year-period, 2010-2019: 8.8% p.a. in USD.

CAGR for 30-year-period, 1990-2019: 8.6% p.a. in USD.

### 20.6.3 Conclusions from GERMANY-USA comparison

The pattern is the same as for the UK stock market in that the performance of DAX was lower than that of the stock market in USA except for the period 2000-2009.

But the performance gap with the US market was considerably smaller than the performance gap between UK and US stock exchanges.

### Period 1990-1999:

The growth rate of DAX in USD was CAGR 13.6% p.a. against 20.4% p.a. average for US stock exchanges. Total return in this period in the US market would have been 540% against 258% in Germany. The ratio of total return in USA to total return in Germany is 2.1 (= 540/ 258).

### Period 2000-2009:

Growth rate of DAX in USD was CAGR 3.6% p.a. against (-) 0.5% p.a. average for US stock exchanges. Total return in this period in the US market would have been (-) 5.0% against 42% in Germany. The ratio of net worth in USA to net worth in Germany is 0.67 (= 95/ 142).

**Period 2010-2019:**

The growth rate of DAX in USD was CAGR 8.8% p.a. against 14.2% p.a. average for US stock exchanges. Total return in this period in the US market would have been 277% against 132% in Germany. The ratio of total return in USA to total return in Germany is 2.1 (= 277/ 132).

**30-year Period 1990-2019:**

The growth rate of DAX in USD was CAGR 8.6% p.a. against 10.8% p.a. average for US stock exchanges. Total return in this period in the US market would have been 2,070% against 1,090% in Germany. The ratio of total return in USA to total return in Germany is 1.9 (= 2070/ 1090).

## 20.7 GENERAL CONCLUSIONS

Migrating your investment from one country to another with a different currency can be highly rewarding depending on the relative growth rates of the stock markets and the development of the exchange rates between the two currencies.

If the stock market performance and the exchange rate development are both favorable, the financial gain that can be achieved by migrating the investment can be many folds. This would have been the case for investors from UK and India who would have invested in US stock markets in the 10 year-periods 1990-1999 and 2010-2019.

Conversely, if the stock market performance and the exchange rate development are both unfavorable, the financial loss that can be suffered by migrating the investment can also be many folds. This would have been the case for investors from USA who would have invested in the UK or Indian stock markets in the 10 years-periods 1990-1999 and 2010-2019.

An important point to be aware of is that the development of the exchange rates between the two currencies can magnify your gain or loss significantly. The depreciation of GBP and the Indian Rupee with respect to USD has substantially increased the gain for investors from these countries who had invested in US stock markets.

Conversely, the exchange rate disadvantage alone would have resulted in a significant loss if US investors had invested in devaluating countries like UK and India.

In short, there is a gold mine to be had if you go beyond the borders of your own country. Or a financial landmine if you cross the wrong border. The great thing about it is that it is all visible to the naked eye, and you only need to learn to look and distinguish between the two. Hopefully, this book will help you with it.

# Chapter 21:

# Ten of the fastest investment highways leading to riches

## Disclaimer

*This book is intended to be a science-based financial book with mathematical and statistical data and analysis. It is intended to provide a largely missing insight into financial mathematics to the reader. It is not meant to be a book on investment advice. The author is an engineer by profession and not professionally qualified or licensed to be a financial or investment advisor.*

*The investment pointers that are given here reflect the personal experiences, opinions, and biases of the author and are intended only to enlighten and widen the knowledge horizon of the reader. They do not in any way constitute any professional investment advice. Before making any investment decisions, the readers are advised to take professional advice from qualified sources.*

## 21.1    START A NEW HIGH-POTENTIAL BUSINESS OR TAKE OVER A START-UP BUSINESS AND MAKE IT BIG OVER TIME

### Rank: 1

This is clearly the investment option with the potential for the highest return, as evidenced by the Billionaires of today.

It could be an innovative business you set up from scratch and build up, alone or together with others, or a business that you take over from someone else at an early stage of development and make it grow big.

Just think of Bill Gates, Jeff Bezos, Michael Dell, Larry Page, late Steve Jobs, and many others who started a business on a small scale, sometimes from garages and dormitories, which grew to become global giants in a couple of decades.

The rate of return of their investments? Let us look at a few.

**Jeff Bezos,** founder of Amazon: His reported $250,000 investment in Amazon in 1994, probably raised from his parents, had grown to a net worth of approximately $200 Billion in August 2020. The after-tax CAGR of his investment in the 26-year period 1994-2020 is 68.7%. p.a. He reportedly owns 11.1% of Amazon.

If his annual tax rate were 10%, his pre-tax CAGR would have been: 76.3% p.a.

If his annual tax rate were 20%, his pre-tax CAGR would have been: 85.8% p.a.

If his annual tax rate were 30%, his pre-tax CAGR would have been: 98.1% p.a.

**Bill Gates**, co-founder of Microsoft: His reported $1 million investment in Microsoft in 1975, reportedly raised from his parents, had grown to a net worth of approximately $120 Billion in August 2020. The after-tax CAGR of his investment in the 45-year period 1975-2020 is 29.7%. p.a.

If his annual tax rate were 10%, his pre-tax CAGR would have been: 33.0% p.a.

If his annual tax rate were 20%, his pre-tax CAGR would have been: 37.1% p.a.

If his annual tax rate were 30%, his pre-tax CAGR would have been: 42.4% p.a.

**Mukesh Ambani**, Chairman of Reliance Industries, India, and the richest man in Asia. His father, Dhirubhai Ambani, laid the foundation for the company in 1958 with $500. Ignoring the split of wealth due to succession and inheritance issues, the $500 investment has grown, in the hands of Mukesh Ambani, to a net worth of approximately $100 Billion in August 2020. The after-tax CAGR of this investment in the 62-year period 1958-2020 is 36.1%. p.a.

If his annual tax rate were 10%, his pre-tax CAGR would have been: 40.1% p.a.

If his annual tax rate were 20%, his pre-tax CAGR would have been: 45.1% p.a.

If his annual tax rate were 30%, his pre-tax CAGR would have been: 51.6% p.a.

**These people got so wealthy by creating their own businesses by investing relatively modest amounts, often raised from family and friends.**

**The pre-tax CAGR of the richest people lies in the range of 40-100% p.a.**

**The after-tax CAGR of the richest people lies in the range of 25-70% p.a.**

Giants are also born as babies, and that also applies to giant businesses. If you can father such a business-baby or adopt one because you miss the needed ingredients or tools or skills to create one, your destination can be one filled with massive wealth like no other.

From the tax point of view, your tax drag can be extremely low, especially when your business is young and growing.

On the negative side, the road to riches may be very bumpy and treacherous, and there is a chance that your Ferrari will crash before you reach your destination. You may be left with no other option than to abandon your vehicle and walk back home in the wilderness, all alone.

The opportunities to start a business with new products or services, especially in the digital arena, are practically limitless.

If you can invest $10,000 and establish a business with a CAGR of 30% p.a., in 30 years, your pre-tax net worth will be $26.20 million. It will increase by a factor of 2,620. If you can invest $1 million instead, your pre-tax net worth can be $2.62 Billion in 30 years and $36 Billion in 40 years.

### 21.1.1   Rate of Return that can be achieved

Pre-tax CAGR is feasible in the range of 20% - 40%. p. a. On average, 30% may be viable.

After-tax CAGR is feasible in the range of 18% - 38% p.a. On average, 27% may be viable.

### 21.2      START A BUSINESS, MAKE IT GROW FAST, AND LET IT BE TAKEN OVER AFTER IT TAKES OFF

Rank: 2

Many young entrepreneurs in the tech sector have got super-rich in a truly short time this way. In most cases, young techies develop an innovative product in the digital arena, and within a short time, giant companies like Google, Microsoft, Facebook, etc., swoop in and grab them paying a stupendous price.

The added value to the acquiring giant justifies such an extreme price, also because a potential competitor would be eliminated that way.

Such start-ups in digital products or services often require only a small initial investment. The investment is mainly in the form of intellectual capital.

### 21.2.1   Rate of Return that can be achieved

When such start-ups get taken over by giant companies, the pre-tax CAGR that can be achieved can be an astronomical 10,000% p.a. or more.

This is a business model coveted and dreamed of by many young entrepreneurial techies.

## 21.3 PARTICIPATE, TAKING AN EQUITY SHARE, IN A HIGH-POTENTIAL NEW BUSINESS

### Rank: 3

If you yourself do not have the many tools and skills needed to start a promising new business all by yourself or together with like-minded partners, you can think about participating in another good business venture by investing in it in exchange for a share of ownership. This is what business angels and start capitalists do on a professional basis, often with great success.

Ideally, such a company suitable for your financial participation would be of the category mentioned above in section 21.2.

You could consider such an investment if an opportunity turns up in the circle of your family, friends, acquaintances, or network.

You could also search actively for such promising but cash-starved start-ups.

From the tax point of view, your tax drag can be extremely low or even zero.

On the negative side, there is a high risk of you losing your investment altogether, but the return on your investment can be sky-high if the venture becomes a success.

### 21.3.1 Rate of Return that can be achieved

Pre-tax CAGR is feasible in the range of 100% - 5,000% p.a. depending on your entry point in the business.

## 21.4 INVEST DIRECTLY IN SELECTED HIGH-POTENTIAL STOCKS THROUGH STOCK MARKET

### Rank: 4

This is probably the best-known and most popular investment vehicle in the big world of investments. It is probably also the most favorite financial sport for many, combining adventure and uncertainty with potentially huge gains or losses.

Warren Buffett is an arch-example of getting super-rich through such investments in stock markets.

For those who take pains to educate themselves and meticulously track and analyze individual companies, the returns can be enormous. On the other hand, there is also the ever-present risk that you may lose a lot of money.

Investing in the stock market is not the proper investment vehicle to build wealth for those who tend to have only a fleeting romance with stocks. This is a vehicle for long-term investment, like in a marriage. Frequent buying and selling will eat away your gains in costs and probably also in additional taxes.

Major stock markets in major countries have rendered, on average, a **pre-tax CAGR of 15% or more** returns per year in the long term in the past half a century, even after epical dips in the 1980s and 2000s and the Covid-stricken 2020.

**But there are numerous companies that have been stellar performers in the stock market, far exceeding the average index returns. This happens all the time, in good and bad economic times. Picking such stocks before they shoot up in price, and selling them before they fall back, is like a sport for many wealthy investors.**

### 21.4.1    Examples of stellar stocks

**Tesla:** Its stock price alone, ignoring dividend yield, increased by a CAGR of 156% p.a. in the 2-year period Sept 2018-Sept 2020. It is a 6.5x fold increase in value in just 2 years.

In the 1-year period Sept 2019- Sept 2020, its stock price skyrocketed by 712% p.a. or 7.12x times.

**Amazon**: Amazon's stock price alone, ignoring dividend yield, increased by a CAGR of 37.5% p.a. in the 23-year period 1997-2020. It is a 1,500x fold increase in value. If you had invested $1,000 in it in 1997, your stock would have been worth $1.5 million in 2020.

In the 3-year period Sept 2017- Sept 2020, its stock price more than tripled with a CAGR of 47.3% p.a. It is still soaring in 2020 despite the Corona pandemic.

**Microsoft**: Its stock price alone, ignoring dividend yield, increased by a CAGR of 28.0% p.a. in the 6-year period Sept 2014-Sept 2020. It is a 4.4x fold increase in value in just 6 years.

In the 1-year period Sept 2019- Sept 2020, its stock price soared by 49% p.a.

**Apple**: Its stock price alone, ignoring dividend yield, increased by a CAGR of 27.8% p.a. in the 6-year period Sept 2014-Sept 2020. It is a 4.3x fold increase in value in just 6 years.

In the 1-year period Sept 2019- Sept 2020, its stock price soared by 101%, p.a. doubling in value.

**ASML** (Nasdaq): The producer of machines for computer chips located in the Netherlands.

Stock price alone, ignoring dividend yield, increased by a CAGR of 20.5% p.a. in the 17-year period 2003-2020. It is a 27x fold increase in value. If you had invested $1,000 in it in 2003, your stock would have been worth $27,000 in 2020.

In 2019 its stock price jumped 91%. It is still soaring in 2020 despite the Corona pandemic.

### 21.4.2 In Summary

An equity investment generally incurs the favorable deferred tax in the form of capital gains tax in most major countries. Dividend-yield also incurs a lower tax than regular income tax in many countries. All in all, from a tax point of view, this is also a favorable investment vehicle for those who aim for exceptionally high net after-tax returns.

When investing in the stock market, migrating your investment abroad to the highest yielding market for your currency must be considered. Migrating your investment can sometimes result in many-fold higher returns. See chapter 20 to learn more about migrating stock market investment.

### 21.4.3 Rate of Return that can be achieved

What is feasible with proper research and effort is the following:

**Pre-tax CAGR is feasible in the range of 20% - 35%. p. a.** On average, 23% may be viable.

**After-tax CAGR is feasible in the range of 18% - 32% p.a.** On average, 21% may be viable.

### 21.5 INVEST DIRECTLY IN BUILT-UP REAL ESTATE IN RAPIDLY GROWING CITY AREAS

#### Rank: 5

This has always been a classical investment vehicle for many people around the world to get wealthy in a tax-favorable way.

The main advantage of using this investment vehicle to build wealth is that you can borrow most of the needed money from a bank or other financial institution using the built-up structure itself as collateral. A residential house or condo is one of the most trusted collaterals by financial institutions worldwide. In many countries, you need to have your own money of only 10% or 20% of the purchase price, and the rest can be borrowed.

The interest on loans for buying real estate is considerably lower than commercial loans in many countries.

Please refer to chapter 10, in which borrowing to invest is analyzed and recommended as a means to get wealthy.

### 21.5.1 Example of leveraging through borrowing

If you borrow $100,000 at 5% interest for 25 years, you will be paying a total of $239,000 as interest to the bank in 25 years.

Assume that your condo appreciated in value at 6% p.a. on average, and the rental yield was 4% p.a. net after deducting maintenance costs. Your rate of return, in this case, would be 10% p.a. (= 6 + 4) for 25 years. That amounts to a total return of $983,000.

After paying $239,000 interest to the bank together with the principal of $100,000, your net worth would be $744,000 (= 983,000 − 239,000).

In this example, your own investment was zero. You got 100% financing from the bank. In practice, however, you might have to put up 10% or 20% of the purchase price.

This example illustrates the power of investing with borrowed money.

This example also illustrates the power of this investment vehicle to enable borrowing 80% to 100% of the required capital.

### 21.5.1.1 You can build a whole real estate empire with borrowed money

With proper structuring and planning, it is possible to build a whole real estate empire with borrowed money. The risk is that it will not be quite stable, and a major financial earthquake like the 2008 financial crisis can shake the empire to collapse like a domino.

## 21.5.2 Rate of Return (ROR)

The return from this category of investments can be hybrid: the regular rental yield on one side and silent capital appreciation on the other.

The rate of return can vary widely from country to country and from city to city within a country. Let us look at the historical rate of return in some countries and cities.

### 21.5.2.1 New York City and USA

**Value appreciation of houses**: Looking at the price development of the 20-year period 2000-2020, you can see that there is quite a lot of variation from area to area, with the middle-class areas appreciating the most. All the areas taken together, there was an average price appreciation of CAGR 5% p.a. with a spread of 3% to 7%.

The period 2000-2020 was one with four major financial shocks, namely, the burst of the dot com bubble in 2000, the 9/11 attacks in 2001, the financial crisis of 2008, and the Corona pandemic of 2020.

Compared to other major cities in USA, New York City scores about the average in the price appreciation of residential real estate. Los Angeles, San Francisco, Seattle, etc., lie towards the top end, and Detroit lies towards the bottom end of price appreciation.

**Rental Yield:** Generally, the average rental yield as a percentage of the value of the house is inversely proportional to the value of the house. In other words, the higher the price, the lower the rental yield.

Within New York City itself, as in all other major cities in USA, there have been wide variations in rental yields. For NY City as a whole, the average rental yield of the 20-year period 2000-2020 lies around 7%. p.a.

Nationwide, the average rental yield in New York City lies around the national average.

**Rate of Return (ROR)**: For New York City, the ROR for the 20-year period 2000-2020 is about 12% p.a. (= 5 + 7). In this respect also, New York City's score is about the national average.

### 21.5.2.2    London and UK

London had a steeper **price appreciation** of residential homes in the period 2000-2020 than New York City. The average value lies around 8% p.a. against 5% for New York City.

**The rental yield**, on the other hand, was lower than for New York City. The average for London was about 4% p.a. against 7% for New York City.

**The average Rate of Return** for London in the period 2000-2020 was about 12% p.a. (= 8 + 4). This is the same as for New York City for the same period.

For the UK as a whole, all three values lie considerably lower than those for London.

### 21.5.2.3    Paris and France

The average values for Paris for the 20-year period 2000-2020 are the same as for London.

The **price appreciation** for the 20-year period 2000-2020 was 8% p.a. as was also for London. The value was higher for London till the Brexit referendum of 2016 but came down after that equaling that of Paris for the 20-year period considered.

The **rental yield** for the considered period was 4% p.a. as was also for London.

Therefore, the **Average Rate of Return** for Paris in the period 2000-2020 was about 12% p.a. (= 8 + 4).

For France as a whole, all three values lie considerably lower than for Paris.

### 21.5.3    Real Estate is a Tax-favourable investment vehicle

From a tax point of view, this is generally a favorable investment vehicle. In many countries, if it is not your own residential home, the rental income may be taxed annually as income tax, but the many tax deductions can lower the tax rate substantially. The capital gain arising out of price appreciation of real estate is generally taxed favorably in most countries, sometimes even allowing price indexing to minimize tax.

We have already seen throughout this book how annual income tax can lead to high tax drag and severe erosion of your potential wealth. Investment in real estate is a way to reduce tax drag substantially.

In addition, the unique strength and popularity of this investment vehicle lie in its ability to get loans to invest in, and that too at favorable interest rates. Therefore, it is also accessible to most people, even in developing countries.

## 21.5.4    Rate of Return that can be achieved

Pre-tax CAGR is feasible in the range of 8% - 16% p.a. depending on many factors like your country and location within the country. On average, 12% may be viable.

After-tax CAGR is feasible in the range of 6% - 14% p.a. On average, 10% may be viable.

## 21.6    INVEST IN EQUITY MUTUAL FUNDS

### Rank: 6

This is probably the easiest and safest way for most people to invest in the stock market. The stock-picking is done by experts and professionals, and therefore, for the individual investor, it is almost as simple as managing a fixed deposit in a bank account.

Overall, the returns for the individual investors are generally not far behind the concerned stock market index. Picking individual stocks, as covered in section 21.4 above, may give you considerably higher returns, but Mutual Funds have a much lower risk profile and require no special skills to access and manage.

Please see chapter 20 for an overview of the performance and comparison of some major stock indices in the world.

Overall, measured in USD or equivalent, the major indices have rendered, on average, a pre-tax CAGR of about 10% or more returns per year in the past 30 years, even after epical dips in the 2000s and now in 2020 due to the Corona pandemic.

When investing in the stock market, migrating your investment abroad to the highest yielding market for your currency must be considered. Migrating your investment can sometimes result in many-fold higher returns.

## 21.6.1    Rate of Return that can be achieved

Tax drag with Mutual Funds may be higher than that for direct investment in equity.

**Pre-tax CAGR is feasible in the range of** 7% - 16% **p.a.,** measured in USD, depending on many factors like your country, currency, and location. On average, 10% may be feasible.

After-tax CAGR is feasible in the range of 6% - 14%. On average, 9% may be viable.

### 21.7 INVEST INDIRECTLY IN REAL ESTATE THROUGH REITS (REAL ESTATE INVESTMENT TRUSTS)

#### Rank: 7

Instead of investing in real estate directly, investing indirectly through investment trusts is an easier route in countries where such trusts are permitted. **It is like a Mutual Fund, but specifically for investing in real estate only.**

Such companies are highly professionalized in managing real estate, which will relieve you of all headaches of owning and managing real estate directly.

A disadvantage is that the management companies take a considerable part of the return on investment on various grounds leaving you with a considerably lower return.

From a tax point of view, it varies from country to country, but effectively, the tax drag may be **higher** than investing directly in real estate as in section 21.5 above as income from REITs may be treated as regular income.

### 21.7.1 Rate of Return that can be achieved

**Pre-tax CAGR is feasible in the range of** 6% - 12% depending on many factors like your country and location. On average, 9% may be viable.

**After-tax CAGR is feasible in the range of** 5% - 10%. On average, 7% may be viable.

### 21.8 INVEST IN GOLD

#### Rank: 8

For many folks around the globe, especially those not infected much by modernity, Gold is almost as sacred as God, and it is in Gold that they do a significant part of their investment. Even though buying gold and keeping it in a box or vault is not really a classical investment, it is the oldest and most classical investment vehicle embraced by everybody from beggar to king throughout the ages.

As far as the speed of wealth-building is concerned, it is not as fast a runner as an investment in stocks, but not far behind real estate or mutual fund.

Gold is a good competitor for all kinds of saving and deposit schemes.

One typical characteristic of Gold is that the price shoots up in times of major crisis in the world but comes down to earth when the crisis abates.

If you can play along with that behavior, Gold has moderate potential for slow wealth building.

**CAGR of gold price in USD in the past 50 years, from Aug 1970 to Aug 2020: 8.3% p.a.**

**CAGR of gold price in USD in the past 13 years, from Aug 2007 to Aug 2020: 8.6% p.a.**

**CAGR of gold price in USD in the past 5 years, from Aug 2015 to Aug 2020: 10.6% p.a.**

**CAGR of gold price in USD in the 20 years from 1983 to 2003: ZERO!**

From the tax point of view, investing in gold is like investing in landed property. Until you sell it and realize a capital gain, there is no tax due in most countries. The tax that becomes due at that point is also the favored deferred tax in the form of capital gains tax.

An alternative way to invest in Gold is to invest in the stock of companies that mine or trade in Gold.

### 21.8.1    Rate of Return that can be achieved

**Pre-tax CAGR is feasible in the range of 5% - 10%.** On average, 7% may be feasible.

**After-tax CAGR is feasible in the range of 4% - 9%.** On average, 6% may be feasible.

But in times of peace and tranquility on earth, Gold goes to sleep, and so also its value.

### 21.9    INVEST IN VARIOUS TAX-EXEMPT SAVING AND INVESTMENT SCHEMES

#### Rank: 9

Most of the countries incentivize saving and investment through tax exemptions, tax deferrals, or tax reductions.

Examples are tax concessions for saving for a pension, buying your own house, mortgage payments, investing in government bonds, etc.

Almost all such schemes have limits on the maximum amount you can save or invest and have other restrictions for withdrawal and use.

The nominal yield rates are generally lower than what you can get with a fixed deposit in the bank. But because of the tax concessions, your net return in the long term can be considerably higher than your net return with a fixed deposit in a bank.

Because of its limited access, limitations on amount, and restrictions of use, in combination with the relatively low net return compared to other investment options like real estate and the stock market, this is not a highway leading you to the kingdom of the rich.

But for those who are addicted to putting their money in a fixed deposit in a bank, this is undoubtedly a better way to raise your relatively low net rate of return by a few percentages or even double it. This is not an investment vehicle that will lead someone with a moderate income to millionairedom within two decades.

### 21.9.1    Rate of Return that can be achieved

This is very variable and depends on the benchmark interest rates set by the central banks from time to time. Generally, the net after-tax ROR can be 1.2x to 2x times higher than what you can get with a fixed deposit in a bank, but with limitations on the amount you can invest.

### 21.10    INVEST IN CRYPTOCURRENCY

#### Rank: 10

As things stood in December 2020, no discussion on wealth-building would be complete without taking investing in cryptocurrencies into account.

The relative newness of the phenomenon, lack of adequate regulation and legal protection in most countries, need for relatively high skills to make a profit by investing in it, and the too high market volatility and related high risks disqualify cryptocurrency as a serious investment vehicle yet, as of end 2020.

However, for all aspiring millionaires, it is an investment vehicle worth tracking closely. For daredevils, there is potential for exceedingly high returns coupled with a substantial risk of significant losses.

### 21.11    THE ROUTE OF FIXED DEPOSIT IN A BANK IS NOT A HIGHWAY TO RICHES BUT A MUD-ROAD TO THE SURVIVAL-HUT

#### Rank: 11

Compared with the ten investment or wealth-building options we have analyzed and ranked above, Fixed Deposit does not qualify to be one among them as it has a net rate of return (net ROR) that is lower than all the others.

Still, fixed deposit is probably the most popular and most used wealth-building vehicle among all the folks worldwide.

Because of high inflation and the consequent depreciation of their currencies in comparison with major reserve currencies like the US dollar and Euro, many countries, especially developing and underdeveloped countries, have been able to offer what looks like attractively high interest rates on fixed deposits.

For example, you may get a 1% interest rate on FD in USA, while you can get 7% in India on a fixed deposit in Indian Rupees. Therefore, it looks hugely attractive to deposit in India instead of in USA. But when the mathematics of exchange rates and interest rates is done, you will notice that the net result is probably only 1% or 2% interest in US Dollar terms, and the 7% interest rate is not of much value to someone living in USA and needing money in USD.

From the tax point of view, Fixed Deposit is the worst in the class too. Generally, in most countries, interest is taxed annually as income tax. We have seen earlier in this book that annual payment of tax is a cascading tax leading to an ever-increasing tax drag, which increasingly drains your net return.

All in all, Fixed Deposit does not make it to the list of the best ten investment or wealth-building options. With fixed deposits, you will be helping the banks to earn more money for themselves than for yourself. See chapter 9 for more details.

\* \* \* \*

## Chapter 22:

# Introduction to software tool YIELDOMETER for computing all investment results instantly

The easiest way to calculate all the results of an investment is to use a software tool in which you can feed the basic raw investment data, and the tool displays all the results instantly.

An extensive computing tool that is based on Microsoft Excel has been developed specifically for this purpose by the author of this book. It was created parallel with the research and calculations that had to be done for this series of books as no suitable and comprehensive software program was available in the marketplace to do all the calculations that were needed.

We have chosen the name YIELDOMETER because what it does essentially is measuring or metering everything that is related to the yield of an investment. Metaphorically, it is like the THERMOMETER for measuring temperature.

However, being a software tool, from the technical point of view, it was not possible to make it part of this e-book. Moreover, it would also have made this book more expensive, defeating the very purpose of this book, i.e., to make knowledge available at a low cost that anybody can afford.

Therefore, the software program will be made available soon as a separate item that can be purchased and downloaded separately.

## 22.1     AN OVERVIEW OF THE CALCULATION PROGRAM

### 22.1.1     Screenshot

Figures 22.1, 22.2 & 22.3 show limited screenshots of 6 out of the 19 main categories of investment results of Yieldometer.

Not all pages and results are shown here with an eye on the size of this book.

### 22.1.2     Input

You need to feed only a minimum of 3 and a maximum of 4 of the following 6 data.

1. **Initial investment amount, in any currency (P).**
2. **Number of periods or years (N).**
3. **Nominal yield rate in % (R).**

4. **Nominal Tax rate in % (T).**
5. **Final amount (Net worth NW or Net yield NY).**
6. **Ratio of the final amount or total return to the initial investment (CAF or CYF).**

You can feed any combination of the 6 input-data and get the results instantly.

## 22.1.3    Output

There is a total of 19 main categories of results with more than 400 individual results.

Categories 1 to 12 calculate and show the results of any investment by feeding data numbers 1 to 4 in the above list. You can choose any mix of values for the four data.

**The first 12 categories of results you will get are the following:**

1. **CAGR (Compound Annual Growth rate) of the initial investment.**
2. **Tax Drag.**
3. **Net worth.**
4. **Gross yield.**
5. **Net yield.**
6. **Tax.**
7. **Net worth Details.**
8. **Gross yield Details.**
9. **Net yield Details.**
10. **Tax Details.**
11. **Extra Loss of Income to Investor due to Annual Tax instead of Deferred tax.**
12. **Loss of Income to Government due to Annual Tax instead of Deferred tax.**

**Categories 13 to 18 will give you the following results.**

**Category 13:** Calculates the initial investment amount needed to reach a targeted net worth or net yield for any set of investment period, yield rate, and tax rate.

**Category 14:** Calculates the investment period needed to reach a targeted net worth or net yield for any set of initial investment, yield rate, and tax rate.

**Category 15:** Calculates the investment period needed to reach a target multiple of the initial investment for net worth (CAF) and net yield (CYF) for any set of yield rate and tax rate. The result will be the same for any investment amount or final amount.

**Category 16:** Calculates the yield rate needed to reach a targeted net worth or net yield for any set of initial investment, investment period, final amount, and tax rate.

**Category 17**: Calculates the yield rate needed to reach a target multiple of the initial investment for net worth (CAF) and net yield (CYF) for any set of investment period and tax rate. The result will be the same for any investment amount and final amount.

**Category 18**: Calculates the multiple of initial investment for net worth (CAF) and net yield (CYF) for any set of investment period, yield rate, and tax rate. The result will be the same for any investment amount and final amount.

### 22.1.4    Stock Market & Foreign Exchange Calculations

Independent of the 18 categories above, there is a separate program to calculate the following:

- Stock market performance as CAGR or Rate of Return in any native currency.

- Conversion of the stock market performance from the native currency to any foreign currency. For example, conversion of Dow Jones performance in USD to performance measured in Euro taking exchange rate variations into the equation.

- Appreciation or depreciation of one currency against another, measured as CAGR (Compound Annualized Growth Rate).

See Figures 22.1, 22.2 & 22.3 for limited screenshots of 6 out of the 19 categories of results.

### 22.2    INTERPRETING THE RESULTS OF CALCULATION

This tool is the easiest, quickest, and best way to analyze and compare various investment options and choose the best one.

### 22.2.1    Choosing the best investment when there are only 2 variables to choose from: yield rate & tax rate

The best investment option is not necessarily the one that gives the lowest Tax Drag percentage or amount, but the one that necessarily gives the highest net yield or net worth in the same span of years and with the same investment amount.

That invariably means the best match between yield rate and tax rate resulting in the highest CAGR (Compound Annual Growth Rate) for net worth. If for investment **A** the yield rate is lower than investment **B**, but the tax rate is still lower, resulting in a higher CAGR for net worth, then investment A is the winner despite its lower yield rate.

Yieldometer can make this rather complex calculation instantly.

## 22.2.2   Choosing the best investment when all 4 parameters are variable

When all four parameters of various investments, namely initial investment, duration, yield rate, and tax rate, vary from one another, comparison and choice become more complex. In such a complex situation also, the best investment may be the one that gives the highest CAGR for net worth, but not necessarily.

That means the highest CAGR alone should not be the criterium for choosing an investment. It should also be supported at the same time by the highest net yield or net worth.

This is because a relatively much smaller project may have a higher CAGR but will give you a much smaller net yield and net worth than a larger project with a CAGR that is a bit lower. Therefore, you may want to go for the bigger project and higher net yield despite the lower CAGR.

Therefore, you need to compare not only the CAGR but also other data before making an investment choice.

Yieldometer will present you with all the data that you may need for any investment sparing you tedious and error-prone calculations.

## 22.3   SPECIAL FEATURES OF THIS SOFTWARE TOOL

Each of the 400+ data that the program generates is **autonomous** and will stand on its own. **Each data is computed using its own original formula and using only the 6 input variables and is not dependent on any other data already calculated in another category.** The advantage of this independence is that there will not be any domino effect if any one of the data gets corrupted for any reason. That error will not be transmitted to any other data.

**This software tool is unique in its category, as is also this book.**

## 22.4   WILL IT WORK ON ALL DEVICES?

The program is based on Microsoft Excel. Therefore, for this program to work properly, it is necessary to have MS Excel installed on your PC or any other device.

| YIELDOMETER: Calculation of Investment Results | | | |
|---|---|---|---|
| NOTE: This calculation is applicable to any currency anywhere in the world. Dollar is used merely as example. | | | |
| **INPUT DATA** | | | |
| 1 **Investment Amount in $ (or any currency), P** | $ | P | 10,000 |
| 2 **Investment Period in Years, N** | Years | N | 30.0 |
| 3 **Gross Yield Rate per annum in percent, R** | % | R | 20.00% |
| 4 **Tax rate in percent, T** | % | T | 25.00% |
| **1 CAGR of Net Worth (Compound Annual Growth Rrate). (= Net CAF, Compound Amount Factor)** | | | |
| 101 **CAGR of Net Worth with Annual tax** | CAGR | % (Ann) | 15.0% |
| 102 **CAGR of Net Worth with Deferred tax** | CAGR | % (Def) | 18.9% |
| 103 **CAGR of Net Worth with NUL tax** | CAGR | % (Nul) | 20.0% |
| **2 TAX DRAG, as % of Total Yield with NUL tax** | | | |
| 201 Tax Drag with Annual tax: Loss of Net Yield as % of Net Yield with NUL tax | Tax Drag | % (Ann/Nul) | 72.4% |
| 202 Tax Drag with Deferred tax: Loss of Net Yield as % of Net Yield with NUL tax | Tax Drag | % (Def/Nul) | 25.0% |
| **3 NET WORTH** | | | |
| a **Net Worth percentage, as % of Net Worth with NUL tax** | | | |
| 301 **Net Worth with Annual tax as % of Net Worth with NUL tax** | NW/ NW | % (Ann/Nul) | 27.9% |
| 302 **Net Worth with Deferred tax as % of Net Worth with NUL tax** | NW/ NW | % (Def/Nul) | 75.1% |
| b **Net Worth Factor (Growth Factor for Net Worth = Compound Amount Factor (CAF) for Net Worth), as multiple of Initial Investment** | | | |
| 303 **Net Worth with Annual tax as multiple of Initial Investment (CAF for Net Worth)** | NW | P-Multiple (Ann) | 66.2 |
| 304 **Net Worth with Deferred tax as multiple of Initial Investment (CAF for Net Worth)** | NW | P-Multiple (Def) | 178.3 |
| 305 **Net Worth with NUL tax as multiple of Initial Investment (CAF for Net Worth)** | NW | P-Multiple (Nul) | 237.4 |
| c **Net Worth Loss** | | | |
| 306 Loss of Net Worth with Annual tax compared to Net Worth with Nul tax, as multiple of initial investment | (-) NW/ P | P-Multiple (Ann) | 171.2 |
| 307 Loss of Net Worth with Deferred tax compared to Net Worth with Nul tax, as multiple of initial investment | (-) NW/ P | P-Multiple (Def) | 59.1 |
| 308 Loss of Net Worth with Annual tax compared to Net Worth with Deferred tax, as multiple of initial investment | (-) NW/ P | P-Multiple (Ann) | 112.1 |

**Figure 22.1. Sample screenshot-1 from calculation program YIELDOMETER.**

| | | | | | | |
|---|---|---|---|---|---|---|
| **e** | **Gross Yield Amount  (Total Return-On-Investment** | | | | | |
| | 413 | **Gross Yield Amount with** Annual tax | GY | $ (Ann) | | 869,490 |
| | 414 | **Gross Yield Amount with** Deferred tax | GY | $ (Def) | | 2,363,763 |
| | 415 | **Gross Yield Amount with** NUL tax | GY | $ (Nul) | | 2,363,763 |
| **5** | **NET YIELD** | | | | | |
| **a** | Net Yield % (Net Return-On-Investment- ROI), as % of Total Yield with NUL tax | | | | | |
| | 501 | **Net Yield with** Annual tax **as % of Total Yield with** NUL tax | NY/ NY | % (Ann/Nul) | | 27.6% |
| | 502 | **Net Yield with** Deferred tax **as % of Total Yield with** NUL tax | NY/ NY | % (Def/Nul) | | 75.0% |
| **b** | Net Yield Factor (Net Return-On-Investment Factor = Compound Yield Factor (CYF) for Net Yield), as multiple of Initial Investment | | | | | |
| | 503 | **Net Yield with** Annual tax **as multiple of Initial Investment (CYF for Net Yield)** | NY/ P | P-Multiple (Ann) | | 65.2 |
| | 504 | **Net Yield with** Deferred tax **as multiple of Initial Investment (CYF for Net Yield)** | NY/ P | P-Multiple (Def) | | 177.3 |
| | 505 | **Net Yield with** NUL tax **as multiple of Initial Investment (CYF for Net Yield)** | NY/ P | P-Multiple (Nul) | | 236.4 |
| **c** | Net Yield Loss | | | | | |
| | 506 | Loss **of Net Yield with** Annual tax **compared to Net Yield with** NUL tax, **as multiple of initial investment** | (-) NY/ P | P-Multiple (Ann) | | 171.2 |
| | 507 | Loss **of Net Yield with** Deferred tax **compared to Net Yield with** NUL tax, **as multiple of initial investment** | (-) NY/ P | P-Multiple (Def) | | 59.1 |
| | 508 | Loss **of Net Yield with** Annual tax **compared to Net Yield with** Deferred tax, **as multiple of initial investment** | (-) NY/ P | P-Multiple (Ann) | | 112.1 |
| **d** | Net Yield Ratios | | | | | |
| | 509 | **Ratio of Net Yield with** Deferred tax **to Net Yield with** Annual tax | NY/ NY | Ratio (Def/Ann) | | 2.72 |
| | 510 | **Ratio of Net Yield with** NUL tax **to Net Yield with** Annual tax | NY/ NY | Ratio (Nul/Ann) | | 3.62 |
| | 511 | **Ratio of Net Yield with** NUL tax **to Net Yield with** Deferred tax | NY/ NY | Ratio (Nul/Def) | | 1.33 |
| **e** | Net Yield Amount | | | | | |
| | 512 | **Net Yield Amount with** Annual tax | NY | $ (Ann) | | 652,118 |
| | 513 | **Net Yield Amount with** Deferred tax | NY | $ (Def) | | 1,772,822 |
| | 514 | **Net Yield Amount with** NUL tax | NY | $ (Nul) | | 2,363,763 |
| **6** | **TAX** | | | | | |
| **a** | Amount of Tax, as multiple of Initial Investment | | | | | |
| | 601 | **Amount of Tax with** Annual tax **as multiple of Initial Investment** | Tax/ P | P-Multiple (Ann) | | 21.7 |
| | 602 | **Amount of Tax with** Deferred tax **as multiple of Initial Investment** | Tax/ P | P-Multiple (Def) | | 59.1 |

Figure 22.2. **Sample screenshot-2 from calculation program YIELDOMETER.**

| 14 | Years (N) needed for Initial Investment (P) to grow to a specific Amount of Net Worth (NW) or Net Yield (NY) | | | | |
|---|---|---|---|---|---|
| | INPUT DATA | | | | |
| 1 | Investment Amount in $ (or any currency), P | $ | P | | 10,000 |
| 2 | Needed Investment Period in Years, N | Years | N | | ??? |
| 3 | Gross Yield Rate per annum in percent, R | % | R | | 20.0% |
| 4 | Tax rate in percent, T | % | T | | 30.0% |
| 5 | Target Net Worth or Net Yield, Amount | $ | $ | | 1,000,000 |
| 6 | NW or NY as Multiple of Investment (= Net CAF or CYF) | Multiple | CAF, CYF | | |

| | | | Years needed for Investment | |
|---|---|---|---|---|
| | NW = Net Worth;  NY = Net Yield | | For Net Worth | For Net Yield |
| | Years needed to reach Target Amount of NW or NY | | | |
| 1401 | Years needed with Annual tax to reach Target NW or NY | years | 35.15 | 35.22 |
| 1402 | Years needed with Deferred tax to reach Target NW or NY | years | 27.20 | 27.25 |
| 1403 | Years needed with NUL tax to reach Target NW or NY | years | 25.26 | 25.31 |
| | Years needed to reach a Fixed Amount of NY or NW | | | |
| 1404 | Years needed with Annual tax to reach NY or NW of $ 0.2 million | years | 22.86 | 23.24 |
| 1405 | Years needed with Deferred tax to reach NY or NW of $ 0.2 million | years | 18.30 | 18.58 |
| 1406 | Years needed with NUL tax to reach NY or NW of $ 0.2 million | years | 16.43 | 16.70 |
| 1407 | Years needed with Annual tax to reach NY or NW of $ 0.5 million | years | 29.86 | 30.01 |
| 1408 | Years needed with Deferred tax to reach NY or NW of $ 0.5 million | years | 23.38 | 23.49 |
| 1409 | Years needed with NUL tax to reach NY or NW of $ 0.5 million | years | 21.46 | 21.57 |
| 1410 | Years needed with Annual tax to reach NY or NW of $ 1 million | years | 35.15 | 35.22 |
| 1411 | Years needed with Deferred tax to reach NY or NW of $ 1 million | years | 27.20 | 27.25 |
| 1412 | Years needed with NUL tax to reach NY or NW of $ 1 million | years | 25.26 | 25.31 |
| 1413 | Years needed with Annual tax to reach NY or NW of $ 2 million | years | 40.44 | 40.47 |
| 1414 | Years needed with Deferred tax to reach NY or NW of $ 2 million | years | 31.01 | 31.04 |
| 1415 | Years needed with NUL tax to reach NY or NW of $ 2 million | years | 29.06 | 29.09 |
| 1416 | Years needed with Annual tax to reach NY or NW of $ 5 million | years | 47.43 | 47.44 |
| 1417 | Years needed with Deferred tax to reach NY or NW of $ 5 million | years | 36.04 | 36.05 |
| 1418 | Years needed with NUL tax to reach NY or NW of $ 5 million | years | 34.09 | 34.10 |
| 1419 | Years needed with Annual tax to reach NY or NW of $ 10 million | years | 52.72 | 52.73 |
| 1420 | Years needed with Deferred tax to reach NY or NW of $ 10 million | years | 39.84 | 39.85 |
| 1421 | Years needed with NUL tax to reach NY or NW of $ 10 million | years | 37.89 | 37.89 |
| 1422 | Years needed with Annual tax to reach NY or NW of $ 20 million | years | 58.01 | 58.01 |
| 1423 | Years needed with Deferred tax to reach NY or NW of $ 20 million | years | 43.65 | 43.65 |
| 1424 | Years needed with NUL tax to reach NY or NW of $ 20 million | years | 41.69 | 41.69 |

Figure 22.3. **Sample** screenshot-3 **from calculation program** YIELDOMETER.

## 22.5    A CAUTIONARY NOTE ABOUT BLINDLY USING SUCH A TOOL WITHOUT UNDERSTANDING THE MATHS BEHIND IT

It will be akin to someone living at the foot of the Himalayas arriving in New York City, hiring a car, and driving to Los Angeles exclusively with the aid of the navigation system without any understanding of the geography of America and not even knowing whether you are driving to the East or West or North or South. It is always good to know where you are and where you are driving to so that even if the lady of the navigation system stops talking, you will still be able to keep going in the correct direction.

The very purpose of this book is to impart some knowledge about the financial landscape that you are driving through in your life. That landscape is also the hunting terrain for thieves and looters in suits, robbers, and Tax Dragons that will suck almost all your financial blood if you fall prey to them.

Therefore, it is strongly advised to go through this series of books first and understand compound interest, tax drag, and many other investment-related matters before relying on any software tool to make investment choices. Equip yourself first with the ability to understand and interpret the data that any software tool will spit out for you. Go through this book first, even if only superficially, so that you have the necessary knowledge to sensibly interpret the investment results that this software tool will present to you.

## 22.6    AVAILABILITY OF YIELDOMETER

Yieldometer, the software program to calculate all the results of investment, will also be released within three months of publication of this first volume of the series.

So also, Volume II, the book on Tax Drag, is expected to be published within three months of publication of this first volume of the series.

If you wish to be notified when Volume II of the book or the software program is available for purchase, please send a note per email to info@dekkaan.com or jacobsebastian@highwaytoriches.info. If you just mention NOTIFY ME or anything similar, that will suffice.

\* \* \* \*

# Chapter 23:

# In Summary

## 23.1    RECAP OF KNOWLEDGE PACKED IN THIS BOOK

This chapter gives a summary of key points that we have learned in this book, but without getting into details.

Please note that the points listed below do not follow the sequential order of the chapters because discussion and analysis of most of the topics are not strictly confined to any singular chapter but are generally spread over multiple chapters. However, the main chapter of each topic is referenced if relevant.

### 23.1.1    Compounding is a playground in 3D or 4D, not 2D (chapter 1)

If simple arithmetic can be considered as a playground in 2D, the mathematics of compounding should be considered as a playground in 3D or 4D.

The two 2D dimensions in which most people perceive, process, and calculate wealth-building are **initial investment** and **yield rate.**

The third of the **3D dimensions** that **adds** power to wealth building is **time**. Time is also the parameter that makes the calculations of wealth-building too complicated for most people.

The fourth of the **4D dimensions,** one that **detracts** from the power of wealth building, is **tax and tax drag,** the notorious twins.

A 4D playground is a lot more complex than a 2D or 3D playground. The rules that apply to a playground in 2D cannot be applied one-on-one to a playground in 3D or 4D because you will have to take also the third and fourth dimensions into account.

If you do not take the 3rd and 4th dimensions into account or do not specify them, you will get convoluted statements like 3% yield rate equals 20% yield rate, etc.

We have treated tax and tax drag as one single entity because tax drag is the shadow of taxation, and they are inseparable. Tax and tax drag are also the parameters that add an extra dimension of complexity to the already complex 3D calculations involving time.

Due to the lack of knowledge, most people think and calculate in simple 2D arithmetic when it is the 3D or 4D mathematics that is required. As a result, they miss the great opportunities that the 3D and 4D worlds of compounding present to create wealth a lot bigger and faster. People not only miss great opportunities, but they also make huge blunders and lose a lot of money due to ignorance.

Chapter 1 explains this topic in more detail with the help of examples.

### 23.1.2 In compounding, a 3% Differential yield rate can be 1,000 times more valuable than a 3% Nominal yield rate (chapter 7)

**Making maximum use of the higher value of differential yield rate forms one of the cornerstones of any serious wealth-building program.**

As we have seen in examples 1.2.3 and 1.2.4 in chapter 1, a 3% differential yield rate can be more valuable than even a 20% nominal yield rate.

The differential yield rate is not only more powerful than the nominal yield rate, but two differential yield rates with the same numerical value are also never equal in compounding. A 1% differential yield rate is never equal to another 1% differential yield rate.

In the kingdom of Compounding, no one is equal. Everyone is ranked.

If you are talking about a 1% differential yield rate, its rank and value depend on where it is positioned. If it is the 1% that lies between 16% and 17%, it is a lot more valuable than the 1% that lies locked between 6% and 7%.

If it is the differential 3% that lies between 20% and 23%, it is a lot more valuable than the nominal 3% that lies locked between 0% and 3%, as we have seen in examples 1.2.3 and 1.2.4 in chapter 1.

Most people are not aware of such a huge difference in the value of net worth between two yield rates that carry the same digital value, i.e., 3% as in examples 1.2.3 and 1.2.4.

A good understanding of this phenomenon is necessary to make full use of it to build your wealth bigger and faster.

Those who have knowledge of this, like you in examples 1.2.3 and 1.2.4, will get richer faster, and those who lack this knowledge, like your neighbor in those examples, will lose a lot of money without even being aware of the loss.

Chapter 7 is devoted to exploring this phenomenon of differential yield rate in detail.

### 23.1.3 Relationship between time-period and growth of wealth (chapter 5)

If your investment doubled in a time period of 5 years, in 10 years, your net worth will increase by a factor 4x, i.e., the square of 2; in 15 years, your net worth will increase by a factor **8x,** i.e., the third power of 2; in **20 years** your net worth will increase by a **factor 16x**, i.e., the fourth power of 2, and so on.

The time period it takes for you to double your net worth from **$100 to $200** will be **the same** as for doubling your net worth from $100 million to $200 million or for Jeff Bezos to go from **$200 Billion to $400 Billion.**

For every **equal increase in time-period**, for example, 5 years each, your net **worth will increase by a constant factor**, for instance, 3.052x times each if the yield rate is 25%. This constant is the Compound Amount Factor (**CAF**).

Chapter 5 is devoted to this **exponential relationship** between time-period and growth of wealth and their inter-relationship with yield rate and initial investment.

### 23.1.4    Relationship between yield rate and growth of wealth (chapter 6, 13)

If you want to reach a net worth of, for example, $1 million, and you double the yield rate, you will be able to reach your **targeted net worth** in a little **more than half the time**. If you triple the yield rate, you will reach your target in a little more than one-third of the original time.

If you double the yield rate, your **actual net worth** in the **same period** will grow by a factor that is a little **less than the square of the initial growth factor (CAF value)**. If you triple the yield rate, your net worth in the same period will grow by a factor that is considerably less than the third power of the initial growth factor (CAF value).

The relationship between an increase of yield rate and the corresponding increase of net worth is **not strictly exponential** as is the case with time-period but falls short of it. In mathematical jargon, the relationship is **Polynomial.**

It is not the yield rate but the **time-period that is always king** in the kingdom of compounding.

Chapters 6 & 13 are devoted to this relationship between yield rate and growth of wealth and their inter-relationship with time and initial investment.

### 23.1.5    Relationship between initial investment and growth of wealth (chapter 12)

The power of initial investment to accumulate wealth is tremendous.

If your target is to **maximize wealth in a specific time period**, and if the initial investment is doubled, the final amount will double in the same time period. If it is tripled, the final amount will be tripled. The relationship between **initial investment and final amount** is **linear.**

For example, if your Amazon shares worth **$2,000** would double in value to **$4,000** in 3 years (with a yield rate of 26.0%), your neighbor's $2 million would double to $4 million also in 3 years, and Jeff Bezos' **$200 Billion** would also double to **$400 Billion** in 3 years.

While you would have earned $2,000 in 3 years, Jeff Bezos would have earned $200 Billion using the very same instrument. The factor of difference is 100 million.

**The only reason for Jeff Bezos' 100 million times higher gain is his 100 million times higher Initial investment at the start of the 3-year period we considered.**

Give it another 3 years, and it would all double again. Your $4,000 would become $8,000, and Jeff Bezos' $400 Billion would become $800 Billion.

As increasing the initial investment, after maximizing the yield rate, is the only instrument available to you to build huge wealth in a given time span, you should always maximize your initial investment.

Borrow and invest if you can, but borrow sensibly.

However, if your target is to reach a **specific amount of net worth in the shortest possible time period, for example, $1 million,** a doubling of initial investment will deliver only a relatively small reduction in the time period needed to reach your targeted final amount. For example, timesaving will be only **13.1%** for doubling the initial investment from **$5,000 to $10,000** to reach a net worth of $1 million, irrespective of what the yield rate is.

To achieve another equal reduction in time-period, you will have to double the investment again, i.e., increase it to 4x times the original amount.

The relationship of time-period with initial investment is one of **exponential increase of initial investment for equal decreases of time-period.** You will need to double the initial investment every time to get an equal reduction in the time period.

Chapter 12 is devoted to this relationship between initial investment and wealth and their inter-relationship with time and yield rate.

## 23.1.6    Tax and Tax Drag (chapter 18)

When interest gets compounded annually, your wealth grows exponentially. In the same way but working in the opposite direction, your potential wealth decreases exponentially when the negative effect of tax withdrawals gets compounded annually. **This negative compounding of your tax withdrawals is what is known as Tax Drag.**

The negative impact of tax drag on your net worth can be enormous and much bigger than most people are aware of. Most people are not even aware of the very existence of tax drag.

For example, if you have been paying **30% annual tax** on an investment with a **20% yield rate,** in an active wealth-building span of **40 years, you will be losing 87.2%** of your potential wealth to tax drag. Your net **worth would be only 12.8%** of what you could have had if there was no tax at all. Your net worth without tax drag would have been **$7.8 million** instead of only **$1 million** with tax drag.

Tax drag is discussed in <u>section 3.4</u> and further elaborated in <u>chapter 18</u> of this book.

Tax drag is treated elaborately in Volume II of this series of books, and it is titled **Tax Drag, the dragon that eats up your wealth.**

### 23.1.7  Migrate your stock market investments to the foreign market with the highest return when measured in your domestic currency (chapter 20)

In <u>chapter 20</u>, we looked at the performance of some of the major stock markets in the world and compared some of them with each other after converting the performance values to one and the same currency.

The aim of the comparison was to help us determine which country or which stock market would have given us the highest rate of return. A typical question we wanted to answer is this: was it better, for example, for someone living in London to have invested in the stock market in USA than in the domestic stock market in London?

The depreciation of one currency with respect to the other makes comparing of two markets complex. **We have developed formulas to take this into account and to make calculations for comparison of performance accurately.**

We have made this analysis and comparisons for stock markets in USA, UK, Germany (EU), and India for the past many years.

The conclusion is that by investing in a different stock market and currency than your own domestic market and currency, sometimes **returns of many folds or hundreds of percentages more could be realized,** especially if your **native currency was losing value** with respect to other major currencies.

In the decade 2010-2019, residents of **UK** could have increased their average rate of return from **5.8%** p.a. by investing in FTSE-100 to **16.6%** by investing in **USA,** all measured in **GBP.** That would have given a total return that is **4.8x times higher** in the 10-year period.

For **Indians,** the increase would have been from **11.0%** in Bombay Sensex to **19.4%** in **USA,** all measured in **INR.** That would have given a total return that is **2.66x times higher** in the 10-year period.

Measuring past performances and comparing them is easy. But predicting whether the same trend would continue is a difficult one. But making pairs of some countries like UK-USA, India-USA, etc., are relatively safe bets. If you ignore this highway to wealth building, you will be missing a gold mine.

## 23.1.8    Investment vehicles that can take you to millionairedom and beyond (chapter 21)

**A fixed deposit** is a donkey-cart on a muddy road to millionairedom, which will never take you to millionairedom in **25 years** unless you have at least **a quarter of a million** to deposit at a **5.7%** interest rate and **zero tax**. With a **20% income tax rate**, you will need a deposit of about **$0.33 million** to reach a net worth of $1.0 million in 25 years. On a scale of 1 to 10 for investment vehicles, fixed deposit scores the lowest with just **1 point out of 10 and is ranked the lowest at position 10.**

On the opposite end of the spectrum, **setting up your own business** in innovative fields is the Ferrari that can take you to Millionairedom or Billionairedom in the shortest possible time. This investment vehicle scores the highest with **10 points and is ranked 1 (one).**

There are 8 other investment vehicles analyzed shortly in this book, with scores ranging from 2 to 8, some of which can also take you to millionairedom and beyond in a relatively short time.

All these investment vehicles are explored briefly in chapter 21 of this book.

## 23.1.9    An uncomfortable truth: Money always flows from bottom to top, and the rich will always get richer by virtue of the laws of mathematics (chapter 17)

Just as the natural flow of water is from top to bottom, the natural flow of money is always from bottom to top, from the poor to the rich.

The rich are not to be blamed for it. It is the result of a mathematical phenomenon caused by **irrefutable mathematical laws.**

Simplistically stated, the end-result of the laws is that **if the wealth of the rich and the poor doubles in, say, 5 years, the wealth-gap between them, measured in dollars, will also double. The wealth-gap will, therefore, grow exponentially with time, just as wealth will increase exponentially with time.**

In addition, there are 5 major reasons why the percentual growth rate of the wealth of the rich will be much higher than that of the poor and will not be equal as assumed in the statement above. This, together with the exponential growth of the wealth gap caused by mathematics as stated above, **will result in a double or triple exponential growth of the wealth gap between rich and poor.**

If left wholly unchecked, the wealth gap between rich and poor will grow ever wider, and most of the wealth in the world will be in the hands of a few in the long term.

It is only the governments that are to be blamed for failing to recognize this mathematical reality and install effective wealth-pumps to keep an equitable balance of wealth between the top and bottom layers of society.

Chapter 17 is devoted to the mathematical laws that lead to this uncomfortable truth about the wealth distribution in the world and the tax measures that governments should take to maintain some equilibrium.

### 23.1.10 The dirty secret: With your deposits, banks may be earning more money for themselves than they let you earn for yourself (chapter 9)

With the Term Deposits that you place with the banks, the banks may be making more money for themselves than they let you make for yourself.

Recall our discovery in section 23.2 that a 3% differential yield rate can be more valuable than a 20% nominal yield rate. The problem with bank deposits is that the bank always takes the smaller-looking, higher-valued differential yield rate for themselves, leaving you with the larger-looking, lower-valued nominal yield rate. That is how banks and their shareholders get richer with your money and at your cost.

Why not earn it all for yourself? Or why not go an extra step and copy what the banks do?

Chapter 9 is devoted to this shocking discovery.

Chapter 10 is devoted to copying banks' earning model by borrowing to invest.

### 23.1.11 Borrowing to invest is one of the fastest highways to millionairedom and Billionairedom (chapter 10)

In example 1.2.3 in chapter 1, we had seen that by borrowing $10,000 from your neighbor at a 20% interest rate and investing it at a 23% yield rate, you had earned a total return of $2.61 million in 30 years. This was achieved without any investment of your own.

Even if you have some money to invest, why not maximize your return by maximizing your investment also through borrowing? Returning to the example, if you had borrowed $1 million instead of only $10,000, your total return would have been $261 million.

When you borrow to invest, you magnify your potential to build wealth.

All the huge companies of today, and almost all the super-wealthy people, created their huge wealth by using other people's money. You can also replicate them to millionairedom.

Do not be held back by a lack of money to invest. Borrowing can also be a great way to get on the highway to riches.

Do the complete math using the actual amounts and numbers involved before making investment decisions. **Using percentages alone, or ratios alone, can be totally misleading.**

In chapter 10, we have analyzed the mathematics of borrowing to invest.

### 23.1.12 Tax paradise may be a fool's paradise: Tax evaders may be losing more money than they save on tax, thus paying out of their own pocket to lose money and get labeled as criminals (chapter 19)

It is also due to the lack of knowledge that some people break the laws and evade tax, even with lawfully earned money, thinking that they are ultimately saving a lot of money. Yes, they may be saving the tax, but many of them would surely be losing a lot more money than what they save on tax. The loss is incurred because of a leak through a hole in the 4D world of compounding, a hole that they do not even know exists.

Just think of the loss if the tax evader accepts a lower 20% yield rate instead of 23% as in our example 1.2.3. In the long term, **the earnings with a 20% yield rate are less than half of the earnings with a 23% yield rate.** Most tax evaders do not know that a 3% differential yield rate can mean a loss of 50% or more in total return. This loss is more than a capital gains tax of, for example, 30%, which may apply if the money was invested in tax-deferred investments like real estate.

Moreover, dubious investments with black money will always yield considerably less than transparent investments with white money. The loss because of this in the long term will be more than 100% of what they ultimately earn, as is the case in the example with a 20% and 23% yield rate. Think also of the drag caused by periodic fees for hiding the money, loss due to exchange rate, etc.

In essence, in the long term, tax evaders lose a lot more money than they save on taxes, pay from their own pocket for secretly arranging such lossy schemes, pay for adding the label "criminal" as an invisible prefix to their names, pay for converting white money into a thinner bundle of difficult-to-spend black money, and pay for losing their sleep. The unlucky ones get caught, lose everything, and may end up in jail. The cause? Lack of insight into the effects of compounding.

In addition, the risk of your black money getting embezzled by unscrupulous middlemen and money managers in obscure tax paradises is also relatively high, leaving you with little or no legal recourse.

However, corrupt politicians and other criminals with ill-gotten money may not be deterred by the shock of this revelation and are likely to continue their criminal path. But pure tax evaders should really take note and reverse gear.

Chapter 19 was devoted to this shocking revelation for tax evaders.

### 23.1.13  What will it take to generate $1 million net worth? (chapter 11)

In chapter 11, we considered **various combinations of initial investments and yield rates** and analyzed **how long it would take** to accumulate a net worth of $1 million.

We analyzed how the needed time to reach a net worth of $1 million would change when initial investments and yield rates are changed.

In that chapter, we developed an **investment matrix** giving the time-period that will be needed to reach a net worth of **$1 million for various combinations of initial investments and yield rates.**

We have also made graphical presentations of the various combinations of investment parameters to make at-a-glance reading possible. These tables and graphs will make your choice of investment easier even without doing any calculation.

**We have seen that, by doubling the initial investment, you double your final amount in the same time period.**

But by doubling the initial investment, you gain only a fraction (3.8 out of 21.5 years, for example) of the original time-period to reach your specific target of $1 million. **The decrease in time with an increase in initial investment is logarithmic. In other words, the initial investment needs to be increased exponentially to achieve equal reductions in the time needed to reach your targeted net worth.**

**If the yield rate is increased, the time needed to reach the targeted net worth decreases almost linearly, with an increasing lag.**

### 23.1.14  Aim for $10 Million or 100 Million net worth instead of just 1 Million (chapter 16)

The time and effort it takes to go from **$10,000 to $1 million** are the same as it takes to go from **$1 million to $100 million**. Why not then go for the highest feasible net worth?

In chapter 16, we have made several investment matrixes for various combinations of initial investments, yield rates, and years needed to reach net worth varying from $0.1 million to $1,000 Billion.

By analyzing them, we come to the following conclusions and recommendations.

**Maximize the amount of your investment, even by borrowing if the risk is low.**

With a **25.9%** yield rate, your investment will grow **10x** times in **10 years**, **100x** times in **20 years**, and **1,000x** times in **30 years**.

With a **25.9%** yield rate, if you invest **$10,000** today, in 20 years, you will have a net worth of **$1 million**. But if you can invest **$1 million** today, you can have **$100 million** in 20 years.

**Time-distance from $1 million to destination $100 million is the same as the time-distance from $10,000 to destination $1 million. Therefore, it is prudent to go for the highest achievable target!**

Therefore, even if you do have enough money to invest to reach a targeted net worth of $1 million, and the investment is a safe one, borrowing to maximize your investment can become your Ferrari on the highway to Billionairedom. See chapter 10 for details about borrowing to invest.

Almost all super-wealthy individuals and companies have grown so big mostly with other people's money. With only your own money saved from an average salary, the chance of you becoming a multi-millionaire is tiny.

### 23.1.15    Annual tax versus Deferred tax (Income tax versus Capital Gains tax)

Income tax is an annual tax, and Capital Gains tax is a deferred tax in most countries.

If you are paying 30% deferred tax or capital gains tax instead of 30% annual tax on your 40-year investment with a 20% yield rate, your net worth would be 70% of your tax-free wealth instead of only 12.8% with annual tax.

Your net worth after 40 years with deferred tax would thus be 5.47x times bigger than your net worth with annual tax.

If you cannot get tax exemption or reduction for your investments, you should aim to qualify for deferred tax or choose an investment class that allows for deferred tax. Real estate is typically one in that category.

Needless to say that, not only Tax Rate but also Tax Drag must be one of the most critical components that must be assessed meticulously prior to any investment.

### 23.1.16    Annual tax instead of Deferred tax is equally disadvantageous to the government as it is to the taxpayer

By imposing annual tax instead of deferred tax, the government would also be missing, just like you, extra income, which it would have otherwise got. The percentual loss of additional income to the government and to you will be equal.

Replacing annual tax with deferred tax would be facilitating citizens to invest and build more wealth, and as a result, they would ultimately be paying more tax than with annual tax.

If it was 30% deferred tax or capital gains tax instead of 30% annual tax or income tax on your 40-year investment with a 20% yield rate, your net worth would have been 70% of your potential wealth instead of only 12.8% with annual tax.

Your net worth after 40 years with deferred tax would thus be 5.47x times higher than your net worth with annual tax.

The tax revenue that the government would receive from you with deferred tax would also be 5.74x times higher than the revenue from the annual tax.

The overwhelmingly prevalent system of annual tax debilitates investments and the creation of wealth and ultimately makes the citizens, as well as the government and the country as a whole, poorer. It is a lose-lose tax system for the government as well as for the taxpayer, the creator of wealth. It is a far-from-intelligent system and will take intelligent and far-sighted politicians to change it.

The software program **Yieldometer** will automatically calculate and present all these tax-related data for any given set of investment parameters.

A specific chapter in volume II of this book series is also devoted to analyzing this little-known fact that the government is also an equal loser with the system of annual taxes.

### 23.1.17  Investment with deferred tax (capital gains tax) may give you a higher net worth than a tax-free investment

Which of the two investments should you choose: a 30-year investment with a 20% yield rate and 30% deferred tax or a tax-free investment with an 18.5% yield rate?

The answer is: you will be better off with the 20% yield rate and 30% deferred tax.

Likewise, for a 10-year investment period, you will be better off with an investment at a 10% yield rate and 20% deferred tax than a tax-free investment at an 8.5% yield rate.

Most people will be choosing tax-free investments rather than investments with higher yield rates and tax, thereby losing money due to the lack of mathematical insight.

As emphasized in this book, never make investment decisions based only on percentages, but always based also on actual amounts.

This book has shown to you, in chapters 14 and 15, how to calculate the net worth of any investment using CAF and CYF tables or get the investment results instantaneously using the software program **Yieldometer** as explained in chapter 22.

### 23.1.18  Compound Amount Factor (CAF) table (chapter 4)

Using a computer or calculator, we can calculate precisely how much an investment of $1 would have grown to for any combination of yield rate and investment period. The value is called the Compound Amount Factor (CAF) for that combination of yield rate and time-period. The third dimension in our virtual 3D world of compounding, i.e., time, is thus incorporated in the CAF value.

As our aim is to be able to make investment decisions even without a computer or complex calculations, a full matrix-table of CAF values has been calculated and presented in this book in **Appendix-A**. The yield rate ranges from 1% to 100%, and the time-periods from 1 year to 60 years.

**To calculate the final amount for any amount of initial investment, we only need to multiply the initial investment with the CAF value.** It is that simple.

If there is no tax involved, the initial investment multiplied by the CAF value will give you the net worth directly.

Chapter 4 is devoted to CAF values and CAF table together with other values and tables.

## 23.1.19    Compound yield Factor (CYF) table (chapter 4)

This table is very identical to the CAF table. The only difference is that this table will give you the total return or cumulative interest instead of the final amount for $1 invested for any combination of yield rate and time-period.

The only difference with values in the CAF table is that all CYF values are lower in value by exactly one (1.00).

If you multiply the CYF value with the initial investment, you will get the net yield (tax considered zero) instead of net worth.

A full matrix-table of CYF values has been calculated and presented in this book in **Appendix-B**.

Chapter 4 is devoted to CAF & CYF values and tables.

## 23.1.20    Using CAF and CYF tables to assess and compare investment results (chapter 14)

This book (Volume 1) will show you a pretty simple way to arrive at the investment results you want using only CAF and CYF tables. Simply looking at and comparing the values in the tables without even performing any calculation is often enough to assess and make investment comparisons and decisions.

You will be able to calculate the total return, net return, net worth, tax, and other relevant investment data using only the CAF and CYF tables and a simple calculator doing just addition, subtraction, multiplication, or division.

After going through volume 2 of the **Highway to Riches series**, which is titled **Tax Drag, the Dragon that eats up your wealth**, you will also be able to calculate tax drag and other tax-related investment data using these tables.

The easiest way to calculate all these and many other investment data instantly is to use a suitable software program. **Yieldometer** is such a software specifically developed for this purpose by the author of this book.

Chapter 4 is devoted to CAF & CYF values and tables.

Chapter 22 is devoted to the software program Yieldometer.

Appendix-A shows the full CAF table.

Appendix-B shows the full CYF table.

### 23.1.21    Learn to make your route plan to reach $1 Million or more net worth using CAF or CYF table (chapter 15)

In chapter 15, we have learned to make the calculations needed to add one or more million dollars EXTRA to your net worth using the CAF and CYF tables appended to this book.

For any investment, there are five primary variables that you must decide upon and fix to enable you to make the calculations. Those variables are:

1. Initial investment ($P$).
2. Number of years ($N$).
3. Yield rate ($R$).
4. Tax rate ($T$).
5. Net yield ($NY$) or net worth ($NW$) that you want to add.

After fixing 4 of the 5 variables at the desired level first, we can calculate what the value of the fifth variable needs to be in order to meet the set values of the other 4. We can do this using only the CAF or CYF tables and a simple calculator, thus without any software program.

We can do this in turn for all 5 variables.

Doing the necessary calculations manually this way serves a double purpose.

1. Learn how to do the necessary calculations using only the CAF and CYF tables and a simple calculator.

2. Understand the various characteristics of compounding and their impact on wealth-building.

### 23.1.22    Taking a loan with your Term Deposit as collateral is a recipe for losses (chapter 8)

When you have a term deposit or other assets in a bank and need money for a major purchase as a house or car, and the bank advises you not to take your deposit but take a loan instead so that you can also benefit from tax deductions, most of the time you will end up losing money and the bank will be the only one profiting.

Worst still, you may even become an instrument in the hands of the bank to siphon off tax money from the government, which will ultimately flow to the bank.

If you have money in the bank, borrowing at an interest rate higher than what you get on your deposit is always a path leading to losses irrespective of whether or not you get tax advantages.

Chapter 8 is devoted to this unethical practice.

### 23.1.23 Volume 2 of this book series: "Tax Drag, the dragon that eats up your wealth" (chapter 18)

A complete treatise of tax and tax drag is given in Volume 2 of this series of books. The reasons for treating them in a separate volume are the following:

- Reducing tax drag is of paramount importance to wealth building as almost everyone in almost every country is affected by tax and tax drag. Their impact on wealth building is much bigger than what the nominal tax rate suggests.

- The investment scenarios and the mathematics involved are more complex with tax drag than investment without tax. When tax drag is also involved, your financial world becomes a 4D world, and you will need 4D glasses to see everything clearly. Volume 2 of the book series will serve you as your 4D glasses.

- If tax drag was included in this volume, this book would have become double this size, making it too unwieldy to manage, publish and read easily.

Volume 2 of the book is titled **Tax Drag, the Dragon that eats up your wealth**. The manuscript is already prepared, and the book will be published soon.

A fundamental understanding of the characteristics of compounding, as presented in Volume-I of the book series, is necessary to understand tax drag and everything that is presented in volume 2. Skipping this volume 1 and jumping to volume 2 is disadvised even if you are a graduate in Mathematics.

After going through volume 2 of the book series, you will be able to adapt your investment options to reduce tax drag and reach your targeted net worth much faster. Ultimately, you will have a net worth that is many folds bigger than you would have had as a tax-slave.

With volume 2 of the book series dedicated to tax matters, tax aspects are not discussed in detail in this Volume 1 of the series. The tax rate was assumed zero for calculations in this volume of the book unless specified otherwise.

An introduction to tax drag is given in section 3.4 and chapter 18 of this book.

### 23.1.24 Yield-o-meter, the investment software (chapter 22)

Instead of assessing investment options using tables and calculators, the software Yieldometer will instantly calculate an array of **400+ data for any set of investment parameters**.

Input needed is any three or more of the six parameters, namely, initial investment, number of years, yield rate, tax rate, targeted net worth, and target CAF or CYF value.

An introduction to Yieldometer is given in chapter 22 of this book, together with screenshots of some of the results that the software will calculate and present to you.

Basic knowledge of the topics presented in volumes 1 and 2 of this series of books is needed to understand and sensibly interpret the data that Yieldometer will calculate and present to you for any wealth-building plan. It is for that reason that the software will be released only after the publication of also volume 2 of this series.

### 23.1.25   This book is littered with more such gems of insight

This book, and volume 2 of this series, are littered with secrets and wisdom like the ones sketched above. They will fundamentally change the way you look at money and wealth building. You will have a third eye that will spot opportunities to build wealth for yourself instead of only seeing others build wealth and wondering how they did it. You will be able to choose tailor-made investment vehicles and devise intelligent plans to build wealth and reach your targeted net worth much faster than you had thought possible. In the long term, you will have a net worth that Is many folds bigger than what you would have had without this book.

Einstein had once qualified the effect of compounding as the eighth world-wonder!

**If you landed in this final section after having gone through this book and absorbed the essence of what is covered, you will understand 100% why Einstein said so. By the end of Volume 2, you will appreciate it 200%, and you will have developed a third eye to see wealth-building in its full depth in 4D and a set of brains that can think in 4D.**

### 23.2      THE WEALTH MULTIPLIER FORMULA: $W_{(K)} = W_{(1)} K^2$

Probably the most famous scientific formula in the world is Albert Einstein's $E = MC^2$. Explained in very simplified terms, it states that matter **M,** such as the nuclear particles of an atom, can be converted into energy **E** (heat), and the exchange rate for that conversion is the square of the speed of light **C**. The speed of light is about 300,000 km/s or 186,000 miles/s, and the square of it is 90 Billion and 34.6 Billion, respectively. With such an astoundingly high conversion factor, you need only a tiny bit of matter (Uranium, for example) to produce an enormous amount of energy in the form of heat. This is what lies at the heart of the nuclear bomb, as well as all those billions and billions of heat-emitting bright stars in the universe, including our own Sun.

Though at an infinitesimally smaller scale, there is an analogy between creating energy from matter and creating much bigger wealth from smaller wealth. The formula for wealth-building can be written as follows.

$$W_{(k)} = W_{(1)} K^2$$

In this formula, **K** stands for **Knowledge level, W**$_{(1)}$ stands for **Wealth** at Knowledge **level 1**, and **W**$_{(k)}$ stands for **Wealth** at Knowledge **level K**,

If you have a knowledge level of 1 in wealth building, which we assume to be the global average, your growth of wealth will also be equal to the global average because the value of $K^2$ is equal to $1^2$, which is also merely 1.

But if you have a knowledge level of **10** in wealth building, which equals the caliber of multimillionaires and Billionaires, your growth of wealth will be equal to **100x times** the global average because the value of $K^2$ is equal to the square of 10, which is 100.

If the average person with a Knowledge level of 1 succeeds in increasing his wealth from $1 million to **$10 million** in 20 years, the person with a Knowledge level of 10 will succeed in increasing his wealth from $1 million to **$1,000 million** in 20 years.

## 23.3     BON VOYAGE!

My endeavor has been, and also my hope is that this book will have helped you to raise your level of knowledge in wealth-building substantially, enabling you to increase your net worth at least 25-fold in your lifetime compared to what your net worth would be without the knowledge and insight contained in the pages of this book.

**Bon voyage! Have an exciting ride on the Highway to Riches!**

\* \* \* \*

# APPENDIX-A:

## Compound Amount Factor (CAF) table

| Compound Amount Factor (CAF) table, page 1 | | | | | | | | |
|---|---|---|---|---|---|---|---|---|
| **Year (N)** | **Yield Rate ( R )** | | | | | | | |
| | 1.00% | 1.50% | 2.00% | 2.50% | 3.00% | 3.50% | 4.00% | 4.50% | 5.00% |
| 0 | 1.000 | 1.000 | 1.000 | 1.000 | 1.000 | 1.000 | 1.000 | 1.000 | 1.000 |
| 1 | 1.010 | 1.015 | 1.020 | 1.025 | 1.030 | 1.035 | 1.040 | 1.045 | 1.050 |
| 2 | 1.020 | 1.030 | 1.040 | 1.051 | 1.061 | 1.071 | 1.082 | 1.092 | 1.103 |
| 3 | 1.030 | 1.046 | 1.061 | 1.077 | 1.093 | 1.109 | 1.125 | 1.141 | 1.158 |
| 4 | 1.041 | 1.061 | 1.082 | 1.104 | 1.126 | 1.148 | 1.170 | 1.193 | 1.216 |
| 5 | 1.051 | 1.077 | 1.104 | 1.131 | 1.159 | 1.188 | 1.217 | 1.246 | 1.276 |
| 6 | 1.062 | 1.093 | 1.126 | 1.160 | 1.194 | 1.229 | 1.265 | 1.302 | 1.340 |
| 7 | 1.072 | 1.110 | 1.149 | 1.189 | 1.230 | 1.272 | 1.316 | 1.361 | 1.407 |
| 8 | 1.083 | 1.126 | 1.172 | 1.218 | 1.267 | 1.317 | 1.369 | 1.422 | 1.477 |
| 9 | 1.094 | 1.143 | 1.195 | 1.249 | 1.305 | 1.363 | 1.423 | 1.486 | 1.551 |
| 10 | 1.105 | 1.161 | 1.219 | 1.280 | 1.344 | 1.411 | 1.480 | 1.553 | 1.629 |
| 11 | 1.116 | 1.178 | 1.243 | 1.312 | 1.384 | 1.460 | 1.539 | 1.623 | 1.710 |
| 12 | 1.127 | 1.196 | 1.268 | 1.345 | 1.426 | 1.511 | 1.601 | 1.696 | 1.796 |
| 13 | 1.138 | 1.214 | 1.294 | 1.379 | 1.469 | 1.564 | 1.665 | 1.772 | 1.886 |
| 14 | 1.149 | 1.232 | 1.319 | 1.413 | 1.513 | 1.619 | 1.732 | 1.852 | 1.980 |
| 15 | 1.161 | 1.250 | 1.346 | 1.448 | 1.558 | 1.675 | 1.801 | 1.935 | 2.079 |
| 16 | 1.173 | 1.269 | 1.373 | 1.485 | 1.605 | 1.734 | 1.873 | 2.022 | 2.183 |
| 17 | 1.184 | 1.288 | 1.400 | 1.522 | 1.653 | 1.795 | 1.948 | 2.113 | 2.292 |
| 18 | 1.196 | 1.307 | 1.428 | 1.560 | 1.702 | 1.857 | 2.026 | 2.208 | 2.407 |
| 19 | 1.208 | 1.327 | 1.457 | 1.599 | 1.754 | 1.923 | 2.107 | 2.308 | 2.527 |
| 20 | 1.220 | 1.347 | 1.486 | 1.639 | 1.806 | 1.990 | 2.191 | 2.412 | 2.653 |
| 21 | 1.232 | 1.367 | 1.516 | 1.680 | 1.860 | 2.059 | 2.279 | 2.520 | 2.786 |
| 22 | 1.245 | 1.388 | 1.546 | 1.722 | 1.916 | 2.132 | 2.370 | 2.634 | 2.925 |
| 23 | 1.257 | 1.408 | 1.577 | 1.765 | 1.974 | 2.206 | 2.465 | 2.752 | 3.072 |
| 24 | 1.270 | 1.430 | 1.608 | 1.809 | 2.033 | 2.283 | 2.563 | 2.876 | 3.225 |
| 25 | 1.282 | 1.451 | 1.641 | 1.854 | 2.094 | 2.363 | 2.666 | 3.005 | 3.386 |
| 26 | 1.295 | 1.473 | 1.673 | 1.900 | 2.157 | 2.446 | 2.772 | 3.141 | 3.556 |
| 27 | 1.308 | 1.495 | 1.707 | 1.948 | 2.221 | 2.532 | 2.883 | 3.282 | 3.733 |
| 28 | 1.321 | 1.517 | 1.741 | 1.996 | 2.288 | 2.620 | 2.999 | 3.430 | 3.920 |
| 29 | 1.335 | 1.540 | 1.776 | 2.046 | 2.357 | 2.712 | 3.119 | 3.584 | 4.116 |
| 30 | 1.348 | 1.563 | 1.811 | 2.098 | 2.427 | 2.807 | 3.243 | 3.745 | 4.322 |
| 31 | 1.361 | 1.587 | 1.848 | 2.150 | 2.500 | 2.905 | 3.373 | 3.914 | 4.538 |
| 32 | 1.375 | 1.610 | 1.885 | 2.204 | 2.575 | 3.007 | 3.508 | 4.090 | 4.765 |
| 33 | 1.389 | 1.634 | 1.922 | 2.259 | 2.652 | 3.112 | 3.648 | 4.274 | 5.003 |
| 34 | 1.403 | 1.659 | 1.961 | 2.315 | 2.732 | 3.221 | 3.794 | 4.466 | 5.253 |
| 35 | 1.417 | 1.684 | 2.000 | 2.373 | 2.814 | 3.334 | 3.946 | 4.667 | 5.516 |
| 36 | 1.431 | 1.709 | 2.040 | 2.433 | 2.898 | 3.450 | 4.104 | 4.877 | 5.792 |
| 37 | 1.445 | 1.735 | 2.081 | 2.493 | 2.985 | 3.571 | 4.268 | 5.097 | 6.081 |
| 38 | 1.460 | 1.761 | 2.122 | 2.556 | 3.075 | 3.696 | 4.439 | 5.326 | 6.385 |
| 39 | 1.474 | 1.787 | 2.165 | 2.620 | 3.167 | 3.825 | 4.616 | 5.566 | 6.705 |
| 40 | 1.489 | 1.814 | 2.208 | 2.685 | 3.262 | 3.959 | 4.801 | 5.816 | 7.040 |
| 41 | 1.504 | 1.841 | 2.252 | 2.752 | 3.360 | 4.098 | 4.993 | 6.078 | 7.392 |
| 42 | 1.519 | 1.869 | 2.297 | 2.821 | 3.461 | 4.241 | 5.193 | 6.352 | 7.762 |
| 43 | 1.534 | 1.897 | 2.343 | 2.892 | 3.565 | 4.390 | 5.400 | 6.637 | 8.150 |
| 44 | 1.549 | 1.925 | 2.390 | 2.964 | 3.671 | 4.543 | 5.617 | 6.936 | 8.557 |
| 45 | 1.565 | 1.954 | 2.438 | 3.038 | 3.782 | 4.702 | 5.841 | 7.248 | 8.985 |
| 46 | 1.580 | 1.984 | 2.487 | 3.114 | 3.895 | 4.867 | 6.075 | 7.574 | 9.434 |
| 47 | 1.596 | 2.013 | 2.536 | 3.192 | 4.012 | 5.037 | 6.318 | 7.915 | 9.906 |
| 48 | 1.612 | 2.043 | 2.587 | 3.271 | 4.132 | 5.214 | 6.571 | 8.271 | 10.40 |
| 49 | 1.628 | 2.074 | 2.639 | 3.353 | 4.256 | 5.396 | 6.833 | 8.644 | 10.92 |
| 50 | 1.645 | 2.105 | 2.692 | 3.437 | 4.384 | 5.585 | 7.107 | 9.033 | 11.47 |
| 51 | 1.661 | 2.137 | 2.745 | 3.523 | 4.515 | 5.780 | 7.391 | 9.439 | 12.04 |
| 52 | 1.678 | 2.169 | 2.800 | 3.611 | 4.651 | 5.983 | 7.687 | 9.864 | 12.64 |
| 53 | 1.694 | 2.201 | 2.856 | 3.701 | 4.790 | 6.192 | 7.994 | 10.31 | 13.27 |
| 54 | 1.711 | 2.234 | 2.913 | 3.794 | 4.934 | 6.409 | 8.314 | 10.77 | 13.94 |
| 55 | 1.729 | 2.268 | 2.972 | 3.889 | 5.082 | 6.633 | 8.646 | 11.26 | 14.64 |
| 56 | 1.746 | 2.302 | 3.031 | 3.986 | 5.235 | 6.865 | 8.992 | 11.76 | 15.37 |
| 57 | 1.763 | 2.336 | 3.092 | 4.086 | 5.392 | 7.106 | 9.352 | 12.29 | 16.14 |
| 58 | 1.781 | 2.372 | 3.154 | 4.188 | 5.553 | 7.354 | 9.726 | 12.85 | 16.94 |
| 59 | 1.799 | 2.407 | 3.217 | 4.292 | 5.720 | 7.612 | 10.12 | 13.42 | 17.79 |
| 60 | 1.817 | 2.443 | 3.281 | 4.400 | 5.892 | 7.878 | 10.52 | 14.03 | 18.68 |
| | 1.0% | 1.5% | 2.0% | 2.5% | 3.0% | 3.5% | 4.0% | 4.5% | 5.0% |

| Year (N) | Yield Rate ( R ) | | | | | | | | | |
|---|---|---|---|---|---|---|---|---|---|---|
| | 5.50% | 6.00% | 6.50% | 7.00% | 7.50% | 8.00% | 8.50% | 9.00% | 9.50% | 10.00% |
| 0 | 1.000 | 1.000 | 1.000 | 1.000 | 1.000 | 1.000 | 1.000 | 1.000 | 1.000 | 1.000 |
| 1 | 1.055 | 1.060 | 1.065 | 1.070 | 1.075 | 1.080 | 1.085 | 1.090 | 1.095 | 1.100 |
| 2 | 1.113 | 1.124 | 1.134 | 1.145 | 1.156 | 1.166 | 1.177 | 1.188 | 1.199 | 1.210 |
| 3 | 1.174 | 1.191 | 1.208 | 1.225 | 1.242 | 1.260 | 1.277 | 1.295 | 1.313 | 1.331 |
| 4 | 1.239 | 1.262 | 1.286 | 1.311 | 1.335 | 1.360 | 1.386 | 1.412 | 1.438 | 1.464 |
| 5 | 1.307 | 1.338 | 1.370 | 1.403 | 1.436 | 1.469 | 1.504 | 1.539 | 1.574 | 1.611 |
| 6 | 1.379 | 1.419 | 1.459 | 1.501 | 1.543 | 1.587 | 1.631 | 1.677 | 1.724 | 1.772 |
| 7 | 1.455 | 1.504 | 1.554 | 1.606 | 1.659 | 1.714 | 1.770 | 1.828 | 1.888 | 1.949 |
| 8 | 1.535 | 1.594 | 1.655 | 1.718 | 1.783 | 1.851 | 1.921 | 1.993 | 2.067 | 2.144 |
| 9 | 1.619 | 1.689 | 1.763 | 1.838 | 1.917 | 1.999 | 2.084 | 2.172 | 2.263 | 2.358 |
| 10 | 1.708 | 1.791 | 1.877 | 1.967 | 2.061 | 2.159 | 2.261 | 2.367 | 2.478 | 2.594 |
| 11 | 1.802 | 1.898 | 1.999 | 2.105 | 2.216 | 2.332 | 2.453 | 2.580 | 2.714 | 2.853 |
| 12 | 1.901 | 2.012 | 2.129 | 2.252 | 2.382 | 2.518 | 2.662 | 2.813 | 2.971 | 3.138 |
| 13 | 2.006 | 2.133 | 2.267 | 2.410 | 2.560 | 2.720 | 2.888 | 3.066 | 3.254 | 3.452 |
| 14 | 2.116 | 2.261 | 2.415 | 2.579 | 2.752 | 2.937 | 3.133 | 3.342 | 3.563 | 3.797 |
| 15 | 2.232 | 2.397 | 2.572 | 2.759 | 2.959 | 3.172 | 3.400 | 3.642 | 3.901 | 4.177 |
| 16 | 2.355 | 2.540 | 2.739 | 2.952 | 3.181 | 3.426 | 3.689 | 3.970 | 4.272 | 4.595 |
| 17 | 2.485 | 2.693 | 2.917 | 3.159 | 3.419 | 3.700 | 4.002 | 4.328 | 4.678 | 5.054 |
| 18 | 2.621 | 2.854 | 3.107 | 3.380 | 3.676 | 3.996 | 4.342 | 4.717 | 5.122 | 5.560 |
| 19 | 2.766 | 3.026 | 3.309 | 3.617 | 3.951 | 4.316 | 4.712 | 5.142 | 5.609 | 6.116 |
| 20 | 2.918 | 3.207 | 3.524 | 3.870 | 4.248 | 4.661 | 5.112 | 5.604 | 6.142 | 6.727 |
| 21 | 3.078 | 3.400 | 3.753 | 4.141 | 4.566 | 5.034 | 5.547 | 6.109 | 6.725 | 7.400 |
| 22 | 3.248 | 3.604 | 3.997 | 4.430 | 4.909 | 5.437 | 6.018 | 6.659 | 7.364 | 8.140 |
| 23 | 3.426 | 3.820 | 4.256 | 4.741 | 5.277 | 5.871 | 6.530 | 7.258 | 8.064 | 8.954 |
| 24 | 3.615 | 4.049 | 4.533 | 5.072 | 5.673 | 6.341 | 7.085 | 7.911 | 8.830 | 9.850 |
| 25 | 3.813 | 4.292 | 4.828 | 5.427 | 6.098 | 6.848 | 7.687 | 8.623 | 9.668 | 10.83 |
| 26 | 4.023 | 4.549 | 5.141 | 5.807 | 6.556 | 7.396 | 8.340 | 9.399 | 10.59 | 11.92 |
| 27 | 4.244 | 4.822 | 5.476 | 6.214 | 7.047 | 7.988 | 9.049 | 10.25 | 11.59 | 13.11 |
| 28 | 4.478 | 5.112 | 5.832 | 6.649 | 7.576 | 8.627 | 9.818 | 11.17 | 12.69 | 14.42 |
| 29 | 4.724 | 5.418 | 6.211 | 7.114 | 8.144 | 9.317 | 10.65 | 12.17 | 13.90 | 15.86 |
| 30 | 4.984 | 5.743 | 6.614 | 7.612 | 8.755 | 10.06 | 11.56 | 13.27 | 15.22 | 17.45 |
| 31 | 5.258 | 6.088 | 7.044 | 8.145 | 9.412 | 10.87 | 12.54 | 14.46 | 16.67 | 19.19 |
| 32 | 5.547 | 6.453 | 7.502 | 8.715 | 10.12 | 11.74 | 13.61 | 15.76 | 18.25 | 21.11 |
| 33 | 5.852 | 6.841 | 7.990 | 9.325 | 10.88 | 12.68 | 14.76 | 17.18 | 19.98 | 23.23 |
| 34 | 6.174 | 7.251 | 8.509 | 9.978 | 11.69 | 13.69 | 16.02 | 18.73 | 21.88 | 25.55 |
| 35 | 6.514 | 7.686 | 9.062 | 10.68 | 12.57 | 14.79 | 17.38 | 20.41 | 23.96 | 28.10 |
| 36 | 6.872 | 8.147 | 9.651 | 11.42 | 13.51 | 15.97 | 18.86 | 22.25 | 26.24 | 30.91 |
| 37 | 7.250 | 8.636 | 10.28 | 12.22 | 14.52 | 17.25 | 20.46 | 24.25 | 28.73 | 34.00 |
| 38 | 7.649 | 9.154 | 10.95 | 13.08 | 15.61 | 18.63 | 22.20 | 26.44 | 31.46 | 37.40 |
| 39 | 8.069 | 9.704 | 11.66 | 13.99 | 16.79 | 20.12 | 24.09 | 28.82 | 34.45 | 41.14 |
| 40 | 8.513 | 10.29 | 12.42 | 14.97 | 18.04 | 21.72 | 26.13 | 31.41 | 37.72 | 45.26 |
| 41 | 8.982 | 10.90 | 13.22 | 16.02 | 19.40 | 23.46 | 28.35 | 34.24 | 41.30 | 49.79 |
| 42 | 9.476 | 11.56 | 14.08 | 17.14 | 20.85 | 25.34 | 30.76 | 37.32 | 45.23 | 54.76 |
| 43 | 9.997 | 12.25 | 15.00 | 18.34 | 22.42 | 27.37 | 33.38 | 40.68 | 49.52 | 60.24 |
| 44 | 10.55 | 12.99 | 15.97 | 19.63 | 24.10 | 29.56 | 36.22 | 44.34 | 54.23 | 66.26 |
| 45 | 11.13 | 13.76 | 17.01 | 21.00 | 25.90 | 31.92 | 39.30 | 48.33 | 59.38 | 72.89 |
| 46 | 11.74 | 14.59 | 18.12 | 22.47 | 27.85 | 34.47 | 42.64 | 52.68 | 65.02 | 80.18 |
| 47 | 12.38 | 15.47 | 19.29 | 24.05 | 29.94 | 37.23 | 46.26 | 57.42 | 71.20 | 88.20 |
| 48 | 13.07 | 16.39 | 20.55 | 25.73 | 32.18 | 40.21 | 50.19 | 62.59 | 77.96 | 97.02 |
| 49 | 13.78 | 17.38 | 21.88 | 27.53 | 34.60 | 43.43 | 54.46 | 68.22 | 85.37 | 106.7 |
| 50 | 14.54 | 18.42 | 23.31 | 29.46 | 37.19 | 46.90 | 59.09 | 74.36 | 93.48 | 117.4 |
| 51 | 15.34 | 19.53 | 24.82 | 31.52 | 39.98 | 50.65 | 64.11 | 81.05 | 102.4 | 129.1 |
| 52 | 16.19 | 20.70 | 26.44 | 33.73 | 42.98 | 54.71 | 69.56 | 88.34 | 112.1 | 142.0 |
| 53 | 17.08 | 21.94 | 28.15 | 36.09 | 46.20 | 59.08 | 75.47 | 96.30 | 122.7 | 156.2 |
| 54 | 18.01 | 23.26 | 29.98 | 38.61 | 49.67 | 63.81 | 81.89 | 105.0 | 134.4 | 171.9 |
| 55 | 19.01 | 24.65 | 31.93 | 41.32 | 53.39 | 68.91 | 88.85 | 114.4 | 147.2 | 189.1 |
| 56 | 20.05 | 26.13 | 34.01 | 44.21 | 57.39 | 74.43 | 96.40 | 124.7 | 161.1 | 208.0 |
| 57 | 21.15 | 27.70 | 36.22 | 47.30 | 61.70 | 80.38 | 104.6 | 135.9 | 176.4 | 228.8 |
| 58 | 22.32 | 29.36 | 38.57 | 50.61 | 66.33 | 86.81 | 113.5 | 148.2 | 193.2 | 251.6 |
| 59 | 23.54 | 31.12 | 41.08 | 54.16 | 71.30 | 93.76 | 123.1 | 161.5 | 211.6 | 276.8 |
| 60 | 24.84 | 32.99 | 43.75 | 57.95 | 76.65 | 101.3 | 133.6 | 176.0 | 231.7 | 304.5 |
| | 5.5% | 6.0% | 6.5% | 7.0% | 7.5% | 8.0% | 8.5% | 9.0% | 9.5% | 10.0% |

CAF **table page** 2

| Year (N) | \| Compound Amount Factor (CAF) table, page 3 | | | | | | | | | |
|---|---|---|---|---|---|---|---|---|---|---|
| | 11.00% | 12.00% | 13.00% | 14.00% | 15.00% | 16.00% | 17.00% | 18.00% | 19.00% | 20.00% |
| 0 | 1.000 | 1.000 | 1.000 | 1.000 | 1.000 | 1.000 | 1.000 | 1.000 | 1.000 | 1.000 |
| 1 | 1.110 | 1.120 | 1.130 | 1.140 | 1.150 | 1.160 | 1.170 | 1.180 | 1.190 | 1.200 |
| 2 | 1.232 | 1.254 | 1.277 | 1.300 | 1.323 | 1.346 | 1.369 | 1.392 | 1.416 | 1.440 |
| 3 | 1.368 | 1.405 | 1.443 | 1.482 | 1.521 | 1.561 | 1.602 | 1.643 | 1.685 | 1.728 |
| 4 | 1.518 | 1.574 | 1.630 | 1.689 | 1.749 | 1.811 | 1.874 | 1.939 | 2.005 | 2.074 |
| 5 | 1.685 | 1.762 | 1.842 | 1.925 | 2.011 | 2.100 | 2.192 | 2.288 | 2.386 | 2.488 |
| 6 | 1.870 | 1.974 | 2.082 | 2.195 | 2.313 | 2.436 | 2.565 | 2.700 | 2.840 | 2.986 |
| 7 | 2.076 | 2.211 | 2.353 | 2.502 | 2.660 | 2.826 | 3.001 | 3.185 | 3.379 | 3.583 |
| 8 | 2.305 | 2.476 | 2.658 | 2.853 | 3.059 | 3.278 | 3.511 | 3.759 | 4.021 | 4.300 |
| 9 | 2.558 | 2.773 | 3.004 | 3.252 | 3.518 | 3.803 | 4.108 | 4.435 | 4.785 | 5.160 |
| 10 | 2.839 | 3.106 | 3.395 | 3.707 | 4.046 | 4.411 | 4.807 | 5.234 | 5.695 | 6.192 |
| 11 | 3.152 | 3.479 | 3.836 | 4.226 | 4.652 | 5.117 | 5.624 | 6.176 | 6.777 | 7.430 |
| 12 | 3.498 | 3.896 | 4.335 | 4.818 | 5.350 | 5.936 | 6.580 | 7.288 | 8.064 | 8.916 |
| 13 | 3.883 | 4.363 | 4.898 | 5.492 | 6.153 | 6.886 | 7.699 | 8.599 | 9.596 | 10.70 |
| 14 | 4.310 | 4.887 | 5.535 | 6.261 | 7.076 | 7.988 | 9.007 | 10.15 | 11.42 | 12.84 |
| 15 | 4.785 | 5.474 | 6.254 | 7.138 | 8.137 | 9.266 | 10.54 | 11.97 | 13.59 | 15.41 |
| 16 | 5.311 | 6.130 | 7.067 | 8.137 | 9.358 | 10.75 | 12.33 | 14.13 | 16.17 | 18.49 |
| 17 | 5.895 | 6.866 | 7.986 | 9.276 | 10.76 | 12.47 | 14.43 | 16.67 | 19.24 | 22.19 |
| 18 | 6.544 | 7.690 | 9.024 | 10.58 | 12.38 | 14.46 | 16.88 | 19.67 | 22.90 | 26.62 |
| 19 | 7.263 | 8.613 | 10.20 | 12.06 | 14.23 | 16.78 | 19.75 | 23.21 | 27.25 | 31.95 |
| 20 | 8.062 | 9.646 | 11.52 | 13.74 | 16.37 | 19.46 | 23.11 | 27.39 | 32.43 | 38.34 |
| 21 | 8.949 | 10.80 | 13.02 | 15.67 | 18.82 | 22.57 | 27.03 | 32.32 | 38.59 | 46.01 |
| 22 | 9.934 | 12.10 | 14.71 | 17.86 | 21.64 | 26.19 | 31.63 | 38.14 | 45.92 | 55.21 |
| 23 | 11.03 | 13.55 | 16.63 | 20.36 | 24.89 | 30.38 | 37.01 | 45.01 | 54.65 | 66.25 |
| 24 | 12.24 | 15.18 | 18.79 | 23.21 | 28.63 | 35.24 | 43.30 | 53.11 | 65.03 | 79.50 |
| 25 | 13.59 | 17.00 | 21.23 | 26.46 | 32.92 | 40.87 | 50.66 | 62.67 | 77.39 | 95.40 |
| 26 | 15.08 | 19.04 | 23.99 | 30.17 | 37.86 | 47.41 | 59.27 | 73.95 | 92.09 | 114.5 |
| 27 | 16.74 | 21.32 | 27.11 | 34.39 | 43.54 | 55.00 | 69.35 | 87.26 | 109.6 | 137.4 |
| 28 | 18.58 | 23.88 | 30.63 | 39.20 | 50.07 | 63.80 | 81.13 | 103.0 | 130.4 | 164.8 |
| 29 | 20.62 | 26.75 | 34.62 | 44.69 | 57.58 | 74.01 | 94.93 | 121.5 | 155.2 | 197.8 |
| 30 | 22.89 | 29.96 | 39.12 | 50.95 | 66.21 | 85.85 | 111.1 | 143.4 | 184.7 | 237.4 |
| 31 | 25.41 | 33.56 | 44.20 | 58.08 | 76.14 | 99.59 | 129.9 | 169.2 | 219.8 | 284.9 |
| 32 | 28.21 | 37.58 | 49.95 | 66.21 | 87.57 | 115.5 | 152.0 | 199.6 | 261.5 | 341.8 |
| 33 | 31.31 | 42.09 | 56.44 | 75.48 | 100.7 | 134.0 | 177.9 | 235.6 | 311.2 | 410.2 |
| 34 | 34.75 | 47.14 | 63.78 | 86.05 | 115.8 | 155.4 | 208.1 | 278.0 | 370.3 | 492.2 |
| 35 | 38.57 | 52.80 | 72.07 | 98.10 | 133.2 | 180.3 | 243.5 | 328.0 | 440.7 | 590.7 |
| 36 | 42.82 | 59.14 | 81.44 | 111.8 | 153.2 | 209.2 | 284.9 | 387.0 | 524.4 | 708.8 |
| 37 | 47.53 | 66.23 | 92.02 | 127.5 | 176.1 | 242.6 | 333.3 | 456.7 | 624.1 | 850.6 |
| 38 | 52.76 | 74.18 | 104.0 | 145.3 | 202.5 | 281.5 | 390.0 | 538.9 | 742.7 | 1,021 |
| 39 | 58.56 | 83.08 | 117.5 | 165.7 | 232.9 | 326.5 | 456.3 | 635.9 | 883.8 | 1,225 |
| 40 | 65.00 | 93.05 | 132.8 | 188.9 | 267.9 | 378.7 | 533.9 | 750.4 | 1,052 | 1,470 |
| 41 | 72.15 | 104.2 | 150.0 | 215.3 | 308.0 | 439.3 | 624.6 | 885.4 | 1,251 | 1,764 |
| 42 | 80.09 | 116.7 | 169.5 | 245.5 | 354.2 | 509.6 | 730.8 | 1,045 | 1,489 | 2,116 |
| 43 | 88.90 | 130.7 | 191.6 | 279.8 | 407.4 | 591.1 | 855.1 | 1,233 | 1,772 | 2,540 |
| 44 | 98.68 | 146.4 | 216.5 | 319.0 | 468.5 | 685.7 | 1,000 | 1,455 | 2,109 | 3,048 |
| 45 | 109.5 | 164.0 | 244.6 | 363.7 | 538.8 | 795.4 | 1,170 | 1,717 | 2,510 | 3,657 |
| 46 | 121.6 | 183.7 | 276.4 | 414.6 | 619.6 | 922.7 | 1,369 | 2,026 | 2,986 | 4,389 |
| 47 | 135.0 | 205.7 | 312.4 | 472.6 | 712.5 | 1,070 | 1,602 | 2,390 | 3,554 | 5,266 |
| 48 | 149.8 | 230.4 | 353.0 | 538.8 | 819.4 | 1,242 | 1,875 | 2,821 | 4,229 | 6,320 |
| 49 | 166.3 | 258.0 | 398.9 | 614.2 | 942.3 | 1,440 | 2,193 | 3,328 | 5,033 | 7,584 |
| 50 | 184.6 | 289.0 | 450.7 | 700.2 | 1,084 | 1,671 | 2,566 | 3,927 | 5,989 | 9,100 |
| 51 | 204.9 | 323.7 | 509.3 | 798.3 | 1,246 | 1,938 | 3,002 | 4,634 | 7,127 | 10,921 |
| 52 | 227.4 | 362.5 | 575.5 | 910.0 | 1,433 | 2,248 | 3,513 | 5,468 | 8,481 | 13,105 |
| 53 | 252.4 | 406.0 | 650.4 | 1,037 | 1,648 | 2,608 | 4,110 | 6,453 | 10,092 | 15,726 |
| 54 | 280.2 | 454.8 | 734.9 | 1,183 | 1,895 | 3,025 | 4,809 | 7,614 | 12,010 | 18,871 |
| 55 | 311.0 | 509.3 | 830.5 | 1,348 | 2,180 | 3,509 | 5,626 | 8,985 | 14,292 | 22,645 |
| 56 | 345.2 | 570.4 | 938.4 | 1,537 | 2,507 | 4,070 | 6,583 | 10,602 | 17,007 | 27,174 |
| 57 | 383.2 | 638.9 | 1,060 | 1,752 | 2,883 | 4,722 | 7,702 | 12,510 | 20,238 | 32,609 |
| 58 | 425.3 | 715.6 | 1,198 | 1,997 | 3,315 | 5,477 | 9,011 | 14,762 | 24,084 | 39,130 |
| 59 | 472.1 | 801.4 | 1,354 | 2,277 | 3,812 | 6,354 | 10,543 | 17,420 | 28,660 | 46,956 |
| 60 | 524.1 | 897.6 | 1,530 | 2,596 | 4,384 | 7,370 | 12,335 | 20,555 | 34,105 | 56,348 |
| | 11.0% | 12.0% | 13.0% | 14.0% | 15.0% | 16.0% | 17.0% | 18.0% | 19.0% | 20.0% |

CAF **table page** 3

| Year | Yield Rate ( R ) | | | | | | | | | |
|---|---|---|---|---|---|---|---|---|---|---|
| **(N)** | 21.00% | 22.00% | 23.00% | 24.00% | 25.00% | 26.00% | 27.00% | 28.00% | 29.00% | 30.00% |
| 0 | 1.000 | 1.000 | 1.000 | 1.000 | 1.000 | 1.000 | 1.000 | 1.000 | 1.000 | 1.000 |
| 1 | 1.210 | 1.220 | 1.230 | 1.240 | 1.250 | 1.260 | 1.270 | 1.280 | 1.290 | 1.300 |
| 2 | 1.464 | 1.488 | 1.513 | 1.538 | 1.563 | 1.588 | 1.613 | 1.638 | 1.664 | 1.690 |
| 3 | 1.772 | 1.816 | 1.861 | 1.907 | 1.953 | 2.000 | 2.048 | 2.097 | 2.147 | 2.197 |
| 4 | 2.144 | 2.215 | 2.289 | 2.364 | 2.441 | 2.520 | 2.601 | 2.684 | 2.769 | 2.856 |
| 5 | 2.594 | 2.703 | 2.815 | 2.932 | 3.052 | 3.176 | 3.304 | 3.436 | 3.572 | 3.713 |
| 6 | 3.138 | 3.297 | 3.463 | 3.635 | 3.815 | 4.002 | 4.196 | 4.398 | 4.608 | 4.827 |
| 7 | 3.797 | 4.023 | 4.259 | 4.508 | 4.768 | 5.042 | 5.329 | 5.629 | 5.945 | 6.275 |
| 8 | 4.595 | 4.908 | 5.239 | 5.590 | 5.960 | 6.353 | 6.768 | 7.206 | 7.669 | 8.157 |
| 9 | 5.560 | 5.987 | 6.444 | 6.931 | 7.451 | 8.005 | 8.595 | 9.223 | 9.893 | 10.60 |
| 10 | 6.727 | 7.305 | 7.926 | 8.594 | 9.313 | 10.09 | 10.92 | 11.81 | 12.76 | 13.79 |
| 11 | 8.140 | 8.912 | 9.749 | 10.66 | 11.64 | 12.71 | 13.86 | 15.11 | 16.46 | 17.92 |
| 12 | 9.850 | 10.87 | 11.99 | 13.21 | 14.55 | 16.01 | 17.61 | 19.34 | 21.24 | 23.30 |
| 13 | 11.92 | 13.26 | 14.75 | 16.39 | 18.19 | 20.18 | 22.36 | 24.76 | 27.39 | 30.29 |
| 14 | 14.42 | 16.18 | 18.14 | 20.32 | 22.74 | 25.42 | 28.40 | 31.69 | 35.34 | 39.37 |
| 15 | 17.45 | 19.74 | 22.31 | 25.20 | 28.42 | 32.03 | 36.06 | 40.56 | 45.59 | 51.19 |
| 16 | 21.11 | 24.09 | 27.45 | 31.24 | 35.53 | 40.36 | 45.80 | 51.92 | 58.81 | 66.54 |
| 17 | 25.55 | 29.38 | 33.76 | 38.74 | 44.41 | 50.85 | 58.17 | 66.46 | 75.86 | 86.50 |
| 18 | 30.91 | 35.85 | 41.52 | 48.04 | 55.51 | 64.07 | 73.87 | 85.07 | 97.86 | 112.5 |
| 19 | 37.40 | 43.74 | 51.07 | 59.57 | 69.39 | 80.73 | 93.81 | 108.9 | 126.2 | 146.2 |
| 20 | 45.26 | 53.36 | 62.82 | 73.86 | 86.74 | 101.7 | 119.1 | 139.4 | 162.9 | 190.0 |
| 21 | 54.76 | 65.10 | 77.27 | 91.59 | 108.4 | 128.2 | 151.3 | 178.4 | 210.1 | 247.1 |
| 22 | 66.26 | 79.42 | 95.04 | 113.6 | 135.5 | 161.5 | 192.2 | 228.4 | 271.0 | 321.2 |
| 23 | 80.18 | 96.89 | 116.9 | 140.8 | 169.4 | 203.5 | 244.1 | 292.3 | 349.6 | 417.5 |
| 24 | 97.02 | 118.2 | 143.8 | 174.6 | 211.8 | 256.4 | 309.9 | 374.1 | 451.0 | 542.8 |
| 25 | 117.4 | 144.2 | 176.9 | 216.5 | 264.7 | 323.0 | 393.6 | 478.9 | 581.8 | 705.6 |
| 26 | 142.0 | 175.9 | 217.5 | 268.5 | 330.9 | 407.0 | 499.9 | 613.0 | 750.5 | 917.3 |
| 27 | 171.9 | 214.6 | 267.6 | 333.0 | 413.6 | 512.9 | 634.9 | 784.6 | 968.1 | 1,193 |
| 28 | 208.0 | 261.9 | 329.1 | 412.9 | 517.0 | 646.2 | 806.3 | 1,004 | 1,249 | 1,550 |
| 29 | 251.6 | 319.5 | 404.8 | 512.0 | 646.2 | 814.2 | 1,024 | 1,286 | 1,611 | 2,015 |
| 30 | 304.5 | 389.8 | 497.9 | 634.8 | 807.8 | 1,026 | 1,301 | 1,646 | 2,078 | 2,620 |
| 31 | 368.4 | 475.5 | 612.4 | 787.2 | 1,010 | 1,293 | 1,652 | 2,106 | 2,681 | 3,406 |
| 32 | 445.8 | 580.1 | 753.3 | 976.1 | 1,262 | 1,629 | 2,098 | 2,696 | 3,458 | 4,428 |
| 33 | 539.4 | 707.7 | 926.5 | 1,210 | 1,578 | 2,052 | 2,664 | 3,451 | 4,461 | 5,756 |
| 34 | 652.7 | 863.4 | 1,140 | 1,501 | 1,972 | 2,586 | 3,383 | 4,417 | 5,755 | 7,483 |
| 35 | 789.7 | 1,053 | 1,402 | 1,861 | 2,465 | 3,258 | 4,297 | 5,654 | 7,424 | 9,728 |
| 36 | 955.6 | 1,285 | 1,724 | 2,308 | 3,081 | 4,105 | 5,457 | 7,237 | 9,577 | 12,646 |
| 37 | 1,156 | 1,568 | 2,121 | 2,862 | 3,852 | 5,173 | 6,930 | 9,263 | 12,354 | 16,440 |
| 38 | 1,399 | 1,913 | 2,609 | 3,548 | 4,815 | 6,517 | 8,801 | 11,857 | 15,937 | 21,372 |
| 39 | 1,693 | 2,334 | 3,208 | 4,400 | 6,019 | 8,212 | 11,178 | 15,177 | 20,559 | 27,784 |
| 40 | 2,048 | 2,847 | 3,946 | 5,456 | 7,523 | 10,347 | 14,195 | 19,427 | 26,521 | 36,119 |
| 41 | 2,479 | 3,473 | 4,854 | 6,765 | 9,404 | 13,037 | 18,028 | 24,866 | 34,212 | 46,955 |
| 42 | 2,999 | 4,238 | 5,971 | 8,389 | 11,755 | 16,427 | 22,896 | 31,829 | 44,133 | 61,041 |
| 43 | 3,629 | 5,170 | 7,344 | 10,402 | 14,694 | 20,698 | 29,078 | 40,741 | 56,932 | 79,353 |
| 44 | 4,391 | 6,307 | 9,033 | 12,899 | 18,367 | 26,080 | 36,929 | 52,148 | 73,442 | 103,159 |
| 45 | 5,313 | 7,695 | 11,110 | 15,995 | 22,959 | 32,861 | 46,899 | 66,750 | 94,741 | 134,107 |
| 46 | 6,429 | 9,388 | 13,666 | 19,833 | 28,699 | 41,404 | 59,562 | 85,439 | 122,216 | 174,339 |
| 47 | 7,779 | 11,453 | 16,809 | 24,593 | 35,873 | 52,169 | 75,644 | 109,363 | 157,658 | 226,641 |
| 48 | 9,412 | 13,972 | 20,675 | 30,496 | 44,842 | 65,733 | 96,068 | 139,984 | 203,379 | 294,633 |
| 49 | 11,389 | 17,046 | 25,430 | 37,815 | 56,052 | 82,824 | 122,006 | 179,180 | 262,359 | 383,022 |
| 50 | 13,781 | 20,797 | 31,279 | 46,890 | 70,065 | 104,358 | 154,948 | 229,350 | 338,443 | 497,929 |
| 51 | 16,675 | 25,372 | 38,473 | 58,144 | 87,581 | 131,492 | 196,784 | 293,568 | 436,591 | 647,308 |
| 52 | 20,176 | 30,954 | 47,322 | 72,099 | 109,476 | 165,679 | 249,916 | 375,767 | 563,203 | 841,500 |
| 53 | 24,413 | 37,763 | 58,206 | 89,402 | 136,846 | 208,756 | 317,393 | 480,982 | 726,532 | 1,093,951 |
| 54 | 29,540 | 46,071 | 71,594 | 110,859 | 171,057 | 263,033 | 403,089 | 615,656 | 937,226 | 1,422,136 |
| 55 | 35,743 | 56,207 | 88,060 | 137,465 | 213,821 | 331,421 | 511,923 | 788,040 | 1,209,022 | 1,848,776 |
| 56 | 43,249 | 68,573 | 108,314 | 170,457 | 267,276 | 417,590 | 650,142 | 1,008,691 | 1,559,638 | 2,403,409 |
| 57 | 52,332 | 83,659 | 133,227 | 211,366 | 334,096 | 526,164 | 825,681 | 1,291,125 | 2,011,933 | 3,124,432 |
| 58 | 63,322 | 102,063 | 163,869 | 262,094 | 417,619 | 662,967 | 1,048,614 | 1,652,640 | 2,595,393 | 4,061,762 |
| 59 | 76,619 | 124,517 | 201,559 | 324,997 | 522,024 | 835,338 | 1,331,740 | 2,115,379 | 3,348,057 | 5,280,290 |
| 60 | 92,709 | 151,911 | 247,917 | 402,996 | 652,530 | 1,052,526 | 1,691,310 | 2,707,685 | 4,318,994 | 6,864,377 |
|  | 21.0% | 22.0% | 23.0% | 24.0% | 25.0% | 26.0% | 27.0% | 28.0% | 29.0% | 30.0% |

Compound Amount Factor (CAF) table, page 4

CAF **table page 4**

| Year (N) | | | Yield Rate ( R ) | | | |
|---|---|---|---|---|---|---|
| | 35.00% | 40.00% | 45.00% | 50.00% | 60.00% | 70.00% |
| 0 | 1.000 | 1.000 | 1.000 | 1.000 | 1.000 | 1.000 |
| 1 | 1.350 | 1.400 | 1.450 | 1.500 | 1.600 | 1.700 |
| 2 | 1.823 | 1.960 | 2.103 | 2.250 | 2.560 | 2.890 |
| 3 | 2.460 | 2.744 | 3.049 | 3.375 | 4.096 | 4.913 |
| 4 | 3.322 | 3.842 | 4.421 | 5.063 | 6.554 | 8.352 |
| 5 | 4.484 | 5.378 | 6.410 | 7.594 | 10.49 | 14.20 |
| 6 | 6.053 | 7.530 | 9.294 | 11.39 | 16.78 | 24.14 |
| 7 | 8.172 | 10.54 | 13.48 | 17.09 | 26.84 | 41.03 |
| 8 | 11.03 | 14.76 | 19.54 | 25.63 | 42.95 | 69.76 |
| 9 | 14.89 | 20.66 | 28.33 | 38.44 | 68.72 | 118.6 |
| 10 | 20.11 | 28.93 | 41.08 | 57.67 | 110.0 | 201.6 |
| 11 | 27.14 | 40.50 | 59.57 | 86.50 | 175.9 | 342.7 |
| 12 | 36.64 | 56.69 | 86.38 | 129.7 | 281.5 | 582.6 |
| 13 | 49.47 | 79.37 | 125.3 | 194.6 | 450.4 | 990.5 |
| 14 | 66.78 | 111.1 | 181.6 | 291.9 | 720.6 | 1,684 |
| 15 | 90.16 | 155.6 | 263.3 | 437.9 | 1,153 | 2,862 |
| 16 | 121.7 | 217.8 | 381.8 | 656.8 | 1,845 | 4,866 |
| 17 | 164.3 | 304.9 | 553.7 | 985.3 | 2,951 | 8,272 |
| 18 | 221.8 | 426.9 | 802.8 | 1,478 | 4,722 | 14,063 |
| 19 | 299.5 | 597.6 | 1,164 | 2,217 | 7,556 | 23,907 |
| 20 | 404.3 | 836.7 | 1,688 | 3,325 | 12,089 | 40,642 |
| 21 | 545.8 | 1,171 | 2,448 | 4,988 | 19,343 | 69,092 |
| 22 | 736.8 | 1,640 | 3,549 | 7,482 | 30,949 | 117,456 |
| 23 | 994.7 | 2,296 | 5,146 | 11,223 | 49,518 | 199,676 |
| 24 | 1,343 | 3,214 | 7,462 | 16,834 | 79,228 | 339,449 |
| 25 | 1,813 | 4,500 | 10,819 | 25,251 | 126,765 | 577,063 |
| 26 | 2,447 | 6,300 | 15,688 | 37,877 | 202,824 | 981,007 |
| 27 | 3,304 | 8,820 | 22,748 | 56,815 | 324,519 | 1,667,711 |
| 28 | 4,460 | 12,348 | 32,984 | 85,223 | 519,230 | 2,835,109 |
| 29 | 6,021 | 17,287 | 47,827 | 127,834 | 830,767 | 4,819,686 |
| 30 | 8,129 | 24,201 | 69,349 | 191,751 | 1,329,228 | 8,193,466 |
| 31 | 10,974 | 33,882 | 100,556 | 287,627 | 2,126,765 | 13,928,892 |
| 32 | 14,814 | 47,435 | 145,806 | 431,440 | 3,402,824 | 23,679,116 |
| 33 | 19,999 | 66,409 | 211,419 | 647,160 | 5,444,518 | 40,254,497 |
| 34 | 26,999 | 92,972 | 306,558 | 970,740 | 8,711,229 | 68,432,645 |
| 35 | 36,449 | 130,161 | 444,509 | 1,456,110 | 13,937,966 | 116,335,497 |
| 36 | 49,206 | 182,226 | 644,537 | 2,184,164 | 22,300,745 | 197,770,344 |
| 37 | 66,428 | 255,116 | 934,579 | 3,276,247 | 35,681,192 | 336,209,585 |
| 38 | 89,677 | 357,162 | 1,355,140 | 4,914,370 | 57,089,908 | 571,556,295 |
| 39 | 121,065 | 500,027 | 1,964,953 | 7,371,555 | 91,343,852 | 971,645,702 |
| 40 | 163,437 | 700,038 | 2,849,181 | 11,057,332 | 146,150,164 | 1,651,797,693 |
| 41 | 220,640 | 980,053 | 4,131,313 | 16,585,998 | 233,840,262 | 2,808,056,078 |
| 42 | 297,864 | 1,372,074 | 5,990,404 | 24,878,998 | 374,144,419 | 4,773,695,332 |
| 43 | 402,117 | 1,920,903 | 8,686,085 | 37,318,497 | 598,631,071 | 8,115,282,064 |
| 44 | 542,857 | 2,689,265 | 12,594,824 | 55,977,745 | 957,809,713 | 13,795,979,509 |
| 45 | 732,858 | 3,764,971 | 18,262,495 | 83,966,617 | 1,532,495,541 | 23,453,165,165 |
| 46 | 989,358 | 5,270,959 | 26,480,617 | 125,949,926 | 2,451,992,865 | 39,870,380,781 |
| 47 | 1,335,633 | 7,379,343 | 38,396,895 | 188,924,889 | 3,923,188,585 | 67,779,647,328 |
| 48 | 1,803,104 | 10,331,080 | 55,675,498 | 283,387,333 | 6,277,101,735 | 115,225,400,457 |
| 49 | 2,434,191 | 14,463,512 | 80,729,472 | 425,081,000 | 10,043,362,777 | 195,883,180,777 |
| 50 | 3,286,158 | 20,248,916 | 117,057,734 | 637,621,500 | 16,069,380,443 | 333,001,407,321 |
| 51 | 4,436,313 | 28,348,483 | 169,733,714 | 956,432,250 | 25,711,008,708 | 566,102,392,446 |
| 52 | 5,989,023 | 39,687,876 | 246,113,885 | 1,434,648,375 | 41,137,613,933 | 962,374,067,159 |
| 53 | 8,085,181 | 55,563,026 | 356,865,133 | 2,151,972,563 | 65,820,182,293 | 1,636,035,914,170 |
| 54 | 10,914,994 | 77,788,237 | 517,454,444 | 3,227,958,845 | 105,312,291,669 | 2,781,261,054,090 |
| 55 | 14,735,242 | 108,903,531 | 750,308,943 | 4,841,938,267 | 168,499,666,670 | 4,728,143,791,952 |
| 56 | 19,892,576 | 152,464,944 | 1,087,947,967 | 7,262,907,401 | 269,599,466,672 | 8,037,844,446,319 |
| 57 | 26,854,978 | 213,450,921 | 1,577,524,553 | 10,894,361,101 | 431,359,146,674 | 13,664,335,558,742 |
| 58 | 36,254,221 | 298,831,290 | 2,287,410,602 | 16,341,541,652 | 690,174,634,679 | 23,229,370,449,862 |
| 59 | 48,943,198 | 418,363,806 | 3,316,745,372 | 24,512,312,478 | 1,104,279,415,487 | 39,489,929,764,765 |
| 60 | 66,073,317 | 585,709,328 | 4,809,280,790 | 36,768,468,717 | 1,766,847,064,778 | 67,132,880,600,101 |
| | 35.0% | 40.0% | 45.0% | 50.0% | 60.0% | 70.0% |

CAF **table page** 5

| | Compound Amount Factor (CAF) table, page 6 | | |
|---|---|---|---|
| Year | Yield Rate ( R ) | | |
| (N) | 80.00% | 90.00% | 100.00% |
| 0 | 1.000 | 1.000 | 1.000 |
| 1 | 1.800 | 1.900 | 2.000 |
| 2 | 3.240 | 3.610 | 4.000 |
| 3 | 5.832 | 6.859 | 8.000 |
| 4 | 10.50 | 13.03 | 16.00 |
| 5 | 18.90 | 24.76 | 32.00 |
| 6 | 34.01 | 47.05 | 64.00 |
| 7 | 61.22 | 89.39 | 128.0 |
| 8 | 110.2 | 169.8 | 256.0 |
| 9 | 198.4 | 322.7 | 512.0 |
| 10 | 357.0 | 613.1 | 1,024 |
| 11 | 642.7 | 1,165 | 2,048 |
| 12 | 1,157 | 2,213 | 4,096 |
| 13 | 2,082 | 4,205 | 8,192 |
| 14 | 3,748 | 7,990 | 16,384 |
| 15 | 6,747 | 15,181 | 32,768 |
| 16 | 12,144 | 28,844 | 65,536 |
| 17 | 21,859 | 54,804 | 131,072 |
| 18 | 39,346 | 104,127 | 262,144 |
| 19 | 70,824 | 197,842 | 524,288 |
| 20 | 127,482 | 375,900 | 1,048,576 |
| 21 | 229,468 | 714,209 | 2,097,152 |
| 22 | 413,043 | 1,356,998 | 4,194,304 |
| 23 | 743,477 | 2,578,296 | 8,388,608 |
| 24 | 1,338,259 | 4,898,763 | 16,777,216 |
| 25 | 2,408,866 | 9,307,650 | 33,554,432 |
| 26 | 4,335,959 | 17,684,534 | 67,108,864 |
| 27 | 7,804,726 | 33,600,615 | 134,217,728 |
| 28 | 14,048,506 | 63,841,168 | 268,435,456 |
| 29 | 25,287,311 | 121,298,220 | 536,870,912 |
| 30 | 45,517,160 | 230,466,618 | 1,073,741,824 |
| 31 | 81,930,887 | 437,886,574 | 2,147,483,648 |
| 32 | 147,475,597 | 831,984,491 | 4,294,967,296 |
| 33 | 265,456,075 | 1,580,770,532 | 8,589,934,592 |
| 34 | 477,820,935 | 3,003,464,011 | 17,179,869,184 |
| 35 | 860,077,682 | 5,706,581,621 | 34,359,738,368 |
| 36 | 1,548,139,828 | 10,842,505,080 | 68,719,476,736 |
| 37 | 2,786,651,691 | 20,600,759,652 | 137,438,953,472 |
| 38 | 5,015,973,044 | 39,141,443,339 | 274,877,906,944 |
| 39 | 9,028,751,479 | 74,368,742,344 | 549,755,813,888 |
| 40 | 16,251,752,663 | 141,300,610,454 | 1,099,511,627,776 |
| 41 | 29,253,154,793 | 268,471,159,862 | 2,199,023,255,552 |
| 42 | 52,655,678,628 | 510,095,203,739 | 4,398,046,511,104 |
| 43 | 94,780,221,530 | 969,180,887,103 | 8,796,093,022,208 |
| 44 | 170,604,398,754 | 1,841,443,685,496 | 17,592,186,044,416 |
| 45 | 307,087,917,757 | 3,498,743,002,443 | 35,184,372,088,832 |
| 46 | 552,758,251,963 | 6,647,611,704,642 | 70,368,744,177,664 |
| 47 | 994,964,853,534 | 12,630,462,238,819 | 140,737,488,355,328 |
| 48 | 1,790,936,736,361 | 23,997,878,253,756 | 281,474,976,710,656 |
| 49 | 3,223,686,125,450 | 45,595,968,682,137 | 562,949,953,421,312 |
| 50 | 5,802,635,025,810 | 86,632,340,496,060 | 1,125,899,906,842,620 |
| 51 | 10,444,743,046,457 | 164,601,446,942,513 | 2,251,799,813,685,250 |
| 52 | 18,800,537,483,623 | 312,742,749,190,775 | 4,503,599,627,370,500 |
| 53 | 33,840,967,470,521 | 594,211,223,462,472 | 9,007,199,254,740,990 |
| 54 | 60,913,741,446,938 | 1,129,001,324,578,700 | 18,014,398,509,482,000 |
| 55 | 109,644,734,604,489 | 2,145,102,516,699,520 | 36,028,797,018,964,000 |
| 56 | 197,360,522,288,080 | 4,075,694,781,729,100 | 72,057,594,037,927,900 |
| 57 | 355,248,940,118,545 | 7,743,820,085,285,280 | 144,115,188,075,856,000 |
| 58 | 639,448,092,213,381 | 14,713,258,162,042,000 | 288,230,376,151,712,000 |
| 59 | 1,151,006,565,984,090 | 27,955,190,507,879,900 | 576,460,752,303,423,000 |
| 60 | 2,071,811,818,771,350 | 53,114,861,964,971,800 | 1,152,921,504,606,850,000 |
| | 80.0% | 90.0% | 100.0% |

CAF **table page** 6

# APPENDIX-B:

# Compound Yield Factor (CYF) table

| Compound Yield Factor (CYF) table, page-1 | | | | | | | | | |
|---|---|---|---|---|---|---|---|---|---|
| **Year** | **Yield Rate ( R )** | | | | | | | | |
| **(N)** | 1.00% | 1.50% | 2.00% | 2.50% | 3.00% | 3.50% | 4.00% | 4.50% | 5.00% |
| 0 | 0.000 | 0.000 | 0.000 | 0.000 | 0.000 | 0.000 | 0.000 | 0.000 | 0.000 |
| 1 | 0.010 | 0.015 | 0.020 | 0.025 | 0.030 | 0.035 | 0.040 | 0.045 | 0.050 |
| 2 | 0.020 | 0.030 | 0.040 | 0.051 | 0.061 | 0.071 | 0.082 | 0.092 | 0.103 |
| 3 | 0.030 | 0.046 | 0.061 | 0.077 | 0.093 | 0.109 | 0.125 | 0.141 | 0.158 |
| 4 | 0.041 | 0.061 | 0.082 | 0.104 | 0.126 | 0.148 | 0.170 | 0.193 | 0.216 |
| 5 | 0.051 | 0.077 | 0.104 | 0.131 | 0.159 | 0.188 | 0.217 | 0.246 | 0.276 |
| 6 | 0.062 | 0.093 | 0.126 | 0.160 | 0.194 | 0.229 | 0.265 | 0.302 | 0.340 |
| 7 | 0.072 | 0.110 | 0.149 | 0.189 | 0.230 | 0.272 | 0.316 | 0.361 | 0.407 |
| 8 | 0.083 | 0.126 | 0.172 | 0.218 | 0.267 | 0.317 | 0.369 | 0.422 | 0.477 |
| 9 | 0.094 | 0.143 | 0.195 | 0.249 | 0.305 | 0.363 | 0.423 | 0.486 | 0.551 |
| 10 | 0.105 | 0.161 | 0.219 | 0.280 | 0.344 | 0.411 | 0.480 | 0.553 | 0.629 |
| 11 | 0.116 | 0.178 | 0.243 | 0.312 | 0.384 | 0.460 | 0.539 | 0.623 | 0.710 |
| 12 | 0.127 | 0.196 | 0.268 | 0.345 | 0.426 | 0.511 | 0.601 | 0.696 | 0.796 |
| 13 | 0.138 | 0.214 | 0.294 | 0.379 | 0.469 | 0.564 | 0.665 | 0.772 | 0.886 |
| 14 | 0.149 | 0.232 | 0.319 | 0.413 | 0.513 | 0.619 | 0.732 | 0.852 | 0.980 |
| 15 | 0.161 | 0.250 | 0.346 | 0.448 | 0.558 | 0.675 | 0.801 | 0.935 | 1.079 |
| 16 | 0.173 | 0.269 | 0.373 | 0.485 | 0.605 | 0.734 | 0.873 | 1.022 | 1.183 |
| 17 | 0.184 | 0.288 | 0.400 | 0.522 | 0.653 | 0.795 | 0.948 | 1.113 | 1.292 |
| 18 | 0.196 | 0.307 | 0.428 | 0.560 | 0.702 | 0.857 | 1.026 | 1.208 | 1.407 |
| 19 | 0.208 | 0.327 | 0.457 | 0.599 | 0.754 | 0.923 | 1.107 | 1.308 | 1.527 |
| 20 | 0.220 | 0.347 | 0.486 | 0.639 | 0.806 | 0.990 | 1.191 | 1.412 | 1.653 |
| 21 | 0.232 | 0.367 | 0.516 | 0.680 | 0.860 | 1.059 | 1.279 | 1.520 | 1.786 |
| 22 | 0.245 | 0.388 | 0.546 | 0.722 | 0.916 | 1.132 | 1.370 | 1.634 | 1.925 |
| 23 | 0.257 | 0.408 | 0.577 | 0.765 | 0.974 | 1.206 | 1.465 | 1.752 | 2.072 |
| 24 | 0.270 | 0.430 | 0.608 | 0.809 | 1.033 | 1.283 | 1.563 | 1.876 | 2.225 |
| 25 | 0.282 | 0.451 | 0.641 | 0.854 | 1.094 | 1.363 | 1.666 | 2.005 | 2.386 |
| 26 | 0.295 | 0.473 | 0.673 | 0.900 | 1.157 | 1.446 | 1.772 | 2.141 | 2.556 |
| 27 | 0.308 | 0.495 | 0.707 | 0.948 | 1.221 | 1.532 | 1.883 | 2.282 | 2.733 |
| 28 | 0.321 | 0.517 | 0.741 | 0.996 | 1.288 | 1.620 | 1.999 | 2.430 | 2.920 |
| 29 | 0.335 | 0.540 | 0.776 | 1.046 | 1.357 | 1.712 | 2.119 | 2.584 | 3.116 |
| 30 | 0.348 | 0.563 | 0.811 | 1.098 | 1.427 | 1.807 | 2.243 | 2.745 | 3.322 |
| 31 | 0.361 | 0.587 | 0.848 | 1.150 | 1.500 | 1.905 | 2.373 | 2.914 | 3.538 |
| 32 | 0.375 | 0.610 | 0.885 | 1.204 | 1.575 | 2.007 | 2.508 | 3.090 | 3.765 |
| 33 | 0.389 | 0.634 | 0.922 | 1.259 | 1.652 | 2.112 | 2.648 | 3.274 | 4.003 |
| 34 | 0.403 | 0.659 | 0.961 | 1.315 | 1.732 | 2.221 | 2.794 | 3.466 | 4.253 |
| 35 | 0.417 | 0.684 | 1.000 | 1.373 | 1.814 | 2.334 | 2.946 | 3.667 | 4.516 |
| 36 | 0.431 | 0.709 | 1.040 | 1.433 | 1.898 | 2.450 | 3.104 | 3.877 | 4.792 |
| 37 | 0.445 | 0.735 | 1.081 | 1.493 | 1.985 | 2.571 | 3.268 | 4.097 | 5.081 |
| 38 | 0.460 | 0.761 | 1.122 | 1.556 | 2.075 | 2.696 | 3.439 | 4.326 | 5.385 |
| 39 | 0.474 | 0.787 | 1.165 | 1.620 | 2.167 | 2.825 | 3.616 | 4.566 | 5.705 |
| 40 | 0.489 | 0.814 | 1.208 | 1.685 | 2.262 | 2.959 | 3.801 | 4.816 | 6.040 |
| 41 | 0.504 | 0.841 | 1.252 | 1.752 | 2.360 | 3.098 | 3.993 | 5.078 | 6.392 |
| 42 | 0.519 | 0.869 | 1.297 | 1.821 | 2.461 | 3.241 | 4.193 | 5.352 | 6.762 |
| 43 | 0.534 | 0.897 | 1.343 | 1.892 | 2.565 | 3.390 | 4.400 | 5.637 | 7.150 |
| 44 | 0.549 | 0.925 | 1.390 | 1.964 | 2.671 | 3.543 | 4.617 | 5.936 | 7.557 |
| 45 | 0.565 | 0.954 | 1.438 | 2.038 | 2.782 | 3.702 | 4.841 | 6.248 | 7.985 |
| 46 | 0.580 | 0.984 | 1.487 | 2.114 | 2.895 | 3.867 | 5.075 | 6.574 | 8.434 |
| 47 | 0.596 | 1.013 | 1.536 | 2.192 | 3.012 | 4.037 | 5.318 | 6.915 | 8.906 |
| 48 | 0.612 | 1.043 | 1.587 | 2.271 | 3.132 | 4.214 | 5.571 | 7.271 | 9.401 |
| 49 | 0.628 | 1.074 | 1.639 | 2.353 | 3.256 | 4.396 | 5.833 | 7.644 | 9.921 |
| 50 | 0.645 | 1.105 | 1.692 | 2.437 | 3.384 | 4.585 | 6.107 | 8.033 | 10.47 |
| 51 | 0.661 | 1.137 | 1.745 | 2.523 | 3.515 | 4.780 | 6.391 | 8.439 | 11.04 |
| 52 | 0.678 | 1.169 | 1.800 | 2.611 | 3.651 | 4.983 | 6.687 | 8.864 | 11.64 |
| 53 | 0.694 | 1.201 | 1.856 | 2.701 | 3.790 | 5.192 | 6.994 | 9.308 | 12.27 |
| 54 | 0.711 | 1.234 | 1.913 | 2.794 | 3.934 | 5.409 | 7.314 | 9.772 | 12.94 |
| 55 | 0.729 | 1.268 | 1.972 | 2.889 | 4.082 | 5.633 | 7.646 | 10.26 | 13.64 |
| 56 | 0.746 | 1.302 | 2.031 | 2.986 | 4.235 | 5.865 | 7.992 | 10.76 | 14.37 |
| 57 | 0.763 | 1.336 | 2.092 | 3.086 | 4.392 | 6.106 | 8.352 | 11.29 | 15.14 |
| 58 | 0.781 | 1.372 | 2.154 | 3.188 | 4.553 | 6.354 | 8.726 | 11.85 | 15.94 |
| 59 | 0.799 | 1.407 | 2.217 | 3.292 | 4.720 | 6.612 | 9.115 | 12.42 | 16.79 |
| 60 | 0.817 | 1.443 | 2.281 | 3.400 | 4.892 | 6.878 | 9.520 | 13.03 | 17.68 |
| **Year** | 1.0% | 1.5% | 2.0% | 2.5% | 3.0% | 3.5% | 4.0% | 4.5% | 5.0% |

CYF **table page** 1

| Year (N) | 5.50% | 6.00% | 6.50% | 7.00% | 7.50% | 8.00% | 8.50% | 9.00% | 9.50% | 10.00% |
|---|---|---|---|---|---|---|---|---|---|---|
| 0 | 0.000 | 0.000 | 0.000 | 0.000 | 0.000 | 0.000 | 0.000 | 0.000 | 0.000 | 0.000 |
| 1 | 0.055 | 0.060 | 0.065 | 0.070 | 0.075 | 0.080 | 0.085 | 0.090 | 0.095 | 0.100 |
| 2 | 0.113 | 0.124 | 0.134 | 0.145 | 0.156 | 0.166 | 0.177 | 0.188 | 0.199 | 0.210 |
| 3 | 0.174 | 0.191 | 0.208 | 0.225 | 0.242 | 0.260 | 0.277 | 0.295 | 0.313 | 0.331 |
| 4 | 0.239 | 0.262 | 0.286 | 0.311 | 0.335 | 0.360 | 0.386 | 0.412 | 0.438 | 0.464 |
| 5 | 0.307 | 0.338 | 0.370 | 0.403 | 0.436 | 0.469 | 0.504 | 0.539 | 0.574 | 0.611 |
| 6 | 0.379 | 0.419 | 0.459 | 0.501 | 0.543 | 0.587 | 0.631 | 0.677 | 0.724 | 0.772 |
| 7 | 0.455 | 0.504 | 0.554 | 0.606 | 0.659 | 0.714 | 0.770 | 0.828 | 0.888 | 0.949 |
| 8 | 0.535 | 0.594 | 0.655 | 0.718 | 0.783 | 0.851 | 0.921 | 0.993 | 1.067 | 1.144 |
| 9 | 0.619 | 0.689 | 0.763 | 0.838 | 0.917 | 0.999 | 1.084 | 1.172 | 1.263 | 1.358 |
| 10 | 0.708 | 0.791 | 0.877 | 0.967 | 1.061 | 1.159 | 1.261 | 1.367 | 1.478 | 1.594 |
| 11 | 0.802 | 0.898 | 0.999 | 1.105 | 1.216 | 1.332 | 1.453 | 1.580 | 1.714 | 1.853 |
| 12 | 0.901 | 1.012 | 1.129 | 1.252 | 1.382 | 1.518 | 1.662 | 1.813 | 1.971 | 2.138 |
| 13 | 1.006 | 1.133 | 1.267 | 1.410 | 1.560 | 1.720 | 1.888 | 2.066 | 2.254 | 2.452 |
| 14 | 1.116 | 1.261 | 1.415 | 1.579 | 1.752 | 1.937 | 2.133 | 2.342 | 2.563 | 2.797 |
| 15 | 1.232 | 1.397 | 1.572 | 1.759 | 1.959 | 2.172 | 2.400 | 2.642 | 2.901 | 3.177 |
| 16 | 1.355 | 1.540 | 1.739 | 1.952 | 2.181 | 2.426 | 2.689 | 2.970 | 3.272 | 3.595 |
| 17 | 1.485 | 1.693 | 1.917 | 2.159 | 2.419 | 2.700 | 3.002 | 3.328 | 3.678 | 4.054 |
| 18 | 1.621 | 1.854 | 2.107 | 2.380 | 2.676 | 2.996 | 3.342 | 3.717 | 4.122 | 4.560 |
| 19 | 1.766 | 2.026 | 2.309 | 2.617 | 2.951 | 3.316 | 3.712 | 4.142 | 4.609 | 5.116 |
| 20 | 1.918 | 2.207 | 2.524 | 2.870 | 3.248 | 3.661 | 4.112 | 4.604 | 5.142 | 5.727 |
| 21 | 2.078 | 2.400 | 2.753 | 3.141 | 3.566 | 4.034 | 4.547 | 5.109 | 5.725 | 6.400 |
| 22 | 2.248 | 2.604 | 2.997 | 3.430 | 3.909 | 4.437 | 5.018 | 5.659 | 6.364 | 7.140 |
| 23 | 2.426 | 2.820 | 3.256 | 3.741 | 4.277 | 4.871 | 5.530 | 6.258 | 7.064 | 7.954 |
| 24 | 2.615 | 3.049 | 3.533 | 4.072 | 4.673 | 5.341 | 6.085 | 6.911 | 7.830 | 8.850 |
| 25 | 2.813 | 3.292 | 3.828 | 4.427 | 5.098 | 5.848 | 6.687 | 7.623 | 8.668 | 9.835 |
| 26 | 3.023 | 3.549 | 4.141 | 4.807 | 5.556 | 6.396 | 7.340 | 8.399 | 9.587 | 10.92 |
| 27 | 3.244 | 3.822 | 4.476 | 5.214 | 6.047 | 6.988 | 8.049 | 9.245 | 10.59 | 12.11 |
| 28 | 3.478 | 4.112 | 4.832 | 5.649 | 6.576 | 7.627 | 8.818 | 10.17 | 11.69 | 13.42 |
| 29 | 3.724 | 4.418 | 5.211 | 6.114 | 7.144 | 8.317 | 9.653 | 11.17 | 12.90 | 14.86 |
| 30 | 3.984 | 4.743 | 5.614 | 6.612 | 7.755 | 9.063 | 10.56 | 12.27 | 14.22 | 16.45 |
| 31 | 4.258 | 5.088 | 6.044 | 7.145 | 8.412 | 9.868 | 11.54 | 13.46 | 15.67 | 18.19 |
| 32 | 4.547 | 5.453 | 6.502 | 7.715 | 9.117 | 10.74 | 12.61 | 14.76 | 17.25 | 20.11 |
| 33 | 4.852 | 5.841 | 6.990 | 8.325 | 9.876 | 11.68 | 13.76 | 16.18 | 18.98 | 22.23 |
| 34 | 5.174 | 6.251 | 7.509 | 8.978 | 10.69 | 12.69 | 15.02 | 17.73 | 20.88 | 24.55 |
| 35 | 5.514 | 6.686 | 8.062 | 9.677 | 11.57 | 13.79 | 16.38 | 19.41 | 22.96 | 27.10 |
| 36 | 5.872 | 7.147 | 8.651 | 10.42 | 12.51 | 14.97 | 17.86 | 21.25 | 25.24 | 29.91 |
| 37 | 6.250 | 7.636 | 9.279 | 11.22 | 13.52 | 16.25 | 19.46 | 23.25 | 27.73 | 33.00 |
| 38 | 6.649 | 8.154 | 9.947 | 12.08 | 14.61 | 17.63 | 21.20 | 25.44 | 30.46 | 36.40 |
| 39 | 7.069 | 8.704 | 10.66 | 12.99 | 15.79 | 19.12 | 23.09 | 27.82 | 33.45 | 40.14 |
| 40 | 7.513 | 9.286 | 11.42 | 13.97 | 17.04 | 20.72 | 25.13 | 30.41 | 36.72 | 44.26 |
| 41 | 7.982 | 9.903 | 12.22 | 15.02 | 18.40 | 22.46 | 27.35 | 33.24 | 40.30 | 48.79 |
| 42 | 8.476 | 10.56 | 13.08 | 16.14 | 19.85 | 24.34 | 29.76 | 36.32 | 44.23 | 53.76 |
| 43 | 8.997 | 11.25 | 14.00 | 17.34 | 21.42 | 26.37 | 32.38 | 39.68 | 48.52 | 59.24 |
| 44 | 9.546 | 11.99 | 14.97 | 18.63 | 23.10 | 28.56 | 35.22 | 43.34 | 53.23 | 65.26 |
| 45 | 10.13 | 12.76 | 16.01 | 20.00 | 24.90 | 30.92 | 38.30 | 47.33 | 58.38 | 71.89 |
| 46 | 10.74 | 13.59 | 17.12 | 21.47 | 26.85 | 33.47 | 41.64 | 51.68 | 64.02 | 79.18 |
| 47 | 11.38 | 14.47 | 18.29 | 23.05 | 28.94 | 36.23 | 45.26 | 56.42 | 70.20 | 87.20 |
| 48 | 12.07 | 15.39 | 19.55 | 24.73 | 31.18 | 39.21 | 49.19 | 61.59 | 76.96 | 96.02 |
| 49 | 12.78 | 16.38 | 20.88 | 26.53 | 33.60 | 42.43 | 53.46 | 67.22 | 84.37 | 105.7 |
| 50 | 13.54 | 17.42 | 22.31 | 28.46 | 36.19 | 45.90 | 58.09 | 73.36 | 92.48 | 116.4 |
| 51 | 14.34 | 18.53 | 23.82 | 30.52 | 38.98 | 49.65 | 63.11 | 80.05 | 101.4 | 128.1 |
| 52 | 15.19 | 19.70 | 25.44 | 32.73 | 41.98 | 53.71 | 68.56 | 87.34 | 111.1 | 141.0 |
| 53 | 16.08 | 20.94 | 27.15 | 35.09 | 45.20 | 58.08 | 74.47 | 95.30 | 121.7 | 155.2 |
| 54 | 17.01 | 22.26 | 28.98 | 37.61 | 48.67 | 62.81 | 80.89 | 104.0 | 133.4 | 170.9 |
| 55 | 18.01 | 23.65 | 30.93 | 40.32 | 52.39 | 67.91 | 87.85 | 113.4 | 146.2 | 188.1 |
| 56 | 19.05 | 25.13 | 33.01 | 43.21 | 56.39 | 73.43 | 95.40 | 123.7 | 160.1 | 207.0 |
| 57 | 20.15 | 26.70 | 35.22 | 46.30 | 60.70 | 79.38 | 103.6 | 134.9 | 175.4 | 227.8 |
| 58 | 21.32 | 28.36 | 37.57 | 49.61 | 65.33 | 85.81 | 112.5 | 147.2 | 192.2 | 250.6 |
| 59 | 22.54 | 30.12 | 40.08 | 53.16 | 70.30 | 92.76 | 122.1 | 160.5 | 210.6 | 275.8 |
| 60 | 23.84 | 31.99 | 42.75 | 56.95 | 75.65 | 100.3 | 132.6 | 175.0 | 230.7 | 303.5 |
| | 5.5% | 6.0% | 6.5% | 7.0% | 7.5% | 8.0% | 8.5% | 9.0% | 9.5% | 10.0% |

Compound Yield Factor (CYF) table, page-2

**CYF table page** 2

| Year | Compound Yield Factor (CYF) table, page-3 | | | | | | | | | |
|---|---|---|---|---|---|---|---|---|---|---|
| | Yield Rate ( R ) | | | | | | | | | |
| (N) | 11.00% | 12.00% | 13.00% | 14.00% | 15.00% | 16.00% | 17.00% | 18.00% | 19.00% | 20.00% |
| 0 | 0.000 | 0.000 | 0.000 | 0.000 | 0.000 | 0.000 | 0.000 | 0.000 | 0.000 | 0.000 |
| 1 | 0.110 | 0.120 | 0.130 | 0.140 | 0.150 | 0.160 | 0.170 | 0.180 | 0.190 | 0.200 |
| 2 | 0.232 | 0.254 | 0.277 | 0.300 | 0.323 | 0.346 | 0.369 | 0.392 | 0.416 | 0.440 |
| 3 | 0.368 | 0.405 | 0.443 | 0.482 | 0.521 | 0.561 | 0.602 | 0.643 | 0.685 | 0.728 |
| 4 | 0.518 | 0.574 | 0.630 | 0.689 | 0.749 | 0.811 | 0.874 | 0.939 | 1.005 | 1.074 |
| 5 | 0.685 | 0.762 | 0.842 | 0.925 | 1.011 | 1.100 | 1.192 | 1.288 | 1.386 | 1.488 |
| 6 | 0.870 | 0.974 | 1.082 | 1.195 | 1.313 | 1.436 | 1.565 | 1.700 | 1.840 | 1.986 |
| 7 | 1.076 | 1.211 | 1.353 | 1.502 | 1.660 | 1.826 | 2.001 | 2.185 | 2.379 | 2.583 |
| 8 | 1.305 | 1.476 | 1.658 | 1.853 | 2.059 | 2.278 | 2.511 | 2.759 | 3.021 | 3.300 |
| 9 | 1.558 | 1.773 | 2.004 | 2.252 | 2.518 | 2.803 | 3.108 | 3.435 | 3.785 | 4.160 |
| 10 | 1.839 | 2.106 | 2.395 | 2.707 | 3.046 | 3.411 | 3.807 | 4.234 | 4.695 | 5.192 |
| 11 | 2.152 | 2.479 | 2.836 | 3.226 | 3.652 | 4.117 | 4.624 | 5.176 | 5.777 | 6.430 |
| 12 | 2.498 | 2.896 | 3.335 | 3.818 | 4.350 | 4.936 | 5.580 | 6.288 | 7.064 | 7.916 |
| 13 | 2.883 | 3.363 | 3.898 | 4.492 | 5.153 | 5.886 | 6.699 | 7.599 | 8.596 | 9.699 |
| 14 | 3.310 | 3.887 | 4.535 | 5.261 | 6.076 | 6.988 | 8.007 | 9.147 | 10.42 | 11.84 |
| 15 | 3.785 | 4.474 | 5.254 | 6.138 | 7.137 | 8.266 | 9.539 | 10.97 | 12.59 | 14.41 |
| 16 | 4.311 | 5.130 | 6.067 | 7.137 | 8.358 | 9.748 | 11.33 | 13.13 | 15.17 | 17.49 |
| 17 | 4.895 | 5.866 | 6.986 | 8.276 | 9.761 | 11.47 | 13.43 | 15.67 | 18.24 | 21.19 |
| 18 | 5.544 | 6.690 | 8.024 | 9.575 | 11.38 | 13.46 | 15.88 | 18.67 | 21.90 | 25.62 |
| 19 | 6.263 | 7.613 | 9.197 | 11.06 | 13.23 | 15.78 | 18.75 | 22.21 | 26.25 | 30.95 |
| 20 | 7.062 | 8.646 | 10.52 | 12.74 | 15.37 | 18.46 | 22.11 | 26.39 | 31.43 | 37.34 |
| 21 | 7.949 | 9.804 | 12.02 | 14.67 | 17.82 | 21.57 | 26.03 | 31.32 | 37.59 | 45.01 |
| 22 | 8.934 | 11.10 | 13.71 | 16.86 | 20.64 | 25.19 | 30.63 | 37.14 | 44.92 | 54.21 |
| 23 | 10.03 | 12.55 | 15.63 | 19.36 | 23.89 | 29.38 | 36.01 | 44.01 | 53.65 | 65.25 |
| 24 | 11.24 | 14.18 | 17.79 | 22.21 | 27.63 | 34.24 | 42.30 | 52.11 | 64.03 | 78.50 |
| 25 | 12.59 | 16.00 | 20.23 | 25.46 | 31.92 | 39.87 | 49.66 | 61.67 | 76.39 | 94.40 |
| 26 | 14.08 | 18.04 | 22.99 | 29.17 | 36.86 | 46.41 | 58.27 | 72.95 | 91.09 | 113.5 |
| 27 | 15.74 | 20.32 | 26.11 | 33.39 | 42.54 | 54.00 | 68.35 | 86.26 | 108.6 | 136.4 |
| 28 | 17.58 | 22.88 | 29.63 | 38.20 | 49.07 | 62.80 | 80.13 | 102.0 | 129.4 | 163.8 |
| 29 | 19.62 | 25.75 | 33.62 | 43.69 | 56.58 | 73.01 | 93.93 | 120.5 | 154.2 | 196.8 |
| 30 | 21.89 | 28.96 | 38.12 | 49.95 | 65.21 | 84.85 | 110.1 | 142.4 | 183.7 | 236.4 |
| 31 | 24.41 | 32.56 | 43.20 | 57.08 | 75.14 | 98.59 | 128.9 | 168.2 | 218.8 | 283.9 |
| 32 | 27.21 | 36.58 | 48.95 | 65.21 | 86.57 | 114.5 | 151.0 | 198.6 | 260.5 | 340.8 |
| 33 | 30.31 | 41.09 | 55.44 | 74.48 | 99.70 | 133.0 | 176.9 | 234.6 | 310.2 | 409.2 |
| 34 | 33.75 | 46.14 | 62.78 | 85.05 | 114.8 | 154.4 | 207.1 | 277.0 | 369.3 | 491.2 |
| 35 | 37.57 | 51.80 | 71.07 | 97.10 | 132.2 | 179.3 | 242.5 | 327.0 | 439.7 | 589.7 |
| 36 | 41.82 | 58.14 | 80.44 | 110.8 | 152.2 | 208.2 | 283.9 | 386.0 | 523.4 | 707.8 |
| 37 | 46.53 | 65.23 | 91.02 | 126.5 | 175.1 | 241.6 | 332.3 | 455.7 | 623.1 | 849.6 |
| 38 | 51.76 | 73.18 | 103.0 | 144.3 | 201.5 | 280.5 | 389.0 | 537.9 | 741.7 | 1,020 |
| 39 | 57.56 | 82.08 | 116.5 | 164.7 | 231.9 | 325.5 | 455.3 | 634.9 | 882.8 | 1,224 |
| 40 | 64.00 | 92.05 | 131.8 | 187.9 | 266.9 | 377.7 | 532.9 | 749.4 | 1,051 | 1,469 |
| 41 | 71.15 | 103.2 | 149.0 | 214.3 | 307.0 | 438.3 | 623.6 | 884.4 | 1,250 | 1,763 |
| 42 | 79.09 | 115.7 | 168.5 | 244.5 | 353.2 | 508.6 | 729.8 | 1,044 | 1,488 | 2,115 |
| 43 | 87.90 | 129.7 | 190.6 | 278.8 | 406.4 | 590.1 | 854.1 | 1,232 | 1,771 | 2,539 |
| 44 | 97.68 | 145.4 | 215.5 | 318.0 | 467.5 | 684.7 | 999.4 | 1,454 | 2,108 | 3,047 |
| 45 | 108.5 | 163.0 | 243.6 | 362.7 | 537.8 | 794.4 | 1,169 | 1,716 | 2,509 | 3,656 |
| 46 | 120.6 | 182.7 | 275.4 | 413.6 | 618.6 | 921.7 | 1,368 | 2,025 | 2,985 | 4,388 |
| 47 | 134.0 | 204.7 | 311.4 | 471.6 | 711.5 | 1,069 | 1,601 | 2,389 | 3,553 | 5,265 |
| 48 | 148.8 | 229.4 | 352.0 | 537.8 | 818.4 | 1,241 | 1,874 | 2,820 | 4,228 | 6,319 |
| 49 | 165.3 | 257.0 | 397.9 | 613.2 | 941.3 | 1,439 | 2,192 | 3,327 | 5,032 | 7,583 |
| 50 | 183.6 | 288.0 | 449.7 | 699.2 | 1,083 | 1,670 | 2,565 | 3,926 | 5,988 | 9,099 |
| 51 | 203.9 | 322.7 | 508.3 | 797.3 | 1,245 | 1,937 | 3,001 | 4,633 | 7,126 | 10,920 |
| 52 | 226.4 | 361.5 | 574.5 | 909.0 | 1,432 | 2,247 | 3,512 | 5,467 | 8,480 | 13,104 |
| 53 | 251.4 | 405.0 | 649.4 | 1,036 | 1,647 | 2,607 | 4,109 | 6,452 | 10,091 | 15,725 |
| 54 | 279.2 | 453.8 | 733.9 | 1,182 | 1,894 | 3,024 | 4,808 | 7,613 | 12,009 | 18,870 |
| 55 | 310.0 | 508.3 | 829.5 | 1,347 | 2,179 | 3,508 | 5,625 | 8,984 | 14,291 | 22,644 |
| 56 | 344.2 | 569.4 | 937.4 | 1,536 | 2,506 | 4,069 | 6,582 | 10,601 | 17,006 | 27,173 |
| 57 | 382.2 | 637.9 | 1,059 | 1,751 | 2,882 | 4,721 | 7,701 | 12,509 | 20,237 | 32,608 |
| 58 | 424.3 | 714.6 | 1,197 | 1,996 | 3,314 | 5,476 | 9,010 | 14,761 | 24,083 | 39,129 |
| 59 | 471.1 | 800.4 | 1,353 | 2,276 | 3,811 | 6,353 | 10,542 | 17,419 | 28,659 | 46,955 |
| 60 | 523.1 | 896.6 | 1,529 | 2,595 | 4,383 | 7,369 | 12,334 | 20,554 | 34,104 | 56,347 |
| | 11.0% | 12.0% | 13.0% | 14.0% | 15.0% | 16.0% | 17.0% | 18.0% | 19.0% | 20.0% |

CYF **table page** 3

| Year (N) | Yield Rate ( R ) | | | | | | | | | |
|---|---|---|---|---|---|---|---|---|---|---|
| | 21.00% | 22.00% | 23.00% | 24.00% | 25.00% | 26.00% | 27.00% | 28.00% | 29.00% | 30.00% |
| 0 | 0.000 | 0.000 | 0.000 | 0.000 | 0.000 | 0.000 | 0.000 | 0.000 | 0.000 | 0.000 |
| 1 | 0.210 | 0.220 | 0.230 | 0.240 | 0.250 | 0.260 | 0.270 | 0.280 | 0.290 | 0.300 |
| 2 | 0.464 | 0.488 | 0.513 | 0.538 | 0.563 | 0.588 | 0.613 | 0.638 | 0.664 | 0.690 |
| 3 | 0.772 | 0.816 | 0.861 | 0.907 | 0.953 | 1.000 | 1.048 | 1.097 | 1.147 | 1.197 |
| 4 | 1.144 | 1.215 | 1.289 | 1.364 | 1.441 | 1.520 | 1.601 | 1.684 | 1.769 | 1.856 |
| 5 | 1.594 | 1.703 | 1.815 | 1.932 | 2.052 | 2.176 | 2.304 | 2.436 | 2.572 | 2.713 |
| 6 | 2.138 | 2.297 | 2.463 | 2.635 | 2.815 | 3.002 | 3.196 | 3.398 | 3.608 | 3.827 |
| 7 | 2.797 | 3.023 | 3.259 | 3.508 | 3.768 | 4.042 | 4.329 | 4.629 | 4.945 | 5.275 |
| 8 | 3.595 | 3.908 | 4.239 | 4.590 | 4.960 | 5.353 | 5.768 | 6.206 | 6.669 | 7.157 |
| 9 | 4.560 | 4.987 | 5.444 | 5.931 | 6.451 | 7.005 | 7.595 | 8.223 | 8.893 | 9.604 |
| 10 | 5.727 | 6.305 | 6.926 | 7.594 | 8.313 | 9.086 | 9.915 | 10.81 | 11.76 | 12.79 |
| 11 | 7.140 | 7.912 | 8.749 | 9.657 | 10.64 | 11.71 | 12.86 | 14.11 | 15.46 | 16.92 |
| 12 | 8.850 | 9.872 | 10.99 | 12.21 | 13.55 | 15.01 | 16.61 | 18.34 | 20.24 | 22.30 |
| 13 | 10.92 | 12.26 | 13.75 | 15.39 | 17.19 | 19.18 | 21.36 | 23.76 | 26.39 | 29.29 |
| 14 | 13.42 | 15.18 | 17.14 | 19.32 | 21.74 | 24.42 | 27.40 | 30.69 | 34.34 | 38.37 |
| 15 | 16.45 | 18.74 | 21.31 | 24.20 | 27.42 | 31.03 | 35.06 | 39.56 | 44.59 | 50.19 |
| 16 | 20.11 | 23.09 | 26.45 | 30.24 | 34.53 | 39.36 | 44.80 | 50.92 | 57.81 | 65.54 |
| 17 | 24.55 | 28.38 | 32.76 | 37.74 | 43.41 | 49.85 | 57.17 | 65.46 | 74.86 | 85.50 |
| 18 | 29.91 | 34.85 | 40.52 | 47.04 | 54.51 | 63.07 | 72.87 | 84.07 | 96.86 | 111.5 |
| 19 | 36.40 | 42.74 | 50.07 | 58.57 | 68.39 | 79.73 | 92.81 | 107.9 | 125.2 | 145.2 |
| 20 | 44.26 | 52.36 | 61.82 | 72.86 | 85.74 | 100.7 | 118.1 | 138.4 | 161.9 | 189.0 |
| 21 | 53.76 | 64.10 | 76.27 | 90.59 | 107.4 | 127.2 | 150.3 | 177.4 | 209.1 | 246.1 |
| 22 | 65.26 | 78.42 | 94.04 | 112.6 | 134.5 | 160.5 | 191.2 | 227.4 | 270.0 | 320.2 |
| 23 | 79.18 | 95.89 | 115.9 | 139.8 | 168.4 | 202.5 | 243.1 | 291.3 | 348.6 | 416.5 |
| 24 | 96.02 | 117.2 | 142.8 | 173.6 | 210.4 | 255.4 | 308.9 | 373.1 | 450.0 | 541.8 |
| 25 | 116.4 | 143.2 | 175.9 | 215.5 | 263.7 | 322.0 | 392.6 | 477.9 | 580.8 | 704.6 |
| 26 | 141.0 | 174.9 | 216.5 | 267.5 | 329.9 | 406.0 | 498.9 | 612.0 | 749.5 | 916.3 |
| 27 | 170.9 | 213.6 | 266.6 | 332.0 | 412.6 | 511.9 | 633.9 | 783.6 | 967.1 | 1,192 |
| 28 | 207.0 | 260.9 | 328.1 | 411.9 | 516.0 | 645.2 | 805.3 | 1,003 | 1,248 | 1,549 |
| 29 | 250.6 | 318.5 | 403.8 | 511.0 | 645.2 | 813.2 | 1,023 | 1,285 | 1,610 | 2,014 |
| 30 | 303.5 | 388.8 | 496.9 | 633.8 | 806.8 | 1,025 | 1,300 | 1,645 | 2,077 | 2,619 |
| 31 | 367.4 | 474.5 | 611.4 | 786.2 | 1,009 | 1,292 | 1,651 | 2,105 | 2,680 | 3,405 |
| 32 | 444.8 | 579.1 | 752.3 | 975.1 | 1,261 | 1,628 | 2,097 | 2,695 | 3,457 | 4,427 |
| 33 | 538.4 | 706.7 | 925.5 | 1,209 | 1,577 | 2,051 | 2,663 | 3,450 | 4,460 | 5,755 |
| 34 | 651.7 | 862.4 | 1,139 | 1,500 | 1,971 | 2,585 | 3,382 | 4,416 | 5,754 | 7,482 |
| 35 | 788.7 | 1,052 | 1,401 | 1,860 | 2,464 | 3,257 | 4,296 | 5,653 | 7,423 | 9,727 |
| 36 | 954.6 | 1,284 | 1,723 | 2,307 | 3,080 | 4,104 | 5,456 | 7,236 | 9,576 | 12,645 |
| 37 | 1,155 | 1,567 | 2,120 | 2,861 | 3,851 | 5,172 | 6,929 | 9,262 | 12,353 | 16,439 |
| 38 | 1,398 | 1,912 | 2,608 | 3,547 | 4,814 | 6,516 | 8,800 | 11,856 | 15,936 | 21,371 |
| 39 | 1,692 | 2,333 | 3,207 | 4,399 | 6,018 | 8,211 | 11,177 | 15,176 | 20,558 | 27,783 |
| 40 | 2,047 | 2,846 | 3,945 | 5,455 | 7,522 | 10,346 | 14,194 | 19,426 | 26,520 | 36,118 |
| 41 | 2,478 | 3,472 | 4,853 | 6,764 | 9,403 | 13,036 | 18,027 | 24,865 | 34,211 | 46,954 |
| 42 | 2,998 | 4,237 | 5,970 | 8,388 | 11,754 | 16,426 | 22,895 | 31,828 | 44,132 | 61,040 |
| 43 | 3,628 | 5,169 | 7,343 | 10,401 | 14,693 | 20,697 | 29,077 | 40,740 | 56,931 | 79,352 |
| 44 | 4,390 | 6,306 | 9,032 | 12,898 | 18,366 | 26,079 | 36,928 | 52,147 | 73,441 | 103,158 |
| 45 | 5,312 | 7,694 | 11,109 | 15,994 | 22,958 | 32,860 | 46,898 | 66,749 | 94,740 | 134,106 |
| 46 | 6,428 | 9,387 | 13,665 | 19,832 | 28,849 | 41,403 | 59,561 | 85,438 | 122,215 | 174,338 |
| 47 | 7,778 | 11,452 | 16,808 | 24,592 | 35,872 | 52,168 | 75,643 | 109,362 | 157,657 | 226,640 |
| 48 | 9,411 | 13,971 | 20,674 | 30,495 | 44,841 | 65,732 | 96,067 | 139,983 | 203,378 | 294,632 |
| 49 | 11,388 | 17,045 | 25,429 | 37,814 | 56,051 | 82,823 | 122,005 | 179,179 | 262,358 | 383,021 |
| 50 | 13,780 | 20,796 | 31,278 | 46,889 | 70,064 | 104,357 | 154,947 | 229,349 | 338,442 | 497,928 |
| 51 | 16,674 | 25,371 | 38,472 | 58,143 | 87,580 | 131,491 | 196,783 | 293,567 | 436,590 | 647,307 |
| 52 | 20,175 | 30,953 | 47,321 | 72,098 | 109,475 | 165,678 | 249,915 | 375,766 | 563,202 | 841,499 |
| 53 | 24,412 | 37,762 | 58,205 | 89,401 | 136,845 | 208,755 | 317,392 | 480,981 | 726,531 | 1,093,950 |
| 54 | 29,539 | 46,070 | 71,593 | 110,858 | 171,056 | 263,032 | 403,088 | 615,655 | 937,225 | 1,422,135 |
| 55 | 35,742 | 56,206 | 88,059 | 137,464 | 213,820 | 331,420 | 511,922 | 788,039 | 1,209,021 | 1,848,775 |
| 56 | 43,248 | 68,572 | 108,313 | 170,456 | 267,275 | 417,589 | 650,141 | 1,008,690 | 1,559,637 | 2,403,408 |
| 57 | 52,331 | 83,658 | 133,226 | 211,365 | 334,095 | 526,163 | 825,680 | 1,291,124 | 2,011,932 | 3,124,431 |
| 58 | 63,321 | 102,062 | 163,868 | 262,093 | 417,618 | 662,966 | 1,048,613 | 1,652,639 | 2,595,392 | 4,061,761 |
| 59 | 76,618 | 124,516 | 201,558 | 324,996 | 522,023 | 835,337 | 1,331,739 | 2,115,378 | 3,348,056 | 5,280,289 |
| 60 | 92,708 | 151,910 | 247,916 | 402,995 | 652,529 | 1,052,525 | 1,691,309 | 2,707,684 | 4,318,993 | 6,864,376 |
| | 21.0% | 22.0% | 23.0% | 24.0% | 25.0% | 26.0% | 27.0% | 28.0% | 29.0% | 30.0% |

CYF table page 4

| | Compound Yield Factor (CYF) table, page-5 | | | | | |
|---|---|---|---|---|---|---|
| Year | Yield Rate ( R ) | | | | | |
| (N) | 35.00% | 40.00% | 45.00% | 50.00% | 60.00% | 70.00% |
| 0 | 0.000 | 0.000 | 0.000 | 0.000 | 0.000 | 0.000 |
| 1 | 0.350 | 0.400 | 0.450 | 0.500 | 0.600 | 0.700 |
| 2 | 0.823 | 0.960 | 1.103 | 1.250 | 1.560 | 1.890 |
| 3 | 1.460 | 1.744 | 2.049 | 2.375 | 3.096 | 3.913 |
| 4 | 2.322 | 2.842 | 3.421 | 4.063 | 5.554 | 7.352 |
| 5 | 3.484 | 4.378 | 5.410 | 6.594 | 9.486 | 13.20 |
| 6 | 5.053 | 6.530 | 8.294 | 10.39 | 15.78 | 23.14 |
| 7 | 7.172 | 9.541 | 12.48 | 16.09 | 25.84 | 40.03 |
| 8 | 10.03 | 13.76 | 18.54 | 24.63 | 41.95 | 68.76 |
| 9 | 13.89 | 19.66 | 27.33 | 37.44 | 67.72 | 117.6 |
| 10 | 19.11 | 27.93 | 40.08 | 56.67 | 109.0 | 200.6 |
| 11 | 26.14 | 39.50 | 58.57 | 85.50 | 174.9 | 341.7 |
| 12 | 35.64 | 55.69 | 85.38 | 128.7 | 280.5 | 581.6 |
| 13 | 48.47 | 78.37 | 124.3 | 193.6 | 449.4 | 989.5 |
| 14 | 65.78 | 110.1 | 180.6 | 290.9 | 719.6 | 1,683 |
| 15 | 89.16 | 154.6 | 262.3 | 436.9 | 1,152 | 2,861 |
| 16 | 120.7 | 216.8 | 380.8 | 655.8 | 1,844 | 4,865 |
| 17 | 163.3 | 303.9 | 552.7 | 984.3 | 2,950 | 8,271 |
| 18 | 220.8 | 425.9 | 801.8 | 1,477 | 4,721 | 14,062 |
| 19 | 298.5 | 596.6 | 1,163 | 2,216 | 7,555 | 23,906 |
| 20 | 403.3 | 835.7 | 1,687 | 3,324 | 12,088 | 40,641 |
| 21 | 544.8 | 1,170 | 2,447 | 4,987 | 19,342 | 69,091 |
| 22 | 735.8 | 1,639 | 3,548 | 7,481 | 30,948 | 117,455 |
| 23 | 993.7 | 2,295 | 5,145 | 11,222 | 49,517 | 199,675 |
| 24 | 1,342 | 3,213 | 7,461 | 16,833 | 79,227 | 339,448 |
| 25 | 1,812 | 4,499 | 10,818 | 25,250 | 126,764 | 577,062 |
| 26 | 2,446 | 6,299 | 15,687 | 37,876 | 202,823 | 981,006 |
| 27 | 3,303 | 8,819 | 22,747 | 56,814 | 324,518 | 1,667,710 |
| 28 | 4,459 | 12,347 | 32,983 | 85,222 | 519,229 | 2,835,108 |
| 29 | 6,020 | 17,286 | 47,826 | 127,833 | 830,766 | 4,819,685 |
| 30 | 8,128 | 24,200 | 69,348 | 191,750 | 1,329,227 | 8,193,465 |
| 31 | 10,973 | 33,881 | 100,555 | 287,626 | 2,126,764 | 13,928,891 |
| 32 | 14,813 | 47,434 | 145,805 | 431,439 | 3,402,823 | 23,679,115 |
| 33 | 19,998 | 66,408 | 211,418 | 647,159 | 5,444,517 | 40,254,496 |
| 34 | 26,998 | 92,971 | 306,557 | 970,739 | 8,711,228 | 68,432,644 |
| 35 | 36,448 | 130,160 | 444,508 | 1,456,109 | 13,937,965 | 116,335,496 |
| 36 | 49,205 | 182,225 | 644,536 | 2,184,163 | 22,300,744 | 197,770,343 |
| 37 | 66,427 | 255,115 | 934,578 | 3,276,246 | 35,681,191 | 336,209,584 |
| 38 | 89,676 | 357,161 | 1,355,139 | 4,914,369 | 57,089,907 | 571,556,294 |
| 39 | 121,064 | 500,026 | 1,964,952 | 7,371,554 | 91,343,851 | 971,645,701 |
| 40 | 163,436 | 700,037 | 2,849,180 | 11,057,331 | 146,150,163 | 1,651,797,692 |
| 41 | 220,639 | 980,052 | 4,131,312 | 16,585,997 | 233,840,261 | 2,808,056,077 |
| 42 | 297,863 | 1,372,073 | 5,990,403 | 24,878,997 | 374,144,418 | 4,773,695,331 |
| 43 | 402,116 | 1,920,902 | 8,686,084 | 37,318,496 | 598,631,070 | 8,115,282,063 |
| 44 | 542,856 | 2,689,264 | 12,594,823 | 55,977,744 | 957,809,712 | 13,795,979,508 |
| 45 | 732,857 | 3,764,970 | 18,262,494 | 83,966,616 | 1,532,495,540 | 23,453,165,164 |
| 46 | 989,357 | 5,270,958 | 26,480,616 | 125,949,925 | 2,451,992,864 | 39,870,380,780 |
| 47 | 1,335,632 | 7,379,342 | 38,396,894 | 188,924,888 | 3,923,188,584 | 67,779,647,327 |
| 48 | 1,803,103 | 10,331,079 | 55,675,497 | 283,387,332 | 6,277,101,734 | 115,225,400,456 |
| 49 | 2,434,190 | 14,463,511 | 80,729,471 | 425,080,999 | 10,043,362,776 | 195,883,180,776 |
| 50 | 3,286,157 | 20,248,915 | 117,057,733 | 637,621,499 | 16,069,380,442 | 333,001,407,320 |
| 51 | 4,436,312 | 28,348,482 | 169,733,713 | 956,432,249 | 25,711,008,707 | 566,102,392,445 |
| 52 | 5,989,022 | 39,687,875 | 246,113,884 | 1,434,648,374 | 41,137,613,932 | 962,374,067,158 |
| 53 | 8,085,180 | 55,563,025 | 356,865,132 | 2,151,972,562 | 65,820,182,292 | 1,636,035,914,169 |
| 54 | 10,914,993 | 77,788,236 | 517,454,443 | 3,227,958,844 | 105,312,291,668 | 2,781,261,054,089 |
| 55 | 14,735,241 | 108,903,530 | 750,308,942 | 4,841,938,266 | 168,499,666,669 | 4,728,143,791,951 |
| 56 | 19,892,575 | 152,464,943 | 1,087,947,966 | 7,262,907,400 | 269,599,466,671 | 8,037,844,446,318 |
| 57 | 26,854,977 | 213,450,920 | 1,577,524,552 | 10,894,361,100 | 431,359,146,673 | 13,664,335,558,741 |
| 58 | 36,254,220 | 298,831,289 | 2,287,410,601 | 16,341,541,651 | 690,174,634,678 | 23,229,370,449,861 |
| 59 | 48,943,197 | 418,363,805 | 3,316,745,371 | 24,512,312,477 | 1,104,279,415,486 | 39,489,929,764,764 |
| 60 | 66,073,316 | 585,709,327 | 4,809,280,789 | 36,768,468,716 | 1,766,847,064,777 | 67,132,880,600,100 |
| | 35.0% | 40.0% | 45.0% | 50.0% | 60.0% | 70.0% |

**CYF table page 5**

| Year (N) | 80.00% | 90.00% | 100.00% |
|---|---|---|---|
| | Compound Yield Factor (CYF) table, page-6 | | |
| | Yield Rate ( R ) | | |
| 0 | 0.000 | 0.000 | 0.000 |
| 1 | 0.800 | 0.900 | 1.000 |
| 2 | 2.240 | 2.610 | 3.000 |
| 3 | 4.832 | 5.859 | 7.000 |
| 4 | 9.498 | 12.03 | 15.00 |
| 5 | 17.90 | 23.76 | 31.00 |
| 6 | 33.01 | 46.05 | 63.00 |
| 7 | 60.22 | 88.39 | 127.0 |
| 8 | 109.2 | 168.8 | 255.0 |
| 9 | 197.4 | 321.7 | 511.0 |
| 10 | 356.0 | 612.1 | 1,023 |
| 11 | 641.7 | 1,164 | 2,047 |
| 12 | 1,156 | 2,212 | 4,095 |
| 13 | 2,081 | 4,204 | 8,191 |
| 14 | 3,747 | 7,989 | 16,383 |
| 15 | 6,746 | 15,180 | 32,767 |
| 16 | 12,143 | 28,843 | 65,535 |
| 17 | 21,858 | 54,803 | 131,071 |
| 18 | 39,345 | 104,126 | 262,143 |
| 19 | 70,823 | 197,841 | 524,287 |
| 20 | 127,481 | 375,899 | 1,048,575 |
| 21 | 229,467 | 714,208 | 2,097,151 |
| 22 | 413,042 | 1,356,997 | 4,194,303 |
| 23 | 743,476 | 2,578,295 | 8,388,607 |
| 24 | 1,338,258 | 4,898,762 | 16,777,215 |
| 25 | 2,408,865 | 9,307,649 | 33,554,431 |
| 26 | 4,335,958 | 17,684,533 | 67,108,863 |
| 27 | 7,804,725 | 33,600,614 | 134,217,727 |
| 28 | 14,048,505 | 63,841,167 | 268,435,455 |
| 29 | 25,287,310 | 121,298,219 | 536,870,911 |
| 30 | 45,517,159 | 230,466,617 | 1,073,741,823 |
| 31 | 81,930,886 | 437,886,573 | 2,147,483,647 |
| 32 | 147,475,596 | 831,984,490 | 4,294,967,295 |
| 33 | 265,456,074 | 1,580,770,531 | 8,589,934,591 |
| 34 | 477,820,934 | 3,003,464,010 | 17,179,869,183 |
| 35 | 860,077,681 | 5,706,581,620 | 34,359,738,367 |
| 36 | 1,548,139,827 | 10,842,505,079 | 68,719,476,735 |
| 37 | 2,786,651,690 | 20,600,759,651 | 137,438,953,471 |
| 38 | 5,015,973,043 | 39,141,443,338 | 274,877,906,943 |
| 39 | 9,028,751,478 | 74,368,742,343 | 549,755,813,887 |
| 40 | 16,251,752,662 | 141,300,610,453 | 1,099,511,627,775 |
| 41 | 29,253,154,792 | 268,471,159,861 | 2,199,023,255,551 |
| 42 | 52,655,678,627 | 510,095,203,738 | 4,398,046,511,103 |
| 43 | 94,780,221,529 | 969,180,887,102 | 8,796,093,022,207 |
| 44 | 170,604,398,753 | 1,841,443,685,495 | 17,592,186,044,415 |
| 45 | 307,087,917,756 | 3,498,743,002,442 | 35,184,372,088,831 |
| 46 | 552,758,251,962 | 6,647,611,704,641 | 70,368,744,177,663 |
| 47 | 994,964,853,533 | 12,630,462,238,818 | 140,737,488,355,327 |
| 48 | 1,790,936,736,360 | 23,997,878,253,755 | 281,474,976,710,655 |
| 49 | 3,223,686,125,449 | 45,595,968,682,136 | 562,949,953,421,311 |
| 50 | 5,802,635,025,809 | 86,632,340,496,059 | 1,125,899,906,842,620 |
| 51 | 10,444,743,046,456 | 164,601,446,942,512 | 2,251,799,813,685,250 |
| 52 | 18,800,537,483,622 | 312,742,749,190,774 | 4,503,599,627,370,490 |
| 53 | 33,840,967,470,520 | 594,211,223,462,471 | 9,007,199,254,740,990 |
| 54 | 60,913,741,446,937 | 1,129,001,324,578,700 | 18,014,398,509,482,000 |
| 55 | 109,644,734,604,488 | 2,145,102,516,699,520 | 36,028,797,018,964,000 |
| 56 | 197,360,522,288,079 | 4,075,694,781,729,100 | 72,057,594,037,927,900 |
| 57 | 355,248,940,118,544 | 7,743,820,085,285,280 | 144,115,188,075,856,000 |
| 58 | 639,448,092,213,380 | 14,713,258,162,042,000 | 288,230,376,151,712,000 |
| 59 | 1,151,006,565,984,080 | 27,955,190,507,879,900 | 576,460,752,303,423,000 |
| 60 | 2,071,811,818,771,350 | 53,114,861,964,971,800 | 1,152,921,504,606,850,000 |
| | 80.0% | 90.0% | 100.0% |

CYF **table page** 6

# APPENDIX-C:

# Expanded Table of Contents

\* \* \* \*

.

CPSIA information can be obtained
at www.ICGtesting.com
Printed in the USA
BVHW051957251121
622517BV00011B/324

9 789083 120300